THE AMERICAN TEMPER

THE AMERICAN TEMPER

 PATTERNS OF OUR INTELLECTUAL HERITAGE

BY RICHARD D. MOSIER

UNIVERSITY OF CALIFORNIA PRESS
BERKELEY AND LOS ANGELES 1952

UNIVERSITY OF CALIFORNIA PRESS

Berkeley and Los Angeles, California

CAMBRIDGE UNIVERSITY PRESS

London, England

Copyright 1952 by

THE REGENTS OF THE UNIVERSITY OF CALIFORNIA

Printed in the United States of America

Designed by John B. Goetz

TO ROSALIND A. MOSIER

The Making of the American Mind

To the Puritans belongs a primitive synthesis of the American mind, in which sixteenth-century Calvinism was gradually transformed in the light of social-contract theory into a religion of reason. To the young republicans of the revolutionary age belongs the pleasure of an early enlightenment, made fresh in the mind by so many recent departures from it. To the transcendentalists belongs a transformation of romantic philosophy into terms suitable to the current American dream. To the pragmatists belongs the creation of a philosophy of technology, with its experimental temper and its instrumentalist purpose. These four have been the main creative moments in the making of the American mind; but none of them, taken by itself, is quite complete, and each can be read in terms of the others. The whole sum of American wisdom may be expressed in a maxim of Bacon, that knowledge is power, if it is accompanied by a question of Whitman, What is the fusing explanation and tie—what the relation between the (radical, democratic) Me, the human identity of understanding, emotions, spirit, on the one side, of and with the (conservative) Not Me, the whole material objective universe and laws, and what is behind them in time and space, on the other side?

The maxim and the question sum up the whole creative contribution of the American mind, and catch in their active union all that America can presently teach. The maxim of Bacon expresses in a phrase a conception of knowledge as technique, and recalls to the mind the current deification of American know-how. The question of Whitman raises an old doubt, now presently forming again in the American mind, whether the conception of the world as machine, generated inevitably by the Baconian conception of knowledge, is adequate to the demands of the spirit and not in the long run hostile to the development of the individual. The history of American ideas is the history of this antithesis between the maxim of Bacon and the question of Whitman. It is the history of their conflict and occasional reconciliation, and it gives rise in each of the major epochs of the American mind to a new synthesis. In Puritanism only God possesses the knowledge that is power, and man is cut off from it by virtue of a primitive apostasy of Adam. In republicanism man recovers his virtue and hence his power of self-government, but must stand as a passive spectator to the world machine. In transcendentalism a new method is discovered for gaining insight into nature's development, and the divinity comes to dwell in individual man. In experimentalism man possesses the power to interfere actively in the development of nature, and by the mastery of its technique gains the ability to control it in the light of human destiny.

But the creative womb of time will one day bear her fruit, and bring to its birth another creative moment in the making of the American mind. Such a moment will reconcile again the antithesis of the maxim of Bacon and the question of Whitman, while summing up the creative contribution of the preceding moments of thought. It will be a moment when the American spirit will once more regain its balance in the flux, discovering in the contradictions of its thought the breeding ground of new and more sprightly children of the American mind. It will be a moment when ideas are on the wing, and the flood of a transition will sweep away the moorings of the mind which previous generations have so laboriously built. The future of the American mind is great because the categories of its thought have not yet been frozen by history into the inviolable, nor by partisan interest into the untouchable. I want to communicate to America this sense of its creativity in the realm of the mind, so that a subsequent generation will not be impervious to the pleasures of the understanding.

To catch then the intellectual temper of each of the transition epochs of the American mind is the purpose of my endeavors. The work of the mind, which is a fruit of long maturing, cannot be easily capsuled in a phrase, or paragraphed by a single vial of thought. But the fundamental ideas which have entered into the making of the American mind have had a singular capacity to enter into wont and use, while awakening the mind from its lethargy and old encrusted superstitions. From Puritanism to pragmatism, from experimental religion to experimental science, the line of thought both embodies and betrays the ideals of former epochs, while breaking through to some new principle of continuity which later ages might build upon. Unless then the continuity of the old and the new, the linkage of past and future, is brought into the focus of current opinion, it will betray itself into action without the protection of contemplation, and into thought without an active outlet for its ideals. The history of American ideas might serve to explain that neither the Puritans nor the Pragmatists could survive the shock of a history that had moved beyond them, because they no longer expressed the ideals to which the American spirit, in its easy hours of self-adulation, had given its sympathies and its undying love.

ACKNOWLEDGEMENTS

I wish to acknowledge my indebtedness to the many scholars whose specialized work has made this present survey possible. Though the original version of my manuscript contained extensive documentation and numerous quotations from the original sources to bolster up my interpretation of our intellectual history, these have been sacrificed in the successive cuttings and revisions through which the manuscript has passed to meet the requirements of publication. Hence, my indebtedness to the original source materials on which, for the most part, this survey was built, has not got adequately expressed in the few quotations which remain. Nevertheless, should any scholar wish to dispute over the grounds of my own bias and judgment, I shall be happy to supply a complete file of references and quotations to bolster up my opinions. On the other hand, it is gladly admitted that what set out to be a scholarly undertaking has now become little more than a series of interpretative essays on the intellectual history of the United States; and it would not be an unusual thing to have some critic point out that other positions, judgments, and evaluations of our intellectual history are not only possible but respectable. I make no claim to having delivered the absolute truth, and only hope that the shortcomings of the present undertaking will stimulate others to a like endeavor but with a more probable success.

My indebtedness to particular authors is threefold. To Professor Perry Miller, upon whom I drew heavily for interpretations of the Puritan mind, and whose unraveling of the complexities of the Federal Theology no doubt found an echo in my work, I am particularly indebted. Professor Miller's *New England Mind* is the pioneering and definitive study of the seventeenth-century Puritan intellectual heritage, beside which my own interpretations of the Puritan mind seem only a faint and far-off echo. To the late F. O. Matthiessen, who provided insights into the character of our native transcendental literature, I likewise owe a great debt. Professor Matthiessen's *American Renaissance* is the most reliable study of the romantic mind, beside which my own pedestrian investigation of our transcendental literature must seem like child's play. To John Dewey, particularly in *The Quest for Certainty,* I am indebted for interpretations of the philosophic significance of the transition from Newtonian to Einsteinian physics and the contradictions which attended it. No doubt the judgments of these three authors have found an echo in my works; but beyond these specific acknowledgements of indebtedness I cannot go, for the present volume was built mainly on my own interpretation of source materials, and hence the three authors to whom I am particularly indebted should not be held responsible for my errors.

For permission to quote copyrighted materials I am indebted to the following publishers: To the Citadel Press, for permission to quote from Thomas Paine, *The Complete Writings,* ed. by Foner; to G. P. Putnam's Sons for permission to quote from Thomas Jefferson, *Writings,* ed. by Ford, James Madison, *Writings,* ed. by Hunt, and John Dewey, *The Quest for Certainty;* to the Thomas Jefferson Memorial Association, for permission to quote from Thomas Jefferson, *Writings,* ed. by Bergh; to Charles Scribner's Sons for permission to quote from Thorstein Veblen, *Science in Modern Civilization* and *The Theory of Business Enterprise;* to Henry Adams, for permission to quote from Brooks Adams, *The Theory of Social Revolutions;* to the Macmillan Co., for permission to quote from John Dewey, *Experience and Education,* and *Democracy and Education;* to Ginn and Co., for permission to quote from Lester Ward, *Psychic Factors in Civilization;* to W. W. Norton and Co., for permission to quote from John Dewey, *Experience and Nature;* to Henry Holt and Co., for permission to quote from William James, *Talks to Teachers on Psychology;* to Appleton-Century-Crofts, for permission to quote from William T. Harris, *Psychological Foundations of Education;* to Longmans, Green and Co., for permission to quote from William James, *Pragmatism,* and *The Meaning of Truth;* to G. P. Putnam's Sons, for permission to quote from Walt Whitman, *The Complete Writings;* to the American Unitarian Association, for permission to quote from Theodore Parker, *Works,* Centenary Edition; to Houghton Mifflin Co., for permission to quote R. W. Emerson, *Works,* Centenary Edition, and John Fiske, *Outlines of Cosmic Philosophy;* to Henry Holt and Co., for permission to quote from John Dewey, *The Public and Its Problems;* to Yale University Press, for permission to quote from W. G. Sumner, *Earth Hunger and Essays,* and John Dewey, *A Common Faith;* to the American Book Co., for permission to quote from Perry Miller and Thomas H. Johnson, *The Puritans;* to Harvard University Press, for permission to quote from S. E. Morison, *The Founding of Harvard Col-*

lege, and C. S. Peirce, *Collected Papers,* ed. by Hartshorne and Weiss; to the Philosophical Library, for permission to quote from Benjamin Rush, *Selected Writings,* ed. by Runes; to Oxford University Press, for permission to quote from Walt Whitman, *Specimen Days in America.*

CONTENTS

BOOK IV

THE MODERN TEMPER

BOOK I

THE PURITAN MIND

"If the manner of this discourse should occasion any disrellish in the apprehension of the weaker reader, because it may seem too Logicall, or Scholasticall, in regard to the terms I use, or the way of dispute that I may proceed, in some places: I have these two things to professe, That Plainesse and perspicuity, both for matter and manner of expression, are the things, that I have conscientiously indeavored in the whole debate: for I have ever thought writings that come abroad, they are not to dazle, but direct the apprehension of the meanest, and I have accounted it the chiefest part of indicious learning, to make a hard point easy and familiar in explication. Qui non vult intelligi, debet negligi. The nature of the subject that is under my hand, is such, that I was constrained to accomodate and conform my expressions more or lesse, in some kinde of suitablenesse thereunto: for in some passages of the dispute, the particulars in their very rise and foundation, border so near upon the principles of Logick: (as whether Ecclesia Catholica Visibilis, was to be attended, as a Totum universale, or Integrale) that either I must resolve to say nothing, or to speak (though as sparingly as I could of such things) as the quality of the things did require. And let any man make a triall, and I do much mistake myself, but he will be necessitated to take the same course, if he speaks to the cause."

Thomas Hooker

CHAPTER ONE

THE DIVINE GOVERNMENT

1. *The Puritan Temper*

There is something of the Puritan in every American, some transcendent standard, some rule of conscience or reason he clings to, which betrays the influence of the primitive Puritan, and calls into high marble relief the most interesting of all whom history has portrayed in her chronicle of character, and painted with her colors of fire and blood. At the beginning of our intellectual life, it was the Puritan above all others who carried the seed of the future, hiding in the ungainly robes of his religion the pragmatism and idealism which carried subsequent generations on high flights of thought. Yankee pragmatism and Puritan idealism are the two sides of the American coin, which united in the New England character for a primitive synthesis of the native mind; and the fruit of this marriage was a pragmatic piety which in its antithesis of action and contemplation carried all before it on a tide of fortune. The Puritan was poised halfway between the poles of a great transition, and drew his inspiration both from the past and from the future, giving to his language the burden of contradiction, and to his thought the motives of despair. In consequence, his character may be somewhat of a problem for the modern interpreter, unless it is remembered that beneath the barbaric feudal language there hid a prescient modern note. For the Puritan was drawn into a fateful hour of history, as the world of feudalism was collapsing and that of capitalism was struggling to take its place; and he entered upon his great adventure with the full knowledge that his piety and his politics must have the approval of God upon them if he was to succeed. To the Puritan, therefore, the drama of salvation, with its quest of certainty, seemed like an economy of redemption, with its promise of success.

The New England Puritan was engaged in a great game of transcendental politics, playing in the market of chance with a sovereign god whose dice are always loaded. He was seeking to wrest from the omnipotent god some stable meaning amidst the flow of time, some line of continuity and insight behind the flux of events. He prayed that God might be an ally in this great empire of time, and professed to believe that he would be singled out for salvation from among the innumerable fallen. He hoped that he might be chosen by the sovereign God as a royal favorite, and sit with an aristocracy of Christian grace in the courts and palaces of a heavenly city. To be thus irresistibly chosen for election to the household of saints seemed to the Puritan the sublimest of conditions; for a mighty sovereign held the future of the Puritan as a secret of His royal heart, and with the prescience of His infinite mind had an irrevocable foreknowledge whether he was predestined either to salvation or damnation. Only by the grace of the omnipotent God, therefore, could the Puritan hope to succeed in his quest of salvation or profit by the economy of his redemption. If then an uncommon piety should mark out the religious experience of the New England Puritan, or an uncommon cruelty betray to us the record of his political success, it should be remembered that he was engaged in a great game of transcendental politics, and caught up in the meshes of an immense economy of redemption.

Thus ensnared by the predeterminism of God, completely absorbed by his quest of salvation, the Puritan was led to establish lines of moral cleavage everywhere, making his own special biases eternally right and all others hopelessly wrong. He was led to make absolute moral decisions, from which, of course, there can be no appeal. He sanctified his own worldly ventures with the authority of God's government, and damned beyond redemption any who stood in the way of carrying out God's purposes. He believed that his kingdom, the colonies rising from the stony and unyielding soil of New England, was supernaturally favored, and that no interference, whether of king or of commoner, or of any worldly power, should stand in the way of his divine experiments. His conscious hopes, his ideas, his prayers even, were all objects of worship, all a part of the onward movement of the Christian experiment. He pursued religion through the imagination, and his faith was the subject of orderly and logical vivisection; he cried out for divine guidance, and believed that holy inspiration was the proper origin for every bold enterprise. He experimented boldly, spoke without hesitation, and acted without compromise, because he believed himself an instrument of holy work, a soldier enrolled in the legions of Christ, a second cause to which the First Cause stood as a prime mover.

His was no fugitive and cloistered virtue; he was no refugee from life's main issues, no hermit or monk concealed from the truth while seeking it. He was a practical idealist, concerned only to gather the fruits of this world while he lived under the transcendent power of the next one; and he professed to judge the affairs of this world in the light of that ideal standard. He was conscious that God had chosen him to do holy work in the service of that royal sovereign to whom he stood as a passive and wholly unworthy subject, and from whom full suffrage could be gained only at the beginning of regeneration, with divine light and holy guidance. He would not brook the weakling, the coward, or the vulgar in this pilgrim's progress of salvation; for he was a soldier enlisted in the legions of his sovereign God to do battle against all evil, and he used as his most critical weapon the standard of that transcendent good which he believed to be treasured up in heaven. He plunged into the midst of practical life, bargained, speculated, and profited, while telling himself that the heart must not be set upon these worldly things, and that he must know how to use wisely the great estate which God has put into his hands. The New England Puritan was a child of two ages, a transition figure—sprung from the loins of feudal society, heir to her ideals, her conceptions, her beliefs, the Puritan nevertheless carried within him the seeds of the future. His outward garments, his accoutrements of belief, were soon to be thrown off for a more modern cut; but he was the model, the prototype, the primitive original, of many who were to come after him. He was the perfect instrument of the nascent capitalism, when that infant needed the perfectionist, the idealist, and the soldier of Christ to bring it forward into life.

2. The Pragmatic Piety

The Soldier of Christ, once enrolled in the legions of his sovereign God, was expected to bear with stoic calm the protracted warfare of the flesh and the spirit, and triumph by the grace of God over the stratagems of a hostile Satan. He was thrust into the trials and temptations of the world in order that his loyalty to the government of God might be tested; and his oath of allegiance, signed and sealed in covenant with God, was put to the test of practice in order to demonstrate the strength of that holy alliance and divine coalition. The Puritan looked upon the past as prologue to his New England experiment, and viewed the lives of men and of nations as unrolled from a single past by the philosophic necessity and strict determinism of God. It seemed that the world was divinely governed, kept upon its course by a holy administration, and presided over by a cosmic king. History became, in the light of piety, not only a record of God's providence but also a drama of salvation. The world machine, having been created by a divine intelligence, was also guided by a divine will, and revealed itself to man as the mechanism of a divine purpose. It was the hope of understanding the divine purpose and of obeying the divine will which inspired Puritan piety and lent to the drama of salvation a sense of cosmic destiny. In this setting the Puritan undertook his great adventure, seeking in its perspectives the resolution of all the knotty intellectual problems descended upon him from the past, and hoping to bring to a tidy reformation the contradictions which gave dialectic vigor to his thought. He was enrolled as a soldier in the legions of his sovereign Lord to do battle against all evil, and he hoped to bring to the point of perfection that faith in practice which was the heart of his piety and the inspiration of his success.

The pragmatic piety led not to monastic retirement and monkish asceticism but to a joyous participation in Puritan struggles. Puritan piety lay in practice, in helping God do His intended work, and not in mystical raptures, not in monkish habits, not in momentary enthusiasms or unreasoning contemplative withdrawals. It led to positive and vigorous action, and manifested the strength of its resolution, by giving to the happy test of practice a metaphysical status which every successful ideology carries with it into the battle of life. At war with the flesh, struggling against the natural man, beset with enemies and defamers, attacked from within by Antinomian enthusiasts and from without by Arminian heretics, the Puritan worshiped his sovereign God. Caught in the act of treason against the divine government, confronted in his conscience by this breach of cosmic law, and convicted of his sins, the Puritan was stirred up to a volcanic release of his energies, and burst through the ordinary tenuous morality of the natural man with the sharp spear of his own absolute resolves. The pragmatic piety demonstrated the allegiance of the Puritan to the divine government, and revealed whether a cosmic king had also reserved for him a cosmic destiny.

3. *The Personality of God*

If then in accordance with the design and decree of God some are irresistibly chosen for election to sainthood while others are just as inevitably predestined to death and damnation, surely the philosophic idea of God must suggest a world in which all things are predetermined, in which all events exist by proxy, where the universal flux of being possesses yet another life beyond that the Puritan daily witnessed. A world in which physical determinism was so obvious must suggest to the Puritan mind a being who has predetermined all existences and events, who foresees and foreknows, who is omniscient as well as omnipotent. The ceaseless flux of events, the invincible flow of causality, whose outcome none but God could foresee, and whose design only He could know, seemed to the Puritan to possess a life of its own, revealing intelligence and will at work in a universe of material change. In this vast economy of redemption, only God could foresee a possible success, and know by an immediate act of His divine intelligence who shall be saved and who shall be damned. The philosophic idea of God which Puritan theology discovered, and to which Puritan piety responded, was the connection of events conceived not in their temporal order but in their logical linkages. The idea of God was the concept of philosophic necessity, generated and sustained by a faith in the inevitable and necessary connection of the events of cosmic history.

Upon the nature and attributes of God, accordingly, the Puritan expended the force of his brilliant imagination, and gave unending hours of silent contemplation to a mystery which he could not know. In his quiet hours of uneasy speculation he struggled for some insight into the divine mystery, sought to comprehend the divine essence, and gave himself up at last to the hopeless predicament into which he had been cast. Arrested in the act of treason against the divine government, brought into the court of conscience, and convicted of his sins, the Puritan was pricked on to determine those laws and gain those insights into the government of God which would guide him to appropriate action and keep him from inevitable sin. For the Puritan lived in a world sustained at each moment by the influx of divine energies, held in its course by the proportions of divine wisdom, and governed by strange forces which mysticism might seek to uncover but which the understanding could not hope to know. He was driven as a passive subject to participate in the predetermined laws of the object; while yet its laws were hidden from him, he was betrayed into transgression and inevitably committed to sin and error by his subjective ignorance and its objective mystery. The active subject-object relation, split apart in philosophy by the conflict of warring classes, left the Puritan with only the species of knowledge but not its hidden essence.

Puritan piety expresses this sense of the predicament of man; it expresses the egocentric predicament in which the subject has lost in its philosophy the object of its search, and seeks to rejoin it, not in the outer world where it might be found, but in the innermost soul of man. Man's ignorance of the hidden essence of the Godhead is the ignorance of the passive subject which cannot gain insight into the immanent laws and iron determinism of the object; and his sense of sin is a feeling of utter frustration that Adam's apostasy has blinded his reason and obscured his understanding beyond the hope of reunion and reconciliation

with the object of his spiritual desire. The Puritan was thus left in subjective alienation from his proper object, God, and dreamed of a time
of innocence or a garden of love in which some primitive ancestor
might have enjoyed the fruits of union and reconciliation. He posits sin
on the original Adam in order to account for his own distempers, and
calls it original sin. He posits a world of supernatural beauty, for thus
he imagines the alienated object, and calls it heaven. He posits a pit and
abyss of eternal fire, as the destiny of those who fall short of reconciliation with the object, and calls it hell. The Puritan wished, in this
dream of a possible reconciliation with the object, to transcend his finite
individuality and subjective selfhood in order to dwell eternally with the
ultimate principle of reality in the infinite mind of God. Hence knowledge of God and of the immortal soul was divine knowledge, and
theology was the queen of the sciences. Theology dealt, accordingly,
with God, the object and end of the soul; with sin, the condition of man
which has cut him off from the object of his quest; and with regeneration, his reconciliation of his subjective inner life with the vast panorama
of divine life dwelling around him.

In the dark reflecting glass of his mind, the Puritan had come to express in a religious way the basic cleavage of subject and object which
lies at the heart of modern philosophy, and which at the beginning revealed itself in the personality of God. A screen of phenomena, a picture of flux and change, had cut the Puritan off from a knowledge of
the immutable laws and unchangeable essence of God; and though this
gap may be bridged in a moment of mystical rapture or supernatural
visitation, the insight gained is momentary only, an incident in the
process of regeneration, when God has willed sainthood for one of his
creatures among the numerous fallen. Perhaps at that moment, or among
the choir of angels in heaven, the saint may share a part of the divine
wisdom, be reunited with the alienated object, and dwell in divine love.
But to all who had not been plucked out of their sins, cleansed of their
depravity, and irresistibly drawn into the household of the saints, knowledge would forever be denied her hidden truth, and the subject in its
passive ignorance would inevitably sin and transgress the immanent
laws of that object from which it had been cut off. Compared with
merely phenomenal knowledge of the natural man, his flesh sinfully
united to his soul, the knowledge which God possessed seemed to the
Puritan perfect, infinite, unchanging, a stable metaphysic in a restless
universe. It was the kind of knowledge the saints aspired to, but which
they could never fully attain. It was a knowledge of things-in-themselves,
without past or future, without addition or diminution, without change

or alteration, such as only God possesses as the cosmic essence or in-created idea of all things.

4. *The Sense of Sin*

From the depths of its imperfection and depravity, the soul conceives the flawless perfection of the imagined God; it dwells upon the possibility of good and of truth and of beauty, and the conviction of some original deprivation, by which the subject has been cut off from the increated good of its object, grows irresistibly. The remorseless logic of events teaches the soul that it is derived and dependent, that it dwells inharmoniously amidst a universal ferment of being, that it has been laggard in its responsibilities and has betrayed its trust. In this moment of recognition it seems as if a sentence of reprobation has been visited upon erring man, that the symbol of Adam's apostasy adequately portrays man's betrayal and his fall; it seems as if all the terrors of an acknowledged imperfection, an admitted sinfulness, all the frustrations of a lost soul, come down as an avalanche upon an old house of flesh, rotten and decayed. Gradually it is realized that man is a fallen creature, that he has cut himself off from the increated good of his heavenly Father, and that he is to be held accountable for his sins and breaches of the trust which God has reposed in him. Now the terrible wrath of the sovereign God seems only an epitome of His justice, and the terrors visited upon the sinful creature only an anticipation of the writhing pains and fiery horrors which are to be his heritage in hell. Finally, the fallen man realizes that without God's supernatural aid and grace there can be no salvation, that the soul's quest for salvation cannot be attained without this visitation of the divine power and influx of the divine energies. The natural man, his flesh sinfully united to his soul, cannot sever this union, cannot rise above his own nature, without the supernatural aid of God.

The union of the soul and sin, which only the supernatural grace of God could sever, originated in the garden of life when Adam in the heat of his apostasy preferred the selfish principles of the natural man, sinfully united to his flesh and appetites, above the divine principle of increated good which God had generously communicated to him. Now these selfish principles belonged to the nature of man and to all his posterity, for Adam had stood as the head and representative of all mankind, and his parliamentary blunder before the royal sovereign had cost his constituents the promise of life eternal. It was this chronology of events which explained to the Puritan why God had condemned all but a handful of the saints to a life of sin and misery and death. It was this conception of sin which set forth the disharmony, the imperfections, and the immoralities that persist in a world that is otherwise so divinely managed. The sense of sin accounted for the accidents, diseases, and the sorrows the flesh is heir to; and the chronicle of apostasy lent cosmic significance to the ceaseless daily triumph of evil in a world whose every event was predetermined by a sovereign God. It followed that however he might try to do good, live a life of holy endeavor, and keep himself by reasonable moderation upon a path of public morality, the Puritan could not hope for success in his quest of salvation, nor for profit in the economy of his redemption, without the supernatural aid and grace of God. Since he had been cut off from God, that increated good of the universe, by an original apostasy of Adam, he no longer possessed the spiritual strength to heal this wound, but must wait until the Lord should confer upon him the divine energy with which to combat evil.

5. *The Covenant of Grace*

The sense of sin involved, accordingly, not simply a natural understanding of man's waywardness, his petulance, his ill-humor, but a penetrating insight into his fallen and corrupted nature, an insight to which one falls heir, in the last analysis, only in the moment of spiritual illumination. The idea of sin suggested that man was a fallen, because he was a natural, creature; that in following the dictates of the body, he denied himself the resources of the spirit; that in living too much in this world, he denied himself access to the next; that in holding too close to temporals, he was refusing life eternal. In all this, of course, man's spirituality, his ideal self, was truly fallen and corrupted; only when conviction of his sinfulness came over man with the absolute and irresistible power of God, and when his whole life had been quickened by this illuminating insight, could he hope to be numbered among the saints, or seek the promise of eternal life. Before the soul in its lethargy can be roused from its sin and death, and the heart engaged in this experimental knowledge of divinity, there must be a right discovery of sin, a penetrating insight into the spiritual composition and accursed nature of human depravity. The illegitimate union of the soul and its sin, by which evil and lesser principles have assumed sovereignty over the temple of the spirit, is the favorite theme of the Puritan theologian. For the imperfections of fallen man are only too well known; his perverseness, his blindness, his ill-humor, are the common stuff of humanity. Once touched by the light of heaven, these plain and simple shortcomings become a sample of that deprivation in man by which he has cut himself off from the object of his quest, and of that primitive apostasy of Adam by which man shares in the punishment for original sin.

The Puritan had plentiful opportunity to observe what John Cotton called "man's perverse sutility in inventing wayes of backsliding." But a greater danger lurked in the hypocrite and saint-seeming deceiver whose outward behavior was a mask of pretense for the evil principles dwelling within. The Puritan was always on guard against the man who should take the doctrine of original sin merely as an invitation to lead a more exemplary life, displaying a correct civil and moral behavior, a life of outward righteousness, for the sake of nursing the hungry progeny of evil who nestle in his heart. But the Puritan professed to believe that the man of impeccable behavior, who aims at mere civil and moral and external goodness, who regulates his conduct by reason and his dealings with his fellow men by simple honesty, could never retain out of his corrupted nature that complete regeneration that flows from resting in Christ. To guard against this deception of mere civil conformity and conventional correctness, and to give the sinner some assurance of salvation while he is striving for moral perfection, the Puritan insisted that man's resolve to follow the path of Christ be bound by contract, signed by the high contracting parties, God and the sinner, and sealed by the blood of Christ. By this device fallen and corrupted man was drawn into indenture with God as His servant, and granted a probational grace on condition that he perform honestly and faithfully the articles of the contract. "Christ comes to you in his word and Covenant of Grace," wrote Thomas Shepard, "there is his Spirit, his Truth, Goodness, Love, Faithfulness: receive this, you receive him; embrace this, you embrace him; as among ourselves you see great Estates conveyed and surrendered by Bond and Writings."

The movement from status to contract, from feudalism to capitalism, is fully chronicled in the covenant of grace. In the light of covenant theology, the collective guilt of feudal times was transformed into a more personal bond and contract involving individual crime and punishment. The contract with God undertaken in the covenant of grace meant that while men had sinned collectively through their original representation in Adam, they were to be saved individually, predestined to a personal salvation or damnation. By the terms of the covenant of grace, moreover, individual man assumes personal responsibility for the moral law and the ordinances, for the performance of his duties to Christ the redeemer, and for the fulfillment of his obligations under the indenture. The Protestant doctrine of justification by faith was not to be allowed to stand without a corresponding doctrine of works slipped into the covenant of graces, brought home to the sinner by the articles he has signed, and by the blood of Christ wrought into the covenant parchment. The Reformation had abolished the doctrine of works in theory, but retained it in practice; for who would labor in church and state, who would bear the encumbrance of the moral law, and the grievous injunction of the ordinances? The covenant of grace, by tying the Puritan to the articles of his indenture, made the performance of his duties a condition of salvation, and the conferring of grace a condition of redemption.

6. *The Process of Regeneration*

Born in sin and fated to suffer evil, by virtue of a primitive apostasy of Adam, man also yearns for some hope of purification and salvation; and seeks about him the means of regeneration by which his erring faculties, dislocated in their natural frame, will stand again in correct dependence and righteous order. For the Puritan the process of regeneration was a most inviting prospect of speculation, and upon the question of the means of regeneration he exchanged with all other seventeenth-century religious professions a heated theological opinion. Amidst the welter of conflicting religious truths, the Puritan stood firm ground before the allurements of other routes into the gates of heaven. For him, God does not depart ordinarily from the familiar causal order He daily employs, neither in the common providence of His government, nor in the more spectacular demonstrations of His administration. God must enter the soul through the ordinary gate of sense impression, and eventually travel to the heart and will through the understanding. It followed that while God could confer grace instantaneously, by a kind of singular rapture of the spirit, he ordinarily worked men up in choice, as cause by counsel, to a conviction of His influence and visitation. Grace must then endow each of the faculties of the soul separately as it passes along, finally leading the blind will by the enlightened understanding to the right choice. Not only the understanding and the will, but the affections and the appetite also, must be touched by divine grace, and the whole man rectified.

"Therefore if there be no great and remarkable abiding change in persons, that think they have experienced a work of conversion," wrote Jonathan Edwards, "vain are all their imaginations and pretences, however they have been affected. Conversion is a great and universal change of the man, turning him from sin to God. A man may be restrained from sin, before he is converted; but when he is converted, he is not only restrained from sin, his very heart and nature are turned from it unto holiness; So that thenceforth he becomes a holy person, and an enemy to sin. If therefore, after a person's high affections, at his supposed first conversion, it comes to that in a little time, that there is no very sensible, or remarkable alteration in him, as to those bad qualities, and evil habits, which before were visible in him, and he is ordinarily under the prevalence of the same kind of dispositions that he used to be, and the same things seem to belong to his character; he appears as selfish, carnal, as stupid, and perverse, as unchristian and unsavory as ever; it is greater evidence against him, than the brightest story of experiences that ever was told, is for him. For in Christ Jesus neither circumcision, nor uncircumcision, neither high profession nor low profession, neither a fair story, nor a broken one, avails any thing; but a new creature." [1]

From this theological position it followed that grace was not miraculous and instantaneous, but had its own peculiar chronology in which each of the faculties is rectified and renewed. It happened, accordingly, that the Puritan viewed regeneration as a process, as a piece of cosmic history, in which ultimately the whole soul of man is enkindled and embraced. The Puritan wished particularly to avoid the twin heresies of Pelagianism and Arminianism on this question of regeneration, for these two departures from orthodoxy generally placed a kind of ability in the will to accept or reject the righteousness that God offers man. To have accepted the Pelagian or Arminian position would have obscured piety and brought a deluge down upon the temple of truth; for such an opinion, an impolitic heresy, was an affront to the sovereignty, to the supernatural royal power, of the divine king. If then the understanding had followed the last dictate of the will, without a former gracious confederation of its own, regeneration would have become a stroke of policy within the parliament of choice, a mere matter of free will, which would have thrown into the discard all the elaborate Puritan speculation on the doctrine of original sin. At the other extreme lay the antinomian radicals who would have the affections touched in a moment of enthusiasm and supernatural visitation, throwing off the ordinances and converting the machinery of salvation into a lawless contingent power. The acceptance of either position would have taken supernatural power out of the household of the saints, and the ministers would have been outflanked by visitations which they could neither analyze nor control. In truth, the Puritan was a religious pragmatist who gave cosmic sanction to his instrumental values, while yet claiming that these values were instrumental only as divine means.

7. *The Economy of Redemption*

The means of regeneration are of course divine [means], but in this operation God does not ordinarily violate the natural order of cause and effect; for though the power of grace extends across the abyss of time by an immediate act of God, it flows normally through the stream of causality and emerges visibly as the strength of the saint in His regeneration. But behind the mechanical show of cause and effect, as a background of its endless puppetry, lurked the mystery of the divine purpose and the power of the divine will. The decree of God in predestining some to salvation and others to damnation expressed in a theological way the fact that the achievements of men and their ultimate success depend, not so much upon any innate virtue or intelligence they possess, nor yet upon the exercise of their abilities or the freedom of their wills, but rather upon a course of events whose inevitable connections were known but to God and whose final outcome no man could foresee. The doctrine of predestination was a theological essay on the fact that man can neither control nor understand all things, and that in the long run the values of things, the increated good of all commodities, will be established by the operation of a cosmic market and finally judged by a cosmic king. The Puritan therefore believed that through his autonomous choices he was bringing about predetermined effects, engaging himself in a predestined history; and as an instrument of the divine will, he was energized to do the world's work, pursuing in the market of chance a predetermined scheme of price-fixing known ultimately but to God.

In consequence, Puritan theology contains a double paradox—on the one hand, the doctrine of predestination led to vigorous exertion and a cosmic optimism; and on the other hand, as a patient of God's determinations, the Puritan felt himself most truly the agent of his own free will. It was argued that man, a created agent and second cause, is one among a number of secondary causal agencies by which God works His sovereign will and carries out His monarchical designs. God has therefore given man a causal virtue, argued the Puritan, by which the sovereign operates to produce His predetermined events, and manages the flow of His efficacy and causal power. God not only fulfills His purpose and satisfies His will, but also employs as His instruments those secondary causes which stand as effects to God's own primary causal power. In this manner God has undertaken to honor man with the dignity of being an instrument of His holy will. God has made man His agent, and has given him a causal virtue and ability, so that he might produce God's predetermined effects. The Puritan was thus caught up in the causal efficacy and power of God; he was thus enmeshed in a vast economy of redemption, and was truly a humble citizen of that divine government. He believed himself caught up in the underground connections and mysterious linkages by which a flow of divine power was communicated across the cosmic abyss between cause and effect, and that he possessed, by virtue of His position, a secondary causal power which was a necessary link in the great chain of universal being.

We are thus brought to the heart of Puritan theology, and to the inner meaning of Puritan dialectics. If we waive for a moment the theological dress of this Puritan paradox, strip off its religious garments, strike out the pious phrases, the paradox will stand naked before us as the familiar philosophic problem of freedom and necessity. Man has effective free will, argued the Puritan; he has a causal virtue and aptitude which as a created agent and second cause is necessary to produce its appropriate effects. These effects God could have produced immediately by the sovereign power of His holy will; but He chose rather to confer an instrumental dignity upon man, and so, in this sense, conferred upon him a secondary or instrumental freedom of the will. But what is thus freedom of the will from the perspective of man is from the cosmic perspective simply the predeterminism of God. *Man's freedom is God's necessity*—this is the heart of Puritan theology, the essence of Puritan thought, the paradox upon which a later generation was to stumble and lose its way. Starting then with the conception of the predeterminism of God, the Puritan was driven from his major premise that the world is divinely governed to the minor premise that he is a predestined instrument of the divine will, and hence to the conclusion that man's freedom is God's necessity. It was a mighty syllogism designed to fortify the Puritan in his struggles; and it proved an effective ideology, for history discovered the Puritan to be no common adversary when it entrusted him with the . fulfillment of the sovereign will of God, and he was hardly the man to be disturbed by the blood of heretics or the rustlings of a cavalier.

CHAPTER TWO

THE CHRISTIAN COMMONWEALTH

1. *The Puritan Politics*

The sovereignty of God might have gone unchallenged had it not been that the sovereignty of man was for the moment a political issue. The Puritan was caught up in the great transition of political theory from monarchical to parliamentary conceptions of government, and his political ideas express the compromise position to which he aspired. If then he left the mother country at the moment when the parliamentary cause seemed lost and government by contract defiled, he by no means intended to introduce anarchy after his migration to America. Caught thus in a compromise position between the political doctrine of consent and the theological doctrine of God's sovereignty, the Puritan effected a synthesis in which the people consent to the government that is set over them by divine administration and bind by their social contract a common dedication of the Christian state to the holy purposes of reformation. It followed from this eclectic doctrine that the people consent to the government which God has set over them, and that the magistrates rule the Puritan commonwealth with as divine a claim as that of the feudal king. The compromise was an uneasy one, and lasted only so long as the theological doctrine of God's sovereignty was not jostled by the Arminian doctrine of free will. When at last the parliamentary rules of choice granted an autonomous sovereignty of the will to man, and presupposed his free consent to the government that was set over him, the days of the saints were numbered and their theory of Christian aristocracy became as outmoded as the pretenses of the feudal king.

In medieval theory, it will be remembered, the state is explained as a necessity engendered by the sinful and corrupt state of man, a necessity which by no means precludes however that some should enjoy its prerogatives. The state is divine, a part of God's ordinance for repressing the fatal taint of evil in all men. The Puritans, however, were caught up in the great transition from feudalism to capitalism; and their political theory, reflecting this change from status to contract, is filled with the unhealthy contradictions which attended it. As medieval theory had begun its analysis on the thesis of original sin, the Puritan theory stated its reformation at that point. In Puritan theory the doctrine of original sin undergoes a marvelous transformation in which Adam stands as the federal head or representative of all mankind, so that his constituents suffer from the parliamentary blunders of their representative. When Adam broke the covenant, accordingly, the legal responsibility was imputed to his descendents and constituents. In brief, it was the rotten-borough system; for Adam stood for all in his district, even for those who did not vote for him. Human nature had nevertheless contracted this legal responsibility by imputation from Adam, and man was henceforth the receiver in bankruptcy of the debt which Adam had contracted with God.

The Puritan analysis of original sin, therefore, provided eminently plausible grounds for the otherwise mysterious doctrine of predestination. To keep faithful to the bond or mortgage, to live in repentance for an original violation of its terms, and to keep the moral law and subsequent commands of God seemed to the Puritan a perfectly agreeable explanation of the doctrine of election. Meantime, however, the Puritans had developed a theory of redemption as the basis of their covenant of grace. As Adam had stood as the federal representative of mankind in the covenant of works, so Christ had stood as the representative of mankind in the covenant of redemption. God covenanted with Christ that if he would pay the price for the redemption of the faithful, they should be discharged of their debt. Thus God and Christ, for the purpose of underwriting the covenant of grace, had incorporated a body of regenerate Christians. As the corporation had been driven into bankruptcy by Adam's apostasy, the incorporated saints had thus filed their papers and assets, and had bound themselves by a new contract in preparation for starting out again under new management. It happened, accordingly, that a church was conceived as a corporation of saints, and the state as the proper organ for an aristocracy of Christian grace.

Puritan political theory, still half-feudal in its forms, sought to counter the feudal claim to rule by divine right by an equally grandiose claim to the divinity of the social contract. Puritan theory argued that the covenant of grace was conferred by Abraham on his seed, so that political societies must be incorporated under this covenant. The state still has the seed of divinity in it, but it can be formed only upon the consent of the people congregated under it. In the feudal view, the state is necessary because of original sin, and the depravity of man becomes a positive buttress for the coercive arm of the law. Even Calvin, living in the era of the absolute monarchs, believed that obedience should be enjoined by a government of the righteous, and punished with fire and sword those who deviated from the discipline of the consistory. But once the Puritans had secured their charter from King Charles, removing themselves from the long arm of his mighty prerogative, they invested it with the old feudal sanctity, so that the magistrates might rule with the same divine grace which had bedecked the courts of the absolute king. Following the Puritan removal to the wilds of America, therefore, the premature modern notes of contractualism and consent were magisterially whittled down. The consequence was that the magistrates considered themselves to represent God rather than the people, and claimed that God had consented, through the people's suffrages, to their most excellent administrations.

The theory of state worked out in New England was a composite of the feudal and the modern, with the feudal notes predominating as the result of the piety engendered by a practical situation. God created, out of the community of the regenerate, an aristocracy of Christian grace, a will to moral obedience and a sense of communal kinship. The regenerate thereupon combine their several wills into one socially inclusive and unified regenerate will, and thus incarnate the divine will and the covenant of grace into a new social contract which had the approval of God upon it. Theoretically, the people consent to this government; but they can after all consent only to a divine government, chosen in Christ. The Lord thus frames a people to a willing and voluntary subjection to the magistrates whom he has appointed through the people's suffrages. The law of God is thus incarnate in the Christian state, and hence ministerial injunction and magisterial law rested upon the same level of moral obedience. It happened, accordingly, that the Puritan state was in reality Plato's rule of the wisest and best, unified by the Christian doctrine of election and made plausible by an aristocracy of Christian grace. The democratic ideals carried in the seed by the migrants to New England were at best premature modern notes which the magistrates and ministers, by one device or another of a political theory rooted in the feudal past, were able to subvert and destroy. Until divinity was rooted out of the state and political theory purged of its feudal past, the magistrates must lay their claim to stewardship over the Christian state on a right as divine as that of the English king, and discover in the doctrine of consent a choice of God in their own administrations.

2. *The Christian Aristocracy*

The conception of an ethical aristocracy to rule over the Christian state was an easy deduction of the Puritan leaders from the theological doctrine of divine election; and if the oligarchy seized upon it as a divine sanction to their endeavors, we should little wonder to find a warrant for it in Scripture and a Mosaic model as precedent. The immigrant Puritan gentlemen who settled at Massachusetts Bay found in the aristocracy of Christian grace the means of rejecting alike the pretension to divine rule indulged in by the Stuart monarchs—a necessary heritage of the feudal epoch—and the democratic pretensions of the populace, who would make grace accessible to all men on equal terms by declaring that God dwells in the heart of every true believer. The Calvinist doctrine of divine election was admirably suited, accordingly, to express the compromise position to which the Puritan leaders aspired; and if they were concerned to challenge the Stuart claim to rule by divine right with their own pretensions of being the elect of God, they were likewise concerned to reject the democratic implications of the doctrine that God grants His supernatural aid to all true believers in Christ. Pressed by the Arminian claim that man had it in his power to accept or reject divine grace, the Puritan leaders reasserted their fundamental belief in the sovereign election of God; and bedeviled by the Antinomian doctrine of the inner light, they replied that supernatural grace was not accessible to all men on equal terms. Translated in the light of the political struggles then going forward in England, the Puritan emphasis upon divine election meant that he rejected, on the one hand, the sovereignty of man in the rule of the state and, on the other, the equal right of all to participate in its government. Fashioned by the caste society of old England, half-feudal in their conceptions, the Puritan leaders were by no means prepared to give up the aristocratic principle after migrating to the New World.

When such men are endowed with religious zeal and granted corporate powers by the terms of their charter, when they regard themselves as instruments of the divine will and take into their hearts the discipline of Geneva and the iron will of God, then the Christian utopia may be expected to raise its coercive arms against all intruders, and exercise over the lives of its citizens a large measure of the authority which God has reposed in its hands. If, beyond the power normally resident in such as are the elect of Christ, the good Lord lets drop a special call that they be armed in the spirit for their endeavors, and to that end binds them in covenant to the performance of their proper duties, then the saints will not take their responsibilities lightly when the sea of troubles and the storms of dissension, common to so perilous a venture, rush in upon them. To such as undertook to govern the model commonwealth, the ideal of the Christian magistracy must early have formed in their minds. Even before leaving England, while they were still leafing through their Genevan bibles, the thought must have entered the minds of the Puritan leaders that the aristocratic principle imbedded in the hard theology of Calvin, and the precious example of his magistracy over the Christian commonwealth at Geneva, were sufficient warrants for the principles to be adopted in laying out the plans and specifications for the holy society in New England.

3. *The Arminian Challenge*

Arbitrary government might live as long as the doctrine of the sovereignty of God went unchallenged. While men lived under the threat of predestination from an absolute monarch, they could not easily challenge the authority of the Christian oligarchy, without at the same time calling into question the sovereignty of God. It happened, therefore, that a number of deficiences in the inherited Calvinist theology soon came to light, and that when the unregenerate pressed for equality with the saints they called into question the Puritan theory of divine election upon which the aristocracy of Christian grace had built their government. Moreover, in laying out the plans and specifications for erecting God's commonwealth in the New World, the Puritan leaders had not reckoned with the problem of ethical absolutism contained as a seedling in the hard shell of their Calvinist heritage. If the events of history are conceived as a chronicle of God's providence, if the acts of the drama of salvation are all prefigured in the mind of the Great Dramatist, and if man plays his assigned and predetermined role under the divine management, in what sense can it be said that man is morally capable of his sins, his crime, and his miseries?

In Adam's apostasy the Puritan could account for the presence of so much evil in a world divinely governed; in the severity of the law he could seek an explanation of the troubles and terrors which flooded in upon man. But there remained, in consequence of the heritage of ethical absolutism, the problem of moral responsibility and, with it, the need to excite man to moral earnestness and sincere endeavor in the face of the pronouncement that these things are not the means of election. Puritan sermons are filled with the complaint that the faithful are neglecting the duty of striving, and decline from any effort of their own to attain righteousness. But this consequence was the logical outcome of the stress on the predestination of man; for it seemed to the laggard that no effort on their part, no election of their own free will, could effect salvation as long as every event and the conferring of every grace remained a part of the predeterminism and absolute sovereignty of God. Sooner or later the New England divines had to face the problem of ethical absolutism contained as a seed in their Calvinist theological heritage, and the occasion pressing for an official solution of this problem came with the rise of the Arminian challenge.

Arminius had asserted the free will of man in accepting or rejecting divine grace, and had thereby punctured the supposed invincibility of the Calvinist armor which protected the sovereignty of God. The significance of the Arminian heresy will not immediately strike the observer unless it is remembered how all the stones of the Puritan church rested their weight upon this one buttress, how every doctrine of Puritan theology was woven in and out of the garment of God's absolute dominion. Unless it is remembered that this theme of God's absolute dominion and sovereignty was central to all the conceptions and theories which framed the Puritan ideology, it can hardly be appreciated that Arminianism represented a challenge not only to Puritan theology but to Puritan politics as well. In asserting man's free will to accept or reject divine grace, Arminius had in effect dethroned the mighty God; he had rebelled against the divine government, had brought the infinite within the range of the finite, and had deflated the sovereignty of God in an effort to elevate the dignity of man. Arminianism asserted the sovereignty of man at the expense of the sovereignty of God and, in so doing, put within the power of man the reconstruction of life out of death and sin and misery. In attempting to grant man some responsibility in his moral endeavors, Arminius had extended the range of man's dominion and had effectively whittled down the feudal title of God to that ancient domain. The Arminian heresy was naturally popular wherever men wanted not only freedom of will but freedom of trade, and is clearly an advance over Calvin's half-feudal notions; but with this single weapon, should it prevail widely enough, Arminius could have brought the amazing theoretic edifice of Puritanism crashing to the ground.

Arminius might thus have struck a mighty blow at the Boston oligarchy which had come to rule the colonies clustered around Massachusetts Bay; for when Arminius asserted the additional heresy that if man would improve his talents and make the most of the means put into his hands God would not withhold His grace, he was clearly taking what seemed from the perspective of New England a fatal step toward secularism, the first step in a movement which comes to fruition in the Enlightenment. In asserting the doctrine that God does not withhold His grace from those who exert themselves morally, Arminius had with one stroke dignified man with moral responsibility and granted an ethical individualism which is clearly lacking in Calvin. Arminianism made salvation depend upon human effort, exalted initiative and individual enterprise, thus forcing God's supernatural aid and His power and dominion more and more into the background. Because Arminianism democratized divine grace, making it accessible to all men on equal terms—provided only that they display the sovereign virtues of individual enterprise and moral responsibility—it became a heresy and abomination to the Boston oligarchy; its effect was to break open the house of the saints and to admit to the ranks of the Christian aristocracy a host of ungracious commoners.

In brief, the political consequences of the Arminian heresy spelled out the fate which sooner or later would overtake the saints in a freer environment. If put into effect in New England, the hold of the Boston leaders would have been broken, and the model Christian commonwealth would have deteriorated in the hands of a natural aristocracy, formed of those who displayed boldness and enterprise, who in time would have come to supplant the aristocracy of Christian grace. The rule of the magistrates and ministers was linked together by an orthodox bond, and so a religious heresy was as intolerable as a political revolt. The authority of the commonwealth, the Puritan maintained, must be invested only in the elect of Christ; for if simple worldly virtues should come to supplant the supernatural dignity of divine grace, and worldly men aspire to power, the church would degenerate and the state fall into the hands of a lesser sovereignty than that of God.

4. *The Federal Theology*

The sovereignty of God might have gone unchallenged had it not been that the sovereignty of man was at the moment a political issue. The parliamentary struggles were now upon the political horizon, and rule by divine right was being challenged through rule by natural right. It happened, therefore, that the theological issues which accompanied these battles fell under the mantle of their causes, and issued forth from the womb of time as creative attempts to undermine Calvinist orthodoxy without pretending any departure from it. Calvin had framed his doctrine in the era of divine right, in the age of the absolute monarchs, and had therefore graced the sovereign God with some of the attributes of a sovereign king. Divine right must presuppose and include the right to dispose of the persons and properties of the subject, for without such an absolute sovereignty the divinity of the right will be impaired. This condition was reflected in Calvinist theology, for the absolute God, by divine right, predestines some to salvation and others to eternal damnation. It happened, accordingly, that this condition had become an abomination and snare to the bourgeoisie. Their condition, on the contrary, presupposed freedom of will, the sovereignty of man in framing the destiny of his person and property. The property of the subject was by right inalienable, but could be alienated through free consent to a contract equally binding upon both parties.

The theological problem of the age, then, was to reserve moral responsibility and freedom of will to man without impairing or diminishing the sovereignty of God. The Arminian heresy arose as a partial solution of this contradiction; for Arminius declared that the efficacy of grace depends on the will of man, by virtue of a native liberty, and therefore that man could accept or reject divine grace when it was proffered. He insisted, further, that if man improved his talents, made the most of his abilities, and attempted to live according to the rule of righteousness, God would not withhold His grace. In brief, Arminianism was offering encouragement, inducements, and freedom of will; it was asserting the dignity and sovereignty of man against the divine sovereignty and absolute dominion of God. All the conditions demanded by the new religion were thus met; for man, under these new terms, subscribed to the government of God out of his own free will and consent, and his industry and talent were rewarded in proportion as his native abilities worked up the substance of life into a suitable commodity for salvation. The absolute monarch of Calvinism had thus become a parliamentary monarch of Arminianism, ruling under conditions specified by national charter or contract.

These necessary conditions of the age were also met by another creative attempt to jostle the old Calvinism by a new assertion of native liberty. Antinomianism was the common possession of radical sectarianism in the theological debates that preceded the English civil wars. Whether in Anabaptist, Quaker, Ranter, or Leveller, or in Mistress Hutchinson, it took the form of the belief that the union of the elect with the Holy Ghost was immediate and intimate. The Antinomian believed that God dwells in the heart of all true believers in Christ, and that such as have this intimate union have assurance of salvation. In brief, while Arminianism struck at the doctrine of election by making it accessible to the free will and natural liberty of man, Antinomianism struck at it by making divine grace accessible to all men on equal terms. Antinomianism was equivalent to the assertion that

God must treat all His subjects as equals, must not sort out the aristocracy of the elect by any supernatural favoritism, must not grant a
monopoly on success to the merchant princes who graced the sovereign
courts. In Arminianism, therefore, the monarch may rule only by the
consent of the ruled; in Antinomianism, he must treat all who are ruled
on equal terms, granting assurance of success and salvation, not to any
aristocracy of Christian grace, but to all who believe and subject themselves loyally to his government. Both the Arminian and the Antinomian
heresies, then, may be looked upon as attempts to democratize divine
grace, to confine this infinite supernatural power within the limits of
the conditions necessary to the emerging social order.

   The Federal Theology of the New England Puritans was an attempt,
not only to counteract these twin heresies, but also to meet the conditions and resolve the contradictions out of which they had grown. It
was founded on the belief that God and man had drawn up a contract,
bond, indenture, or mortgage, the essence of which was voluntary
agreement on both sides, to a document attested and sealed. It presupposed that man has applied for a charter of liberties from the divine monarch. God, because He wishes to treat men as rational creatures,
voluntarily enters into covenant with them. The Federal Theologians
insisted that God has always dealt with man in this way; for, although
the covenant of works was broken by Adam, the Lord initiated a new
covenant with Abraham, a covenant of grace. The terms of this new
mortgage or contract stipulated that men, for their part, are to walk
in good faith, and that God, for His part, will give assurance to those
who so walk in faith and live in righteousness. In brief, the Puritan had
entered into an agreement with God, promising assurance of salvation
to men and assurance of faith to God. The two conditions of the new
theology have thus been met; for God, without sacrificing His sovereignty, has condescended to treat men as equals, to encourage them in
their endeavors by granting assurance of salvation, while man has entered into the contract of his own free will and consent.

   This interpretation of the covenant of grace by the New England
divines had softened the blow of predestination without disturbing its
ultimate truth. Protestant orthodoxy had insisted that salvation was by
faith rather than by works, and the new covenant in Abraham had in
truth made faith an article of its agreement. In keeping the people
to the moral law, however, so that there might be no breach of the commandments in spite of assurance given in the covenant of grace, the
divines insisted that God had incorporated into the covenant of grace
a covenant of works, not indeed as the conditions of salvation, but as

the rule of righteousness. This bit of Puritan casuistry insured that those in the covenant of grace, the visible elect, would not lead an unsanctified life; it made clear that while man met the conditions of faith and repentance in the covenant of grace, he was not thereby free from the original covenant of Adam, and must inevitably fulfill the demands of God in that ancient covenant and pledge himself in payment of the full debt of the law. The Puritans had thus met all the conditions demanded by the new theology without for one moment abandoning their orthodoxy; for they had granted the free will and consent of man to the contract, had bound God to its performance, granting assurance in return for faith and repentance, without for a moment impairing the rule of the elect over the unregenerate, or the moral law of God in the lives of men. It was an uneasy compromise and lasted only so long as the ignorance of men prevented them from finding out how much of a compromise it was.

But for the moment the Federal Theology was an effective answer to the Arminian challenge and the Antinomian heresy. By this ingenious piece of divinity, accordingly, Arminianism was directly confronted and Antinomianism was put to rout. The covenant theology emphasized, on the one hand, the voluntary nature of the agreement between God and man, and hence asserted man's free will and consent to the contract; and on the other hand, the covenant theology made the point that God had instigated the deal, had struck off the bargain, so that His sovereignty was not lost, nor was the doctrine of election or that of predestination seriously impaired. The saints are still saints, the elect are still elected; but their status is contractual, and they have entered into the contract of their own free will and consent. Nor is God's absolute providence and dominion impaired, because the offer of the covenant and the aid of supernatural grace comes from Him. In brief, the absolute monarch of feudalism has granted a bill of inalienable rights in order to qualify himself for government under the covenants of capitalism.

5. *The Social Contract*

To make clear how much ingenuity was exercised in maintaining the rule of the Christian oligarchy, we have only to explore further into the labyrinths of Federal Theology, for its premature modern notes hardly suited its outlandish feudal dress. The Federal Theology was one of those recondite and technically perfect ideologies thrown up in the movement of history from a static feudal order to a dynamic cap-

italist one, and its feudal notions are so skillfully harmonized and inter-
woven with its modern notes as to baffle the investigator in tracing out
its complex themes. In the Federal Theology, it will be remembered, the
original sin of Adam had been modified from a permanent and invariable status between serf and lord—such as had obtained in feudal
theory—into a simple breach of contract, for which, of course, any indentured servant or bonded laborer could in Puritan times be punished.
In traditional theory Adam's depravity was held to be communicated
to all his descendants by inheritance; in his fall, all had by imputation
fallen with him. In the Federal Theology, however, it is maintained
that Adam stood only as the Federal representative of man in the legislature of the divine government, and that, in his breach of contract, all
who had underwritten and guaranteed him before the Lord were jointly
responsible for the betrayal of his trust. Although the effect of this
variation on the traditional theme of original sin left the matter of man's
current depravity untouched, the Puritan had in his subtlety transformed
the nature of the Fall from a matter of strictly feudal inheritance and
tenure to one of personal guilt and responsibility in breach of contract
punishable by law. It happened, accordingly, that the Puritan was able
to negotiate with the Lord in this business, whereas his feudal predecessors had been hopelessly bound by Adam's apostasy.

The covenant of grace made possible, as we have seen, the binding
of God to treat with His creatures as with rational and autonomous
beings who by their voluntary consent enter into His mortgage or bond.
At this point, in transforming the nature of Adam's sin, the Federal
Theologians added a clever covenant of redemption, in which Christ,
of his own free will and consent, offered to fulfill the covenant of works
and to atone for the imputed sin of man. The effect of the covenant of
redemption was to placate God's justice, so that God could mercifully
receive the saints for their faith in the light of supernatural grace. But
in volunteering to act as the scapegoat for man, Christ bound God in
contract to bestow grace upon those for whom he was about to die. Adam
had stood as the Federal representative of man in the original breach of
contract between man and God; but now Christ stands as the Federal
representative of the elect in the atonement, so that negotiations over
the broken bond had now reached a new and encouraging stage. It
happened, therefore, that the Federal Theologians interpreted the Scriptures as if God the Father and God the Son had drawn up an everlasting
compact concerning the redemption and salvation of prospective saints.
The covenant of works is now to be fulfilled by a mortgage on the life
of Christ, and the covenant of grace is assured by that capital outlay.

By this investment in the Trinity, the Puritan had worked out a novel and ingenious contract to salvage the souls of the elect, and he had bound God and Christ irrevocably to assure the eternal life.

The consequences of this social-contract theory for setting up God's commonwealth in New England and in justifying the rule of the saints were momentous; and in this respect, too, the oligarchy were called upon to exercise their casuistry in a way that puts to shame the clever hosts of modern apologists. At the outset the Puritan was faced with the contradiction that contractual theory called for government by the consent of the governed, constitutional limitations on the prerogatives of the governors, and the voluntary submission of the people of their rulers; but traditional theory, following St. Augustine, required that governments be divinely instituted, that governors and magistrates hold their authority as from God, and that the state had originated out of the depths of man's depravity, to repress the evil beast within. The result of these contradictory requirements was, of course, an impossible compromise in which it was maintained that governments exist upon the suffrages of their people, but that elected representatives rule by divine right. Rule by the consent of the governed was accordingly transformed into a divine sanction for magistracy; and it was maintained, with a certain metaphysical consistency, that: "In regular actions of the creature, God is the first agent; there are not two several and distinct actions, one of God, another of the people; but in one and the same action, God, by the people's suffrages, makes such a one governor, or magistrate, and not another." [2]

It happened, accordingly, that the social-contract theory of the New England Puritan involved him in the premature modern admission that government is by consent of the governed, while at the same time his feudal heritage required that the state be divinely instituted, and left to his discretion the means by which consent might be extracted through the people's suffrages. The people consent to the Puritan government erected by their suffrages; but they can after all only consent to a divine government, chosen in Christ. The Lord thus frames the people to a willing and voluntary subjection to the magistrates whom He has appointed through the people's suffrages; and the law of God, by virtue of the people's choice, becomes incarnate in the Christian state. The state still has a seed of divinity in it, and the magistrates rule by a right as divine as that of a feudal king; but God, by virtue of the many covenants he has signed with his chosen people, has come to rule by the consent of His governed, and will hold His people personally liable for any breach of the divine contract. The modern requirement that the state has its origin in a social contract and exists by the consent of those who are governed was thus balanced by the feudal requirement that the state is divine and its rulers rule by virtue of God's choice in their most excellent administrations. In political theory, as in every department of life, the Puritan revealed himself as a transition figure, the living contradiction of a contradictory age, an empty category into which God poured the full vial of his wrath.

CHAPTER THREE

THE PURITAN LIFE

1. *The Congregational Principle*

The Boston migrants shared, not only religious principles and purposes, but stock in the Massachusetts Bay Company. They were Cambridge men, disciples of Peter Ramus and Calvin, followers of the Federal Theology of Ames and Perkins, and they no doubt possessed at the moment of their coming over common preconceptions on the matter of ecclesiastical polity. The problem of church government had for them resolved itself into the means of incorporating a company of Christians, so that the purity of their worship and the observation of the ordinances of Christ might be promoted. The regenerate thereupon form a company for the orderly worship of God; and, satisfied that they are all men of sound faith, they covenant together, forming out of their compact a church. A congregation of saints thus formed is in its nature autonomous, and no bishops, archbishops, synods or assemblies may assert coercive power over them. The principle of congregational autonomy parallels the principle of corporate autonomy, for the saints own a common share in the means of salvation. The principle of congregational autonomy, while it assured the independence of the churches from the coercive arm of bishops, did not of itself provide for a democratic fellowship of all true believers in Christ, but rather legalized the means by which the saints were assured of their salvation.

The original members of the newly congregated church will receive into fellowship, accordingly, only those whom they judge to be within the covenant, and will expel those in whom they have been deceived; the members of the corporation of Christ will elect ministers and officers, appropriate church funds, and determine policies by their suffrages. A true church is thus a congregation of saints, submitting to the rule of Christ in the public observation of the ordinances out of their own freewill and regenerate choice. This collection of visible saints, incorporated by the covenant into church fellowship, seemed to the Presbyterian wing of the Puritan party to exclude from membership and salvation the majority of those who attended church services and paid their dues to righteousness, but who were not admitted to the exclusive inner circle of the corporation. The Presbyterians preferred to believe that a true church should include the whole nation, so that the matter of election and damnation might be left to God. They professed, as all true Christians might, that they could find no warrant for a company of incorporated saints in Scripture; and they believe that Christ had ordained a universal visible church organized out of the body of inhabitants of each nation. To the New England congregationalist, however, it seemed that Christ had given the administration of his ordinances and the keys of his kingdom only to particular churches, which might become visible by their bond or covenant. The church covenant, by incorporating a particular proprietary of religious opinion, gave visible embodiment to the covenant of grace in which the saints owned a common share.

The result was a congregational system of church government particularly adapted to the problems of ecclesiastical polity as they were faced in the wilderness of New England. Each town had its church, and each church its congregation of visible saints. Around these sanctified persons was gathered the unregenerate mass of the people. The body of unincorporated inhabitants was to attend church services, lend their low wits to a sermon exhortation, and support the minister in his pulpit and the magistrate on his throne. The inhabitants—the plain people dwelling around—inspired by the hope of regeneration and of admission to the visible aristocracy, faithfully performed audience for the learning and piety of their ministers and sat obediently before the groaning admonitions of their magistrates. But the keys of the kingdom were in the hands of an aristocracy of Christian grace, and no one might gain admittance to the heavenly city without the approbation and judgment of the saints visibly assembled. For the New England divines professed to believe that the covenant of grace included and sustained the church covenant. The ordinances, which were after all so many means or signs of regeneration, could be received only in church fellowship, and hence the means of salvation could be shared only by the company of incorporated Christians.

The Presbyterians had objected that the New England church covenant made membership a condition of salvation; and this was truly the plight of the unregenerates who were pressing for spiritual and political equality with the saints. But the Puritans rejoined that the church covenant only included, presupposed, and made visible the covenant of grace; that indeed, it was the covenant of grace which was the condition of election, not church membership as such. For the Puritan community, then, an inward condition of faith was transformed into an outward consociation of the faithful; the thin white flame of Christian piety was clothed with a visible and political form, and its power was mobilized as the purest heart of the community. The social conscience was thus assembled through the church in the form of a profession of faith, so that the ministers and magistrates, in the performance of their holy work, might enjoy a plebeian suffrage for the policies which they had already determined secretly in their private though incorporated wills. "The government of the church in regard to the body of the people is democraticall; in regard of the elders aristocraticall; in regard of Christ, truely monarchicall." These words of Thomas Hooker sum up the congregational polity of the New England Puritan, and reveal how piety and politics might confederate together for the purpose of perpetuating the rule of the saints.

2. The Means of Salvation

The question of regeneration had led the Puritan quite inevitably to the position that God does not ordinarily depart from the natural order of causes in bringing about His intended efforts. It therefore appeared to the Puritan that regeneration was a process of spiritual growth, a piece of cosmic history, in which the whole soul of man is caught up in a vast and irresistible economy of redemption, and drawn inevitably to a predestined salvation. The conscience, then, must be engaged by causality, and this power must transmit itself over common ground of causal connections until it emerges again in human causal action. Hence, among the ordinary means of conversion, the Puritan placed the sermon as of outstanding importance, and one generally employed by God to effect His transcendent work. The Puritan sermon was addressed to the understanding, with the hope that it would do its transcendent work through the will; and to the sermon, accordingly, as to all other ordinary means, the Puritan attached both a natural and a supernatural causality, the former being the efficient order of causes and effects, and the latter being the necessary and wholly mysterious connection between them. The sermon might arouse the spirit to regeneration, or leave its auditors slumbering in their sins. Meantime, the magistrates and ministers, who could discourse with equal eloquence on natural or supernatural means of conversion, were assured that visible election, with its corollary of public confession and ministerial examination, would stay from the congregation of the elect all those who professed a saving knowledge of Christ but who in their judgment were not genuinely elected. The doctrine of means was thus the final sword put into the hands of the saints that they might keep the house of the Lord in good order. It had served to banish from the temple of truth the liberal spirits who professed to be visited immediately by supernatural grace, and it might indeed be a suitable instrument with which to keep the minister in his pulpit and the magistrate on his throne.

It happened, therefore, that while the means might be ordinary they could not be common; for if supernatural grace should prove so weak an instrument of election that each individual could accept or reject it as his private will determined, or if, on the other hand, some Antinomian rebel should imagine that his high affections were a sign of the supernatural visitation, little would be left of the doctrine of election, and a vulgar democracy might creep into the commonwealth of God. To prevent such a catastrophe, the elect had to possess, not only their own graciousness, but the means by which others might claim equally a portion of that high spiritual estate. If then the saints were to rule by a right as divine as that of the English king, or by a means as secure as that of an Anglican bishop, they would have to set themselves up as God's chosen, as those predestined not only to salvation but to dominion over the consciences of men. They would therefore argue that they had been elected to high Christian estate by the decree of an absolute sovereign God, and that they had been lifted to this higher plane of the spirit by an invincible causality. The saints had been lifted to salvation, they argued, not by their own righteousness and striving for moral perfection, but rather by the absolute command and unchangeable decree which God had predetermined from the beginning of time.

Incorporated by the highest legal power, sustained in their endeavors by the most intricate metaphysic, the Christian aristocracy could not fail of success, either in this world or in the world to come. Though the means of regeneration were natural, they could not be common, for the gates of heaven were forever closed to those who had not received the approbation of the saints. Bound by the social contract to the public good, tied by the church covenant to the congregational will, linked in irrevocable bond and mortgaged to God by the covenant of grace, the Puritan found himself without recourse except to perform his public duties and maintain his holy charge. A society thus bound together, a society united by economic, political, and religious hoops of steel, will seek to maintain the great chain of being in the commonwealth, the natural order of rank and class, as God Himself maintains it in the universe, and with a complete sense of its divine sanctions. The lower orders of society will accordingly be restrained, differentiations of rank and class will grow up in manners, dress, and social privileges; and such a society, seeking to preserve its holy charge, will constantly be on guard against backsliding and the laggard heart.

3. The Commonwealth of Man

To portray the life of man, not only as it was in nature, but as it might seem in the drama of salvation, the Puritans built their human psychology somewhat after the structure of the cosmos. Man is a microcosmos who repeats at a lower level the same history which the macrocosmos displays. Though the soul of man, according to theology, might have been infused by God, the body was its momentary attachment and hindrance. Yet this soul is a trinity of the vegetative, animal, and rational natures which the macrocosmos describes; it repeats the great chain of being, in seried dependence of faculties, and is at last another representation of that hierarchy of things which is contained in reality. Medieval psychology had taught the Puritans to revere this great hierarchy, and it was some time before they realized that they must reconstruct this inheritance in the light of a more balanced and harmonious commonwealth of man. The feudal psychology, then, must be reconstructed by the Puritan taste; the hierarchy in church and state, reflected in psychological theory, must now be modified in the light of the Christian commonwealth which man truly inhabits.

For the most part, however, the Puritans accepted the substance of scholastic psychology. It had accounted for the hierarchy of being by examining the hierarchy of faculties which were thought to dwell in the soul of man. Any object such as the contemplative soul might chance upon impresses in the senses an image or replica, a phantasm or species, of that thing. This phantasm is then carried to the central chamber of the brain, to the common sense; then, common sense, distinguishing among the various phantasms or species, relays them to the imagination or the fancy, located somewhere in the front of the brain. This faculty of imagination, duly informed by common sense, then judges and compares the different phantasms or species, meanwhile holding them as they sway the sensual inclination in their capacities to act as objects of desire. Meantime, reason or understanding summons the phantasms before its judgment seat from either the imagination or the memory, determines the right and the true, and sends the image representing its decision, by the agency of the animal spirits, along the nerves to the will. The will, dwelling always in the heart, embraces true images as the good to be pursued, and commands the sensitive appetite, which consists of affections and passions, to transmit the impulses to the muscles by the proper emotions.

This eclectic theory, a stew of ancient doctrines, permitted the Puritans to explain regeneration in terms that were common to psychology and theology, and lived for a while in the house of orthodoxy before it was fully grasped that scholastic psychology was unsuited by virtue of its many defects to shadow forth and image the commonwealth of man. It followed that the work of the imagination was, for the Puritans, a crucial point in this ancient psychology. By virtue of its influence on the reason, will, and affection in presenting desirable or undesirable images of things as objects of desire, the imagination seemed ultimately to determine the will. Thus for the Puritans, who above all wished that the passions and the imagination should not pervert the understanding, the order and dependence of the various faculties became a pressing question. In Puritan theory, then, it was insisted that images should be approved by the reason because they are true, and by the will because they are good, so that the pursuit of the good, the true, and the beautiful might not be disrupted by ungainly passions or a weak imagination. Now in this incongruous affair, the Puritans were caught between the predeterminism of God and the self-determination of man; and if any semblance of moral responsibility was to be salvaged from medieval theory, the supremacy of the will must be assured.

In order to assure an appropriate dependence in the faculties, then, it had to be asserted, as with Willard and Edwards, that the will follows the last dictate of the understanding. This strategy salvaged both the reason and the will from the encroachments of the diseased imagination, and yet gave assurance that the will in its actions is formally subordinate to the understanding. But suppose that the understanding should follow the will, as proposed by John Cotton; the will would have gained full responsibility only at the expense of reason, and would have blinded what God clearly intended should be the ruling faculty in the commonwealth of man. Piety demanded conviction and assent as well as truth, and theology could not depart from the most pertinent teaching of the Scriptures. These contradictions in psychological theory must evidently have arisen because the Christian commonwealth was not identical with a feudal estate. In brief, medieval theory required that reason be lord of the soul, and the hierarchy insisted that the understanding must be the highest link in the great chain of being. But at long last the spirit of individualism was abroad in the world, and it demanded that the will or desire be a balancing factor in the commonwealth of man.

The compromise, for the Puritans, came when it was realized that will and the understanding coöperate in the commonwealth of man. Psychology in its faculty dress was henceforth modeled after parliamentary theory. The reason is a kind of upper chamber, and the will a chamber of deputies. But passion, which represents the unruly democratic mob, must likewise be subordinate to these houses of parliament, finding its appropriate role when the affections are described as instruments of the will. The faculty psychology furnished, accordingly, a cast of political characters for the parliamentary drama which was being unrolled. Orthodoxy could not suffer itself to lose its essence, however, and so insisted that sanctification must follow justification, that moral perfection required an infusion of divine grace. Religion had taught them, said the Puritans, not to destroy but to improve the faculties, so that when all faculties attend to their private functions, the commonwealth of man prospers and flourishes in the sight of God. To mutiny against this empire of reason, to break out in insubordination, was to derange the commonwealth. Hence it is, as Hooker said, the imagination which lends to the passions objects of mutiny and false desire; the imagination is the true forge of villainy, the warehouse of wickedness, the magazine of mischief. The apostasy of man has put a malignancy in the faculties which only the strictest discipline of orthodoxy can subordinate the control. In the unregenerate man the commonwealth has turned to riot and discord, the parliamentary harmony is dissolved, and the vain faculties issue forth in petty separate rebellions. Only the iron discipline of orthodox, inspired by the irresistible grace of the sovereign God, can hope to bring harmony to these mutinous subdichotomies, provincial rebellions, and separatist tendencies dwelling in the commonwealth of man.

4. *The Antinomian Tragedy*

No other event in the crowded calendar of New England history is as illustrative of the alignment of Puritan psychology and Puritan politics, of the Puritan theory of harmony in the commonwealth of man, as the mighty storm provoked by the outbreak of Antinomian enthusiasm and the consequent tragic days that attended it. The Antinomian tragedy illustrates what great care must have been taken by the elect to preserve their erring people from the ravages of enthusiasm and the diseases of the imagination. For the teachings of Mistress Hutchinson represented a revolt against the empire of reason, a mutinous subdichotomy in the faculties, a separatist movement dwelling in the commonwealth of man. If we examine into the list of eighty-two opinions, "some blasphemous, others erroneous, and all unsafe," we shall discover that what was at issue during those tragic days was the revolt of religious individualism against the corporate unity of the Puritan church-state organization. But Antinomianism represented to the Puritan a false psychology, a derangement of the proper order of the faculties, and the dependence of the reason and will upon high affections and diseased imagination. When therefore the storm burst over New England as the clouds of Mistress Hutchinson's opinions gathered upon the horizon, the clergy, who had come in for some of her worst charges, rose up in arms against this intrusion of raised affections into the empire of reason and the understanding. "A company of legal professors," she said, "lie poring on the law which Christ hath abolished." Believing herself to be subject to divine revelations, trusting to none but the promptings of the divine light within, declaring the ministers to be under a covenant of works—that they were professing only legal Christianity, and not the genuine spirit of Christ—Mistress Hutchinson raised a foment among ministerial authorities, who recognized in her teachings an open door to revolt from the rule of magistrate and minister. The fierce jealousy aroused in the breast of the orthodox clergy, proud possessors of propriety in opinion and of power in the churches, can hardly be imagined. Lay preaching, if it should spread widely in the land, and degenerate into mere enthusiasm, might encumber all, loosening the hold of the saints over the yeomanry, and opening the doors of the temple to every democratic upstart and imagined possessor of the spirit.

These threats to orthodoxy came at a moment when John Winthrop and the reactionary party had been driven from office by young Henry Vane, protector of the deputies in their struggle for legislative autonomy. The time was ripe for the usual combination of magistrates and ministers to deflect from its course this rising tide of popular enthusiasm, which might undermine their prerogatives. John Cotton had suggested a friendly meeting with the other ministers in order to resolve quietly the points of difference among them, and Mistress Hutchinson, though reluctantly, finally accepted. There she was betrayed into several unripe opinions—among them, that few of the ministers had the seal of the spirit upon them, that they were under a covenant of works, and had departed from the true path of Christ. The heresy was now spreading to alarming proportions, for a political party had been organized combining Antinomianism in religion with the popular cause in politics. The stronghold of the popular party was Boston, but that capital was also strongly entrenched with Winthrop and his faction, who controlled a majority in the legislature. So strong was the influence of the saints that they were successful in blocking the appointment of the Anti-

nomian John Wheelwright to a Boston church. Meantime, John Wheelwright had taken to the preaching of his Antinomian errors from another pulpit, and so was arraigned in court on the charge of treason.
The court convened as a jury composed of his adversaries, followers of
the reactionary party of Magistrate Winthrop. Although the citizens
petitioned in Wheelwright's behalf and the radical breeze was beginning to blow into a storm, the conservatives were determined to punish
the offender. Meantime, the period of elections was nearing, so Winthrop and his party removed the government to Cambridge, where, co-
erced by the ministers from the outlying towns, a majority was wrung
from the populace to elect Winthrop governor. The first fruit of this
reactionary success was a law forbidding strangers to reside in towns
more than three weeks without consent of two of the magistrates, for
it was known that a strong party of enthusiasts was sailing from Britain,
and the orthodox wished to make certain that the coercive power of
the state could be exercised to exclude them and their heretical opinions
from the Christian commonwealth.

That the danger of Antinomianism involved not only default from
orthodox opinions, but the threat of separatism and independency as
well, is attested to by the notes Winthrop himself made on the tragedy.
Antinomianism involved, he noted regarding a speech of Wilson, "the
inevitable danger of separation, if these differences . . . were not speed-
ily remedied, and laid the blame upon these new opinions. . . ." John
Cotton had in the meantime come to see the error of his ways, and
indulged in an orgy of confession and wailing for his heretical opinions, while he turned over to the authorities all his former friends whom
he suspected of harboring antinomian ideas. Yet, on the day of election,
which saw the triumph of Winthrop and the reactionary party, it was
admitted that the differences between orthodoxy and heterodoxy could
hardly have been detected by the ignorant voters. "Mr. Cotton . . .
stated the differences in a very narrow scantling," wrote Winthrop; and
Mr. Shepherd, preaching at the day of election, brought them yet nearer,
so as, except men of good understanding, "and such as knew the bottom
of the tenets of those of the other party, few could see where the difference was." [3] Meantime, Wheelwright had been arraigned before the
legislature along with a numerous body of offenders; but the legislature,
proving itself unable to attach the charge of treason to these conscientious
Christians, was dissolved, and new elections were held, for the purpose
of stuffing the assembly with more compliant tools of the reactionary
party. All were summarily dealt with, but most cruelly of all in the case
of Mistress Anne Hutchinson, the author of these misfortunes. The
action against her was led by Winthrop himself, much to the glory of

his party, and in the service of the continued rule of the saints. Subjected to the cruel stings and blows of the ministers, big with child, exhausted and nearly out of her mind, she was banished from the wilderness Zion, only to meet a bloody fate at the hands of the Indians. Most significant of all, John Cotton gave testimony against her, a complete renegade and shuffling Christian before the mighty power of the Winthrop party. After Vane had sailed for England, the last protection of the Antinomians was gone, and vengeance, such as the Lord might require, reigned in New England.

5. *The Rhetoric of God*

Against the Antinomian enthusiast, however, the Puritan might charge that his sudden conceits dripped from his tongue poorly digested; or that the heat of his argument was greater than its fuel. For the Puritan himself was convinced that mere enthusiasm without discipline and without learning was not a suitable embellishment for a sermon. The sermon had the work of God in it, and should be labored over in disciplined tranquility, lest a loose tongue and an empty head pour fourth from the Devil's workshop. Truth is seldom rawly delivered and eloquence is simply a revelation of the truth. Antinomian eloquence, on the contrary, stemmed from such a spiritual anarchy within that it could only express contempt for the settled order without. Such eloquence might be treason, if allowed to persist; for the enthusiasts address the imagination and the sensible soul, rather than the rational and immortal part of man. Moreover, Antinomian eloquence does not address itself to the use of doctrine; it is enthusiastic without being pragmatic, and eloquent without being pious. But the Puritan sermon was ordered by a triumvirate of pragmatic exposition; and doctrine, reason, use followed one another as inevitably as the sequences of a natural order. Yet if beauty is the causality of order, the relationship of means to ends, there was some beauty in the Puritan sermon, expressing in a homely way the conception of the divinity which it served.

The Puritans were opposed because of their piety to the vainglorious rhetoric and humane helps of the formal sermon; and they had no taste for the exotic words and high-flown notions, the metaphysical jargon, of the Anglican peroration. But they were, nevertheless, students of rhetoric, of a disciplined eloquence that would flow with plain style straight to the hearts of the people. The Puritan abhorred the carnal eloquence of the Anglicans as a style unfit for pastoral care; and he reprobated those strained metaphors, handsome allusions, and lofty expressions which glossed the formal cathedral sermon. But the Puritan approved a restrained eloquence, which might be more than table talk, plain yet not vulgar, and suited to the capacities and tastes of his audience. A plain style, he thought, might indeed be eloquent as a means of regeneration, and could rest upon that dignity. The rhetoric of God, then, had its fit end, which ought to affect the use of it—the communication of His glory and fullness—in a divine manner of speaking.

In preaching, accordingly, the proper rule to follow is the plain style; a simple, plain, and perspicuous style will make "that preaching best wherein was most of God, least of man, when vain flourishes of wit, and words were declined." Moreover, as beauty refers to the essence of things, to the intelligible principles of them, and is allied to divinity through its diverse representations, so the ministers must follow a plain style, whose only elegance is simplicity; for a work of the Devil is found in sermons strung with beads of wit, or ornamented with finely wrought phrases, or loaded down with the weight of learned quotations dragged from original texts in Latin, Greek, or Hebrew. The consequences of such a loaded style have been described with typical Puritan pointedness: "I have sometimes admired at this: Why a company of gentlemen, yeomen, and poore women, that are scarcely able to know their A.B.C. yet they have a minister to speake Latine, Greeke, and Hebrew, and to use the fathers, when it is certain, they know nothing at all. The reason is, because all this stings not, they may sit and sleepe in their sinnes, and goe to hell hoodwinckt, never awakened." [4]

6. The Sense of Beauty

The Puritan, nevertheless, was not untouched by aesthetic interests; his sense of beauty was kindled by his perception of the order, design, and harmony of the universe, to which perfect cause, as we have seen, he frequently dedicated himself. But because in Puritan literature the sense of beauty is subordinate to the sense of purpose, and because intelligible ends transcend their external representation, the aesthetic quest has seemed in the Puritan curiously distorted and repressed. His preoccupation with the traditional problems of theology, with sin, grace, and regeneration, though they may seem removed from the concerns of beauty, were in fact the categories into which the aesthetic interest deposited her ideal forms. In truth the Puritan conception of sin is that of a fugitive beauty whose loss is the undoing of man, and the Puritan conception of regeneration is almost that of her wonderful presence. The modern interpreter will probably never discover by what insights the saints came to dwell in harmony with a premised unity living in the events and existences around them; but it would seem that an imagined generality which lived for a moment in a transient particularity might haltingly echo a reminiscence of a former and more ideal self from which, in the days of apostasy, she had been cut off. Sin, as Thomas Hooker wrote, had defiled the beautiful frame and harmony which God first implanted in the order of Being.

Beauty is thus allied to divinity; it is the representation of the divine purpose in the eternal harmonies of things, or the order of nature represented in the light of her intelligible ends. If then the ideal unity, which the order of nature represents when she is studied in the light of divinity, is taken as a positive good, it may enter into the composition of other things, lending out of itself the means of their government and direction. Pragmatism and idealism had thus fused again in the Puritan conception of beauty; for the great chain of being has a utility by virtue of its order. The Puritan sought, accordingly, to represent the external form in the light of the internal principle, to confederate the disparate elements which premised unity, and to incorporate the common bonds which seemed to speak of divine love. Puritan art expressed a practical piety; its connection with values, judgment, and its representation through significant form, endow it with the office of intelligence. To the Puritan, therefore, art was a handmaiden to divinity; its peculiar office was to embody in significant form the essence of things, as a truth to which all things ultimately refer. But the truth, which is not in an anarchy of contradiction, possessed also an order which was the visible embodiment of its increated good. It happened, therefore, that pragmatism and idealism had once more come to terms in the sense of beauty; for that which is orderly possesses a utility by virtue of its order, and a premised unity, which must be an absolute good, by virtue of the harmony of its parts.

Here then was a creative synthesis of that beauty which was a cause of all things with that beauty which expressed its design, purpose, or fulfilled intent. In seeking to transcend by art the limitations of the natural man, the Puritan felt himself reaching out for God, giving to the soul that stimulus which seemed to come from divine sources, but which was just as much embodied in the material representation of its essence. The useful was beautiful not merely because it was useful, an error into which the pragmatists of a later day unwittingly fell, but because also it was the embodiment of the stream of cosmic history, the thread of continuity which philosophic necessity had made the premise of a cosmic unity and absolute good. To this source, accordingly, the Puritan traced all conscious art; for therein dwelt the standard which the perfectionist seeks in his moments of perfection, and the artist, when he fulfills the promise of his art. Art was representative divinity; and the sense of beauty, a name for the language of the soul when she saw herself transcendently in the stream of cosmic history. In brief, pragmatism and idealism were the two facets of a common ground of underground connections and mysterious linkages by which the premised unity of the cosmos came to express, not only the philosophic necessity of a formal logic, but also the mysticism which faith in practice had inadvertently bred.

CHAPTER FOUR

THE MAKING OF PURITANS

1. *The Educational Reformation*

The Protestant Reformation was followed by an educational recon-struction; for the first generation of reformers was inevitably drawn into an attack, not only upon the popish corruptions of Christianity, but also upon Catholic scholasticism, the intellectual bulwark of the feudal classes. The revolt from the medieval church involved the reformers in a critique of the social privileges of the priesthood, and carried in its vitriolic train a criticism of the monopoly of education and culture which the feudal ruling classes had enjoyed. With Luther this attack took the familiar form of justification by faith, with its corollary of Bib-lical authority rather than Papal interpretation; and Calvin's attack upon carnal and corrupted reason was the religious expression of the assault upon Papal infallibility. The revolutionary doctrine of the priest-hood of all believers, intended by the reformers to upset the monopoly of salvation enjoyed by the Roman priesthood, ultimately rested re-ligion on the foundation of individual judgment, and brought to the leaders of the Protestant movement a flood of problems. It left to a second generation of reformers the problem of reconciling the revolu-tionary thesis with the practical task of building new churches and organizing new social commonwealths. At the same time, the revolu-tionary doctrine of the priesthood of all believers, intended by Luther to counteract the priestly monopoly of the Mother Church, implied, when carried to its logical conclusion, that no specially trained and educated ministry need be organized to spread the gospel. The conse-quences of these revolutionary ideas would have been disastrous to the Protestant movement, had not the means been found ready at hand for causing the believers to coalesce into churches, synods, and assemblies. Piety and reason, religion and learning, had somehow to be reconciled in a new Protestant scholasticism; and a new universe of knowledge must somehow be organized. The new Protestant synthesis must not, on the one hand, rest salvation entirely in the hands of carnal and corrupted reason, an error in which both Catholics and Anglicans sometimes shared; and on the other, must not neglect the necessary Protestant emphasis on faith and piety as outward signs of the supernatural visitation.

It had long been clear, accordingly, that the Protestant doctrine of justification by faith and its corollary idea of a priesthood of all believers implied that the congregation itself could elect a minister from one of its number of faithful, and that no particular qualification need be enforced beyond the requirement of faith and piety. In such radical form, of course, the Protestant doctrines represented an attack, not alone on the Catholic monopoly, but also upon the social privileges which the university-bred classes enjoyed. It happened, then, that the Puritan was faced with the problem of building a new Protestant synthesis in which reason and faith could be reconciled; he must find a secure place for learning in religion, and must somehow justify the new social and clerical privileges cast up by the Protestant movement. In brief, faced with the practical necessity of building new Christian commonwealths rather than with the luxury of enunciating revolutionary Protestant doctrines, the second generation of reformers found itself faced with a common task of organizing its churches and of providing for a trained and literate ministry. The Puritan, like other practical reformers, had to get the world's work done without appearing to sacrifice the revolutionary doctrines of Protestantism. He had to educate leaders for church and state, and maintain them at public charge, with all the social privileges pertaining to their office, while pretending that these things alone were not the key to salvation. He had to defend the place of learning in the reformed religion, while emphasizing that learning is not the instrument of salvation, nor the cause of election among men.

Practical tasks, then, rather than revolutionary principles, explain the adherence of the Puritan movement to the alliance of religion and learning, reason and faith. The Puritan ruling class of magistrates and ministers, supported in their offices by the mercantile saints with whom they were allied, and now secure in their hard-won social privileges, were constantly faced with the danger that radical sects might remind the people of the revolutionary ideas imbedded in the reformed doctrine, thus upsetting the order which God had ordained in church and state. To the preservation of such a divine order, Puritan education was dedicated; it served the very real need of Puritan orthodoxy. To provide an educated and university-bred ministry for the government of the churches, and to offer a gentleman's education for the magistracy who were to rule the state, Harvard College was founded. But with this jewel set as a diadem at the apex of the system, a classical preparatory school became a necessity; and for the understanding of magisterial injunction and ministerial law, an elementary school to teach the rudiments of literacy and the fundamentals of the catechism was henceforth required. The Puritan insistence upon learning as a necessary ally of religion, and the haste with which he laid out a public system of schools, should be taken chiefly in the light of the political struggles attendant upon the Protestant reformation. The populace must be taught to read the Bible, and from its premises the magistrates and ministers were to draw off the substance of their arguments. When pronounced as the will of God, the wishes of the magistrates and ministers could be made effective instruments of social action; for the tribunal of magistrates and ministers—the aristocracy of Christian grace—had as its peculiar function to discern the duties and govern the action of all members of the Christian commonwealth. If then the magisterial office required that Christian duties be pronounced as the word of God, and if the minister's role required that he search the Scriptures for a sacred buttress to magisterial law, little should we wonder that dialectic skill and sacred casuistry were attainments highly prized in Puritan society. The tortuous road of the Puritan casuist led him to gather just and certain inferences from scriptural premises, and to warrant his little kingdom of achievement with the sacred pledge of God.

2. *The Puritan Education*

The Bible, so long devoured by the false glosses and corrupted by the faulty linguistic attainments of the medieval saints, had now become not only the holy restored word of God, but a constitutional document of the Protestant movement. The Bible was the fundamental law to which all parties of the reform movement would inevitably appeal, and upon the assertions of which the will of the magistrate would ultimately have to be justified to the people. It happened, accordingly, that when various of the radical sects thrown up by the Cromwellian disturbance insisted that the revolutionary principles of the Protestant movement be carried to their logical conclusion, that, among other things, a university-bred ministry enjoying special social privileges be abolished, the New England Puritan hastened to defend the union of religion and learning. In the view of the radicals, however, the universities had become dens of ensnaring syllogistic priests, the temples of pompous professors of divinity, whose very learning was the Devil's own hellish brew. The radicals called, not only for the separation of church and state, but also for the separation of church and school; they insisted, according to the logic of the Separatist movement, that they were not hostile to education as such, but rather to defiling pure religion with human inventions.

While these struggles were going forward in England, there was issued from New England a pamphlet explaining the reasons for setting up Harvard College, a pamphlet which set forth the views of the colonial Puritan leaders on the vital problem of the relation of religion and learning. The Separatist radicals had called, it will be remembered, not only for the separation of church and state, but also for the separation of church and school; but this program was the very antithesis of the philosophy of the Puritan saints, for they professed only to reform certain of the heritages which the Anglican church had taken over from the Mother Church at Rome. It happened, accordingly, that the pamphlet describing *New England's First Fruits* was a political lancet intended to pierce the unsavory rumors that had been spread in England about the colonial venture, and to establish the position of the colonists on the vital question of the relation of religion and learning. The significance of *New England's First Fruits,* then, should be sought in the light of the struggles then going forward in England. The establishment of Harvard College provided the Puritan with a fresh opportunity to remind his enemies that he professed a hardy dislike of the principles of Separatism.

Religion, the Separatist argued, has no need of learning to prepare the way for Christ; and he professed to have no quarrel with learning when it was properly restricted to its own sphere. The universities, the sectarian radicals contended, were centers of heathenism, where pagan philosophers and obscene poets added to the natural corruptions of the vain lads in attendance. By concealing divinity in a thicket of exposition and exegesis, in syllogistic traps and vain cloaks of learning—argued the radicals—the reactionary clergy hope to deter the common people from study and inquiry into these matters, seeking thereby to keep their privileges over the poor and humble seekers of God. To the Puritan, however, it seemed that this radical attack upon learning must proceed either from ignorance or from a desire to swallow up the revenues and endowments with which benefactors had supported the Puritan cause in the universities. Meantime, the Antinomian outbreak which followed in the train of Mistress Hutchinson's teachings made it clear that behind the radical attack upon the learned ministry small fires of revolt against magisterial rule were being kindled. One of the disciples of Mistress Hutchinson was overheard to say: "I had rather hear such a one that speakes from the meere motion of the spirit, without any study at all, than any of your learned schollars, although they may be fuller of Scripture." [5]

Charles Chauncy, arguing the cause of orthodoxy, wrote that the secular arts and sciences, now purged of their popish errors, could safely be taken to the aid of Scripture study, a knowledge of the arts and sciences having proved useful in setting forth Scripture doctrines. Harvard College, then, was from the first an institution whose aims were broader than the training of the ministry; its leaders intended to offer a humanist's course in the liberal arts for the gentlemen who were destined to rule the commonwealth. But Harvard became, from the moment of the radical Antinomian attacks upon learning, a bulwark against religious and social radicalism, a fortress of orthodoxy in a sea of troubles. Before she was touched by the liberalizing influences astir at the turn of the century, Harvard ears had been assaulted by this orthodox theme in her commencement addresses, one of which argued: "The ruling class would be subjected to mechanics, cobblers, and tailors; the gentry would have been overwhelmed by lewd fellows of the baser sort, the sewage of Rome, the dregs of illiterate plebs which judgeth much from emotion, little from truth; we should have seen . . . no flashing sparklets of honors; the laws would not have been made by *senatus consulta,* nor would we have rights, honors, or magisterial ordinances worthy of preservation, but plebicites, appeals to base passions, and revolutionary rumblings, if these our fathers had not founded the university." [6]

3. The Higher Learning

Bearing all the traditions and laden with all the fruits of higher learning in the Middle Ages, Harvard College sprouted in the soil of New England, a pitiful outpost of the intellect in a wilderness Zion. It was from the first, however, a society of scholars, a collection of books, a temple of learning; for as the scholars of the Middle Ages were potential priests, the scholarly armory of the Roman church, so the vestments of learning at Harvard, the vain lads and carping tutors, were designed for service in church and state. But an important difference attaches to Harvard which entitles us to view her in the perspective of the reformation, as a child of Trent, the consummation of the Protestant need to train a learned ministry to combat the monopoly of consciousness of the feudal church. Harvard was essentially a school of Christ, which, sharing in the pagan joys, cultivated the pagan arts; her founders, so they said, dreaded to leave an illiterate ministry to the churches, or an untutored magistracy to the courts. The curriculum was, accordingly,

Christ and the liberal arts, the Bible and pagan letters, the divinities and the humanities; and in these it was discovered that Hebraism and Hellenism might dwell together, that the *liber homo* was a man inspired with the truth that should make Puritans free.

Harvard was constructed somewhat after the Cambridge model, for most of her founders, and indeed the literate leadership of the Massachusetts Bay Company, had been bred in that den of Puritan revolt, nurtured in that nest of Calvinist tutelage. Although Puritanism was a party name rather than a moral standard, there was from the first a significant appendage of precisionists within that body, calling upon the faithful to cling to the moral law as well as the word of Christ. The wolves of Geneva, the Marian exiles, had brought back the harsh Calvin with them from their sojourn in Switzerland, determined to ram the rod of that saint down the throat of every backslider and erring Christian. But Cambridge had changed in the interim, her scholasticism and musty learning all but banished by the influx of bourgeois lads who wished to be educated like gentlemen. But both Hebraism and Hellenism could combine in the Cambridge parent and yield a fruit even to the wilderness Harvard, because Moses aimed at virtue in the moral law and Aristotle at morality in the life of a gentleman. It happened, therefore, that with a judicious interpretation Aristotle's ethics might seem a branch of the moral law, and the gospel of Christ a treatise on the vocation of virtue.

But the Cambridge model possessed, too, a lesson which the migrants learned before their coming over. Forewarnings of subsequent Antinomian outbreaks had revealed themselves at Cambridge, where a radical wing of the Puritan party contested the union of school and church, the moral law and the inspiration, the covenant of works and the covenant of grace. And the fruit of these issues was to possess the conservative wing of the Puritan party with the notion that Antinomianism was hostile to learning, denying to the gospel of Christ and the inspiration of the prophets those morsels of pagan reason which the gentry in the practice of their craft had found so useful. Viewed in such a perspective, the rebellious Antinomian spirit might be hostile, not only to learning, but to the rule of the saints. The gentlemen who founded Harvard College formed a band of stockholders in the corporation of Massachusetts Bay. If then the corporation of scholars should be severed from the corporation of saints, and the corporation of the elect from the corporation of the stockholders, it would provide plentiful ground for uncommon expectations, leading in some of the choicest spirits to a desire for authoritarian conformity on the part of the scholars and of careful tutelage on the part of the saints. The dangers of the Anti-nomian breach in the wall of party discipline were subsequently illus-trated in the controversy over the teaching of Mistress Anne Hutchinson. Her nimble wit and voluble tongue inspired, she said, by immediate revelations of the spirit, had gathered an untutored flock about her, telling them what questions to ask of their ministers, what answers to give in the courts. She denied good works, the validity of the moral law, and listened only to the voice of divine illumination within. It followed from this Antinomian teaching that however one sinned or broke the moral law, the law of Moses, or the injunctions of the magistrates, the illumined one was predestined to be saved.

This Antinomian teaching was, of course, disastrous to the rule of the saints, and raised up a defiant spirit in the indentured servants who had followed by the coercion of contract the elect who ruled the wilder-ness corporation. It was a break in party discipline, a threat to the or-ganized churches, an ideological deviation from corporate rule; and if it had been carried widely enough in New England, it would have proved equally disastrous to the plans of the founders of Harvard Col-lege. It was clear enough that if she had the revelation of the spirit, then the saints had it not; that if she was the oracle of heaven, then the elect could not hope to enter those gates; that if her teaching was not in error, then the truth, which should be whole, could not indeed dwell with the founders of Harvard College. The outcome of this famous religious rebellion, the banishment of the schismatics, and the due and proper punishment of the offenders is well known to all the sons of Harvard. But according to Professor Morison, the "majority" made a clever po-litical move in transferring the court of elections to Newtown in order to prevent the "schismatic Bostonians" from full attendance at a demo-cratic trial of Mistress Hutchinson's teachings, and, as a result of this "clever political move," Winthrop was elected governor, confirming once more that truth was the possession of the elect, that the saints alone could be visited by the divine and spiritual light.[7] By this stroke of political good fortune, then, the elect were confirmed in their election and the saints in the possession of their truth; though it had raised the specter, not only of religious rebellion, but of Antinomian politics as well. It happened, accordingly, that the higher learning was preserved in the colony of Massachusetts Bay, the Separatist tendency defiled, and the Antinomian spirit was banished from the household of the saints. The temple of learning, as Franklin subsequently called it, had gone through its preliminary skirmish in the defense of truth, leaving to the churches a literate ministry, and to the courts a handful of Harvard saints.

4. *The Humanist Temper*

In Puritan humanism, that remarkable union of Hellenism and Hebraism, the colonists preserved the store of secular knowledge, and turned
the sayings of the ancients to theological account. There were voices like
Milton's in the colonies—minor voices it is true; but if they did not soar
so high as the English singer, they were nevertheless engaged in the
common task of justifying the ways of God to man, of creating a Protestant culture wrought of Renaissance humanism and Reformation Hebraism. For the Puritans were the heirs not only of the Reformation
but of the Renaissance. They were drinkers from the cup of Plato at
Emmanuel College, Cambridge, while they sojourned awhile in the
mother country. Now, come at last to the wilderness Zion, they set it
down so succeeding ages could be assured, that they too carried the
humanist taste into the task of salvation. The way of learning which
lay open to the Puritan had already been marked out by his Renaissance
predecessors, so that the Puritan, upon his arrival in New England, was
already in the possession of the main outline of the humanist program.
But the humanist learning had ultimately to be justified in the light
of the soul's quest of salvation. If the Puritan was heir to the Renaissance, with its humanist ideal, its devotion to classical scholarship, its
Platonic conceptions, he was even more the child of the Reformation,
in whose reformed gospel of grace he bathed the light of his spirit.
The religious quest, therefore, was not to be subordinated to the love
of learning; nor could the mere humanist secure satisfaction in heaven.

The Renaissance humanist had not so hastily devoured the classical
treasures that he had been forgetful of medieval rhetoric; and the Puritan was not so great a child of the Reformation as to be forgetful of the
pleasures of Renaissance literature. Whether in the Yankee person or
among the Puritan lads at Harvard College, a certain grandeur of expression is achieved when ancient morality is fused with scriptural art;
and the rolling orchestral rhythms of Biblical meter, when they are
joined by the stately march of classical prose, produce in their beholder
some simple and yet majestic harmony which even to modern ears has
a subtle persuasion and a strange eventful charm. The Renaissance humanist, after he had combined scholastic rhetoric with the lessons to
be learned from the newly discovered manuscripts of Cicero and Quin-
tilian, purged the former of its centuries of indigestible accretions, and
gave to the art of rhetoric a new dignity which was comparable to the
new status of the individual man. Rhetoric, logic, and theology became,
accordingly, the new triumvirate of Puritan scholasticism, and the liberal

arts were decked out in reformed divinity as the appropriate dress of educated gentlemen. At Harvard College the Renaissance ideal of the gentleman flourished alongside the Puritan moral intensity, producing at that
college an educational program which fused Hellenism and Hebraism in
a new encyclopedic and practical ideal. "Gentlemen must be educated
like gentlemen," declared Tutor William Brattle; and of course the
Puritan gentleman combined in a single personality the qualities of the
humanist scholar who labors in love over the manuscripts of Greece and
Rome, with those of the theologically erudite scripturalist who could
argue with the Devil if need be, and sometimes did.

The current of humanism thus carried in the wake of the Puritan
reform movement no doubt increased the tensions in the Puritan mind
between piety and reason, between revealed religion and reasonable religion, between the morality of reason and the morality of sanctification.
Of the pagan philosophers, Plato came closest to expressing the ideal of
the theocratic state; and the pagan moralists were used abundantly to
reinforce Scripture lessons. But while the Puritans built their own reformed theology, welcomed the humanist current of criticism against
the barbarism and darkness of the feudal ages, and attacked Catholic
Aristotelianism, they retained, without being aware that new adjustments were called for, some part of the scholastic heritage itself. The
subjects taught at Harvard throughout most of the seventeenth century
were actually the seven liberal arts reformed under the influence of Peter
Ramus and cast into encyclopedic form by his disciples. History, chronology, and mathematics, with patches of the new divinity added by
theological texts, modified the older circle of the arts, it is true; but the
essence of the curriculum was contained in the magical seven. What
contributed most to the educational reformation effected by the Puritan, however, was the new method and discipline of Peter Ramus. Under his influence a new basis was laid for Puritan scholasticism, and the
arts and sciences were brought into a great encyclopedia of learning. It
happened, accordingly, that while the Puritan was a humanist as well
as a reformer, the practical realities of theological dispute and political
controversy forced him to spend his energies upon the construction of
systems, until at last the humanist temper was all but devoured by the
scholastic mind.

5. *The Ramist Discipline*

The method by which the Puritan was to carry out his program of
reformation among the inherited liberal arts, and with which he hoped

to purge the sciences of their scholastic subtleties and popish errors, he discovered in the dialectic of Peter Ramus. By requiring that logical progression and rhetorical transition be illustrated from classical writings, that the movement of language be demonstrated by the movement of things, Ramus opened up to the student of the classics a new road to the employment of the humanist knowledge in his quest of salvation. When the educative process—the discipline of natural intelligence—is discovered to be wholly logical, the liberal arts become so many fields of logical deployment and exercise. In addition, Ramus provided a method or dialectic of systematic dichotomy in which distinctions and distributions could be represented, and in which the architecture of thought could be shown; he put into Puritan hands an ideal instrument for setting forth received truth in a new and convincing manner. Education then seemed to the student a voyage of discovery, a journey into the temple of the arts, a systematic exploration of the geography of the sciences. The dialectic of Peter Ramus provided a method of setting forth clearly, simply, and with abundant classical allusions the intelligible order which was assumed to lie at the heart of the universe. Through *didactia,* the educational discipline, the mind was settled in the received rubrics and classifications, so that pupil and tutor could travel together over the terrain of the liberal arts. Logic, of course, became the basic discipline of this new education method; for it enabled the disciplined mind to order ideas and concepts in appropriate relations in the hierarchy of being, making the universe at last an intelligible realm into which the mind could penetrate.

In all this, of course, Ramus had drawn upon the heritage of Renaissance Platonism. The concepts which are developed in the mind as the result of the dialectic progression of the Ramist method represent the true order of being, the reality of which the world is composed. The soul contains an intuitive knowledge of eternal truth, the disciples of Ramus insisted; and while this knowledge was obscured and benumbed by the primitive apostasy of man, it surges back under the influence of an appropriate discipline, partly restoring the powers enjoyed in the days of purity. Knowledge, then, is a kind of remembrance in which the soul picks up an echo of its former self, after the educational discipline has enabled it to call forth the ideas which lie at the heart of all things. The soul comes to see its innate correspondence with the world, perceives itself in the order or hierarchy of being, and dwells, so to speak, with the eternal. When President Charles Chauncy told his students at Harvard that the arts and sciences are in the right sense scriptural learning, that physics, politics, rhetoric, and astronomy, "in the true sense and right meaning thereof are theological and Scripture learning, and are not to be accounted as humane learning," he was expressing the central theme of Puritan educational theory. Under the influence of the Ramist discipline, the Puritan interpreted God as art; and the attempt of the human mind to uncover the order of the universe was to the Puritan a measure of his understanding of the divine wisdom. All the arts and sciences were thus composed into one body of knowledge, and all were handmaidens to divinity. The liberal arts were drawn together in a new systematic pattern, encyclopedias of the arts were constructed, and a new Puritan scholasticism was prepared to defend its authors from the corruption of rival systems.

It remains for us only to note that Puritan education, like Puritan piety, was immensely practical. To minds unfettered by scholastic thought, it may appear that the new Puritan scholasticism suffered from all the defects of contemplation that the older Catholic synthesis was heir to. But the influence of Ramus on Puritan education accentuated its normal tendency toward emphasizing the practical. The discipline it provided was a practical and moral discipline, in which discovered intelligible ends, making the world a more congenial stimulus for the soul, encouraged its mediation of the normal order of God's government. Puritan education placed man in the center of natural processes, making of the Puritan not only an observer but a participant in the drama of salvation. The world of the Puritan was both ordered and meaningful; for knowledge and being were one, and the Puritan mind, happy in the conception, believed it could penetrate some of the secrets of divine wisdom. Though the orthodox Puritan never reached the point of believing that human salvation could be attained without divine intervention, the educational reforms of Peter Ramus had widened the domain of human understanding, and had prepared the Puritan mind for the acceptance of the triumphs which were to come with a succeeding generation. Because Puritan education played so important a role in the economy of redemption, because a disciplined intelligence was so much better fitted for the voyage of the world than one untrained, the main goal of this discipline was the discovery of the ways of God's acting, and the subjection of the will to His government. It happened, accordingly, that Puritan education was the effective instrument, not only of building a new scholastic synthesis, but of subjecting the mind to ways of thought already made familiar by the rule of magistrate and minister. The scholastic mind was the inevitable outcome of a government of the orthodox, forced upon the New England Puritans by the incessant theological disputes and political struggles into which history had cast them.

6. *The Problem of Knowledge*

The truth, which so long lay locked up in the secret repositories of Rome, must now become the possession, if not of every man, at least of those disciplined minds which had resolved to free it from the medieval monopoly that so long professed to honor it. But the Puritan who had promised to lay open the truth to every man was himself an unhappy compromise between the medieval spirit and the modern temper. His theory of knowledge, therefore, lay halfway between Rome and Geneva; it was an uncritical mixture of scholastic science and Puritan theology, but with so sharp a weapon as the dialectic of Ramus the Puritan hoped one day to set the compromise right. Ramus had not fully challenged the traditional epistemology, however; for he believed that the soul abstracts the intelligible forms that arise from the heart of things. Nevertheless, his logic had made clear that human reason was competent to deal with the whole province of knowledge, if only chastened by the Ramist dialectic, and had curiously asserted that arguments and things are identical. Unless thought and being are identical, accordingly, the Ramist logic and Puritan theology might very well collapse in the sea of contradictions.

Puritan theory, therefore, argued that man possesses a natural intelligence for apprehending the forms of experience. The mind of man, though unhappily distorted by the Fall, discovers the truth in things because it is attuned to respond to them. The intellectual principle in man, therefore, corresponds to the intelligible principle incarnate in nature. The Puritan was not prepared to argue for innate ideas, but he was willing to describe an innate faculty, a kind of primitive dialectic, which the disciplined mind might generate and sustain. Sense is the first teacher, but she is subservient to the rational principle which manifests itself by abstracting the forms of experience. Ideas are thus the images of things formed in the soul by the divine power. It remained only to keep this rational principle of the natural man well within the bounds of the universal intelligence, lest man, glorying in his newly won freedom, should forget the divine mind in which all dwell.

But this view of the nature of human knowledge is combined with a program of humanism, so that the encyclopedic thirst of the Renaissance can show forth its classical interests as a demonstration of things that are of God. Since, however, all the arts and sciences had to be reduced by the Ramist method to unity, which provided a distinct logical framework, there could be no metaphysics apart from logic. The Puritan developed the doctrine of *technologia,* accordingly, in order that all the arts might conduct to the ends enunciated by God. Invention or discovery, as Ramus called the first part of logic, was literally a search for revealed ends; while judgment or disposition placed these discoveries in order according to the Ramist method. It happened that the Puritan exercised his caution in these matters, lest he should presume too much upon the hidden essence of the godhead; and he professed only to be discovering the revealed ends, not the secret will. This distinction is the heart of the Puritan compromise between theology and science, and it rests upon the dualism between the reflection of the divine mind in nature and essence of the divine mind itself.

The basic premise of *technologia,* therefore, is that finite ends are comprehended in the arts, that revealed ends could be reached if not the hidden purpose. Art is conceived, accordingly, as the rule of the divine government, its outer bureaucracy, though not its inner and secret administration. Nature continuously reveals and reflects the wisdom of God, and the arts are prisms of that divine intelligence. But the end of knowledge is action, for the reports of divine intelligence which the Puritan professes to receive he construes as *eupraxia,* the rule of good conduct. Art itself was first in the mind of God; then, archetypally, in the decrees of God; then, entypally, in created objects; finally, actypally, in the mind of man. But all art conducts uniformly to the rule of good conduct and right reason. The physical world—so long an object of disdain, distorted by the glosses of the saints—has become but a shadow and symbol of the hidden spiritual essence. Ideas are thus the exemplars of things in the mind of God, and the arts radiate a divine wisdom; for all things should conform to their essence or end, the preëxistent platform of ideas in the mind of God.

The quest of truth had become for the Puritan the search for essence; and if this adventure is mainly Platonic in its themes, the Puritan could argue that the pagan essences are godless while his are in the divine mind. Science hastens to her full glory, because she reflects the wisdom of God; and the classical arts and literatures are devoured with the humanist's encyclopedic thirst, because they likewise conduct man to appropriate ends. In his theory of knowledge, accordingly, the Puritan had reconciled the diversities of theology and science, of humanism and Hebraism, of faith and reason, which underlay the seventeenth-century world view. Scholasticism, which had intermittently undertaken the same compromises, had nevertheless issued in a nerveless contemplation. The Puritan theory, on the contrary, was from first to last a program of action; for *technologia* bound the arts to practice, and issued in a vigorous discipline. Yet, because the Puritan was a man of piety as well as of reason, the physical universe remained but a copy of the ideal, the natural of the supernatural; and the cosmic energies, which might have been turned to naturalistic account, radiated instead a divine wisdom.

To know a thing as it is in itself, then, was for the Puritan to know its essence; for while he dwelt in a real world he aspired to an ideal one, and, like the transcendentalist of a later epoch, read natural history as a cosmic fable. The physical or visible world remained a screen between the intellect and the realm of essence, even though, in that intermediary world, man might learn to command the objects of knowledge. But the mysterious thing-in-itself, which drove the romantic philosophers of a later epoch to a search of the soul of knowledge, was not for the Puritan the least mysterious. While the essence of God remained forever hidden, the essence of things was revealed to him, so that the Puritan, while he dwelt in a mortal realm, felt in touch with the manifestations of one that was eternal. The problem of knowledge was solved for the Puritan the moment he realized that a program of action must be energized with an appropriate metaphysic, and that the hazards of this world were as nothing to those who had an open-sesame to the wisdom of God.

CHAPTER FIVE

THE WORLD OF NATURE

1. *The Puritan Dialectic*

The heart of action, because it lies in resolution, may seem to an un-prejudiced observer to contain a seed of freedom in it. But this con-clusion would prove unripe for those who were committed before ob-servation to a theory of the universe in which all things hang upon a great chain of being fashioned according to the divine order and sov-ereign will of God. The Puritan, for his part, had committed himself to such a theory, and it only remained for him to discover in the order of nature a preëxistent platform of ideas, an increated realm of essence, where Plato might have left his old ideal forms. Plato's cosmic myth did not quite represent the whole of reality for the Puritan, however, for the Platonic ideas have a godless existence, as we have noted, while the Puritan realm of essence was the wisdom of a divine mind. As Plato had required the study of dialectic on the part of the rulers of his utopia, so the Puritan asked that the prospective saint sharpen his logical faculties in anticipating his elevation to a higher spiritual plane. On this plane, it was discovered, the increated essence of God might be revealed with the aid of divine grace, and the rational principle of the mind would be refurbished with the help of divine wisdom. It followed that the dia-lectic faculties were the chief treasures of man, while reason, because of the demands of piety, represented the remnant of divinity within.

Reason, that noble capacity of man, was unhappily impaired in the Fall; and man, struggling with brutishness and inevitable error, only occasionally purged the reason by the dialectic and brought into the commonwealth of man the proper subordination of inferior principles. It was felt, therefore, lest man despair of final refuge through the light of reason, that some might retain a piece of that ancient capacity, and, particularly in moments touched by divine grace, recover out of the fog

of sin the light of reason and truth. Dialectics alone, without divine
grace, would not essentially save man from the ignobility and pressure
of his hellish end; but it might, by the authority of the remnant of
divinity within, carry him to such a surge of perception on the sea of
truth that he could hope thereby for some glimpse of the divine intelligence. In truth, logic was found an inevitable tool once the Protestant
mind had declared its reliance upon the authority of revelation; and
the Puritans insisted especially upon the practice of that humane art.
It was accordingly indispensable to Protestant theology that the latent
reasoning of God, here or there obscured by Scripture reference or
heavenly innuendo, might be drawn by subtle reason from the mystic
passages.

The Puritans, for their part, were happy in the possession of so sharp
a tool with which to ward off the waves of enthusiasm and religious
frenzy which accompanied the Protestant revolt. The free working and
maneuvers of the spirit, so inconstant in their manifestation and so difficult in their sincerity, might be judged in the light of reason, by
suitable professors of the congregational way, when the unwary were
taken up in vain enthusiasms and drowned in stormy blasts of affection. This orthodox position, as we have seen, was under constant attack by the sectarian radicals, who desired, not indeed that unreason
should prevail, but that university dialecticians should be detained from
the preparation of syllogistic snares to capture those unpledged but to
God. But Puritanism defended logic as the dianoetical faculty, the dis-
coursing ally of man, without which the Bible might succumb to the
democratic impulses of diversity, and be taken up here and there by any
new pledge of inspiration. Unreasoned and fantastic to them seemed
those abnormal workings of the antinomian spirit whose pathology did
not fit into the Puritan creed; and that creed, they confessed, was contained not only verbatim in the Bible but drawn also as a deduction
therefrom. It happened, accordingly, that the Puritan insisted on the
authority of reason as well as of revelation, and carried to the high peak
of orthodox casuistry a dialectic skill that puts to shame the clever hosts
of modern apologists.

In the current of their casuistry they discovered the work of Peter
Ramus an invaluable tool. Ramus regarded the Aristotelian-Thomistic
science of the medieval universities as a mere forensic flourish; for indeed logic had been frozen by history into eternal categories, and logic
chopping had been carried to the high point of art. When Ramus chose
as his thesis the forgeries or false glosses on Aristotle—this pagan saint
the Roman church had claimed its own—he began a reformation of the
art of logic which corresponded to the social and religious reformation

of which he was the dialectic part. Ramus substituted for the traditional categories and predicables what he called arguments, that is, whatever is affected by the arguing of something else. The logician, argued Ramus, should analyze these arguments, discover the radii of their connections, and dissolve the formal categories into a mechanical series of things. His work, accordingly, occupied the same ground in logic that Renaissance science represented when opposed to traditional physics. The essence of his reformation of logic was to dissolve the eternal forms into a mechanism of purpose, so that a logical determinism may be unrolled from the beginning, just as the world is pictured by the science of the time as a predetermined flow of events. At the same time, Ramus's dialectic introduced the classification of arguments by dichotomy; starting thus with the material of any art, it was first divided into its mutually exclusive parts and then further dichotomized until exhausted. By this logic, then, the universe of being was split into realms of contradiction, so that the Puritan might well exclaim with Thomas Hooker: "The consequence is beyond dispute, for contradicents divide the breadth of being."

Bacon might object that from the Ramist dichotomies issued only the dry husks of learning, covering the empirical seeds; but the Puritans were convinced that logic had become thereby the most general and useful of the arts. A ground scheme of the divine intelligence, such as the unwitting student might never chance upon, was thus laid out as if by election; for logic began with discovery mediated by disposition and ordered by method. Truth was henceforth to be discovered, routed from her hidden lair, and driven into contradiction by the mechanical dichotomy of her parts. To the traditional three figures of the syllogism, therefore, Ramus added the hypothetical and disjunctive, and laid particular stress on the disjunctive mode of logical inclusion by which the determinism, or rather predeterminism, of the universe might be noted. Truth, which parallels the order of nature, and indeed represents its increated realm of essence, must itself be ordered, so that method may proceed from universals to particulars in a perfectly ordered rational chain. It thus seemed that the great chain of being might be paralleled by a great chain of logic, with the result that logical order was a transcription of the divine order. Truth which was discovered dialectically was in fact a logical copy of the predeterminism of God, and could only issue in a conviction of the predestination of man. If invention discovers the essence of a thing, disposition places it in the right order, according to the rules of the dialectic art. It happened, accordingly, that the Puritan conceived truth as something finished, perfect, and complete, which needs only to be discovered and disposed by an appropriate dialectic; and the enjoyment of that truth, as the chief end of man.

2. The Order of Nature

The commentary which nature provoked in the Puritans was a happy compromise between science and faith. The natural order of causes and effects was conceived as the ordinary power of God, while piety did not deny that a perfectly free cause could, if need be, transcend the limits of its own causality. The Puritan could thereby celebrate the ordinary providence of things, while happily entertaining the effects of a beneficent special providence which had brought him the fruits of some secret design. The secret will of God might be forever hidden, but there remained the revelation and the book of nature which God with His immanent design had written. There remained to the Puritan after the Fall two great sources of truth, the faculties of intelligence within and the world of nature without, both of which declared that experience was under the decree and inspiration of the will of God. A world so gloriously mechanical is not without its inspiration to mysticism, and if nature is to the Puritan first of all a self-contained machine, the serried effects of a continuous causality, it might also be a map and a shadow of the spirit. Nature, then, might lead to piety; and science to faith. Indeed, for the Puritan these outcomes were predetermined by his theological commitments.

Both science and theology might speak of a judicious determinism; for science illustrates necessity by arguing from necessary causes to necessary effects, and theology insists that this necessity mirrors also a moral necessity which corresponds to the mechanical. In such a view, the good —provided only it shadows forth some moral truth—might then be identical with the useful, and an ethical pragmatism could justify any means which God might put into profitable hands. The Puritan could let no opportunity escape which might bring him profit from the natural providence of things; but if this natural order should be disrupted by some overwhelming providence or special design, he finds himself at least in the possession of some moral truth which he has abstracted from it. There is then no end to the lessons which science and morality offer to a mind disposed by discipline to hear them. The order of nature was no less mechanical for being moral, nor less inspiring to piety for being so necessary. To one disposed like the Puritan to seventeenth-century mechanical materialism in his view of nature, a continuous and inevitable causality seemed only to prove the existence of a perfectly necessary First Cause. But the operation of this cause in the production of its intended effects always implied for the Puritan a design on the part of the First Cause, and hence an intelligence and a will appropriate to an infinite and eternal Being.

Puritan physics capably absorbed the new science of the seventeenth century into its inherited theology; for by the doctrine of second causes, through which God acts by ordinary causal means, the Puritan could adjust any new evidence concerning the world machine or the order of nature to the dogma of his faith. The world of Calvin and of the Puritans was a world in which no chance, accident, or contingency enters; it was a world of predeterminism and necessity. To God, the first cause, all things are foreseen, and are immutably ordered. God is simply the predeterminism of events, the stretch of causality which works continuously through cosmic history. With such a conception, as we have seen, the conscience might be engaged by causality, and the conduct ordered according to a moral necessity; for, the will which engages man in his various sublunary acts follows the counsel of his understanding, and draws out of God's necessity an apparent ethical responsibility and secondary freedom of the will. This freedom is, however, only apparent; for by definition nothing could happen outside of God's will or intent, or beyond the scope of His sovereignty. The will of God predetermines all events, yet man himself, like all natural agents, possesses that secondary and derived power by which contingent effects are brought about. This bit of Puritan casuistry simply meant that contingency is an aspect of necessity; it was theological strategy for preserving free will and moral responsibility in man in the face of the glaring fact that all his acts are predetermined. In truth, the Puritan view is nothing less than mechanical materialism in theological disguise. Man has an apparent and secondary freedom which is in fact identical with God's necessity.

These obvious implications of Puritan theology led him to define clearly in his physics the distinction between the theological materialism which he was in fact preaching and the various kinds of pagan and seventeenth-century materialisms which were flourishing about him. He was especially concerned to show that his doctrine was not like that of Spinoza or Hobbes; and he objected particularly when he was charged with Epicureanism or Stoicism. In Epicureanism the Puritan saw simply the doctrine of chances, in which all things fall out fortuitously; and in Stoicism he discovered an ancient fatalism, in which even God is tied to the connection of secondary causes. In the Puritan view, however, God is superior to physical reality, to the mechanical causality of matter, and can transcend the province of secondary causality to work at first hand His special providences and extraordinary effects. Nature was thus both the connection of necessary causes with necessary effects, a world machine, and the symbol of a moral allegory, the scene of the drama of salvation. The conception of the world as a machine was hopelessly confused with the drama of salvation, so that truth might give birth to a moral law, and the divine government be fashioned by a cosmic constitution. Freedom of will, in the Puritan view, was simply a secondary causal agency, a contingency in virtue of a primary causality, and hence not inconsistent with the predeterminism of God. Man ordinarily acts as cause by counsel, but, in any case, he can accomplish with his freedom only what God has willed. Causality is God's will manifested in the action of secondary natural causes, but collapsed by God's timelessness into one infinite and immediate act. Nevertheless, the distinction between the world considered theologically and the world considered physically had its uses; for it permitted the Puritan that duality of freedom and necessity, of God's primary causality and nature's derived effects, without which Puritan theology would not be a living doctrine. If nature is a machine which grinds out natural necessity it is also a table of commandments which makes man's deliberations no less preordained. Caught thus between natural necessity and moral responsibility, the Puritan could be no other than that living contradiction which makes of all history a moral biography and of all physics a natural theology.

3. *The Cambridge Platonism*

The immediate background of Puritan scientific thought was Cambridge Platonism, whose distinguished votaries included Henry More and Isaac Barrow, the immediate predecessors of Newton in the Cambridge well of neo-Platonic waters. At Cambridge a revived Platonism, designed to combat the growing materialism of the seventeenth century, lived in harmony with a mathematical interpretation of nature, and indeed inspired it. The principal role played by geometry in the mathematical interpretation of nature had led the Cambridge Platonists to conceive of God as extended substance, incorporeal but none the less real. Struggling against the materialism of Hobbes and the dualism of Descartes, the Cambridge scientists adopted the current mechanical materialism in their interpretation of nature, but gave it an extended spiritual dimension in their interpretation of reality. Matter itself was simply a compound of atoms, which, though inert, were moved by spirit. In the beginning, God impressed a common quantity of motion on matter, giving to the world machine a uniform motion and direction, which was influenced however by mysterious gravitational forces and the unforeseen collision of its atoms. As nothing can exist without extension, however, spirit must be a geometrical dimension of substances, alienated, so to speak, out of their bodies and dwelling in a nether world of proportion, figure, and motion. But the associations and separations of the atoms of matter, the phenomena of gravity, are the vicarious power of God on matter, a mysterious force which holds all planets in their course and balances with an uncommon harmony the divergent parts of the world machine.

Behind the realm of sensible appearance, then, lies a realm of essence, the spirit of nature, which manifests itself as the vicarious power of God on matter. The qualities of matter are accordingly the attributes of God, with extension the most prominent characteristic of His geometrical realm. As extension is the property of every existing thing, it seemed a fair conclusion of the Cambridge scientific school that extension was the absolute essence of things, a property which not only defined them but gave them being. The old antinomy of essence and existence had thus been resolved in a new and exhilarating fashion; for it seemed that God, by virtue of His omnipresence, must be absolute extension. Moreover, it was found that since the various parts of the world machine were unified by definite mathematical relations, then the spatial relations of objects must be the proportions of divine wisdom. It happened, accordingly, that the predecessors of Newton at Cambridge had prepared the way for his famous mathematical interpretation of nature by making extension the essence of existence, and existence the essence of extension. The geometrical properties of space thereby lent themselves to piety, by giving to religion a measure of divine presence. Space, then, was the divine presence, and all objects and events had their existence by virtue of their suspension in God.

The continuity of space was the divine presence; but the shadows of substantial things, immersed in time, might also decay and dissolve, leaving for the absolute spirit no relative manifestation. In facing this problem, the Cambridge Platonists reduced the continuity of space and the continuity of time to one form of continuity—that of motion. The problem was not only of interest to science, but was vital to religion, because the divine presence, in touch with every quarter of the world by virtue of its extensive existence, could not have created the world without having given to the particles of matter some inalienable properties of their existence. The outcome of these investigations not only attributed to space a divine continuity, a continuous extension, but also attributed to time a similar continuity, and reduced both forms of continuity to a common form. The result for piety meant that absolute space and absolute time had been welded into a common form of absolutism, namely, the absolutism of God. To such as had reason to cling to the old Calvinism, the new science made an overwhelming appeal. It had been established scientifically that God is an infinite and eternal Being—infinite as to His unlimited extension, and eternal as to His unlimited time.

In the light of Cambridge Platonism, then, the continuity of space (extension) and the continuity of time (duration) are reduced to a common form of continuity—that of absolute motion. Though the result of these developments was to prepare the way for their culmination in the scientific synthesis of Sir Isaac Newton, a more immediate gain accrued to religion; for it was clear that motion, which imparts the qualities to matter according to mechanical philosophy, is closely associated with the concept of God. Indeed, God was an absolute necessity to the world view constructed at Cambridge, for Newton, in common with his predecessors, considered matter inert, incapable of motion without the intervention of God. The Puritan theory of the predeterminism of God never had a more profound philosophic justification; for God was the creative life of the world machine, the creator as well as the sustainer, in His infinity and eternity, of all the motions by which the world machine was kept in operation. The mechanical materialism which was a common assumption of seventeenth-century science had thus acquired a spiritual dimension, and the Puritan found a confirmation not only for his pragmatism but also for his idealism, while once more he gathered into the household of the saints all in the way of science that might serve his faith.

4. *The Geometry of God*

There were days of sundered conscience when the world seemed to exist only in the divine mind, when it was caught up in that continuum of absolute space and eternal time which the Cambridge scientific school had described. There followed an attempt, both pathetic and divine, to bring the world once more within the focus of God's understanding, so that piety might be revived and faith renewed in the light of the philosophy which Cambridge science had bequeathed the world. It happened, therefore—since science had made space absolute, and since God Himself was infinite—that piety was inclined to identify the absolute space with the absolute God. Jonathan Edwards, in the interest of piety, did not hesitate to follow the Cambridge school in their deification of space. "It is self-evident I believe to every man, that Space is necessary, eternal, infinite, and omnipresent. But I had as good speak plain: I have already said as much as that Space is God." [8] From this conception it followed that everything which takes place in absolute space must also take place in absolute or eternal time; so that everything, all events and existences of the material world, must exist in absolute space and absolute time, the conception of which can only occur in a mind that is equally absolute and infinite, namely, the mind of God. The Puritans therefore attributed to space a divine presence, and to the properties of being, extension, figure, motion, color, because they were perceived by consciousness, the perception of a universal consciousness, a divine mind. Jonathan Edwards, perceiving the causal power and efficacy which seemed to inhere in inert matter, attributed it not to the substance of matter but to the spirit of nature. "Deprive the world of light and motion and the case would stand thus with the world," he wrote: "There would be neither white nor black, neither blue nor brown, bright nor shaded pellucid, no opake, nor noise or sound, neither heat nor cold, neither fluid nor wet nor dry, hard nor soft, solidity nor extension, nor figure, nor magnitude, nor proportion, nor body, nor spirit, what then is to become of the universe? Certainly it exists nowhere but in the divine mind."

The basic philosophic tenet of the idealist mind, the dependence of being on being known, thus acquired a new content from the philosophies of Cambridge science. The dependence of being on being known was for them, however, a dependence upon God, whose causal power and the radii of whose divine wisdom were in no way impaired by the mathematical interpretation of nature which led the Cambridge school into its curious geometry of God. "A state of nothing," wrote Edwards, "is a state wherein every proposition of Euclid is not true." It followed that the formal logic of philosophic necessity would drive the conception of being into contradiction without the premise of a divine cause and a universal consciousness with which to confer upon it the creative spirit of life. The immaterialist was unable to conceive of the creation of matter without consciousness, or of the motion of its inert substance without spirit. Without the premised unity of a universal consciousness, without the intelligence and will of a divine mind, without the radii of divine wisdom in the geometry of God, the world would collapse into an absolute nothing and perish amidst a flood of contradiction. "Let us suppose," wrote Edwards, "for illustration this impossibility that all the spirits in the universe be for a time deprived of consciousness, and God's consciousness at the same time intermitted. I say the universe for that time would cease to be." It followed that substance was dependent for its existence upon spirit, and that matter should perish without mind.

In this perspective piety could be renewed, because it mattered little to science whether religious philosophers thought of material existences and events as "the proportions of God's acting" or as the motion of the world machine. It is all the same, argued Edwards, whether objects exist in the divine mind or whether they exist "in the same manner as is vulgarly thought." To interpret the order of cause and effect (the order of nature) as proportions of divine wisdom (as a measure of the divine excellence) had indeed a certain value to those philosophers who wanted to deify the self-regulating powers of nature in the interest of laissez-faire economics and republican politics. At the same time, this interpretation of Cambridge science lent itself to Puritan Platonism and recalled many of the departed to the ancient faith, thus blocking the movement toward atheism and deflecting the deists from their course. For Edwards the lesson of the new science was that it reinstated Puritan idealism, and lent itself to Puritan piety, in the interest of the divinity of the New Lights. Under his influence, the Platonic theory of divine love was brought once more to life, until it seemed that appearance was a deception and a firmer reality lay behind the phenomenal screen. The Puritans thus renewed their traditional tendency to see behind the gross shell of material things the shadow of being, and behind the intercourse of events the beauty and excellence of the art of God.

The mechanistic presuppositions of Puritan scientific thought had therefore generated the idealism of its philosophy. It resulted in a theological materialism in which the qualities of matter are aspects of the personality of God, and gave birth to a pragmatic piety which was no less pious for being material nor less pragmatic for being spiritual. The fusion of these divergent aspects of the Puritan world view was a necessity brought about by the conception, on the one hand, that matter was a dead or inert substance, and on the other, that spirit alone was free. In brief, the mechanical materialism of the New England Puritan produced a corresponding philosophic idealism and drove him into a sea of contradiction. The solution of the main problem raised by seventeenth-century science, for the New England Puritan as for many other seventeenth-century philosophers, was the supposition that the motion and causal efficacy of matter were impressed upon the atoms at the moment of creation and subsequently sustained by the influx of divine energies. In common with Newton and the Cambridge scientific school, the Puritan attributed the principle of gravity and other mysteries of the world of material change to a "most subtle spirit." Edwards and Cotton Mather and other metaphysicians of the American mind were similarly inclined to attribute to matter the passivity of an object that is known, while giving to a universal consciousness, a divine mind, the creative power and causal efficacy of a knower.

5. *The Cosmic Constitution*

The world of nature thus seemed to the New England Puritan a demonstration of God's active power, as the essences or ideal forms abstracted from its scene appeared to him as a demonstration of God's wisdom. Nature was the observable and recordable part of the divine government, a segment of the universe in which God habitually acted by means and agencies rather than directly. Causes and effects, represented as the logical mechanism of God, were in reality secondary to the First Cause, God Himself. The Ramist dialectic, aided by Cambridge Platonism, made it possible for the Puritan to receive the latest scientific intelligence of the world of nature, to resolve it logically, and to comprehend the results of observation and experiment as parts of the economy of redemption. The mechanism of nature was therefore identical with the logic of God, and the divine wisdom was equivalent to the sovereign power. The world of nature was accordingly dependent upon the concurring influences of its Creator for its operation and continued existence.

The attempt to discover behind the power of the second cause the inevitability of the First Cause was the heart of Puritan physics; and Puritan theology rested no less directly upon the argument of philosophic necessity. The sovereignty of God was in fact, not the effect, nor yet the secondary cause which preceded it, but the necessary connection between them. In terms of Puritan physics, then, God was not the world machine, but the universal reign of law which kept it on its course; for behind the world machine stood the concursive causality which made its operations necessary. It is this background of physics which made the Puritan argument for the predeterminism of God and the predestination of man seem so irresistible. God was the creation of logical necessity, the necessary connection between events, which could not have been otherwise than it was. From this it followed that the mechanical world, the world of matter, or what the Puritan called the realm of second causes, stood dependent upon a more primary world of causality obeying immutable and universal law.

The operation of the universe, the world of nature, betrayed its divine governance, the concursive influence of its creator. To the Puritan, therefore, it seemed the universe was governed by a cosmic constitution, presided over and created by a cosmic king. The science of physics thus combined with the science of theology to confirm the Puritan in his piety; for his piety was in fact the symbol of his loyalty to the divine government, of his faith in a cosmic king and in the reign of cosmic law. It is this faith in the inevitable reign of law, in a cosmic constitution presided over by an omnipotent sovereign God, which is the essence of Puritan religion. It is a faith in the necessary connection, in philosophic necessity, which the Puritan denominated "God," and which a subsequent generation lost to scepticism because it seemed hostile to the causal efficacy and free will of man. In attributing primary causal power only to God, beside whom the ordinary mechanical efficacy of natural causes seemed secondary and at times unreal, the Puritan had unwittingly erected a barrier to progress which a subsequent age of industrialism had at last to destroy. For the Puritan, however, the world was governed by a cosmic constitution, which was no less arbitrary for being legal and no less authoritative for being divine. For him, indeed, the divine government was of necessity an arbitrary government, and the world of nature was an impeccable machine.

6. *The Realm of Essence*

Wandering thus far through the mazes of Puritan metaphysics, we discover that we have at long last stumbled upon the realm of essence. The Puritan, confronted by the universal flux of being, has made his characteristic rupture in its movement, defined and described its terms, and expressed in a theological way his dialectic intent. The new program of Puritanism was mainly Platonic in its themes, and conceived the world of matter as but a copy of counterpart of an ordered hierarchy of ideas existing in the mind of God. Logic, therefore, set forth the order of things in terms of their essences, and these became the ideas or realities upon which the world of change seemed to rest. The essences, however, exist latently in the human intelligence; knowledge is a kind of reminiscence, and the soul contains in the germ an intuitive knowledge of these eternal truths. Thinking is thus, under the tutelage of logic, an unveiling of ideal forms, which, when completed in pairs and contraries, and arranged dialectically in their essential unity, make up the architecture of reality, the superstructure of the divine. The sum total of truth, the complete system of essence, exists only in the mind of God; while man, through the sharpening of his reason or with the aid of divine grace, shares in some part of it. The world of matter is flux and change; that of essence is eternal. Such was the metaphysics of Puritan science; such was the philosophy of the New England divines.

We are thus brought back to the point from which we set out; we are brought back to the central theme around which Puritan theory continually oscillates and upon which it finally rests. The Puritan carried his political program into the realm of metaphysics, and constructed his hierarchy of essences with the same care that he lavished upon the rule of the elect. He was engaged in a great game of transcendental politics, and in attempting to deal on fairly equal and negotiable terms with the great monarch whose impotent subject he was, he erected a theory which hedged the divinity about with contracts and rules, making him intelligible, for all His unpredictable power, to the finite mind of man. In the light of contractualism and consent, the Puritan was committed to hold man morally responsible and contractually liable for his stubborn sinfulness and error, and this presupposed an efficacious choice on the part of man as he struggled for redemption. But in confronting the problem of free will, the Puritan could not charge full responsibility for salvation upon the natural man, for to do so would have meant encroaching upon the sovereign power of God. Neither could he deny, however, that man had some capacity toward regeneration, without disappointing those who had put their faith in the ability of man to make reasoned choices and effect determinate ends. Caught thus between the sovereignty of God and the sovereignty of man, between the demands of piety and the duties of moralism, the Puritan worked out his patchwork of compromise, and condemned to the usual contradiction his philosophy of God.

The hesitant steps the Puritan had taken in this direction were in fact the first steps in a long process of reconciliation by which God is transformed from an arbitrary feudal monarch into a benevolent parliamentary king. The decent and orderly God who rules in the light of a cosmic constitution, and manifests himself in the regular and recurrent order of nature, who works through familiar instruments and agents and carefully observes the normal causal relations of his government, was a wonderfully appealing and dramatic figure, the creation of Puritan pragmatism. But piety demanded also a wayward and lawless feudal monarch, the heritage of rule by divine right, who cared little what his plans might cost his worldly subjects, and carried his designs with no concern for the torment of his pawns. The God of Puritan piety was a governor of contingencies, whose interference with the normal operation of events brings to nought the calculated risks of man. The benevolent despot whose actions are regulated by constitutional law is the God of the Yankee, the creation of Puritan pragmatism; and the lawless feudal monarch who interferes in an unpredictable way with the normal order of nature was the God of the Puritan, the creation of Puritan idealism. This living contradiction, which only a more enlightened age would remove, was the paradox of Puritan character and the source of those double antinomies which gave dialectic vigor to his thought. The Puritan was a contribution of the old world and the Yankee a creature of the new; but it was inevitable in the steps the Puritan had already taken that the Puritan would come into conflict with the Yankee, while the waning of Puritanism would mark the rise of a revolutionary generation.

CHAPTER SIX

THE WANING OF PURITANISM

1. *The Death of Absolutism*

When a succeeding age had grown more enlightened, and the Puritan heritage had split along the lines of its major cleavage, its piety fled into the arms of the evangelical churches, and its rational core into an enlightened worship of reason and nature, after its pragmatism had grown too cold to stir the heart. The waning of Puritanism and the rise of religious rationalism, by loosening the bonds of the ancient faith, had thus prepared the colonial mind for the revolutionary ideas of the eighteenth century. The deity, who had heretofore enjoyed an impeccable austerity, was now dragged into the disputes of men, examined of his pretensions and stripped of his antique powers. In Puritanism, it will be remembered, God enjoyed an absolute sovereignty and dominion over the lives of men and of nations, with the consequence that man's freedom of will and his sovereignty over nature were correspondingly limited. But the revolutionary fires were burning upon the political horizon, and the absolutism of the Puritan God proved no less objectionable than the absolutism of the English king. The deistic faith of the eighteenth century proposed to limit the powers of both monarchs, confining the absolute God to the constitutional law of the cosmos, and the absolute King to the restrictions of a social contract. Man would thereby enjoy a corresponding freedom of the will—which was presupposed to bolster up the doctrine of government by consent—and a corresponding sovereignty over nature—which was needed to carry home to his small proprietary the means of independence.

It happened, accordingly, that the absolute sovereign God of the Puritan underwent a marvelous transformation corresponding to the political consciousness of men. The cosmos was interpreted after the image of a monarchy among the Puritans of the seventeenth century, though with certain significant anticipations of social-contract theory, it is true; then in the eighteenth century, the cosmos was fashioned after the architecture of a republic, with an impeccable harmony and balance of its forces, and a cosmic constitution shadowing forth the universal reign of law. Finally, the easy optimism of the nineteenth century began to picture the cosmos in the manner of property accumulation, with an immanent God at the heart of the process and a divinity dwelling in the heart of individual man. The winds of political doctrine had thus blown a fresh breeze through the American mind at every instance of a major transition; for it cleansed the mind of notions that were no longer right, and purified the faculties for the reception of ideas which it was next to inspire. The Puritan God was blown out of his cosmic throne only to dwell as an immanent divinity in the heart of man, and from the Puritan heritage the revolutionary generation drew not only a religion of reason but also a religion of the heart. Stripped of his antique powers, deprived of each of his prerogatives, the absolute sovereign God of Puritanism had no recourse but to enter as a weakened prince into the temple of individualism, and there to seek refuge. Religion and politics would henceforth measure their strides together, walking toward a common goal, ordained it seemed by a deity who was a creature not only of the struggle of ideas but of the struggle of men.

Unless some such secular interpretation of sacred history is given, it will be difficult to understand the conclusions of the orthodox, and even more difficult to perceive why a revolutionary generation should reject not only an absolute God but also an absolute King. When Samuel Willard summed up the orthodox faith inherited from the seventeenth century, he argued that all who were truly faithful should stand against the temptation of eighteenth-century rationalism. Those who sought to overthrow the doctrine of the absolute sovereignty of God, he said, wished only to establish an uncontrolled sovereignty in the will of man. Similarly, Jonathan Edwards's exposition of the sovereignty of God, inspired by a new and genuine piety, and refurbished by the scientific materials available in the age of Newton, could not stem the tide of opinion demanded by the doctrine of consent. The revolutionary age demanded that both the absolute God and the absolute King must henceforth rule by the consent of their governed. The absolutism of God was thus dissolved in the absolutism of man. The religion of reason triumphed over the waning Puritanism, and drew from a weakened God a bill of inalienable rights; while the piety which had once inspired the indomitable Puritan fled into the arms of evangelical religion and bred a sentimental religion of the heart.

The struggle against the absolutism of the English king thus had as its corollary a struggle against the absolutism of the Puritan God, and in the measure that the colonists wrested sovereignty from their English monarch, they secured it also from their cosmic King. The doctrine of passive obedience and nonresistance, so long taught by the clericals as a corollary of their conception of the absolute dominion of God, was now pronounced a fabulous invention and snare, a deception of the people, a stratagem of the imperial council to deprive the people of their rights. The revolutionary temper, aroused by the stirring winds of political doctrine against the principle of absolutism, could no more tolerate the principle in a sovereign God than it could in a sovereign King. The doctrine of passive obedience and nonresistance to higher powers was discovered to be a deception of the priestcraft, the royal roguery of divine right, the senile insinuation of the clericals, a slander upon the natural rights of man, an outrage perpetuated in the provinces for the purpose of keeping the colonials in submission to the royal brute of England. The tyrant and the cleric, clubbing together for the purpose of deceiving the people, were issuing their pronouncements as if from a divine source, commanding by divine right what the people hold by natural right. The defense of the revolutionary cause became, accordingly, a defense of natural rights; for the rights of nature are more primitive and authoritative than the commands of men.

The revolutionary temper had thus issued in a new naturalism, which, inspired by a mathematical interpretation of nature, seemed at once more reasonable and more pious than the unreasonable superstitions inherited from the feudal ages. An enlightenment was bred from a new science of causes which followed in the wake of the Newtonian confirmation of a mathematical universe, and gave birth to a promising science of mechanics. Thus aided in its revolutionary cause by a scientific warrant for its most generous hopes, the age broke forth in all its new-found joy, worshiped in the temple of nature and prayed openly to the goddess of reason. Nature and reason symbolized for the age the two most important fundamentals of its revolutionary faith; for nature, because of her harmony, balance, and order, could be trusted to regulate herself; and man, by virtue of his claim to reason, was proved to be capable of self-government. In nature and reason, accordingly, the enlightenment found the symbols of its faith—on the one hand, in a laissez-faire, self-regulating capitalism, and on the other, in a republican government founded upon consent and based upon individual choice. But before self-government could be proclaimed as a cosmic principle, either in the realm of nature or in the society of man, the absolutism of the Puritan God must be swept away, and the doctrine of predestination confined within the four walls of the consociated churches. For as long as the sovereignty of God went unquestioned, the sovereignty of man would remain in doubt. The waning of Puritanism and the rise of religious rationalism, by loosening the bonds of the ancient faith, prepared the way for the revolutionary ideas of the eighteenth century, and brought the absolutism of God into question for the sake of a newly discovered faith in man.

2. *The Government of God*

The conception of God as an arbitrary, despotic sovereign, a product of the aristocratic society of the sixteenth century, had now to come face to face with the benevolent, utilitarian God of the eighteenth century. In this transition from the arbitrary feudalistic monarch to the benevolent capitalistic king, the work of Jonathan Edwards represents a creative compromise; for while the need of Puritanism for a sovereign and absolute God is preserved, virtue—and hence the power of self-government —becomes the reward, of both those who are supernaturally visited and those who strive for moral perfection. In this creative defense of Calvinism, Edwards introduced a new conception of the government of God, so that the sixteenth-century need of absolutism is preserved alongside the eighteenth-century need of republicanism. Edwards's delight in the sovereignty of God had already led him, as we have seen, to describe the whole course of nature as an arbitrary constitution. In this way he had preserved both the faith of the Enlightenment in the immutable reign of law and the faith of Puritanism in the necessary and arbitrary connection of events. At the same time, under the influence of Cambridge Platonism, he conceived matter to be inert, and required the intervention of God at each instant to keep the world machine upon its course. By this strategy the sixteenth-century requirement of absolutism had been preserved alongside the eighteenth-century requirement of a government by law, so that the absolutism of God, with its faith in the necessary connection of events, had been transformed into an arbitrary constitution, with its faith in the universal reign of law.

A further step in this creative theology was taken when Edwards conceived of true virtue as "benevolence to Being in general." In order to get the true standard or measure of anything, Edwards seemed to be saying, it is necessary to take the perspective of "Being in general" as the point of departure. By this innovation Edwards had introduced the notion that the judgment of anything ought to be undertaken in the light of a transcendent standard, and in the perspective of God. In the light of this standard, accordingly, because it is not mean, provincial, or selfish, one could be led to true virtue, to benevolence to Being in general. Edwards contrasted the "love of complacence," the love of self, with the "love of benevolence," which is derived from love of God. By this distinction Edwards had established that natural and social morality—the morality of the self and of society—is only a natural and a secondary virtue, not a primary one like true virtue, or benevolence to Being in general. It follows from this distinction that without true virtue things cannot be appreciated for what they truly are, and their truth cannot really be known. True virtue is thus a benevolent regard for an object as a part of an inclusive whole; and love of God implies a consent of the heart and of the will to its course and constitution. Thus it happened that Yankee pragmatism and Puritan idealism had once more been fused in a creative synthesis of the American mind.

Here then was a creative compromise, not only of the sixteenth-century theology with an eighteenth-century need, but also of an eighteenth-century rationalism and the cosmic optimism and transcendental consciousness of the nineteenth century. Edwards was the creative thread of continuity between the Puritanism and transcendentalism, and the link by which republicanism was joined both to its past and its future. In the theology of Edwards, God had in fact become identical with the cosmic constitutionalism which became so much a part of nineteenth-century thought; and the rationalists of the eighteenth century, the disciples of republican religion, were building also on the concept of universal law, on the notion of a self-regulating economic and natural order. It was the contribution of Edwards to have united these diverse conceptions without sacrificing either the sovereignty of God or the piety which is a necessary expression of man's recognition of His government. In the wake of this creative theology, however, followed the swirl and eddies of endless controversy; for in this matter, as in so many others, Edwards was hopelessly misinterpreted and misunderstood. The critics of the new divinity betrayed their own entanglement with the needs of the age, and, unable to rise above it, as Edwards had done, confused the metaphysical notion of a divine constitution with their own crying need for a benevolent and pragmatic God.

The theological issues of the age had thus come to fruition in the conception of God. The liberal Calvinists, starting with Edwards's idea of benevolence to Being in general, were inclined to emphasize an abstract moral law, a cosmic constitution, supposed to lie at the heart of the universe, and by the terms of which the moral governor would finally judge man either for salvation or damnation. The conception of Edwards had led to a cosmic constitution, also; but with Edwards the doctrine was primarily metaphysical, one of philosophic necessity, in which the predeterminism of God and the predestination of man expressed the

absolute space-time perspective of Cambridge science. The liberal theologians who opposed the new Calvinism were inclined more and more
toward a benevolent and utilitarian deity whose goal was the happiness
of mankind and whose means was the freedom of the will. It happened,
accordingly, that the twin demands of the age, moral responsibility in
men and democracy in their redemption, were met equally by the creative defense of Calvinism and by the rational theology which opposed
it. Meantime, however, Calvinism in its most virulent form became the
possession of popular religion, so that the abstract theological attempts
to rescue it were doomed by the enthusiasm of the popular cause. The
way had been prepared for the transition, however, even among those
normally orthodox, from the wrathful God of Calvin, renewed in the
beatitudes of Edwards, to the benevolent God of the young republic,
upon whom destiny had for the moment lavished her warm smile.

The government of God had thus been transformed by the government of man; and the monarchy of the sixteenth century, with its heritage of absolutism, gave way to the republic of the eighteenth century,
with its heritage of constitutionalism. Underlying the movement toward
liberal religion was the old demand that individual initiative and moral
striving, the psychological equivalents of republicanism, should have
some place in salvation of men; and underlying the evangelical revival
was the old need, inherent in the aristocratic principle of divine election,
that there should be a greater democracy in the redemption of men.
When therefore the orthodox disciples of Calvinism recognized beneath
the cloak of liberal religion the small fires of smouldering revolt from
the divine government, they hastened to the defense of the ancient orthodox doctrines, defending against the liberals the conception of the
sovereign and absolute dominion of God. But where the social environment enjoined not only equality of opportunity but also the profitable
rewards of success to those whose individual initiative and private enterprise had given them the courage to hazard the main chance, the
sovereignty of God had now to be limited so that it might not interfere
with the natural rights of man. It happened, accordingly, that where
the government of God had become an impediment to the advancement
of the new social order, the divine decrees of the feudal monarch were
transformed into the legal principles of a constitutionalist king.

3. *The Universalist Revolt*

In passing from the conception of the feudal monarch to the constitutionalist king, liberal theology was driven to raise again the vital question
of regeneration. However much the orthodox might hedge on the

question and hide behind the robes of their ecclesiastical prestige, Puritanism would seem to have been lacking in a number of particulars regarding the salvation of men. The age actually demanded a new democracy in the salvation of men, a new equality of opportunity in their redemption. The compromises with the older orthodoxy which followed the creative attempt to reconcile the need of the new age with the heritage of the old were for the most part only devious and stubborn departures from the traditional positions. In one way or another, however, theology was forced to grant a reluctant province to the dignity and sovereignty of man. Whether in the form of granting a new efficacy to the means of salvation, or in the form of a treatise on the religious affections, the older generation of theologians was gradually driven from its orthodox position. With private enterprise and individual initiative enjoined by the economy of capitalism, these things could not long be denied to the economy of redemption; and similarly, with equality of opportunity demanded by the enterprise of life, a democracy in redemption could not long be denied to the enterprise of salvation.

It was the tendency of the universalists who followed the teachings of Charles Chauncy, therefore, to stress the fact that Christ through his atonement had put all men in a position to be saved, and this was a religious version of the republican doctrine that all men are created equal. The advantages which a mercantile aristocracy formerly possessed as the royal favorites of God were now brushed aside by the doctrine of republican religion that all men have equal opportunity to be saved. Both the Calvinists, who defended the Puritan doctrine, and the Universalists, who attacked it, were trying to turn God's sovereignty and feudal lordship into a moral government. The concern of the disciples of Calvinism, in their creative defense of the aristocratic principle, was that the moral government of God should be upheld and the dignity of divine law established through the salvation only of those irresistibly chosen by the moral governor. Where the evangelicals and universalists had transformed Christ's sacrifice into a universal redemption of mankind, the Calvinists transformed the gospel of love into the gospel of justice, and the moral law into a cosmic constitution. In either case, the aristocratic principle of divine election was under attack from the republican principle of universal salvation; and as it turned out, the creative Calvinists of the new age could save their doctrine only by modifying it in the light of republican and constitutionalist principles. Thus it happened that the aristocratic doctrine of divine election was gradually transformed by republican religion into the equal right of all men to the means of salvation. The royal favorites of the absolute monarch had become the parliamentary assemblage of a constitutionalist king.

4. *The Pietist Revolt*

Although religious individualism had been the heart of the Puritan revolt and of the Protestant movement generally, little room for its expression had been found in the wilderness Zion. The Puritans, for the sake of the orderly management of the Christian state, had emphasized the church-social covenant, repudiating all attempts to set up direct communion with God. Hence the covenant of grace, or individual contract with God, was congregationally embodied in church order; for church order, as we have seen, was the ecclesiastical bulwark of the standing order of society and of the Christian aristocracy of the state. It happened, moreover, that Ramist Platonism had embodied God's will both in the social order and in natural law, so that the representatives of this divine order, the repositories of this divine will, had been loath to permit any individualist deviations from the rule of the saints. But these traits of Puritan thinking, strongly fortified in the trials of the Christian state, and increasingly called upon to defend the rule of the magistrates and ministers, segregated the Christian utopia from Quakers, Anabaptists, and Antinomians, enthusiastic sects of political and religious individualists, who more often than not sacrificed enlightenment to enthusiasm and church order to personal revelations. It happened, accordingly, that the standing order in church and state were called upon to emphasize sober religion and an enlightened mind rather than "raised affections," thereby rejecting religious individualism, personal mysticism, and all private revelations which were not credited by the saints.

As Puritanism waned, however, and as the control of the magistrates and ministers faltered, this repressed side of the hungering spirit, especially after European pietism had migrated here, swept large parts of the populace into an outburst of religious enthusiasm known as the Great Awakening. This outburst of religious enthusiasm and sectarian frenzy, which marked the revolt of the backcountry from the political control of the town gentry, seemed at first an attempt to return to the piety of the fathers, now waning in the land; but as the outburst progressed and removed itself further and further from the control of the established churches, it spread beyond the confines of the congregational empire and engrossed the whole nature. Strange and untutored, the migrant ministers took it up, and pastoral leadership passed to a host of charlatans; while backcountry politicians were not above taking up the new enthusiasm as a means to ends not enjoined by Holy Scripture. The Pietist revolt, then, was an outbreak of religious individualism, so long fettered by the standing order of the New England churches; but it was also a revolt of the backcountry producers from the stringent controls of the mercantile aristocracy which ruled from afar. It was a revolt, not only against the ruling elders of the church, but also against the ruling oligarchy of the state; and in this religious disguise, it was the first step in a movement which culminates in the American Revolution.

By a strange paradox of history, the creative theology of the Pietist revolt was furnished by one who intended only to buttress the waning faith of the fathers. Influenced by the new learning of the Enlightenment, in contact with the ideas of Hutcheson and Locke and Newton, Jonathan Edwards set out to reconcile the new learning with the old theology. Influenced also by Continental pietism, and under the intense personal experiences of the Great Awakening, Edwards soon became the leader of the "New Lights," for whom he furnished an empirical philosophy of religion. From Locke's emphasis on experience as the ultimate source of ideas, and from Hutcheson's doctrine of the moral sense, Edwards argued that God must be experienced before He can be understood. He had thus returned piety to orthodoxy and mysticism to faith, giving to the abstract science of theology that living and vital sense of the presence of God from which it had long since departed; and in so doing, Edwards had made possible once more an individualist's interpretation of religion of such proportions that the basis might be laid for a common faith. In insisting that God must be experienced before He can be understood, Edwards had opened up varieties of religious experience to an equal plane of being with those the saint had so long monopolized; and he had made possible, though he himself did not follow this lead, a kind of democracy in the redemption of man by which the aristocracy of Christian grace was quite effectively whittled away.

5. *The Unitarian Revolt*

The Unitarian revolt had long been preparing in New England; for the liberal tides of opinion, carried on the stream of universalism and evangelicalism, had sooner or later to take a rationalist form. Unitarianism rejected the Trinitarian formula, of course; but it rested ultimately upon a benevolent conception of God and an exalted conception of man. It inquired into the moral powers of the human being, citing as the cause of moral perfection, not the supernatural aid, but only the supernatural example; and its outcome was self-government, moral perfection without supernatural aid, the government of the self without the government of God. It happened, accordingly, that the Unitarian revolt was one form of the revolt in religion against sixteenth-century Calvinism, and that, like other questions involved in the waning of Puritanism, it reflected republican principles within the scope of religion. But the underlying issue that sprang up in the wake of the Unitarian revolt was the question of Christ's divinity, whether Christ was merely a man of many excellencies or a god. If the former alternative is accepted, it follows that Christ's divinity is not a necessary mediation in the salvation of man, but that man can hope for moral perfection without supernatural aid, though he might still need the supernatural example.

No wonder the orthodox frowned upon this liberal tide. Once the divinity of Christ is questioned, the divinity even of God may be open to doubt. For the saving grace and supernatural aid of God, which had inspired the piety of the Puritan fathers, their Unitarian descendents had substituted simply the ethical teachings and the philosophy of Christ —a kindly humanitarianism invoked by the example of the Redeemer. The defenders of orthodoxy saw clearly that the real issue was the question of Christ's divinity; for upon that dogma the whole structure of Christianity rested. Once call into question the divinity of Christ, and the sanctity of the whole Christian system might be open to doubt. But the Trinitarian formula, as defended by the orthodox, led to the mystery of the atonement, why God in Christ should suffer for the salvation of others, and in particular for those whom he had already predestined, by the transgression of Adam, to suffer the torments of sin and death. The mystery of the atonement seemed to the Unitarians contrary to all sound morality; contrary, that is, to a rational, calculating morality such as the eighteenth-century was inclined to credit.

Self-sacrifice in Jesus, except merely as a demonstration of the resolution of his will or of the excellency of his virtue, now seemed contrary to the right of life, liberty, and property; for the divinity of Christ conflicted with the sovereignty of man, whose encompassing powers and freedom of will were presupposed by the new republican goals of life, liberty, and property. But to the defenders of orthodoxy, it seemed, the Unitarians were overlooking the ruined state of man, granting him an efficacy and a power not permitted to so depraved a creature; it seemed they were bent upon making human intelligence the guide to morals, denying minute regulations, the divine law, upon which a moral government must rest. But the Unitarian possessed a benevolent conception of man, in whom dwelt, it was said, elements of the divinity. Thus, it happened that the Unitarian revolt, questioning the divinity of Christ, and by indirection the government of God, was led to confer upon men some parcel of that divinity they had secretly denied to their God, and which now they wished to appropriate as a capital immunity to themselves.

6. *The Sovereignty of Man*

In the waning of Puritanism all the pristine doctrines of orthodoxy had been stripped of their pretenses and denied their antique powers. The final issues of the theological battles in which the heritage of the past and the needs of the present had been joined came down at long last, not to the government of God, but to the government of man. The issues were thus joined not only upon the battlements of theology but in the open fields of politics, because the Puritan heritage had called into question the fundamental presupposition upon which republicanism was to be built. Unless the presupposition of freedom of will is granted, the sovereignty of man over his person and property, which were the ends that republicanism proposed to effect, would inevitably fall short of attainment. The Puritan had always subjected the will to its appropriate position in the hierarchy of faculties, and under the tutelage of an ancient faculty-psychology had denied the will its native liberty. When the proponents of republican religion set out to challenge Puritanism, therefore, they focused their main attack upon the serfdom of the will as portrayed in the old Calvinism, and called before the bar of reason the denial of native liberty to this representative of man in the parliament of choice. The sovereignty of man, with its presupposition of freedom of will, became the rallying cry of republican religion, bringing to a final point of disintegration the forces of Puritanism which had momentarily rallied to protect the heritage of the fathers.

In Puritanism, it will be remembered, the will bears a serf-like relationship to its overlord, the understanding, so that the fundamental position of the fathers on the freedom of the will was that it had not merely rights, which were secondary and derived, but also obligations, which were primary and inevitable. Although the Puritans had taken the first hesitant steps in an assertion of the sovereignty of man, they were deflected from this course because of their piety and out of respect to the sovereignty of God. The theological problem of the age for the apologists of Calvinism, therefore, was to find new and more convincing grounds for denying the will its native liberty, and to assert once again the superiority of the understanding. In the theological battles in which the issue was joined, the work of Jonathan Edwards stands out once again as a creative compromise. He begins his analysis by denying the faculty-psychology, in which the will, because it is a part of a hierarchy, bears subordinate relations to the other parts; then he brings his great intellect to bear on the problem of erecting a more functional theory of man. In Edwards's inquiry into the freedom of the will, therefore, the will's freedom is denied because it is a facet of a larger functional unity of the human being. The error of the republicans, on the other hand, was that they took the will as a separate faculty while dissolving the feudal hierarchy in which it had been immersed in favor of a sovereignty over itself. The strange paradox of the age therefore was that the "liberal" theologians, those who were in the forefront of the fight for freedom of will, employed the feudal faculty-psychology to buttress their arguments, while Edwards, who attempted to defend the temple of orthodoxy, developed an empirical and functional theory of man.

In all this Calvinistic casuistry, however, Edwards was unavoidably opposed to the conception of freedom of the will. It was essential to Puritanism and to the omnipotence of God that the will be kept in bondage to the understanding, so that the ruling faculty might seem more spiritual and hence superior to the objects of the will's desire. Edwards drew a distinction, accordingly, between moral behavior, which involves motivation and preference, and physical or natural behavior such as might be discovered in the world of matter. In the latter, he wanted to express the iron determinism of matter, a natural necessity; and in the former, he wanted to demonstrate the logical connection of ideas, a philosophic necessity. But it will be remembered that in Puritan philosophy the Ramist Platonism had embodied God's will both in the social order and in natural law, with the result that Edwards was able to reduce both forms of necessity to a common divine necessity. Hence, he wrote, the difference between natural and moral necessity, "does not lie so much in the nature of the connection, as in the two terms connected." Here then was a revival of the Puritan idea of the necessary connection of events, which in turn was closely associated with the concept of God. In Puritanism, causality was a metaphysical principle as well as a demonstrated fact, and it led, whether in ethics or physics, to the same world of philosophic necessity, which inevitably denied freedom of the will. Moral and natural necessity are therefore identical, wrote Edwards, insofar as they are instances of philosophic necessity, which is "nothing else than the full and fixed connection between the things signified by the subject and predicate of a proposition, which affirms something to be true." In brief, the world of Edwards, as of the Puritan fathers before him, was a world of strict determinism, in which freedom of the will in man can only be an aspect of philosophic necessity in God.

Edwards had, however, raised the crucial issue of the age, the issue upon which all other aspects of controversy actually turned; and he had raised it in such form that, while righteousness was encouraged, the faith of the Puritan fathers in the predeterminism of God and the predestination of man had been sustained. But the disciples of freedom, the apostles of republican religion, could not understand how moral responsibility could be held unless moral freedom could be granted; and as God had by now been transformed into a moral governor, the young republicans wanted not only the freedom and the responsibility but the means of salvation thrust into their hands. The complaint of the liberal theologians against Calvinism, even in the creative form in which Edwards had cast it, was that it made of the spiritual or moral world the same kind of mechanism which science proclaimed in the physical world. While the liberal theologians were inclined to grant Edwards a certain amount of moral obligation by virtue of the moral governor and his cosmic constitution, they could hardly stomach the cavalier way in which he had fused moral and natural necessity in a common philosophic necessity. But the Calvinists saw clearly what the Puritan fathers had known long before, that, unless the government of God is preserved, that of man would crumble into a chaos of choice and an anarchy of free will, while it denied the authority and the divine right of the government of God.

With the issue posed in this form, whether they would choose the sovereignty of God or the sovereignty of man, the republicans did not long hesitate. Puritanism had buttressed the aristocratic principle in church and state, and out of respect to the absolutism of God seemed a defense also of the arbitrary government of the English king. The waning of Puritanism, therefore, had clarified the major issue of the dispute, and had brought to the fore the mysterious Puritan doctrine of the will's serfdom in the hierarchy of the faculties. In its search for a presupposition upon which to rest its new social order, accordingly, it was essential to the republican cause that Puritanism be destroyed. The sovereignty of God was thus being challenged by the sovereignty of man, and the unlimited absolute prerogatives of the divine monarch were being modified in the light of newly discovered natural and inalienable rights of his man. The controversy over freedom of the will was the crucial issue of the whole epoch, because republicanism presupposed the sovereignty of man over his person and property, and presumed that a moral governor would inevitably be obliged to reward those who possessed true virtue and were carried by their moral initiative to a high tide of success. It happened, accordingly, that where the Puritan heritage had become an impediment to the advancement of republicanism, the absolutism of the feudal monarch was transformed into the constitutionalism of the capitalist king.

BOOK II

THE AMERICAN
ENLIGHTENMENT

"The United States of America have exhibited, perhaps, the first example of governments erected on the simple principles of nature; and if men are now sufficiently enlightened to disabuse themselves of artifice, imposture, hypocrisy, and superstition, they will consider this event as an era in their history. Although the detail of the formation of the American governments is at present little known or regarded either in Europe or America, it may hereafter become an object of curiosity. It will never be pretended that any persons employed in that service had interviews with the gods, or were in any degree under the inspiration of heaven, more than those at work upon ships or houses, or laboring in merchandise or agriculture; it will forever be acknowledged that these governments were contrived merely by the use of reason and the senses, as Copley painted Chatham; West, Wolf; and Trumbull, Warren and Montgomery; as Dwight, Barlow, Trumbull and Humphries composed their verse, and Belknap and Ramsay history, as Godfrey invented his quadrant, and Rittenhouse his planetarium; as Boylston practised inoculation, and Franklin electricity; as Paine exposed the mistakes of Raynal, and Jefferson those of Buffon, so unphilosophically borrowed from the despicable dreams of De Pau. Neither the people, nor their conventions, committees, or sub-committees, considered legislation in any other light than as ordinary arts and sciences, only more important. Called without exception, and compelled without previous inclination, though undoubtedly at the best period of time, both for England and America, suddenly to erect new systems of laws for their future government, they adopted the wise method of a wise architect, in erecting a new palace for the residence of his sovereign. They determined to consult Vitruvius, Palladio, and all other writers of reputation in the art; to examine the most celebrated buildings, whether they remain entire or in ruins; to compare these with the principles of writers; and to in-

quire how far both the theories and models were founded in nature, or created by fancy; and when this was done, so far as their circumstances would allow, to adopt the advantages and reject the inconveniences of all. Unembarrassed by attachments to noble families, hereditary lines and successions, or any considerations of royal blood, even the pious mystery of holy oil had no more influence than that other one of holy water. The people were universally too enlightened to be imposed on by artifice; and their leaders, or more properly followers, were men of too much honor to attempt it. Thirteen governments thus founded on the natural authority of the people alone, without a pretence of miracle or mystery, and which are destined to spread over the northern part of that whole quarter of the globe, are a great point gained in favor of the rights of mankind. The experiment is made, and has completely succeeded; it can no longer be called in question, whether authority in magistrates and obedience of citizens can be grounded on reason, morality, and the Christian religion, without the monkery of priests, or the knavery of politicians."

John Adams

CHAPTER SEVEN

THE REVOLUTIONARY TEMPER

1. *The Origin of the State*

The waning of Puritanism had prepared the colonial mind for the reception of the revolutionary ideas of the eighteenth century, and by calling into question the absolutism of an omnipotent God had demonstrated the fraud of an omnipotent King. Before a genuinely revolutionary temper could be harried out of the colonial environment, however, habits of thinking long rooted in feudal soil had to be torn up by the roots, and the cause of revolution linked with the cause of mankind. Fashions of thinking that were no longer right gave the indelible impression that the newer ideas of the revolution must be wrong, and the appearance of the revolutionary ideas raised at first a formidable outcry in defense of custom. But custom itself proved not to be an unyielding host when the revolutionary temper spread through the colonies, and the fraud of tyranny was exposed as a heritage of the canon and feudal law. The path of the revolutionary propagandists had thus been marked out for them—they were to expose the fraud of monarchy, banish the remnants of feudalism from government and religion, and bring into the open the imperial designs of Great Britain to reduce the colonies to slavery. To unite in a single regiment, the enemies of America and the enemies of mankind; to prove that the cause of independence was enlisted in the cause of progress; and to establish in one rank the forces of evil and the regiments of the king, was the path the revolutionary propaganda took.

In establishing the fraud of monarchy and the artificial claims of the feudal aristocracy, the revolutionists traced the origin of the state, and demonstrated by its origin, causes, and sequence, that society had been artificially encumbered by despotism. The state originated out of natural society at a certain point in its development where moral virtue failed and its single purpose was diffused by the struggling wants of individuals. To form a just and clear notion of the origin of the state, accordingly, we must take ourselves back in imagination to an original state of nature in which all men were free and equal. In this state of natural liberty, however, many things were wanting; and at last the unmanageable contest of wills generated by an unchecked native liberty threatened to break forth in civil warfare. It soon became clear that the lack of moral virtue would have to be supplied by an organized state through which competing wills could be harmonized and the conflict of interests resolved. Society was therefore to some extent a natural and inevitable product of human association, while government was produced by wickedness and existed as a kind of necessary evil. Government was accordingly a measure of human shortcomings, of the failure of virtue on the part of an original human society. "Government, like dress, is the badge of lost innocence," wrote Paine; "the palaces of kings are built upon the bowers of paradise."

Such governments as have arisen of necessity from an original state of nature have been formed, however, not out of social compact, but rather out of force, fraud, and deception. A race of conquerors and kings thus arose whose power was seized from the people by fraud, deception, and violence, and the hereditary succession of whose line constituted an artificial aristocracy perpetuated by the same means which had brought it honor. Driven to justify themselves in the perpetuation of their power, the artificial nobility played upon the ignorance of the people, invented the priestcraft, and created the deception of rule by divine right. The necessity of this deception created a temporal union of church and state, through which the priest was kept in his pulpit and the magistrate on his throne. "The key of St. Peter, and the key of the Treasury, became quartered on one another, and the wondering, cheated multitude worshipped the invention." It followed that governments had not been founded on the common interests of society in a social compact of all who consented to be governed by general and necessary principles; but rather on violence, fraud, and deception—the common repertory of an artificial aristocracy and a fraudulent king.

2. *The Natural Rights*

The natural rights which man had lost as the result of the fraud of the king and the deception of the priestcraft had now to be established as inalienable, as the private right of the individual to sovereignty over himself. Certain rights were considered alienable, and were surrendered to government for their general protection and greater facility, but could not, except by the consent of the individual, be sundered from their possessor. It therefore seemed that the true office of the legislator was to conserve, not to invade, the rights of man, and measured by this standard, the imperial policy of Great Britain appeared as an invasion of English liberties. In tracing the origin of the state from a primitive natural society, accordingly, the revolutionary philosophers were concerned that the principle of the social contract, with its corollary doctrine of government by consent, should be the basis upon which private rights might be surrendered to society. Most of the revolutionary theorists, however, reserved a special bill of inalienable rights which could not be so surrendered, even under the general principles of a constitution, and for the protection of which governments were to be instituted among men. "There are rights which it is useless to surrender to the government," wrote Jefferson, "and which governments have yet always been found to invade. These are the rights of thinking, and publishing our thoughts by speaking and writing; the right of free commerce; the right of personal freedom." [9]

The question which was uppermost in the minds of the revolutionary philosophers, however, was the origin of private property out of a state of primitive communism, and the subsequent invasion and sequestering of the right of private property by the deceptions of the priestcraft and the fraud of monarchy. As the meaning of the right of property was broadened to include not only personal estates but personal liberties, the possession of sovereignty over oneself, and over the possessions which were a manifestation of the sovereignty over oneself, it eventually included almost all the original natural rights. Freedom of speech, of the press, of commerce, of assembly, of religion, were all eventually considered as adjuncts of the basic right of private property. The inalienable rights which were the basis of man's freedom and dignity, and which an obstreperous tyrant insisted upon invading, were all to be traced at long last to the fundamental right of property, and seen as manifestations of the basic sovereignty of man over himself. The inalienable rights were therefore those which could not be surrendered to any government without reducing man to slavery, and which a government erected on the consent of the governed would seek to preserve rather than to destroy. It therefore fell to the lot of the revolutionary philosophers to trace in the evolution of society the origin of those positive and natural rights of life, liberty, and property which were—and of right ought to be— inalienable and inviolable, but which the despotism of the English king sought to invade and destroy.

"In the early savage state of society," wrote Thomas Cooper, "it is manifest, however, that the necessity of combination among the weak to protect each other against the strong, would give origin to associations of men, and develop the first germ of political communities. This is manifest among our American Indians. They have no written laws; but exclusive property in all things that their state of society requires to be made so, has been forced upon them by its obvious expediency, and enjoined by all on each other. Land, being in abundance compared to the population, has never become the object of exclusive property among them, except a large district claimed as the hunting ground of the tribe. Property implies the existence of capital. The deer skin, the parched corn, the jerked venison, of an Indian cabin, the cabin itself, is the property of the owner; being the result of his own labour, and his accumulated savings out of former acquisitions. He had labored beyond what his immediate necessities called for, and his wealth consists of that which has not been consumed. He may now labour for what is merely convenient, during the time his accumulated food will maintain life. All *capital,* then, from the very outset of society, is the result of saving and accumulation. He may make bows and arrows, or he may trap beavers and otters for their skins; he may exchange these for some article wanted or wished for. Hence the origin of *barter,* and of *exchangeable value.* The capital thus accumulated is wealth. His anxiety to be protected in the enjoyment of this wealth and that similar anxiety of others in like circumstances, induce them to propose regulations binding upon each other for that purpose; hence the origin of *laws.* It is to exclusive property therefore (and to the institution of the marriage contract which emanates from it) that we owe everything valuable which society has bestowed upon mankind." [10]

The capital immunities were the immunities of capital; and the revolutionary philosophers traced the history of private right in their effort to prove that the fundamental rights of society had been invaded by the tyranny of the English king. The philosophy of natural rights therefore presupposed that man was capable of self-government, of sovereignty over himself, and that he could not alienate this sovereignty, except by a social contract, without reducing himself to abject slavery. There emerges from the body of revolutionary writings, accordingly, a clear meaning of despotism and, from its meaning, of the consequences which at all costs the revolutionary leaders sought to avert. Arbitrary government, which from the time of Winthrop had increasingly been called into question, was now to be summoned for a final indictment before the bar of reason. Arbitrary government, by cutting man off from participation in a government of his choice, denied his right of private judgment, denied his sovereignty over himself, and by that inevitable consequence, placed him upon the level of the animal. Despotism meant, above all other things, a government of whatever form which denied the sovereignty of man over himself, and in that denial called into question his right to his life, his liberty, and his estate. Despotism meant in its essence a denial of freedom of the will, and hence of the efficacy of morality and reason; it meant that the properties which were the result of the free exercise of man's abilities could be alienated without his consent, and, by some ancient principle of hereditary right, that the fruit of his labor could be taken from him to enrich an artificial nobility and fill the coffers of the king.

3. *The Attack on Monarchy*

The doctrine of rule by divine right had now to be countered with the argument of natural right, and the pretenses to divinity on the part of the king balanced by an equally divine justification of the revolutionary cause. In this phase of the attack on monarchy, Jonathan Mayhew advanced with his rationalist legions, slaughtering with their own weapons the clerical mercenaries who sought to defend the divinity of the king. The doctrine of divine right, in virtue of which infamous doctrine people who professed to be religious could not resist the tyrannous usurpations of their king, Mayhew discovered as the excuse of absolutism for imposing a slavery upon the minds and hearts of the people. "No people are under a religious obligation to be slaves, if they are able to set themselves at liberty," he wrote. If the scriptural rule is true, that kings have their authority from God, it does not follow that they have authority to do mischief, but only that which reason approves and nature will support.

The scriptural argument that Christians should obey their king because he rules for the common welfare, Mayhew sets aside with his doctrine of resistance to tyrants; for a departure from Christian benevolence, he argues, is enough to relieve Christians from the duty of supporting an un-Christian ruler. "If it be our duty, for example, to obey our king merely for this reason, that he rules for the public welfare— which is the only argument the apostle makes use of—it follows, by a parity of reasoning, that when he turns tyrant, and makes his subjects his prey to devour and destroy, instead of his charge to defend and cherish, we are bound to throw off our allegiance to him, and resist." The right of resistance to tyranny had thus been given a Christian perspective, and made to bear service in the cause of Christ. It was a resuscitation, or rather continuation, of the Puritan doctrine of resistance to tyrants, and it breathed some of the old Puritan fire, now almost a century since the forefathers of Mayhew had employed it as an ecclesiastical weapon in their revolt from the impious reign of King Charles. At one stroke, therefore, Mayhew had united the cause of Christ with the cause of the colonies, the history of the Puritan rebellion with the prospect of a colonial revolt; and the doctrine of resistance to tyrants, spreading widely in the land, added a fiery argument to the general attack on monarchy.[11]

In thus uniting the cause of independence with the cause of human progress, the propagandists of the revolution joined battle with the monarchical system, explaining by its origin, sequence, and power that the sovereignty which kings enjoy was in the first instance gained by fraud. If the sovereignty of the king is an illegitimate power wrested from a primitive sovereignty which the people in a kingless age enjoyed, then it might be shown that the institution of monarchy was the seat of all the revolutionary troubles, and an attack upon the throne a proper origin for the bold enterprise of independence. Government by kings, wrote Paine, "was first introduced into the world by heathens," and is "the most prosperous invention of the devil ever set on foot for the promotion of idolatry." Feudalism in government is on the same footing with feudalism in religion, the consequence of fraud and deception, which can only issue in idolatry and corruption. "That the Almighty hath here entered his protest against monarchical government is true," wrote Paine. "And a man hath good reason to believe that there is as much of kingcraft as priestcraft in withholding the scripture from the public in popish countries. For monarchy in every instance is the popery of government." The earliest monarchs, argued Paine, were not much better than the principal ruffian of some restless gang, the predatory prototype of later usurpers of the throne, the cannibals of power, devouring the sovereignty which by right of nature belonged once to their humble followers. Hereditary right soon arose as the excuse for such arbitrary power, and conferred upon the descendents of the first monstrous plunderer the fruits of his impious depravations.

The success of the claim to hereditary right over the spoils of the first plunderer may be explained, wrote Paine, because "many submit from fear, others from superstition, and the more powerful part shares with the king for the plunder of the rest." After the lapse of a few generations, however, hereditary right was easy to sustain because the king, in league with his circle of priests and soothsayers, undertook "to trump up some superstitious tale conveniently timed, Mahomet-like, to cram hereditary right down the throats of the vulgar." Moreover, "original sin and hereditary right are parallels," because "the doctrine of original sin, which supposes the free will of all men lost in Adam," presupposes also a first society in which men retained their free will and full sovereignty. The sovereignty of kings is therefore part of that vast plunder which the monarchy has stolen from the people, while bishop and priest hide beneath the cloak of original sin the free will and full sovereignty which they have helped the monarch steal from the primitive virtue of man. The claim to divinity in the king and to sainthood in the priest have equally the origin of pilfering and plunder, and are equally a mask for a common tyranny.[12]

4. *The Attack on Feudalism*

Having exposed the fraud of monarchical government and the sequestering of its tyranny beneath the lubrication of holy oil, the colonists now turned their attention toward the feudal system as the fruitful mother which had given birth to the progeny of absolutism. In a remarkable essay on the canon and the feudal law, John Adams exposed the machinery of dominion, and the origin out of military conquest of the specious claim to proprietary estates. By the canon law, wrote Adams, the Roman clergy had established an admirable system for the aggrandizement of their own order; and by the feudal law a system was devised by which Europe could be kept under the perpetual reign of a military encampment. These opinions, formed in the revolutionary heat of an independent cause, invested the common attack on monarchy and feudalism with the accents of a promised progress, and urged upon mankind that they set aside forever the canon and feudal systems of tyranny. As the canon law was designed to foster the depredations of the canonical clergy, so the feudal law was fashioned to justify the plundering of the feudal aristocracy. Both the canonical clergy and the feudal aristocracy enjoyed a common tyranny over the horde of their humble followers, depriving them of that inalienable sovereignty and free will which by the rights of nature and of man had always belonged to them. Feudalism, then, was a curious system of absolutism, which granted not only a monopoly over lands but also a proprietary over opinions, and enjoined upon all a common allegiance to this tyranny on the threat of damnation in hell. But neither the holy oil nor the doctrine of divine right could keep the young republicans from penetrating to the heart of the feudal system and exposing the tyranny of the canon and feudal law.

The object of this attack on the canon and the feudal law was to establish that the allegiance of the colonies to the crown was merely a formal one, descended, like the principles of primogeniture and entail, from the long practice of feudal ages. The king of England, accordingly, had no more than a feudal claim to the properties of America; and private property was held by a right more inalienable than the right of the feudal king. The taxing of the property of the subject without his consent was, therefore, a resurrection of the old tyranny in the disguise of parliamentary act. Subsequent analysis proved also that parliament itself had no right to tax the properties of Americans for any but a regulatory purpose, and that a tax on colonial property designed to raise revenue for the mother country was naked despotism. It therefore seemed to the colonists that the mother country, instead of creating the conditions for the free transference and alienation of property, was in fact promoting a policy of arbitrary restriction and regulation upon the commerce and wealth of the colonies. The mother country was in fact calling into question that very sovereignty of the colonists over their lives, opinions, and estates which they had assumed to be an established principle of English liberty. This step appeared to promise the introduction of feudal tyranny, in which no man could by right hold his property except in fealty to his king. The colonists were therefore raised to a revolutionary pitch, and promised to banish the remnants of feudalism —the heritage of the canon and the feudal law—not only from an absolute God but also from an absolute King.

5. *The Cause of Independence*

The cause of independence had now been united with the cause of mankind, and freedom had been declared the prerequisite of progress. It remained only to rehearse the specific list of grievances against Great Britain, and to declare the causes which impelled the colonists to enter upon a final act of separation from the mother country. It remained to demonstrate that the imperial policy of Great Britain, the pensioners, the placemen, the machinery of imperialism, the parliamentary exactions and disciplinary taxes, were an inevitable ingredient of British policy, never to be relieved by any hope of reconciliation, or mitigated by any royal promise. Before the revolutionary spirit could finally be raised to a defiant pitch, it had to be demonstrated that a policy of open resistance, of defiance to the imperial ministry and its illegal acts, was the only hope of those who wished to remain free. The entrance of Great Britain upon a bold new imperial policy provoked a provincial storm, and demonstrated the revolutionary thesis beyond all question. When news arrived of an act in which the parliament proposed to carry out this new policy, not only retaining but also enlarging upon the old duties and restrictions on trade with America, and moreover, not as an act of regulation but as one of revenue, the colonial mind burst forth with its fiery protest. When the significance of the new policy broke upon the Americans, a literary storm broke loose, threatening to shatter the last moorings of the colonies to the mother country, and carrying in its vitriolic train all who thought or dared speak out against the new policy.

The new imperial policy reminded the colonists of the long history of dispute over the rights of the colonial legislatures; for the cause of independence, with its argument for freedom of trade, had as its political corollary a claim to local home rule. Colonial history was filled with the raucous conflict between provincial assemblies and royal governors, between rights subsumed under charter privileges and obligations categorized as royal prerogative. It was the basic conflict between imperial policy and local home rule which broke forth with all its bitterness whenever the colonials assumed that charter privileges had been based upon the consent of the governed. But in the course of the somewhat vitriolic controversy over the rival claims of imperial policy and local home rule, the argument based upon the social-contract theory received an uncommon extension, until at last it seemed that the principle of consent of the governed might be interpreted as an argument of complete independence and final separation from the mother country. The interpretation which the colonial mind gave to the social-contract theory and its corollary doctrine of government by consent included a larger measure of local home rule than the imperial councils found congenial to their policies.

The revolutionary philosophers were not above using the English constitution as a basis for their arguments when it suited their purposes; for by the stratagem of placing the argument for local home rule and the doctrine of consent on the foundation of the grand and venerable constitution of England, they deprived Tories of their arguments, and turned the weight of veneration and tradition in favor of the colonial cause. The English constitution thus did service for Tory and for Whig, and without discrimination lent its body of laws to partisan interpretation. It could be made to serve equally the advocates of the king or the partisans of revolution. The addresses, remonstrances, and petitions sent to parliament were themselves couched in the language of the law, and won praise for their brilliance and cogency even where they could not be honored. The revolutionary philosophers had learned their rights from the fundamental law and were loathe to give up so fundamental a privilege. The Tory argument for adherence to the crown, which rested upon the assumption of a balance of powers and upon virtual if not actual representation of the colonists, was ignored by the Whigs in favor of emphasis upon the rights guaranteed by the constitution that the property and liberty of Englishmen should not be invaded except by consent. By this strategy of advocacy, the Whigs had turned the Tory veneration of the English constitution to their own account, resting their case not upon its harmonies but upon its list of imprescribable rights.

In order to refute the arguments of reconciliation with Great Britain, therefore, the patriots undertook an analysis of the cause of independence, and advanced in serried array the final points upon which the battle of arms should be joined. "As Europe is our market for trade," wrote Paine, "we ought to form no partial connection with any part of it. It is the true interest of America to steer clear of European connections, which she can never do, while, by her dependence on Britain, she is the makeweight in the scale of British politics." The lesson of colonial experience was clear that continued dependence upon Great Britain would strangle the commerce of America and deprive her property of a capacity for growth. "America is only a secondary object in the system of British politics. England consults the good of this country no further than it answers her own purpose. Wherefore, her own interests lead her to suppress the growth of ours in every case which doth not promote her advantage, or in the least interferes with it."

The hope of the future would seem to lie in a new union of the colonies, where nature might make a fresh start in guaranteeing the rights which tyranny had defamed and imperialism encumbered. The object of this new union of independent states ought to be, since these things are denied by the English tyrant, "securing freedom and property to all men, and above all things, the free exercise of religion, according to the dictates of conscience." These rights, granted by nature to all men, cannot be alienated, except at the price of slavery; for security to property, to conscience, and to persons, are objects of governments so universally recognized that whoever opposes them commits "a kind of atheism against nature." Finally, besides the securing of these natural rights, the cause of independence is the cause of freedom of trade, and of that condition of the free market which sustains and protects the native liberties of man. "The freedom of trade, likewise, is, to a trading country, an article of such importance, that the principal source of wealth depends upon it; and it is impossible that any country can flourish, as it otherwise might do, whose commerce is engrossed, cramped and fettered by the laws and mandates of another—yet these evils, and more than I can here enumerate, the continent has suffered by being under the government of England. By an independence we clear the whole at once—put an end to the business of unanswered petitions and fruitless remonstrances—exchange Britain for Europe—shake hands with the world—live at peace with the world—and trade to any market where we can buy and sell." [13]

6. The Declaration of Independence

A declaration of causes, concerted with a haunting yet stately rhythm, gives to the Declaration of Independence that sense of natural law, which, when stated, seems only to dissolve the illegitimate allegiance to the British crown which pomp and circumstance had foisted upon an innocent and suffering people. For a declaration of causes is not rebellion, nor yet the severance of bonds which nature has established and ordained. Besides a list of specific grievances, the Declaration enumerates certain self-evident truths; and these, in the light of nature and reason, could be no more than those that nature herself might lisp in the wanton days of her youth. So nature, seemingly primitive and innocent in her laws, just because she was so unerring and invariable, was addressed in public remonstrance against the king of Britain, and against all kings who took arms against natural right and natural law. The young republicans, assembled in the councils of reason, recorded truths transcribed from nature, and self-evident to all who possessed reason. "We hold these truths to be self-evident," the young republicans wrote, "that all men are created equal; that they are endowed by their creator with certain unalienable rights; that among these are life, liberty & the pursuit of happiness; that to secure these rights governments are instituted among men, deriving their just powers from the consent of the governed; that whenever any form of government becomes destructive of these ends, it is the right of the people to alter or to abolish it, and to institute new government, laying its foundation on such principles and organizing its powers in such form, as to them shall seem most likely to effect their safety and happiness."

Now here was not only a political philosophy but a governmental metaphysic. Here are set down principles believed to lie at the heart of nature, where rights inalienable descended to man by right of being man. Whereas it was thought that animal natures were governed only by instinct and appetite, so it was concluded that rational choice, the government of reason, pertained to man alone. The institutions of government, therefore, are and of right ought to be derived from the consent of the governed. Now as man prefers life to death, liberty to tyranny, and happiness to despair, so also he can give his loyalty and his honor only to the state that secures these rights. Experience had shown that the silent sequesterings of tyranny have reduced man to a state of inexhaustible obedience, and that a long train of abuses and usurpations, evincing a design to reduce man to absolute despotism, can but rekindle the demands of freedom in his heart. Nature rebels at tyranny and reason abhors a despotism—such is the philosophy of the Declaration.

Continued grievances multiplied and instanced as empirical evidence of a desperate design, having as direct object the establishment of an absolute tyranny over the colonial states, are thus submitted to a candid world. The facts which evidence a conspiracy against nature on the part of the English king are then enumerated; and it is concluded that these, far from being singular instances and exceptions, the accidental repertory of a tyrant, are in fact the manifestation of a design, not only to render the colonies subservient, but to deprive the people of their rights. "A prince whose character is thus marked by every act, which may define a tyrant, is unfit to be the ruler of a free people." When therefore men are assembled to debate with nature of the profligacy of a tyrant, they mark out and sustain the primitive natural law which no despot can entirely disrupt or consume. The Declaration abides, then, not with temporal laws but with eternal ones, not with the simple expedients of experience but with ontological perspectives and unshaken truths. Its claim to the scriptures of the heavens is the same as that of the despot whose divine right it sought to displace. Social reformers always seize upon some primitive metaphysic when they desire to wrench the world from its habitual perspectives and build once more a picture of reality closer to the great idea that drives them on.

The document rests, then, like the philosophy of the whole epoch, upon the conception of an inviolable order of nature, an order which a despotic king and greedy parliament persistently sought to disrupt and control. Divine right could only be countered by natural right; and if a modest middle-class atheism accompanied the Declaration, or if at best a mild deism sat in the assembly, God was at least at an infinite remove from the scenes of council and would not arbitrarily interfere in the legitimate and natural designs of men. As the princes of feudalism had ruled by divine right, the counselors of capitalism must lay claim to some equally powerful metaphysic. The document was composed, accordingly, as a record of experience, whose transcriptions of natural law had finally embodied in a political form the breath and being of reality. The lantern of the Enlightenment had revealed the illusion that the way of religion lay in revelation, or that the way of politics lay in faith. The Declaration supposes, and rests on the assumption, that all men are free to order their actions and dispose of their possessions and persons as they think fit. It was a declaration, not only of independence, but of a new philosophy of nature; and it was a call, not only to revolution, but to a new way of life.

CHAPTER EIGHT

THE WORLD OF NEWTON

1. *The Age of Reason*

The triumph of the revolutionary cause had prepared the colonial mind for the reception of the ideals of scientific enlightenment, which were spreading in the learned parts of the globe. The Newtonian synthesis of science interpreted nature mathematically, and in proportion as it spread, justified the principles of harmony and balance which were to form the foundation of the American constitutions. The metaphysics of Newtonian science furnished the enlightened with a world hypothesis for their venture into republicanism, and justified their search for self-evident principles in the science of government. Now at last science and reason had triumphed with the revolutionary cause, banishing alike the imperial restrictions of the English monarchy and the feudal restrictions of medieval science. The mind unfettered sought the means of enlightenment, and celebrated with its ideals the republican way of life. Reason was deified and nature worshiped in her harmonies, while a self-regulating economy of nature promised the reign of universal law. The republic was to be built on the foundation laws of the universe, and enjoy with God an indefinite existence; truth had become the ally of man, and the new age was acclaimed the age of enlightenment and reason.

Science now promised the endless prospect of success, and no secret of nature appeared beyond the power of reason and experiment. The world had opened its gates to the vista of unlimited progress, while the human mind proved itself capable of the most extended inquiries. No barriers remained to man's conquest of nature; no restrictions were left to cramp the powers of the human mind. Mechanism spoke with her bold claims, and natural philosophy took up her endless play of cause and effect as the latest scientific achievement. To an age so visibly immersed in the fable of cause and effect, and which secretly nursed its private motives for desiring to apply universal mechanics on a universal scale, the new science of mechanics appeared as a singular invention of God for the happiness and prosperity of man. The universe was interpreted mechanically, leaving to the imagination the source of its power; the world was a machine, and the science of mechanics promised to open new vistas of progress to the struggling mind. With the science of mechanics in his pocket, the natural philosopher, like Archimedes, thought he could move the world. "The man who proportions the several parts of a mill uses the same scientific principles as if he had the power of constructing a universe," wrote Paine; "but as he cannot give to matter that invisible agency by which all the component parts of the immense universe have influence upon each other and act in motional unison together, without any apparent contact, and to which man has given the name of attraction, gravitation, and repulsion, he supplies the place of that agency by the humble imitation of teeth and cogs." [14]

The universe was one vast machine operating according to the principles of the cosmic constitution which lay at the heart of nature. Newton had legalized the machinery of the universe, converting it from a lawless contingent power into an efficient and regular machine obeying universal and immutable law. The Puritans had worshiped a lawless, contingent, and arbitrary power, while the young republicans restricted the arbitrary interference of God in the self-regulating economy of nature by the laissez-faire presuppositions of their science. The world-machine, described by Newton and popularized for the vulgar by a host of disciples, trailed the imagination to its hiding place and stirred a happy response in republican hearts. A series of events—particles of matter in motion, so related to one another that all combined to achieve a single remarkable result—seemed the essence of benevolence in operation, and of reason in motion. The stupendous machinery of the universe, offering by its harmony the hope of a life of reason governed by law, seemed at last to the enlightened to invite the endless prospect of progress and the infinite hope of republican success. While the young republicans were busy composing the constitution of the American government, Newton was occupied writing the constitution of the world government; and the result in both cases was favorable to the republican cause.

Gone was the neat little claptrap feudal universe, the fixed points and the stars, the fabulous architecture of the heavens, the cathedral-like, hierarchical universe of the Middle Ages. In its place Newton had placed a world machine, a government of law, which rested on a cosmic constitution. In the infinite motion of the universe, the endless swirl of planets, the revolving compass of solar systems and stars, Newton had discovered the self-evident mathematical principles which governed it; amidst its endless action and reaction, the sequence of events, the churning of secret and yet untold forces, man stood alone and unafraid. The immensity and grandeur of it all, far from overwhelming him, seemed rather an object of adoration and piety than of pessimism and despair. The world was not only harmonious, but beautiful in its harmony; it was not only self-regulating, but benevolent in its operation. Then followed a celebration of the new ideals, while the young republicans deified the goddess of reason and worshiped at the altar of nature. Telescopes were set up in the streets that man might wonder at the harmony of the stars and study the laws of the planet's roll; churches were converted to the study of scientific principles; and a religion of nature, with its adoration of a reasonable universe, spread in the wake of the enlightenment. In proportion, then, as the enlightenment spread, and the enslavement of the mind to the train of ancient venerable prejudices relaxed, the brave new world emerged. It was a world which gloried, not only in the constitution of America, but also in the constitution of the universe; and both ventures into constitutionalism meant that the feudal fogs had been cleared from the mind of man, the medieval distemper purged from his soul; that at long last he could live under a government of law, no longer subjected to the arbitrary will and dangerous caprices of a lawless feudal monarch or a whimsical absolute king.

2. *The World Machine*

The Newtonian scientific synthesis, it will be remembered, formed a consistent scheme of mechanical philosophy. It was a new form of the prevailing mechanical materialism, built up on an atomistic basis, including a corpuscular theory of light. The theory of light had always been a problem of natural philosophers, but Newton's apparent reconciliation of the older contradictions seemed an adequate atomistic account of the phenomena and hence formed an apparently impregnable fortress in the Newtonian synthesis. All particles of matter behaved according to a simple law of motion which determined the movements of each particle. Given an initial start, the creation of the atoms out of nothing by an act of God, the universe was apparently self-regulating, beating out its paths of absolute time and space with accustomed regularity, like a huge watch which, once wound up, repeats its pattern to the end of time. God thus appeared in the universe as abstract force or substance deprived of all the attributes of personality; for in fact it was increasingly regarded as a mark of imperfection for the world engineer to correct the errors of his world machine once he had designed it and set it in operation. This was expressed in the laws of the conservation of matter and energy; a given quantity of energy and matter, put into the machine by God in the act of creation, maintains its absolute quantity through innumerable variables of time and space. It thus appeared that the world machine could manage its own affairs and repeat its endless cycles without the interference of God. This was the position of the deistic faith of the eighteenth century, which regarded God's own interference with his laws as a mark of imperfection in the author of nature, the designer of the world machine.

Newton himself, however, did not quite adopt the deistic position; for, under the influence of Cambridge Platonism, he regarded space as the divine presence, and substance as a measure of divine regulation. Newton's caution in these matters was soon forgotten in the general popularity of the deistic position, so that the eighteenth-century rationalists increasingly relegated God to the position of an abstract spectator of the world machine. God was a sovereign limited by constitutional law to presiding over the councils of the republican gentlemen who possessed absolute rights which could not be alienated. This motion contrasted with the Puritan conception of the world; for, it will be remembered, the Puritans insisted that motion required a constant expenditure of force, quite apart from the abstract monistic law governing such forces. The Puritan universe, accordingly, needed a continual inflow of the divinity as prime mover, to keep it in operation; and this position was in fact a measure of Puritan lethargy in separating themselves from medieval conceptions and disengaging themselves from scholastic Aristotelianism. Newton's world, however, increasingly gave the disciples of reason the basis for deleting the Puritan God from the universe, inevitably pushing them to deism, atheism, and scepticism in religion.

The Puritans had maintained piety largely by insisting, not only on the universal reign of God's law, but also on the necessity of his continual emanation of himself, the diffusion of his force and energy throughout the universe. Once deprived of the theory of emanations, Puritan rationalism could come to terms with deism; and in fact later generations of Puritans, living under the influence of the Newtonian science, denounced deism in theory but accepted it in practice. Jonathan Edwards alone saw the necessity of preserving the theory of emanations from the incursions of deistic rationalism and built the divinity of the New Lights on this ancient principle. But whether the mysterious force of gravity was interpreted as the divine emanation of God's power, or merely as an expression of the abstract monism of the reign of universal law, it followed from the developments of Newtonian science that the world was a vast machine, whose particles of matter associated or separated according to the mechanical principles which the great scientist had reduced to mathematics. In place of the Puritan divine emanations of power, flooding into the universe, giving it light and motion and quality, the eighteenth-century disciples of reason discovered Newton's equations of motion and concluded that God existed only as a mathematical principle, the abstract monism of the reign of universal law. But in the world of Newton the young republicans had found a scientific justification for their faith in republicanism. The immutable order of nature upon which the republicans pinned their hopes for a balanced government and the economists for a laissez-faire capitalism, was justified ultimately by the metaphysics of Newtonian science. For Newton provided the young republicans with a picture of the universe which would sustain their faith, not only in the self-government of man, but also in the self-regulation of nature's economy.

3. *The Method of Newtonian Science*

Newtonian science had thus brought to completion a mechanical interpretation of nature which had been in preparation since the days of Galileo; but with Newton the new philosophy received a particular form and was carried in the wave of the current ideology. The essence of the new scientific method, wrote Newton, is "from the phenomena of motions to investigate the forces of nature, and then from these forces to demonstrate the other phenomena." It happened, accordingly, that Newton was the heir not only of the mathematical interpretation of nature but of the experimental method. Equations of motion derived from mathematical analysis could thus be given empirical verification and ultimate synthesis. But the principles of natural philosophy had taken a mechanistic form, one which science would not throw off for two hundred years. "I wish we could derive the rest of the phenomena of nature by the same kind of reasoning from mechanical principles," wrote Newton; "for I am induced by many reasons to suspect that they may all depend upon certain forces by which the particles of bodies, by some causes hitherto unknown, are either mutually impelled towards each other, and cohere in regular figures, or are repelled and recede from each other; which forces being unknown, philosophers have hitherto attempted the search of nature in vain; but I hope the principles here laid down will afford some light either to that or some truer method of philosophy." [15]

The method of analysis by which science had thus progressed to a mechanical interpretation of nature relied in its preliminary stages upon mathematical analysis. All the qualities, hitherto richly expressed in nature's operations, were eliminated; the qualitative uniqueness of nature was reduced to quantity, rendering the colors and hues of nature, the tastes and the sounds, the exclusive property of the subjective consciousness of man. The rich teleological universe of Aristotle and his scholastic commentators had become the universal property of the individual consciousness; all the occult qualities and substantial forms were banished from the universe as the genteel ethical wisdom of Greek natural philosophy was transformed into a mechanics of bodies and its form reduced to equations of motion. Following in the wake of Newton's famous demonstration, accordingly, all the intellects of Europe and America were immersed in a mathematical interpretation of nature. Because mathematics lends to scientific statement the precision and grandeur of expression which is wanting in ordinary language, when language carries the freight of the infinite in finite expression, its popularity was immediate and its practical demonstration overwhelming. Minds unschooled in any other art and long absent from the university dens of dialectic, hastened to the certainty of demonstration and precision of belief which mathematics would lend to any science.

In the wake of the disenchantment of absolutism and amidst the general wreckage of authority in government, it appeared to the apostles of reason that reason herself, which all men could possess on equal terms, must stand in the place of arbitrary governments and authoritative institutions. Newton had opened the way for the foundation of a new science of government, by placing before man the force of self-evident propositions and axiomatic truth. What better device, then, could imagination strike upon and the enlightened mind conceive, than that of resting authority on propositions, on facts, which were themselves self-evident, which carried their own authority as a testament to their existence? Mathematics lends itself to such self-evident propositions and maxims; its truth appears to depend not upon the interpretation of individuals, but upon an evidence exterior to themselves. Newton, of course, was the contemporary exemplar of the mathematical ideal, but the ancients were not without reason, before the dark ages of scholasticism intervened, and Euclid seemed to carry his own authority.

4. *The Problem of Knowledge*

Newtonian science had thus declared its allegiance to the methods of natural philosophy; it proposed to listen to the arguments of deduction, while framing only such hypotheses as would be empirically verified. But the ultimate empiricism of Newtonian science—proceeding from effects to causes—and its general method, inevitably produced a republic of nature in which causes would exist before the law on an equal plane with effects. The method of empiricism, of learning from experience, disclosed itself as the source, not only of those secondary qualities which had been relegated to the sphere of human consciousness, but also of those primary qualities which defined the objects of natural philosophy. Here then was the beginning of that transition in philosophy which culminates in Kant, with whom nothing remains of the object of knowledge but the mysterious thing-in-itself. It appeared to the disciples of Newton as an inevitable outcome of his scientific method that primary qualities were as much the deduction of sense experience as the secondary, and could as well be confirmed by experience.

The outcome of the Newtonian method was thus to attribute to individual particles the properties which they possessed as members of a cosmic republic, giving the protection of universal law to the private properties of the particular individuals. In the beginning, argued Newton, God gave to these primitive particles of the universe such properties as were appropriate to his end in creation. The world was composed of ultimate primitive particles, which change only when separating from one another or when forming new associations. In brief, the Newtonian method had produced an appropriate metaphysic of individualism, in which the primitive pluralism of the universe was preserved and the world-machine kept impeccably on its course by the universal law of God. Meantime, all the rich qualities of the world, all its uniqueness and qualitative wealth, had become the private property of the individual particles who were the citizens of this cosmic republic. Their rights, in being inalienable, could be severed only upon the supposition of a cosmic constitution, through which they entered into association and combination.

The outcome of the new method of science was the discovery that, though we learn only from experience, listen only to the arguments of induction, we are shut off from phenomena by a screen; we are spectators and observers but not participants in the world of primitive particles. This raised the problem of knowledge in a particularly acute form, because, following Newton's famous discussion of the problem in the *Opticks,* the question arose whether man might simply mirror nature and become once again the prisoner of his own egocentric predicament. Following the weight of learned opinion in his day, Newton had declared that the mind of man is locked up in his body and has only sense contact with the outside world. Motions from external objects are conveyed to the sensorium by the nerves, from which motions are transmitted to the muscles by the animal spirits. Man is thus separated from phenomena by a screen, the complex mechanism of communication with the outside world, which inevitably reflects not the reality but the appearance of nature. Vibrations of sound or color on the various media of the senses transmit the image or message to the sensorium of the mind, where it is delivered by the animal spirits to the muscles. The real world had grown suddenly cold and distant; denied those sensuous qualities of existence which had been appropriated by man, she hid her naked mechanism behind a screen of phenomena, and would only open her secrets and reveal her charms to those who possessed the mathematical key to her buried treasures.

These speculations of Newton on the problem of knowledge were the immediate scientific background of the question as it was raised by the enlightened of America. The problem of knowledge had arisen with the revolution, when it was realized that the scientific materialism which was the outcome of the new science seemed inconsistent with the life of thought. The age of reason was indebted for its solution to the age of faith; for it seemed only the height of wisdom, since God had set the planets on their roll, that He might also have endowed matter with consciousness and body with mind. This was in fact no solution at all, for the age of mechanism had denominated man a machine, but was then at a loss to account for that innate spiritual principle, by which, through his acts of choice and intelligence, man was capable of self-government. Granted the mechanist presuppositions of science, man was a machine ruled by the inevitable necessity of nature and determined by occult outside forces in every act of his existence. But granted the republican presuppositions of politics, man was a rational animal, capable of choice and the free exercise of his abilities to effect determinate ends, and hence qualified for self-government and the life of reason. The solution of the contradiction took the form either of a confession of absolute ignorance on the problem of how inert matter could think, or else of attributing thought as an inalienable property imparted to man by God at the beginning of creation.

5. The Problem of Newtonian Science

The conception of nature that was derived from Newtonian science was thus one of masses in motion, moving in accordance with immutable mathematical laws in space and time, and under the influence of regular forces and accelerations. Mass was the conception of a physical body and was equivalent to its weight. Irregular motions of bodies, however, Newton was inclined to attribute to some mysterious force, deflecting the particles of matter from their ideal course. Every body tends to remain in its state of rest or of uniform motion in a straight line; but since under the application of equal forces different bodies accelerated differently, they were regarded as possessing *vis inertiae,* which is the mathematical characteristic measurable by the acceleration imparted by a given external force. When bodies were spoken of as masses, therefore, this additional quality of *vis inertiae* was attributed to them. Hence the discovery that the same mass has a different weight at different distances from the center of the earth led ultimately to Newton's formulation of the law of gravitation, which united in a single theory the realm of astronomy and the domain of mechanics.

Every body in the world system thus tends toward every other body directly in proportion to the product of their masses, and inversely in proportion to the square of the distance from their centers. Now if this law is to be taken universally, differences among the particles of matter must be eliminated from consideration, and all treated as equal before the law, except with respect to the mathematical properties or quantities stated in the application of the law. In brief, the necessary requirement for an equal treatment of all particles before the law was the supposition that the world machine possessed the properties of absolute time, space, and motion. The effect of this venture into the absolute was to translate nature into an immutable order, and to lend to the young republicans the hope of a self-regulating natural economy. The supposition that all things are placed in time as to order of succession and in space as to order of situation, could only result in a conception of absolute time and space, which were in turn the components of absolute motion.

The central problem of Newton's absolute conception of space, time, and motion was now revealed; for unless we can find a body at absolute rest we cannot possibly calculate absolute motions. The conception of motion as absolute was, however, basic to the whole theory; for absolute time and absolute space were derived from the conception of absolute motion. Apparently, then, sensible bodies do not move with reference to absolute time and space, but only with reference to themselves. Absolute motion was therefore an abstraction from relative motion and existed only in the boundless sensorium of the mind of God. This outcome of Newtonian science was congenial to Newton's background of Cambridge Platonism, and not at all hostile to piety. God was the absolute conception in the mind of the scientist, and the presupposition and the superstructure of Newtonian science. "And these things being rightly dispatched," wrote Newton, "does it not appear from phenomena that there is a Being incorporeal, living, intelligent, omnipresent, who in infinite space, as it were his sensory, sees the things themselves intimately, and thoroughly perceives them, and comprehends them wholly by their immediate presence to himself; of which things the images only carried through the organs of sense into our little sensoriums, are there seen, and beheld by that which in use perceives and thinks. And though every true step made in this philosophy brings us not immediately to the knowledge of the first cause, yet it brings us nearer to it, and on that account is to be highly valued." [16]

The hypothesis of God proved a universal solution of the problems to which Newtonian science had given rise; but meantime another aspect of Newton's theory was proving equally convenient as a solution of its problems. The theory of light proved a particularly convenient receptacle for all the occult qualities that could not be banished from nature; for the eye, which perceived the light, was after all a property distinctively human and private. Newton believed that his experiments on refraction had banished color as a quality of objects. In the theory of light, then, the doctrine of secondary qualities was clearly established; for outside the human brain they had no real existence, though the vibrations or motions of bodies seemed to produce certain rays or propagate certain motions. Outside, however, the world was cold, dark, mysterious, an endless scene of particles in motion, of their attraction and repulsion, of their association and separation. The warm and sensuous qualitative richness of the world had been reduced to the form of cold, cash-valued, rational quantity. The outcome was that the qualities of matter were the contribution of the knower in the familiar subject-object relation, and that the empiricist presuppositions of Newtonian science had given rise to an early form of idealism. Henceforth man was cut off from the object of knowledge by a phenomenalist screen, and completely dependent for his knowledge upon his private sensations.

6. Beginnings of Idealism

The ruthless stripping of quality from the object had as its outcome the acquisition of quality by the subject, and the way to transcendentalism was thus laid open to a succeeding generation of American philosophers. All the rich qualitative uniqueness of the universe was thus taken up into the province of subjectivity, and when that exploded from the infinity of its predatory act, the body of quality was transferred to the subjectivity of God. The movement by which matter was stripped of all qualities, which then became the private possession of individual minds, may be illlustrated in the case of Jonathan Edwards, who argued that quality disappears mysteriously into private consciousness, either of man or of God. But for him the outcome was, not only that colors and other qualities could not exist outside the mind, but also that the bodies themselves must have their existence by virtue of their conception in some mind. It followed that substance was dependent for its existence upon spirit, and that body could not exist without mind. The beginnings of transcendental idealism were thus laid in the eighteenth century, and philosophy had come to an inevitable idealism as the result of the presuppositions of mechanism from which it had started out.

Edwards was quite unable to conceive of the abstract coercive force of universal law without a corresponding principle of divine energy or power to act as prime mover in the atomistic universe which Newtonian science was creating. Space was to the Puritan the divine presence, but the motion of the particles in their course, and their deflection through gravitational force, were closely identified in the minds of the Puritans with the emanations of God. Newton had employed the hypothesis of God as the last thesis of his stupendous treatise on nature, also; but with him the particles acquired the power of motion at the moment of their creation, and while for all theoretical purposes they were suspended like all material objects in God's boundless sensorium, still the intervention of God in the motions of the particles was increasingly regarded by Newton's disciples as an unnecessary step. With Edwards, however, the universe, though a mechanism, requires the continuous intervention of God as its source of motion and its prime mover. True to his Puritan heritage, he was unable to conceive of the abstract coercive force of universal law without a corresponding principle of divine energy to keep the world machine in motion, and so required the continuous emanation of divine power as the prime motion or First Cause of all secondary motions and effects.

Edwards alone of all the philosophers who sprang up armed with the Newtonian synthesis did not permit himself to degenerate into positivism; for he perceived the tendency of the empiricist critique of tradition to leave man with no beliefs beyond those confirmed by his immediate experience, a tendency, it need not be said, which might in the end prove hostile to piety. Edwards therefore defended the metaphysical substance of his own treatise on the will, in which he had come to the conclusion, as we have seen, that man's freedom is God's necessity. But this conclusion could only be confirmed by a philosophy which aspired to insights beyond the immediate empirical perceptions of man, and so Edwards was drawn into a defense of metaphysics in the interests of piety, while his contemporary peers were denouncing metaphysics as a branch of monarchical apologetics and feudal obscurantism. His defense of metaphysics as a legitimate perspective of the inquiries of natural philosophy was in part the outcome of his effort to revive Puritan idealism, but the contradictions into which he was driven prepared the way for a succeeding generation of transcendental philosophers, and established a path of continuity by which subsequent American thinkers could be led into transcendentalism without entering through the abstruse philosophy of Immanuel Kant.

CHAPTER NINE

THE RELIGION OF NATURE

1. *The Science of Theology*

The progress of science had shattered all hope of returning to the superstitions of the feudal ages, and made impossible even a return to sixteenth-century Calvinism or seventeenth-century Puritanism. Granted the conception under which the movement of the enlightenment went forward, namely, that the study of nature is the study of God, it followed that once the old theology had been laid aside, and the rubbish of superstition discarded, there might yet remain a true theology. The religion of nature was born of the attempt to rescue from the dying supernatural faith a part of natural belief to which reason might listen to and the enlightened mind attend. A science of theology, once its truth was discovered, might then correspond to a science of morality, and both lend enchantment to the art of a happy and virtuous life. Natural philosophy, mathematical and mechanical science, would then be a source of tranquil pleasure, and the study of those sciences would become the study of true theology. Despite the gloomy dogmas of the priests and the discouraging obscurity of superstition, the study of science would teach man to know and admire the glories of the creation, and lend his sympathies and allegiance to the divine origin of the world machine. What would then remain of all former theology would be simply a system of principles and laws derived from science, the book of creation written in a scientific manner. The author of nature, having inscribed the laws of nature in his sacred book of creation, intended that the enlightened of mankind should seek for true theology in its pages, and gather from the petty dogmas of the seventy jarring sects the kernel of cosmopolitan truth which each contains. The science of theology therefore dedicated itself to the laws of nature as revealed in the book of Newtonian physics, and criticized in the light of reason the feudal obscurantism and gross superstitions which it had inherited from more primitive ages.

The conflict of the new religion of nature and the old religion of superstition was immediate and apparent, and the ingenuity of two hundred years of modern philosophy has been lavished upon their reconciliation. But in the eighteenth century these new philosophies were less hesitant; they entered the lists boldly as opponents of the old theology in the warfare of science and religion, and proposed only to substitute a religion of nature for the obscure dogmas which had descended upon them from feudal ages. To banish from religion every form of superstition, and from science every facet of myth; to drive the priest from his pulpit, and his church from the affairs of the state; and consequently, to purge from the mind every barrier to its enlightenment, was the form which the attack upon the old theology took. Addressing themselves as disciples of the religion of reason or as apostles of the religion of nature, the enlightened gentlemen of the eighteenth century plunged into the warfare of the new science and the old theology. The old theology was banished and the new science reigned supreme; for the supernatural religion inherited from more primitive ages stood in the way of a deification of reason and a worship of nature, and so was dismissed from the company of the enlightened, only to stand unfabled and unfrocked as the enemy to man.

2. *The Critique of Revealed Religion*

The age of reason could no longer accept—and therefore not condone—the divine revelations upon which the various world religions had for so many ages rested. Inspired by the new faith in reason, in the ability of man to carry forward a critical account of his origin, nature, and destiny, the citizen and citizeness proceeded to an attack upon the ancient inspirations. The churches which had claimed for themselves a divine authority, and which had countered the progress of the republican movement by appeals to the supernatural, had now to meet the combined assault of the radical intellectuals. Before the authority of reason could triumph, the authority of revelation had to be destroyed; before the legality of the state could be accepted, the pretenses of the church had to be subjected to criticism. Regiments of the enlightened assembled to join battle with the wavering hosts; all society was caught up in the movement, until every tinker's apprentice was on terms of intimate familiarity with the arguments against revealed religion.

In the forefront of the attack, Thomas Paine demonstrated that every natural church based its authority on the pretense of a special divine commission from the hand of God, signed and sealed like any diplomatic mission, and delivered to certain individuals to be communicated to the mass of mankind. The Jews with Moses, the Christians with Christ, and the Turks with their Mahomet were alike open to the charge, and equally came in for a common attack. The world religions, inspired by their diverse books of revelation, had come at last to a claim upon the same divine commission, so that it was difficult to know whose truth was apocryphal and whose was a diplomatic invention. The whole of Christian theology seemed to the young republicans a curious admixture of heathen mythology and the beliefs of the Jews, and it occurred to them to inquire whether the Mosaic commandments had been inspired by a heavenly source or were rather the outcome of the trials of Israel and the Mosaic economy. "The commandments carry no internal evidence of divinity with them," wrote Paine; "they contain some good moral precepts, such as any man qualified to be a lawgiver, or legislator, could produce himself, without having recourse to supernatural intervention." [17]

The story of creation might be traced by any competent scholar or linguist, and the disparities of which it was composed laid bare by any of the young republicans. Christian theology seemed to them an encyclopedia of idolatry which had grown up amidst centuries of indigestible accretions, and which the young republicans found uncongenial to their cause. Revealed religion had thus become opposed to reasonable religion, and the religion of supernature contrary to the religion of nature. The revelations upon which authority was based seemed the inventions of priests, and the miracles and prophecies with which revealed religion abounds appeared as witnesses in evidence of a horrible fabrication. Absolutism in government and dogmatism in religion rested alike upon a spurious foundation, which it was the business of the enlightened to dispel. Christianity rested, like other world religions, upon the inventions of its priestcraft and the idolatry of its humble followers. The original gospel of Christ had been distorted for the purposes of revenue and corrupted to justify the exactions of popery. It had been the scheme of the Christian church, "to hold man in ignorance of the Creator, as it is of governments to hold man in ignorance of his rights. The systems of the one are as false as those of the other, and are calculated for mutual support." [18]

Jefferson joined in the universal chorus of dissent from revealed religion, questioning every tenet, because, as he argued, if there is a God, he must be a rational one, who would not want false speculations and dreams set up after his name. Give to God the homage of reason, he wrote to a young republican, and call out the weapons of the mind to combat the evil idolatry which has ensnared the world. Consult also the laws of nature to see whether any inspired prophet or dreamy saint has contradicted those immutable principles upon which the whole fabric of the world rests, and which, if there is a God, are surely his creation. Search too into the bottomless pit of doubt, so that if the mind survives its dark abyss it will be returned to its owner richly rewarded by a new faith in natural law and human progress. "Your own reason is the only oracle given you by heaven," wrote Jefferson, "and you are answerable not only for the rightness but for the uprightness of your decision." But many who undertook this voyage into doubt never returned to the older faith, even in any of its new disguises and current forms, but drifted finally into the seas of scepticism where atheism and its brother deism lingered to trap the most courageous and vigorous of the questioners.

Then followed a current of anticlericalism which rushed forward, flooding in upon the chain of ancient prejudices, superstitions, and priest magic. John Adams had no less scorn for the priestcraft of the Church of England than he did of the popecraft of the Church of Rome. "Very often shepherds that are hired to take care of their masters' sheep go about their concerns and leave the flock to the care of their dogs," he wrote. "So bishops are appointed who oversee the flock of Christ, take the fees themselves but leave the drudgery to their dogs, that is, curates and understrappers." No less ridden by the train of officialdom and the hierarchy of soul-savers than the Church of England, the Church of Rome similarly promulgated a dogma which made salvation impossible to any who were not of their faith. "The Church of Rome has made it an article of faith that no man can be saved out of their church, and all other religious sects approach to this dreadful opinion in proportion to their ignorance, and the influence of ignorant or wicked priests." [19]

Not only the priestcraft, but the word of God, the Holy Bible, stands quite by itself in this age of science and reason as a book called into question by the disparities of its composition, and by the wrangling of theologians over its interpretation. Reflecting upon the fact that the seventy jarring sects based themselves upon seventy antagonistic interpretations, the young republicans were led to reject as fiction what could not be established as fact. To the enlightened gentlemen of the age of reason nothing was too sacred to be examined before the bar of reason, and nothing was too authoritative to justify itself in the light of human experience. Because they were engaged in struggles designed to throw off the weight of political authority, of absolutism in government, they were concerned also to attack religious authority, absolutism in religion. As the authority of the sects depended upon the word of God, it seemed the height of wisdom to examine it in the light of reason, and to dispel from the awakening mind the ghosts of superstition and idolatry with which it abounds. The bourgeois gentilhomme could tolerate no authority but the authority of experience, and no writings but those of the book of reason. When the mind had once cast off authority in every field, when to an age of absolutism in government and dogmatism in religion had succeeded an age of republicanism in government and of reason in religion, the mind thus enlightened could no longer accept lightly the cathedral of superstition, the host of wicked lies, or the massive tomb of immorality, in which the priests had so long imprisoned the simple ethical wisdom of the philosophy of Christ.

3. *The Gospel of Christ*

In the degree that the age of reason lifted from the life of Jesus the fables and miracles with which history had endowed his personality, his teachings were revealed as the epitome of benevolence and his morality was shown to be the essence of republicanism. The radical intellectuals, having destroyed the mythological basis of belief in Christ, had only his philosophy to recommend him. It happened, accordingly, that the enlightenment abounds with references, not to the miracles of Christ, but to his gospel; and that it believed, not in his mission, but in his creed. It was discovered that the morality of Christ corresponded to the best systems of morality in all ages, and that he preached an ethical philosophy not immediately hostile to the creed of the middle class. Christ was seen as a virtuous and amiable man, whose perfections were only an exemplar of the virtue to which the young republicans should aspire. Though his system of morality was addressed to men universally, it was soon discovered that it fitted quite well the creed of republicanism; that indeed, Jesus was perhaps the first man to recommend the republican form of government to the assembled hosts at Galilee.

The accounts of the miracles of Christ—the claim of his supernatural personage, of his divinity and the magical efficacy of his mission—must of course be discounted as fabulous, as the invention of priests to steal the filthy lucre of the peasantry. As to the miracles of Christ, wrote Paine, it was evident that "the tellers of this party of the story had this advantage, that though they might be credited, they could not be detected." It was difficult, moreover, to credit the account of Christ's supernatural resurrection from the dead; for this and like performances, "so far as relates to the supernatural part, has every mark of fraud and imposition stamped upon the face of it." When therefore the philosophers of the Enlightenment had finished with their critique of the supernatural, nothing remained to believe except that Christ was a historical personality endowed, like them, with a fanatic faith in republicanism and the quality of man.

There was moreover a significant difference between the gospel of Jesus and the dogmas of Calvin which the radical philosophers were inclined to bring out, a difference for which the whole revolutionary struggle, the battle of ideas, may be said to have taken place. The philosophy of Christ presupposed the free will and moral efficacy of man; it presupposed the fundamental propositions of republican government, namely, the sovereignty of man over himself. Calvinism, on the contrary, had never been willing to grant this elementary proposition of republican faith; for, as we have seen, the basis of the absolutism of Calvin's God had been the debasement and subjection of man. When the gospel of Jesus was read in the perspective of republicanism it seemed to sustain the faith of the age of reason in self-government and moral perfection. The republicans, though they were willing to grant God the proportions of infinity and the wisdom of eternity, were loathe to part with any of the pristine liberty in the will of man, against which the universal necessity of Calvinism and the absolutism of monarchical government had seemed so foreboding. The attempt to attribute sovereignty to man without encroaching upon the eternity or infinity of God occupied the best minds of the age and proved to be a problem solved only by a theological dualism which separated God, the creator, from the world machine, which he had created. But for the moment, the genteel ethical wisdom which the republicans associated with the gospel of Christ seemed a confirmation of that faith in self-government and the infinite perfectability of man which the age of enlightenment had resolved to call its own.

4. *The Deist Faith*

Out of the general wreckage of superstition and the vitriolic attack on revealed religion, what faith remained to a reasonable man, that might yet be accounted religion? Such a question confronted the Enlightenment, and through the Enlightenment, the world citizens who had destroyed feudalism in religion. Paine dedicated his fascinating critique of the old theology, *The Age of Reason,* to this question, realizing that in the cold light of rationalism many things which had been destroyed might drag with them into oblivion the few kernels of truth that religion might still contain. His work was necessary, wrote Paine, "lest in the general wreck of superstition, of false systems of government and false theology, we lose sight of morality, of humanity and of theology that is true." It would be wrong, moreover, to mistake the faith of the deist for the scepticism of the atheist, to say that because the deist rejected the priestly monopoly of religion, because he rejected authoritarianism, dogmatism, and absolutism in religion, he was thereby transformed into his opposite. The age searched for a republican religion, and deism, with its belief in the one true God, seemed an appropriate expression of the new ideals.

If through the process of analysis we decompose the elements of which deism was compounded, we find that the enlightened gentlemen of the age of reason were following in their deistic faith the presuppositions of Newtonian science. Belief in the one true God was required, because without it there would be no absolute point of reference from which to verify Newton's calculations; and in Paine's famous phrase, whoever would disbelieve in God while in the possession of the new science would commit "a kind of atheism against nature." Deism was in fact a religion of nature, for it presupposed that the hand of the creator had imparted an initial velocity of motion to the primitive particles of the material system; and it was also a republican religion, for its faith in a final judgment was only an expression of the belief that virtue would be rewarded, that moral initiative and ethical enterprise would in the long run prove their worth. It followed from these elements of the deist faith that man was capable of self-government and moral perfection, and that he could be trusted with the regulation of his own affairs. Deism was, then, on all counts, not only the religion of republicanism and the religion of nature, but it was also a religion of reason. It was, like Unitarianism, a faith in God that had been generated by a faith in man.

5. The Concept of God

Once religion had been purged of superstition and piety drained of the fabulous, there remained to the age of reason the only proof of God's existence that reason would accept. A mechanical conception of nature, with its order and sequence, its causes and effects, led inevitably to the notion of a First Cause, a first term in the sequence of events by which other events were managed, and to which all effects were ultimately related. The world machine seemed to suggest to the young republicans a design that was favorable to their endeavors and a cause which rewarded benevolence. But their conception of God was derived from first principles as well as first causes; for the immensity of the creation, which, by a happy benevolence, provided man with sustenance and instruction, also provided in its universal machinery for the instrumentalities of human progress. The God of the young republicans was thus both benevolent and pragmatic. In the course of the transition from feudalism to capitalism, God had become the means rather than the end, and the machinery of the universe lent itself to human technique rather than to divine contemplation. The technical power of God, and the instrumental causality by which he moved so many cogs and wheels, became the basis for his adoration and the foundation for the expression his benevolence.

When confronted with the problem of defining this Supreme Being, however, the age flew into the customary extremes of spiritualism and materialism; for God had in fact become identical with the world machine and was either the spirit which moved it or the substance of which it was composed. Jefferson referred to God as "the creator and benevolent governor of the world," or as the Supreme Being who had formed man as a moral agent, worthy of his freedom, and capable of self-government. But he also wrote that: "the fathers of the church of the three first centuries generally, if not universally, were materialists, extending it even to the creator himself; nor indeed do I know exactly in what age of the Christian church the heresy of spiritualism was introduced." [20] But the progress of the enlightened in their revolt from revealed religion would have explained to Jefferson that curious ecclesiastical history by which the heresy of spiritualism was introduced into the Christian churches. For the enlightened gentlemen of the age of reason repeated the defection from an original materialism by virtue of the mechanism of their science, which generated the idealism of their religion.

Starting then with the concept of God as First Cause, the abstract coercive force of immutable natural law, and the metaphysical presupposition of Newtonian science, the enlightened gentlemen of the eighteenth century were led to the perception that if there is a First Cause there must be a final design. In addition to the natural order, accordingly, the enlightened were driven to posit a moral order. As the conception of a natural order had given rise to the religion of nature, so the concept of a moral order gave rise to the religion of reason. The former had issued in the conception of God as the abstract monism of universal law, while the latter issued in the conception of God as a moral governor. The religion of nature, with its worship of the universal reign of law, was paralleled by the religion of reason, with its deification of moral government and its promise that virtue should be rewarded. The concept of God as a moral governor was based, therefore, upon the ability of man to lead a life of reason. The moral governor occupied a place in the moral world similar to that occupied by the mechanical governor in the physical world, and was a conception required by the republican demand that man be infinitely perfectable. The life of reason, with its innate perceptive laws, was founded like the science of Newton on the geometrical proportions of the universe, and inevitably carried the mind forward to the concept of a moral governor, who should reward virtue out of consideration of those who lead the life of reason and obey their innate moral sense of right and wrong.

6. *The Religion of Nature*

Every form of feudal superstition was followed by the religion of reason, and the religion of reason was followed by the religion of nature. Man first in his reason retraced the sequence of events to the First Cause, and then in science and imagination traced them back again to the Last Cause. Science and religion might then seem to rest ultimately upon the same principles of reason and nature, making of all science a natural theology and of all religion a science of causes. "Every science has for its basis a system of principles as fixed and unalterable as those by which the universe is regulated and governed," wrote Paine. "Man cannot make principles, he can only discover them." Such principles are as much the wisdom of God as they are the discovery of man; they constitute a natural theology, a religion of nature. The deification of reason and the worship of nature, leading alike to a religion of nature and a religion of reason, cannot but lead to the notion that this is the best of all possible worlds. As "nothing was made in vain," and as all parts of the universal system fit into the design and harmony of the whole, the prosperous Yankee concluded that God was above all other things benevolent. The wrathful, sovereign God of Calvinism had thus been dismissed in favor of a kindly benevolent father to the middle classes.

The existence of a benevolent God was now established beyond all doubt by the simple propositions and axioms of geometry, and a mathematical theism was bred out of the numerical order which the disciples of reason believed God had established both as to time and to space. Evidence of God's existence could be established no less by scientific principles, by indubitable propositions and unassailable axioms, to which the mind in its reasonable moments was forced to give assent. God was above all else a divine magnitude of proportion and figure, which holds the universe together by His divine presence. God was the fundamental axiom of a geometrical universe; he was in essence a mathematical theorem; and from this reasoning the young republicans could only conclude that nature was a revelation of God. "So certain as God is, we cannot comprehend his essence, eternity or manner of existence, yet as far as we understand nature, we are become acquainted with the character of God; for the knowledge of nature is the revelation of God." God was revealed in the unceasing motion, the eternal flux, as the harmony which holds the universe together, as a force of universal composition and universal law. He was the mysterious force of gravity, within which primitive particles associate and separate, join or tear asunder, at his bidding and command. "If we form in our imagination an idea of the harmony of the universe it is the same as if we called God by the name of harmony." From this harmony it followed also that the deity is benevolent in his productions and humane in his commands, that this is the best of all possible worlds. "If from the composition, texture, and tendency of the universe in general, we form a complex idea of general good resulting therefrom to mankind, we implicitly admit a God by the name of good." But this universal benevolence, this divine good, is extended, for our theorem has committed us to a mathematical theism. God was therefore extended goodness, the axiom of all existence, the fundamental theorem of a universal geometry.[21]

7. *The Religion of the Heart*

If the existence of God is proved by the necessity of a universal geometry, there would seem no room for the birth of quality, the crest of the wave of molecules which marks change, growth, novelty, and development. The problem of quality remained without resolution until the time of Darwin and Hegel, but in the first pathetic attempts of the disciples of reason to deal with it the way was laid open for a passage to transcendental religion. The religion of nature had been caught up in its logical proofs of mathematical theism, and the existence of God had been proved as the outcome of mathematical necessity. The religion of nature had been absorbed in its quest of empirical evidence for the revelation of God, and His existence had been established by the benevolence and harmony which the universal system displayed. It remained only that the religion of reason and the religion of nature should be joined on a common idealistic plane to breed a sentimental religion of the heart. In this transition to transcendentalism, the religion of the heart absorbed the mathematical theism of the religion of reason and the empirical evidence of the religion of nature, then endowed the result of their fusion with a qualitative richness and capacity for novelty which anticipated the evolutionary theism of a subsequent generation.

That mathematical necessity should breed mysticism and the study of nature should produce piety ought not surprise those who are acquainted with the materialism of the primitive Christian fathers or the mechanical syllogisms of the Reformation leaders. With Jonathan Edwards, as with all creative Puritans, mysticism is germinated out of the ground of philosophic necessity, as when a chain of reasoning, symmetrical and harmonious in its parts, elicits an emotional response from the erring philosopher. Such was the experience of Jonathan Edwards as he contemplated the sovereignty of God in the light of the philosophic necessity which was the ground and substance of his existence. The logic that was the groundwork of the Puritan faith in philosophic necessity, the proof that had been the foundation for the existence of God in the age of reason, was now to become a piety and a mysticism and a religion of the heart. With the union of the rationalism of the religion of reason and the empiricism of the religion of nature, in the work of Edwards, the philosophic necessity that had bred the abstract theological God had precipitated also the warm personal God of human affections, the God of piety, of mysticism, and of love. For Jonathan Edwards, who alone reconciled the antinomies of eighteenth-century science and religion, this development was the beginning of a new religion of the heart, the test of whose faith would rest not so much upon a knowledge of abstract divinity but upon the genuine experience of religious emotion and holy affection. The new religion was at once more empirical, more penetrating, and more pragmatic than those that it displaced, and it gloried in change, in the production of quality, as those had not.

From a new conception of piety and the religious sense a new religion of the heart was bred on the grounds of philosophic necessity, and we are brought to the doors of the temple of transcendentalism, where a revolt from reason is announced for the sake of the understanding. Not only a new religious sense, but an empirical sense of indwelling force, of the emergence of novelty, and of the birth of quality, opened wide the doors of the temple of transcendentalism, and left the disciples of reason toying with their theorems in the utter coldness of their perfectly rational world. Idealism had confronted mechanism on its own terms and found it wanting; transcendentalism had confronted rationalism on the field of battle and found it deathly cold. The discovery of the new religion of the heart was that man was the focus of subjectivity and of quality, that all the qualitative uniqueness of the world had been suddenly revealed in his consciousness, or in that of God to which his was akin. From the premises of the age of reason, it was an easy deduction of a succeeding generation of transcendentalists that God dwells in the heart of individual man, that the spiritual life of the universe is paralleled in the growth of the individual. But the empirical piety of the religion of the heart had prepared the way for this discovery by announcing that God must be experienced before he can be understood. Now at long last the mathematical theorems of the rationalist had bred an evolutionary thesis, and the religion of reason gave way before the unbounded optimism of transcendental religion.

CHAPTER TEN

THE STRUCTURE OF GOVERNMENT

1. *The Science of Politics*

The revolutionary period had now opened a vast avenue of study, an inquiry into the nature and structure of governments, which promised to dissolve the immobile accretions of feudal lore under which the priesthood and artificial aristocracy of the Middle Ages had languished in their accustomed security. The science of politics was to be the means of reaching a common end, of bringing before the applause of the world a structure of government resting upon scientific principles. The objects of government were to be studied by facts, observations, and experiments, as a practical embodiment of the laws of nature, according to the rule of reason and the science of experiment. It was believed that the laws of political science might be as infallible as the axioms of Euclidean geometry, and that if the experiment were hazarded of erecting a government upon scientific principles, it might prove to be eternal and unchangeable, like the immutable reign of natural law. The ideal of a government not imposed from the outside of society by the arbitrary whims and despotic caprices of a feudal king, but generated from within by its own natural laws, and gathering its force from the consent of its constituents, seemed to parallel the principle of self-government in nature by which the world machine was kept upon its course and regulated by the reign of its immutable natural law. If then a government should be erected which should have no interest in society beyond the common interest of the several members of its system, the lives, the liberties, and the properties of its citizens would be protected by a common consent. As the principle of self-regulation was embodied in nature by the science of Newton, the principle of self-government was now to be embodied in society by the science of politics.

In the light of this new principle, the contrast could not have been greater between the republican and monarchical forms of government to the middle-class gentlemen who managed the revolution. Stated in its utmost simplicity, the monarchical form was no longer consonant with the development of the "peaceful arts" of manufacture, commerce, and agriculture; it no longer met the needs of the middle class, however much it might please the purses of the pandering courtiers. From monarchy all the evils of politics were derived, and from republicanism all the goods were drawn—monarchy was a maker of wars, a destroyer of commerce, a pillager of produce, an engrosser of revenues; while a republic, by promoting universal society through universal commerce, measured its prosperity, not by the revenues it extorted, but by the small amount of taxes it was obliged to collect. From these things it seemed but the height of wisdom to all who wished peace, prosperity, and abundance, to all except the purse-proud courtiers and the henchmen of monarchy, that a republican form of government be instituted and the science of politics demonstrated by a practical application. The monarchies of the old world had been founded in fraud by the seizure of power, while the republic of the new world was to be founded in consent by the delegation of its power. The sovereignty which had originally reposed in the people was thereby to be delegated to their representatives, and a government was to be erected upon the firm principle of natural right.

The republican form of government, in the absence of the principle of hereditary succession, was to promote the active circulation of public genius in public office; and by its system of representation to bring forward, by a quiet and regular operation, the full capacity and talent of the nation. Of all forms of government, therefore, the republic seemed best suited to the needs and capacities of man, and to the fulfillment of those objects for which governments were designed. "The only forms of government are, the democratical, the aristocratical, the monarchical, and what is now called the representative," wrote Paine. "What is called a *republic,* is not any particular form of government. It is wholly characteristic of the purport, matter, or object for which government ought to be instituted, and on which it is to be employed, *res-publica,* the public affairs, or the public good; or, literally translated, the *public thing.* It is a word of a good original, referring to what ought to be the character and business of government; and in this sense it is naturally opposed to the word *monarchy,* which has a base original signification. It means arbitrary power in an individual person; in the exercise of which, *himself,* not the *res-publica,* is the object. Every government that does not act on the principle of a republic, or in other words, that does not make the *res-publica* its whole and sole object, is not a good government. Re-

publican government is no other than government established and conducted for the interest of the public, as well individually as collectively.
It is not necessarily connected with any particular form, but it most
naturally associates with the representative form, as being best calculated
to secure the end for which a nation is at the expense of supporting it." [22]

The science of government had thus uncovered the republican or
representative form to be the best calculated to protect the interests and
preserve the properties of those who had to bear the expense of supporting it. Government, not only in the ancient states of Greece, but also
in primitive society, had been a simple democracy. But democracy proved
to be contradictory in form, though not in principle, to the extension of
territory and population. Primitive democracy thus afforded the original
data from which a reconstruction in government could begin; and
though it had proved inconvenient in its form to an extension of society, its principle of representation might be preserved to succeeding
generations. Retaining, then, democracy as the ground and principle of
the new form of government, but rejecting the corrupt systems of aristocracy and monarchy, the young republicans arrived at a system of
government which seemed capable of embracing and confederating all
the various interests and every extent of territory and population. It
was this new system of government, uncovered by inquiries into the
origin and nature of states, that the young republicans proposed to
erect in America. It sought to preserve the representation of democracy
without the popular commotion of its immediate form, while retaining
the regularity of more stable systems by embodying the natural interests
of society in constitutional law. What followed from these inquiries into
the science of politics was a republican system which sought to preserve
the inalienable rights of each in the form of the representative or public good of all.

2. The Federalist Mind

The new science of government, the art of political economy, came to
a fruition in those vigorous years in a single publication, *The Federalist,* which, quite apart from its interest as a reflection of a contending
faction in the great debate over the Constitution, is of peculiar interest
also as revealing the state of mind of the men who most directly brought
the great document through the fires of controversy. *The Federalist,*
therefore, is the basic document of those fruitful years of controversy,
a bible of political economy, a textbook of the science of government.
Its presuppositions were those of the founding fathers; its arguments
were those of the leaders of the new government; its sallies of hypothesis

and axioms of politics form the basic philosophy, not simply of a faction in the great debate, but of the men who conceived the structure and laid down the plans and specifications for the new state. The first object of government, declared Madison, is the protection of the inalienable qualities of man, "the diversity in the faculties of men, from which the rights of property originate." The duty of government, the object of legislation, is the reconciliation of the divergent interests which grow out of the different forms of property: "The regulation of those various and interfering interests forms the principal task of modern legislation, and involves the spirit of party and faction in the ordinary operations of government." Government participates in the property interest by virtue of its common object—to provide public councils and a specific code for the adjustment of conflicting interests. Here then, in the conflict of the different forms of property, thought Madison, is the origin of factions in politics: "The most common and durable source of factions has been the various and unequal distribution of property. Those who hold and those who are without property have ever formed distinct interests in society. Those who are creditors, and those who are debtors, fall under a like discrimination. A landed interest, a manufacturing interest, a mercantile interest, a moneyed interest, with many lesser interests grow up of necessity in civilized nations, and divide them into different classes actuated by different sentiments and views." [23]

The solution, then, of the problems of politics and the whole art of legislation, the sum of the science of government, is to erect a constitutional structure which will forever prevent a coalition of the distinct interests into a tyrannous majority whose object might be to deprive a propertied minority of their rights. The structure of government outlined in *The Federalist,* with its dogma of the balance of powers, fully supports the political hypotheses thus laid down. The remedy for the abuses of government, then, is a steady division and subdivision of the powers of government, balancing each against the other, checkmating one by means of the other, balancing as in a perfect mechanism the opposed pieces of the political watch. "The only answer that can be given is, that as all these exterior provisions are found to be inadequate, the defect must be supplied by so contriving the interior structure of government as that its several constituent parts may, by their mutual relations, be the means of keeping each other in their proper places." But republican government should extend its mechanism of checks and balances to the whole of society, preventing an effective majority from ever securing a common interest which would unite them against a minority: "It is of great importance in a republic not only to guard the society against the oppression of its rulers, but to guard one part of the society against the injustice of the other part. Different interests necessarily exist in different classes of citizens. If a majority be united by a common interest, the rights of the minority will be insecure." [24]

A further safeguard was placed upon the mechanism of checks and balances, not only by opposing the various divisions of government in the very structure of government, but also by recruiting the sovereignty of each division from a separate source. The house of representatives was to spring from the suffrages of the people of the various states, a check in the states being provided according as each state saw fit to enlarge upon its qualifications. The senate was to be elected by the legislatures of the states, thus inserting another barrier between the mass of the people and their national representation. The president was to be chosen by the electors selected as the legislatures of the state should determine, a provision which amounted in most cases to placing the election of the president at an infinite remove from the people. Finally, the judiciary was to be chosen by the president and the senate, each of which, already removed by several degrees from direct popular control, was to form further barriers to popular control. The mechanism of government envisaged by the young republicans is thus an intricate mechanism, each step of which removes the machinery of politics further from direct popular control. An expression of the will of the people, especially of a will of the majority of the people in all the states, is thus practically impossible in this federalist scheme. Protection of the rights of property, the essence of the art of legislation, the mainspring of the science of government, thus reveals itself as the main object of the young federalists. Hidden behind the mechanism of government, shrouded in the robes of legality, ensconced behind the representative hierarchy, property could rest secure amidst all the clamor of quarreling factions and noisome classes.

Meantime a further division of powers, as between state and national governments, was designed to effect the same ultimate objects. The authors of the *Federalist* papers envisage a system in which the state governments, though not necessarily in conflict with the federal government, possess certain powers reserved to them by the Constitution which balance those expressly stated as pertaining to the national government. Under this further scheme of check and balance it would be practically impossible for any durable majority to capture the offices of both state and national governments. The strong military arm of the national union would always be available to crush any revolt initiated in the states. Military and naval dominion, designed to protect the states from invasion from without and from rebellion within, the power to levy and collect taxes, providing for common interests of the states through the devotion of such funds to national interest and development, and control over the foreign and interstate commerce of the states, by which protective and discriminatory laws could be enacted favoring native industry and commerce and agriculture—these were the powers which the federalists envisaged as a counteracting boon to the loss of certain state privileges through the adoption of the Constitution.

3. *The Representative Principle*

The theory of republican government demanded that each branch of government should represent the people as a whole, the body politic, and yet that each branch separately was to represent a distinct class in the community. The senate, representing the rich, the well born, the merited, the defenders of property, was the spokesman for this class in government; while the house, representing the poor, the small in property, the humbler members of society, was presumed to be the spokesman for the latter class. The executive chief, the third force, was to represent the balancing principle between the other two, inclining the weight of its sovereignty first to one side and then to the other, as a mediator or umpire, and was presumed to be impartial as regards the representation of distinct classes. It was felt that in this way the interminable war between rich and poor, between the leaders of the few and the representatives of the many, might be composed, and that a distinct sovereignty might be set up to represent the common good. Inveterate party battles, reflected in the quarrels of house and senate, might thus be harmonized, effecting a compromise apparently representing the public good. The defects of all former governments, wrote John Adams, was that conflicting parties had not been "legally separated from one another, nor empowered to control each other." There will ever be a struggle between rich and poor, he wrote, for these parties are indigenous to the natural order of society; but republican government, by representing their distinct interests, might hope to alleviate the bitterness of their struggle.

The party of the rich and the party of the poor, argued Adams, must both be represented in a free government; both must be "represented in the legislature, and must be balanced, or one will oppress the other." Republican government was representative, accordingly, not merely by reflecting the will of the contending parties in the struggle for power, but by balancing and harmonizing these wills, reaching a commonly denominated public good as a happy compromise between the two extremes. "There will never probably be found any other mode of establishing such an equilibrium, than by constituting the representation of each an independent branch of the legislature, and an independent executive authority . . . to be a third branch and a mediator or an arbitrator between them. . . . The great art of lawgiving consists in balancing the poor against the rich in the legislature." The rich should be represented in a senate, he argued, and the poor in a house of representatives of the people. But neither can be "defended by their respective guardians in the constitution, without an executive power, vested with a negative, equal to either, to hold the balance even between them." The executive power was thus a common mediator between the two balanced class forces, and the theory presupposed that the chief magistrate would be an impartial, neutral authority in the ceaseless struggle which inevitably takes place between the contending classes. "Two such parties," wrote Adams, "always will exist, as they always have existed, in all nations, especially in such as have property, and, most of all, in commercial countries. Each of these parties must be represented in the legislature, and the two must be checks on each other. But, without a mediator between them, they will oppose each other in all things, and go to war until one subjugates the other. The executive authority is the only mediator that can maintain peace between them." [25]

The whole scheme of balanced powers, and hence of equal and proportional representation, breaks down once it is realized, however, that each branch of government really has the power to prevent any balancing. The machinery of government is thus distinctly conservative, for unless a happy coincidence brings a common harmony of wills, public action cannot be facilitated, and hence public representation through political action cannot be effected. The fault apparently lay in the presuppositions of mechanism common to an age which indulged in Newtonian science and conceived the science of mechanics to be the foundation of the science of politics. The presupposition was that each of the separate powers was perfectly equal to each of the others, but clearly on that supposition the machinery of government would not turn over at all, its engines dying with every importation of conflicting purposes into each of its separate powers. If each power were to be given an absolute veto or negative over the others, one part of the machinery, by opposing itself to another part, would halt the mechanism, and bring to nought the best purposes as well as the worst. The truth is that the desire to build a representative government contradicted the need to erect a balance of powers, and that republican theory foundered on this contradiction.

The fundamental principle that sovereignty was indivisible was violated by the fundamental provision that its unity was in fact a trinity.

The fundamental principle that republican government was representative of the whole people was contradicted by the fundamental provision that each of the distinct classes of the community was to be separately represented. Meantime, the real repository of sovereignty was not found, nor was the source of ultimate check upon the rampage of government discovered, until the qualifications for suffrage had been broadened, and election made an instrument of the general will. The representative principle was ultimately to be discovered and the democratic provision made, only after each branch of the government, house, senate, and executive, should become representative not of a distinct class, but of the whole people. But this discovery lay yet in the lap of time, and the young republicans could only contribute to the science of government on the basis of mechanistic presuppositions and aristocratic prejudices. Society had not yet been emancipated from government, nor had the representative principle been embodied in a democratic composition of the several branches of government.

4. *The Balance of Powers*

The republicans held simple governments, governments in their pure form, to be obnoxious, and tending to tyranny, whether they were aristocracies, monarchies, or democracies. In such simple governments, where the dominating principle in pure form is nearly achieved, the seat of sovereignty is too well defined, and the various classes and orders of society, in a state of emergency, precipitate a revolution against so clearly defined an object of their oppression. Pure governments, whether monarchical, aristocratical, or democratical in their dominating principle, are thus always disgorging their incipient tyranny; for they cannot afford to brook criticism, are hostile to the freedom of the mind, and cramp the developing powers of the individual. All simple governments, the young republicans argued, thus run into tyranny: monarchy falls into despotism, aristocracy tumbles into oligarchy, and democracy is pushed into anarchy. Beneath them all runs what John Adams called the diabolical iniquity of "unlimited sovereignty, or absolute power," whether in the hands of a despot, an oligarchy, or a mob. This was apparently the chief fear of the republican counselors, for their prescription for good government was harmony, the purity of the several principles of government being submerged in a balance of their powers, the rights of each being conscripted to do service for the rights of all.

Of these, however, it is clear that simple democracy, democracy in its pure form, is the worst of evils, the one most to be avoided in the constitution of the new government. A simple democracy, collected into one popular assembly, such as that of the Athenians, is a dangerous expedient, laying the power of the mob at the instance of the passions of the chamber, corrupting both the legislators and the people, issuing in the devilish broth of tyranny. Democracy, the republicans argued, is a poor keeper of the rights of the people, the most factious, the most corrupt, and in the end, the most tyrannous of all forms of government. Property is endangered by the rule of the mob; the minority is always harassed by the majority; the rich are embattled with the poor; the many lambs finally confide their power to a wolfish tyranny whose despotism is as evil as its power is great. Aristocracy is likewise a dangerous form of government, alike injurious to those who rule and those who are ruled, though some of the terrors experienced in democracy are at least obviated when the aristocratical principle is found in its pure form. Aristocracy is safer, more peaceful, more enduring than democracy; yet it too becomes harsh, oppressive, first provoking then destroying the rebellion of its people. It invariably gains a check over the king by opposing the power of the nobles to that of one of them who has elected himself chief noble; but the king comes to side with the people and incites them against the ruling aristocratical powers. It follows that aristocracy ultimately destroys itself and passes into oligarchy. Monarchy is almost as bad at its extreme as is democracy at the opposite extreme. In monarchy the sovereign power is resident in one person, and hence in its pure form the monarchy is immediately a despotism, encroaching on the rights of its people, destroying the balance which the nobles might have provided, unable to sustain itself but by the naked use of force. Like democracy, aristocracy and monarchy pass insensibly into a common despotism; destroying themselves, they obliterate forever the hope of stable, orderly government such as the young republicans, in the first fruit of their revolutionary hopes, might desire.

It follows from these discoveries of the new science of government that any simple government, any unchecked power, any unbalanced sovereignty, is itself a definition of poor government; and that the opposite principle of a balance of powers, of a harmony of conflicting sovereignties, is by the same definition the prescription for good government. The need for such a balance of the powers of government the young republicans found in the badness of human nature, the taint of selfishness, which caused each man, in the pursuit of his own good, to neglect the good of others. Men invariably sway under the weight of their passions, each man preferring his dinner and his girl before all other things. Neither the love of liberty, a general system of benevolence, nor the influence of philanthropic religion, can be counted on to overcome the equal guilt of all in the common war of each against all. Just as the passions are only balanced and harmonized by the reason, so the conflicting sovereignties of society can only be balanced by a stable and orderly government, a government of reason. "Government is intended to set bounds to passions which nature has not limited," wrote John Adams; "hence the principle end of government, the great art to which the science of government reduces, is to regulate the passions of men by setting up a form of government in which every passion has an adequate counterpoise." [26] The only antidote against the rivalry of divergent sovereignties, the only prescription for attaining "that balance of passions and interests, which alone can give authority to reason," is a government which itself embodies a balance of powers, a government of reason and not of men.

This approach to the science of politics clearly reveals the influence of the science of mechanics; for the principle of balance of power, of the harmonization of sovereignties, is a reflection of the well-known principle of mechanics that action and reaction are equal. Hence the young republicans concluded, and with some support from the world of Newtonian science, that power can only be checked by power; that one passion must balance and check another, rather than overcome it; that each man independently pursuing his own freewill, determined only by the sovereignty of himself, has no other check than that of a balanced and virtuous government which should reconcile the war of each against all. It followed for the republicans that the division of powers must be perfectly equal, for only if equal, could the opposing sovereignties be harmonized. Between two opposing powers of government, one of which is stronger than another, there could be only an unstable equilibrium, a temporary peace, until the omnivorous strength of the one swallowed down the inherent weakness of the other. The prescription for good government then followed automatically; for stability in government, the permanent interests of the whole of society, could only be preserved by an equilibrium among the sovereignties, a balance of the powers of government. A republican government, in brief, was like the world of Newton, a huge machine in perfect equilibrium, endlessly repeating, but never violating, a few stable and harmonious laws. It was no wonder that the young republicans insisted so universally on the principles of mechanism, or that they clung so tenaciously to the picture of the world which the science of mechanics had bequeathed to them; for they were building a government according to those principles which science had discovered to lie at the heart of reality. They demanded no less an authority for the science of government, no less a philosophic buttressing of republican principles, than a cosmic constitution and a republican metaphysic.

5. *The Mechanism of Government*

The principle of the balance of powers, and consequently of the equal and separate nature of the diverse powers which were federated together to form republican government, was, as we have seen, the most fruitful principle which mechanism imported into the science of government. John Adams summed up the principle of balance of powers when he wrote that "there can be no government of laws without a balance, and that there can be no balance without three orders; and that even three orders can never balance each other, unless each in its department is independent and absolute." [27] But if the principle were to be applied with full force it would soon be apparent that the equal power of each constituted a negative on the powers of all, thus realizing in effect the ideal of laissez-faire in politics. The three separate and distinct powers were to be regarded as so many checks on one another, lest the power of one grow omnivorous and swallow down the power of all, and hence as providing the mechanism by which government was to remain free. The executive power, for its part, was to possess a veto over the legislative branches of government, but these, in their turn, could veto legislation initiated by the executive through an adverse vote. It followed that membership in the house, the senate, or in the executive branch of government should not originate primarily from any one of these, but should emerge directly from a representation of the people. Each branch of federated sovereignty is thus the jealous guardian over the other; each is incipiently at war with the other; and the issue of the deliberations of all would likely be a compromise which would not injure any one class of citizens more than any other. The *res publica,* the public good, was accordingly neither a good of the majority nor the good of a minority, but a harmonization of wills created by the compromise enforced by the very mechanism of government.

The mechanism of government might thus prevent the capture of all branches of government by a single party, though theoretically such a step was possible. Combinations of any two of the powers of government against a third was indeed possible, either as house and senate against the executive, or as executive and senate against the house; but it was considered extremely rare that a single party could mobilize all branches of the government. The great desideratum of government thus appeared to be a mechanism embodying distinct powers, each strong enough to prevent the encroachments of the others, and yet not strong enough to encroach itself upon the powers pertaining to the other branches. Were the house and senate counterpoised against one another, the weight of the executive would provide the motive force of legislation; or were the executive entrenched behind a stubborn veto power, the combined weight of the houses of the legislature might coalesce to form the needed power. The machinery of government was thereby forced to repeat itself, endlessly forming its majorities and minorities, continually coagulating its separate sovereignties around a particular issue, and grinding out results as the mechanism of the heavens endlessly repeats its nocturnal orbits. But it was not of itself a mechanism of change, for it presupposed a repetitious cycle of nature with no real change, in which the harmonizing principle, perpetuation of the basic body of law, consigns to oblivion any departure from its fundamental structure. In its structure, therefore, the republic was a mechanism; not simply an instrument of government, but a political machine, the structure of which was determined by the universal reign of law, and regulated by a cosmic constitution.

6. The Theory of Republicanism

The students of the new science of government had now discovered the fundamental principles and axioms of their inquiry. Government was to be separated into three departments, and yet the three were to be harmonized into a single government. Feudalism with its concentrated authority, its monopoly of power, and its arbitrary restrictions on property was opposed by the principle of separation of powers—a principle which was nevertheless the first step in harmonizing the elements of political sovereignty which were believed to reside in each separate division of government. This mystery of the science of government, of a trinitarian separation of the powers of government which yet expressed a unitarian sovereignty in government, Adams appropriately described as a "political trinity in unity, trinity of legislation, and unity of executive power, which in politics is no mystery." [28] The mystery is dissolved, however, when it is realized that the first magistrate will have the power to propose and veto legislation, thus constituting a third source of legislative power in addition to the upper and lower branches of the legislature. The three sources of sovereignty are on principle independent and yet inevitably balanced by reason of their legally prescribed relations to one another; it is a trinitarian power expressed as a unitarian sovereignty, a mystery so great that even the pious cannot decide where the authority of one ends and that of another begins; for, like the persons of the religious trinity, the separate powers of government are but different aspects of one sovereign personality. The young republicans could not have devised a more mysterious formula for protecting the rights of property than a feudal prince for insuring his catholic right to exploit the peasantry.

Theoretically the three components of power are equal; each can exercise its sovereignty only upon the tacit consent of the other sovereignties which are tied to it. Here the principles of monarchy, of aristocracy, and of democracy, the young republicans argued, are harmoniously blended. It harkens back to the philosophic principle of the one and the many, pluralism and monism, with the aristocratic principle embodied as a happy medium between these extremes, which have existed in their purity, the colonists insisted, but rarely in the course of history. In brief, the principle rests on the classic notion of harmony, balance, proportion, and embodies both the pluralism and the monism of the world of Newton. Although the departments of government are separated and theoretically of equal power, a mysterious force, akin to Newton's gravitation, deflects and harmonizes the independent sovereignties, which would otherwise proceed upon their independent courses. By virtue of the definition thus encountered, a despotism is a government in which three independent sovereignties are reposed in one man, particularly if his claim to power be held hereditary; and on this definition alone, the governments of feudalism were all to be considered despotic. A republic, then, is a government in which the people share in sovereignty by virtue of representation, and are equally represented by virtue of the division of the powers of government and their equal claim to sovereignty.

Here, then, the doctrine of equality and the claim to freedom are alike embodied in principle; for the people, being equally subject to fixed and stable laws, by virtue of the social contract into which they have entered by their own free will and consent, share equally in the sovereignty of republican government, but diversely according to the representation which their position in the order of society entitles them. It followed that the Virginia planter and the Boston merchant were represented diversely, by virtue of their regional attachments, and yet equally by virtue of the share in sovereignty which each was entitled to claim. The science of politics was thus accoutred with those ancient and noble accounts of primitive republicanism, in which a diversity of form covers a unitary principle. Republican governments, like governments in general, were found to embody to a greater or lesser degree the monarchical, aristocratical, and democratical principles. In brief, there were found to be degrees of republicanism, phenomenal manifestations of the underlying principle, which diverged from purity according to the circumstances of time and place in their founding. Here was the matter upon which the great debate ultimately floundered; for while all were republican in principle, not all were agreed whether a republican government should be established without embodying some degree each of the monarchical, aristocratical, and democratical principles. The theoretical differences which lie between the Adams-Hamilton school of thought and that of Jefferson and Paine were matters of degree rather than of substance, the one inclining more toward the incorporation of monarchical and aristocratical principles in the republican body politic and the other more toward the inclusion of the full force of the democratical principle within the structure of republican government. In brief, all were republicans, but not all were democrats; and the great debate was enlivened by the weight of authority which should draw a line between these fluid nuances of degree.

The compromise by which a "mixed government" was agreed upon was more nearly in accord with the prevailing views than has been generally recognized. Such a mixed government, though republican in form, would embody aristocratic, monarchic, and democratic principles within it; and yet by that very admixture, by that harmonization of principles seemingly diverse, would provide for permanence and longevity in government by nullifying and canceling out the petty antagonisms and minute subdichotomies to which such diverse principles give rise. Sovereignty thus resided not only in the one (the monarchical principle) and the few (the aristocratic principle) but in the many (the democratic principle); and each of these was to be given its appropriate structure, the monarchic principle in the executive department, the aristocratic principle in the senate, and the democratic principle in the house. While sovereignty theoretically resided in the people as a whole, it took up residence and found a more congenial home in a structure which balanced and canceled out the qualitative differences in this sovereignty, reducing them at last to simple quantitative differences which expressed the compelling will of each separate power. The young republicans had thus discovered in the new science of government that not only are there three simple states in nature, the monarchy, the aristocracy, and democracy; but that the principle of each might be happily mixed in a fourth form, which they dubbed republican government. This republican government, rarely existing in pure form, was in fact inclined ordinarily toward its monarchical, aristocratical, or democratical principle, according to time and circumstance. The most pressing of problems in the scientific study of politics, therefore, was to find just that perfect balance and harmony which should severally cancel out and suppress the latent tendencies to domination of each of these three principles of sovereignty, and which should reduce the qualitative difference of interest to a mere quantitative difference of representation, thus expressing in the will of each the will of all.

CHAPTER ELEVEN

THE MAKING OF CITIZENS

1. The Republican Education

The life of reason, founded on some small pledge of virtue, required a seasoning of knowledge to give it the vitality of life; and the republican principle, founded, so it was said, on the life of reason, asked only that a school of virtue be given its province as a seat of character for the republican life. If by the laws of nature which had proclaimed the rights of man, every man was to become the sovereign of himself, the lord and governor of the provinces of his being, it surely followed that the sovereign should be educated, that the citizen should be sent to school to protect his newly discovered rights. The order of nature had established that each man was to be his own legislator, judge, and avenger, the "absolute lord of his own property," and so it remained to hedge these sovereign rights with the fortress of virtue and the army of personal knowledge. The disciples of reason had taken the position that "the strength and spring of every free government, is the virtue of the people; virtue grows on knowledge, and knowledge on education." It remained only to issue the call for a republican education, a general diffusion of knowledge, by which the people would grow in virtue, in the facility of self-government and the principles of provincial command. This undertaking occupied the best minds of that prolific age, drawing into its circle of proponents, Franklin, Jefferson, Paine, Rush, Knox, Webster, and a host of less famous men. But it was the beginning, not only of a republican education, but of a new Socratic faith that in knowledge lay all the springs of virtue, all the sources of an enlightened government.

The moral principle of the Revolution, the young republicans declared, was to instruct, not to destroy, the foundations of virtue. It was to bring into the temple of learning every species of promise, every hope of a rationally ordered life, and there to inculcate not only the life of reason but the principles of republican government. A republican citizen is, by definition, one who "sees the rationale of the whole system, its origin and its operations." Political science was to be studied in the light of the republican principle; for, Benjamin Rush had written, "the principle of patriotism stands in need of the reinforcement of prejudice, and it is well known that our strongest prejudices in favor of our country are formed in the first one and twenty years of our lives." During these years, the youth were to be instructed not only in matters of common learning, but in the principles of true virtue and the foundations of republican government. They were to absorb the mechanism of character and of habit, acquire the new duties incumbent upon the republican foundations. "While we inculcate these republican duties upon our pupils, we must not neglect, at the same time, to inspire him with republican principles." Thus, by character and virtue, by learning and knowledge, were the new ties to be knotted, the new loyalties to be drawn; and the issue of this republican education, inspired by the opening of the channels of political science so long clogged by priestly monopoly and royal usurpation, was to be a new species of patriotism, loyalty to a country that was republican at its birth.[29]

To examine, then, the principles of public right and the foundations of true virtue upon which the republic had been founded was to be the beginning of the design of republican education; for the Revolution had opened a new class of duties for every American, had opened the channels of liberty through which knowledge and virtue might now flow. "It becomes us, therefore, to examine our former habits upon this subject, and in laying the foundations for nurseries of wise and good men, to adapt our modes of teaching to the peculiar form of our government." But republican government had been designed, above all else, to harmonize the wills, to balance the desires, of the men who had drawn it up; it was in essence a mechanism of compromise, a market-place of ideas, and it rested on a thoroughly mechanical conception of the obligations of government and the duties of its citizens. Similarly, a mechanical conception pervaded the design of education in the young republic, so that a balance might be struck between the machinery of government and the machinery of man. "From the observations that have been made," wrote Benjamin Rush, "it is plain, that I consider as possible to convert men into republican machines."

From the great Montesquieu he had drawn the fundamentals which distinguished republican government from a monarchy, and the republican education from the education of a despotism. "It is observed by the great Montesquieu, that the laws of education ought to be relative to the principles of government. In despotic governments the people should have little or no education except what tends to inspire them with a servile fear. Information is fatal to depotism—in monarchies education should be partial and adapted to each class of citizens. But 'in a republican government,' says the same writer, 'the whole power of education is required.' Here every class of people should know and love the laws. This knowledge should be diffused by means of schools and newspapers; that an attachment to the laws may be formed by early impressions on the mind.—Two regulations are essential to the continuance of republican governments. 'First. Such a distribution of lands, and principles of descent and alienation as shall give every citizen the power of acquiring what his industry merits. Secondly. Such a system of education, as gives every citizen an opportunity of acquiring knowledge, and fitting himself for places of trust.' These are fundamental articles, the *sine qua non* of the existence of American republics. 'Hence the absurdity of copying the manners and adapting the institutions of monarchies.'" [30]

Granted the premise upon which this great experiment in republican education went forward, namely, that the foundations of education in a republic are the principles upon which republican governments rest, it is little to be wondered that each of the states, like so many separate and tiny republics, should appropriate to themselves a function of instruction which was only federally united. Though the designers of the experiment no doubt envisaged a national system of republican education, political principles called for the control of the system to be laid in the hands of the states, where liberties could be jealously guarded and inalienable rights systematically sustained. Jefferson's famous bill for the diffusion of general knowledge demonstrates the federal principle in operation; for it units in one parcel of legislative reforms provisions for the abolition of the remnants of feudal landed property and proposals for establishing a system of schools. This was the essence of republican education—to establish a government to protect the rights of property and to establish a system of schools which should encourage the virtue of its care.

2. *The Critique of Classical Education*

The habit of classical learning, long ingrained by the prejudices of the Renaissance gentleman and the power of the Puritan priest, had now to give way to the utilitarian learning, to a mode of instruction appropriate to the new status and privileges of the citizens of the republic. "The study of the Latin and Greek languages is improper in the present state of society and government in the United States." The classical learning, too long associated with the feudal monopoly of consciousness and the aristocratic principle in education, was to be banished with the other remnants of feudalism, in favor of the republican principle of utility. "While Greek and Latin are the only avenues to science, education will always be confined to a few people." As the republicans had demanded democracy in the redemption of man as the fruit of the revolution in religion, and equality in the government of man as the fruit of the revolution in politics, so they would now demand democracy in the education of man, an equal right to the privileges of knowledge and representation in the parliament of virtue. "It is only by rendering knowledge universal, that a republican form of government can be preserved in our country." In the midst of the process of removing the feudal barriers to the expansion of capitalism by the foundation of a free government, the apostles of reason quite consistently undertook to remove the barrier of ignorance to the expansion of the mind by the establishment of a system of free, universal, public education. A part of that great task required, in the words of a contemporary, that the republicans should "shake off the fetters of those ancient languages," the barrier to science, which clogged by its strange antithesis the flow of freedom in the human mind. In the words of Benjamin Rush, that nation "which shall first shake off the fetters of those ancient languages, will advance further in knowledge, and in happiness, in twenty years, than any nation in Europe has done in a hundred." [31]

If then for the sake of a liberal education a republican gentleman wished to undertake the study of languages, let them be, the age agreed with Franklin, the languages of the modern nations, whose commercial intercourse gives to the linguist a stake in their utility. His own program of moral improvement and self-instruction had let him to concentrate on the modern languages; for he concurred with the opinion of the age that the classical languages were the appendages of a leisure class devoted not to a useful instruction but to a cultivation of their vices. The classical languages, which since the time of the Renaissance had seemed to the awakened mind the source of all knowledge, the possession of which was not only the mark of the scholar but also the sign of the gentleman, had now to bear up in competition with the modern languages. The utility of learning, not its ancient classical lineage, was henceforth the test and standard by which it was to be judged. It happened, accordingly, that in the young republic the dead languages must give way to the living, and the knowledge of the ancients must stand aside for the learning of the moderns.

3. The Utilitarian Learning

The counterpart of the attack on classical education was the prospect of the utilitarian learning, of a mode of instruction which might parallel the civic aim of republican government by producing useful citizens. The promise of a free government, that the people might be free from the exactions of tyranny to devote themselves to developing the resources of the nation, had as its educational expression the promise of a free education, that the people might be free from the tyranny of educational tradition to devote themselves to developing their human resources in the cultivation of every useful art. The utilitarian learning therefore condemned as wasteful the ostentatious pursuit of linguistic prestige by those who lackeyed after the monarchical principle of classical learning. "Under these circumstances, to spend four or five years in learning two dead languages, is to turn our backs upon a gold mine, in order to amuse ourselves catching butterflies." [32] The pursuit of utilitarian learning, if taken up by the schools, would spread useful knowledge through every part of the public, uniting in its adherence to freedom all the arts and all the sciences which minister to man's success.

Following out the principle that to make men free was to make them independent, resourceful, and self-sufficient, able to judge in matters of public right and capable of choice in public wrong, the utilitarian educators argued that useful instruction would increase the progress of the arts of agriculture, the techniques of manufacturing, and the science of commerce. To the economic utility of this mode of instruction would be added a corresponding political utility, raising the weight of the local clamors which should be heard in national councils. "It is certainly laudable to pay due regard to those sciences that tend to enlarge the sphere of world interest, and without which the complicated business of human life cannot be transacted." [33] The tradition of the liberal arts had been examined and found wanting; the tyranny of the classical tradition had been broken. "Indeed," wrote Noah Webster, "it appears to me that what is now called a liberal education disqualifies a man for business." [34]

The utilitarian learning presupposed the Baconian conception of knowledge, that knowledge is power, and carried in its wake a renascence of interest in the technical sciences. Utility was conceived, on the one hand, as a knowledge that would lead to virtue, and hence to self-government, thus preparing the young for their duties as republican machines; and on the other, as a knowledge that is power, a technique of production, by which causes could be set in operation and effects brought about through a correct adjustment of means and ends. The utilitarian educator proposed to unite both these conceptions of useful learning under the heading of power, declaring that the virtue to protect one's life, liberty, and estate, was of the same character as the technical knowledge to produce effects. The utilitarian learning thereafter took a mechanical form and received a narrow interpretation from the current ideology, until at last a subsequent generation called it into question as an experiment in selfishness. But the transcendental education was still below the horizon, and the young republicans were concerned with a pragmatic reformation of the schools. They proposed that the curriculum be reformed, so that it might make useful citizens; for the utilitarian curriculum included the usefulness of practical power as well as the usefulness of republican principles, with which the young citizens were to be indoctrinated. But at long last the heritage of feudalism in education was shattered, the church was separated from the school, and the aristocratic taste for classical education gave way before the republican need of a utilitarian learning.

4. *The Curriculum and the Culture*

Of the subjects which might lend themselves to the republican education and fulfill the promise of the utilitarian learning, the creative minds of the epoch had formed a fairly settled opinion. First in the order of study because it was commended by the very principles upon which the system of republican life was founded was natural history, which, if it might be joined to natural philosophy, would gain the concurrence of nature for the system that was being perfected and the experiment that was being tried in the United States. Natural history, wrote Benjamin Rush, is "the foundation of all useful and practical knowledge in agriculture, manufactures and commerce, as well as in philosophy, chemistry and medicine"; it is the foundation of all subsequent studies and should be begun early in the life of the student, while it is carried through to the highest level of his learning. Geography too might serve as an auxiliary to the study of nature: "It may be perfectly understood by means of cards—globes—maps; for each of these modes of conveying instruction seizes upon the senses and imagination." In place of the ancient languages, French and German, or French and Spanish, will serve the need of a foreign tongue, proving useful in commerce while it is not inelegant in the discourse of polite society. In brief, the student ought to be instructed "in grammar—oratory—criticism—the higher branches of mathematics—philosophy—chemistry—logic—metaphysics—chronology—history—government—the principles of agriculture, and manufactures—and in everything else that is necessary to qualify him for public usefulness and private happiness." [35]

Conscious also of the decay of those ancient republics that neglected to inculcate republican principles into the minds and characters of their youth, Rush emphasized the science of government, a study calculated to establish the superiority of the republican over all other forms of government. "Above all, let our youth be instructed in the history of ancient republics, and the progress of liberty and tyranny in the different states of Europe." As an aid to the study of government, argued Rush, let the student inquire into the history of human progress, noting the defiles by which reason was lured into error and truth held bondage to the hordes of ancient lies. The new era of liberty, now dawning in Europe and America, was not to be overlooked in the design of the curriculum, the architecture of republican studies. But alas! suitable teachers were lacking even for that: "We suffer so much from traditional error of various kinds, in education, morals, and government, that I have been led to wish, that it were possible for us to have schools established, in the United States, for teaching the art of forgetting. I think three-fourths of all our school-masters, divines, and legislators would profit very much, by spending two or three years in such useful institutions." The soul of the republic, which could only live in the characters of its citizens, must expire unless the older generation, raised under the regimes of corrupt and effete monarchies, could purge these errors from their minds, or rear the younger generation in the purity of republican principles. "Accustomed to look up to those nations from whom we have derived our origin, for our laws, our opinions, and our manners; we have retained, with undistinguishing reverence, their errors, with all their improvements; have blended, with our public institutions, the policy of dissimilar countries; and have grafted, on an infant commonwealth, the manners of ancient and corrupted monarchies." [36]

5. The Aims of Education

The aims of education proposed by the advocates of republicanism were invariably linked to social progress and moral improvement. In the light of the idea of progress and the promise of a republican way of life, it was believed that the barriers to the development of the mind had been removed, once the shackles of feudalism and the chains of monarchy had been torn by the Revolution loose from their historical moorings. Education was conceived, accordingly, as the discipline of free men, the acquisition of virtue and the accumulation of knowledge, which, it will be remembered, were considered the foundation of republican government. "Education is the training up of the human mind by the acquisition of sciences inculcated to extend its knowledge and promote its improvement." [37] The faculties of the mind, conferred with unequal pleasure by an otherwise unerring order of nature, were to be strengthened by education and disciplined by the exercises of republican habit. It is plain, wrote Samuel Smith, "that the crude wisdom which nature bestows is unequal to the production and government of virtue, such as man in his pursuit of happiness discovers it to be his interest to practice; and that to insure this desirable object, it is necessary that the original faculties of the mind should be vigorously exercised, extended, and strengthened." [38]

Inspiring youth with the desire of improving their minds, opening up to them the infinite perspectives of development denied to them under feudal and papal systems, had as its object the liberation of the human mind. "The feudal and papal systems were tyrannical in the extreme; they fettered and debased the mind; they enslaved a great portion of Europe." [39] The genuine aim of education underlying the republican principle was that man was to be given the liberty to develop his mind and mold his character in the pursuit of that happiness which the republic had been established to protect and sustain. "The real aim of education is less to give the children positive facts than to keep them constantly developing, working themselves and by themselves to observe and to understand. For that wonderful habit once made part of their lives will never be lost and will grow with the growth of their minds." [40]

6. *The Question of Method*

The revolt from monarchy, from its arbitrary prescriptions and tyrannous exactions, had as its educational expression a clamor not only for a general system of republican education but also for a method appropriate to the new dignity and status of its pedagogical citizens. The attempt was hazarded to call for a republican method of education, a mode of instruction and discipline which should liberate the capacities of individuals. But it was necessary, first, to take into account the native capacities of the pupils, to adopt instruction to their level of development. "From these considerations it would certainly appear most proper, in establishing, or extensively patronizing, a liberal system of education, that it should be generally adapted to the various natural endowments and genius of those who are to be trained up by its discipline." [41] On the question of method, accordingly, the apostles of republicanism gave an almost unanimous answer; education should begin at the level of the capacities of the student and should follow the order of nature in their development. In the organization of instruction, the principle of republicanism will be followed, and pupils will be enlisted in the management of their own affairs. "The principle of obedience will be finer and nobler when they have themselves been the commanding officer. These children will eventually serve the State better, because, having learned to exercise some authority themselves, they will realize the importance of respecting it always." [42]

The republican method, then, proposed that the capacities of pupils for self-government be developed by frequent opportunities to exercise these faculties. The student will accordingly be consulted in matters that affect his interest; he will be drawn into the habit of forming judgments and making choices. "To consult children on all matters on which they may have an opinion seems to be so good a way to form their judgment, to accustom them to decide for themselves and to reason, to give them character, that I would not hesitate to allow them to vote on all matters." Revolting against monarchy in government and against mercantilism in economics, the republicans called for a system of education corresponding to the new status and dignity of the individual man. Rejecting then authoritarianism in politics, they were drawn to reject it also in educational method: "They will exercise their own logic and their minds will become accurate. They will understand objects before they concern themselves with signs and words—which will be given them not as arbitrary forms, but as welcome assistance." Thus, the method of republican education, like the method of republican politics, was designed to train each man as the sovereign of himself.

7. Nationalism and Education

First in importance, though never quite accomplished, was the problem of establishing a national system of schools. The diversity of the states in population, religion, and resources called imperatively for a federation of the state systems into a single national one; but though the literature of the age was filled with the recognition of this need, the jealous character of the several states with respect to matters that had been left by the Constitution in their hands prohibited a solution of the problem. "Great, surely, must be the difference between two communities, in one of which, good laws are executed only in some particular situations, while in others they are almost totally neglected; and in the other are universally established with equal and impartial authority. Such, surely, must be the difference between the effects of education when abandoned to the precarious uncertainty of casual, partial or local encouragement;

and of that which has been established uniformly and generally by the united wisdom and exertions of a whole nation." [43]

Diversity of resources and culture, of religion and life tenures, stood in the way of a national system of schools; but the argument was hazarded that before the European cultures mingling in the land could be blended into one homogeneous culture steps would have to be taken leading to a uniform system of public schools. "In a country circumscribed and situated as the United States of America, a considerable local diversity in improvement, whether with respect to morals and literature, must be the consequence of such a wide extent of territory, inhabited by citizens blending together almost all the various manners and customs of every country in Europe. Nothing, then, surely, might be supposed to have a better effect towards harmonizing the whole in these important views than an uniform system of national education." All the appeals to patriotism, to the pride of progress, to republicanism and virtue, failed to call forth the required effort in the attempt to build from the diversity of the states a federated system; for the appeal for a national system militated against those very principles which the republic had been organized to sustain. The principle of states-rights, jealous of recent Federalist insurgencies, bore her recalcitrance to the last. "On account of the difference of the elements which forms the population of the United States of America, an institution of national education is there evidently more necessary to form a proper character, than it was in the republics of antiquity. This institution is absolutely necessary to make and arouse principles of patriotism to be inoculated in the heart of infancy; to strengthen the bonds of an union which needs to be incessantly solicited, in an immense republic, composed of divers peculiar states." [44]

The principle of separation of church and state, upon which the republic had been founded, discovered its educational corollary in the principle of separation of church and school. Aroused by the revolutionary pamphlets against the priestly monopoly of knowledge, resolved by the bitter debates in colonial legislatures to set an end to the interference of the church in political affairs, the republicans insisted, no less strongly, that if the church was to be separated from the state, then it was to be separated also from the school. "Perhaps there is no circumstance that can be brought to view, in the history of scientific improvement, that has more retarded its progress, or tended to enslave the human mind, than that of admitting any combination to exist between the interests of academical instruction; and the, too often, partial interests of particular religious bodies. On its dissolution the cause of genuine federalism, as much as the cause of science, ultimately depends."

They proposed to abolish the religious qualification for teaching, too long identified in the minds of the republicans with the tyranny of feudalism and monarchical government, just as they had abolished it for the holding of public office. Acceptance of a particular religious creed, an unbearable orthodoxy which bent and clogged the mind, they accounted the surest cause for the rejection of a public professor. "It is a happy circumstance peculiarly favorable to an uniform plan of public education," wrote Knox, "that this country hath excluded ecclesiastical from civil policy, and emancipated the human mind from the tyranny of church authority, and church establishments." [45]

The hope of nationalism and education, the progress of science and of republicanism, were now seen to be united in one vast effort to preserve the national life. The republican education ought to teach, "that there can be no durable liberty but in a republic, and that government, like all other sciences, is of a progressive nature," wrote Rush. "We daily see matter of a perishable nature rendered durable by certain chemical operations. In like manner, I conceive, that it is possible to combine power in such a way as not only to encrease the happiness, but to promote the duration of republican forms of government far beyond the terms limited for them by history, or the common opinions of mankind." The means of preserving republican government beyond its historical term was to be public enlightenment, and in this great task education was to unite with nationalism to inculcate republican opinions. Rush recommended the study of commerce, of the art of political economy, in republican seminaries, because it was "the best security against the influence of hereditary monopolies in land, and, therefore, the surest protection against aristocracy." The plan of a national system of education was therefore to inculcate republican principles, teach admiration for the republican form of government, and devote itself not only to the study of the science of government but also to a mastery of the art of political economy. The great educational experiment upon which the young republic had entered proposed no less than to set aside the historical term that had been established for republican governments, and to lay by the heels the common opinions of mankind which supposed the dissolution and decay of public virtue and the failure of public enlightenment. This was the essence of the republican education; this was the educational philosophy of the young republicans. [46]

CHAPTER TWELVE

THE LIFE OF REASON

1. *The Natural Aristocracy*

The world had now opened the prospect of success, and the barriers erected by an artificial aristocracy had been battered down, so that talent and genius and virtue might flow without impediments to the highest source of attainment, and form of themselves a natural aristocracy. The promise of free government was that nothing should stand in the way of the development of an aristocracy of nature, that society should have in it all the springs of mobility by which men of talent and virtue could be catapulted to success. The attack on monarchy, artificial aristocracy, and hereditary succession had as its goal the liberation of the talents of individuals that they might rise in the social scale in accordance with the laws of nature, and constitute themselves a natural aristocracy. This new class was to be as superior to the feudal aristocracy as the claim of natural right was to pretense of divine right, and it was to be drawn initially not from those who claimed noble distinctions and hereditary allegiances, but of those whose initiative and enterprise, of those whose talent and virtue, carried them by natural right to positions of honor and emolument. The artificial noble of the Middle Ages was then to appear a spurious potentate when compared with the noble of nature. "The artificial noble shrinks into a dwarf before the noble of nature." The courtier who had graced the courts of power, and the monarchs who had managed its thrones, were alike to be displaced by the natural aristocracy, and give way to the rise of the bourgeoisie.

The ideal of an aristocracy of nature was an expression of the positive demand that an aristocracy of talent and virtue should rule; that the bourgeoisie should displace the feudal nincompoops, the royal patentees, the stupid monopolists, who had come to their artificial position by spurious claims. The aristocracy of nature, in brief, was to replace those who had artificially gained their wealth and power; the patrician order of England, the estates held by feudal grant, secured by primogeniture and entail, were to be dissolved in a free circulation and alienation of property, which would lend mobility to the flow of every form of talent and virtue and give all men equally a stake in society. "I agree with you that there is a natural aristocracy among men," wrote Jefferson. "The grounds of this are virtue and talents. Formerly bodily powers gave place among the aristoi. But since the invention of gunpowder has armed the weak as well as the strong with missile death, bodily strength, like beauty, good humor, politeness and other accomplishments, has become but an auxiliary ground for distinction. There is also an artificial aristocracy, founded on wealth and birth, without either virtue or talents; for with these it would belong to the first class. The natural aristocracy I consider as the most precious gift of nature, for the instruction, the trusts, and government of society." [47]

2. The Republican Life

For a society which so wantonly had proclaimed the equality of all men, it must have been a disturbing study to discover that society had its inevitable order, as stable and tranquil as the order of nature. "Nature, which has established in the universe a chain of being and universal order," wrote John Adams, "has ordained that no two objects shall be perfectly alike, and no two creatures perfectly equal." All societies, the young republicans discovered, have their principles of order, their pyramided hierarchies, which God and nature, by the common consent of each and to the natural distress of all, have implanted in the heart of reality. Men are unequal as to birth, wealth, virtue, height, weight, or whatever measure one chooses; and these inequalities are not to be eradicated by some philanthropic legislator in his search for perfect equality. Particularly important was a principle which the young republicans insisted upon—that inequalities of property can never be rectified, for as soon as the legislator declares his artificial equality the hand of God and the order of nature ultimately redivide property on a very real basis of inequality. There is then, quite apart from the artificial aristocracy of the feudal ages, a natural aristocracy, an aristocracy arising by the conjunction of wealth, of virtue, and of knowledge in several persons, and these are the real leaders of society, as distinct from the artificial aristocracy of hereditary right imposed from the outside, and contrary to the spirit of nature, by the feudal principle of divine right.

Such a natural aristocracy, when it rules, rules by natural right, as the feudal aristocracy, buoyed up by its fictitious claims, ruled by divine right. But the natural aristocracy, as John Adams pointed out, does not arise from "artificial inequalities of condition, such as hereditary dignity, titles, magistracies, or legal distinctions," nor from "established marks, as stars, garters, crosses, or ribbons." Titles may be abolished, but distinctions never; for the natural aristocracy arises according to natural law, establishing in each society if it be free the rule of the wisest and best. Thus it was not against aristocracy in principle that the young republicans were arguing, but against the artificiality of the feudal aristocracy which the times had decreed should be supplanted by a republican aristocracy, an aristocracy of nature. Nor did the young republicans object to the hierarchic principle in society; only it should remain a principle of nature and not of men, a law of the universe and not a spurious claim of hereditary succession or divine right.

Although the eighteenth-century science of society does not give a uniform reply on the question of the order of society, it is clear that such an order is recognized, and that the natural aristocracy should have no artificial and unnatural barriers put in its climb to the top of the social order. The natural divisions of society create an upper, a middle, and a lower class, argued the young republicans; and the principle which should obtain in a free society is that there should be no artificial barrier to the passages of a member of one of these great classes into membership in another. Distinctions, where they exist, should be natural distinctions, not imposed by an arbitrary creed, a spurious ideology, or a policy of craft and deceit. Sometimes, when the notion of class conflict was uppermost in their minds, the students of society divided it into upper and lower orders, the rich and the poor, the stable and the unstable. But the predominating conception in all these theoretical divergencies is the definition which gives to the possessors of property a stable will, and to the possessors of the most property a most stable will, and to the possessors of no property no stable will at all, and hence makes them subject to their passions, and thus by definition unworthy to be represented in government.

Basic to such a conception of the order of society is the principle that all elements should be kept in more or less stable equilibrium, balancing the power and influence of the minority of property against the passion and interests of a majority, and by that strategy, provided only that these interests are carefully represented in government, maintaining its stability. Fundamental to the whole theory of government was the idea that the different orders of society, though not equal in rank, distinction, or property, were equally represented in government. Thus, it can be seen that it was no contradiction to the young republicans to declare, on the one hand, that all men are created equal, and on the other, that there is a natural order of rank and class in society, culminating in an aristocracy of nature fit to preside over a republican state. All the contrivances of philanthropic legislators cannot prevent a natural order of rank, distinction, class, and property from arising in society; but by definition a truly free society would treat each of these classes on the same legal basis, thus introducing a spurious equality in principle into an order realistically unequal in distinctions of rank. Here again the young republicans were drawing upon the science of mechanics to establish their science of society, delving into the order of nature to justify their order of society. They devoted themselves to the discovery of principles which should reveal that the action and reaction of the different components of society should be equal, then turned to the problem of embodying their discovery in a government which should provide for the perpetual repetition of the social machine.

3. The Utilitarian Standard

To prove that man was capable of self-government, without the paternalistic tutelage of the king or the absolute morality of the church, the natural aristocracy had to establish a new science of morality. The object of this science—since these things had been denied under the feudal system—was to establish that men are not encumbered with the hereditary taint of sin, by which the efforts of all but a small number of elect had been doomed to futility; but, on the contrary, that their efforts were to be rewarded and their virtues carry their own proclamation. It fell to the lot of the young republicans to give man the possession of an innate moral faculty, by which he could be trusted to choose right from wrong and good from evil without the absolute morality of the church. "By the moral faculty," wrote Benjamin Rush, "I mean a capacity in the human mind of distinguishing and choosing good and evil, or, in other words, virtue and vice. It is a native principle, and though it be capable of improvement by experience and reflection, it is not derived from either of them." The moral faculty was a kind of lawgiver, so that men could be ruled by their own constitutional principles, and the conscience was a kind of supreme court, so that it could rule on the constitutionality of the legislative faculty. The science of morality rested, then, upon the conception of man as a republican machine, whose rational, moral, and physical faculties corresponded to the different branches of constitutional government. But the moral faculty, as Rush noted, was differently conceived and differently named by republican philosophers: "The moral faculty has received different names from different authors. It is the 'moral sense' of Dr. Hutchinson; 'the sympathy' of Dr. Adam Smith; the 'moral instinct' of Rousseau; and 'light that lighteth every man that cometh into the world' of St. John. I have adopted the term of moral faculty from Dr. Beattie, because it conveys, with the most perspicuity, the idea of a capacity of the mind of choosing good and evil." [48]

The inevitable outcome of this doctrine of the moral sense was a drift toward an ethics of intuition. If every man possesses sovereignty over himself, a private property in his own personality, then he is endowed also with an innate perception of right and wrong, and composes his ethics out of intuition. The creator has made the moral sense, "so much a part of our constitution," wrote Jefferson, "as that no errors of reasoning or speculation might lead us astray from its observance in practice." It followed that man was capable of self-government without outside dictation either from the absolute king or the absolute God, and the consequence was that his sovereignty in the parliament of choice could not be contested by forces lying beyond the province of his own constitution. From this line of reasoning, virtue "consists not in the act we do, but in the end it is to effect"; but the outcome was only a utilitarian standard, because a market place of chance intervened between the purpose and the act, and consequences hidden and unintended brought about effects that were not foreseen, thus tearing the young republicans from responsibility for consequences which they had not intended. A subsequent generation of pragmatists was to attempt a reconstruction of the republican doctrine of the moral sense, but it only fell as a result into a new species of utilitarian morality.

What standard then could the disciples of reason retain out of the dissolution of ancient priest injunction and the disintegration of the formulated creed? Only one standard remained to man, a standard suggested by nature and proved in the life of every species. If man possesses a moral sense, a faculty of morals, as much as faculties of perception, memory, cogitation, then it could be argued that the morality inherited from the feudal epochs had been found wanting, while a utilitarian standard of virtue would thus seem the standard to which a disciple of reason should cling. "Some have argued against the existence of a moral sense," wrote Jefferson, "saying that if nature had given us such a sense, impelling us to virtuous actions, and warning us against those that are vicious, then nature would have designated, by some particular earmarks, the two sets of actions which are, in themselves, the one virtuous and the other vicious. Whereas, we find, in fact, that the same actions are deemed virtuous in one country and vicious in another. The answer is, that nature has constituted utility to man, the standard and test of virtue." [49]

4. *The Ideal of Laissez Faire*

The utilitarian standard was in fact an ethical expression of the underlying ideal of laissez-faire. That ideal, indeed, was the underlying source of republican freedom and American individualism, and presupposed that every man is the best judge of his own business. The most solid axiom of the science of politics, argued Thomas Cooper, is *pas trop gouverner*—do not govern too much; and he summed up the ideal of laissez-faire by paraphrasing Franklin: "Perhaps in general, it would be better if government meddled no further with trade than to protect it, and let it take its course. Most of the statutes or acts, edicts, arrets, and placards, of parliaments, princes, and states, for regulating, directing, or restraining trade, have we think, been political blunders, or jobs obtained by artful men, for private advantage, under pretence of public good. When Colbert assembled some wise old merchants of France, and desired their advice and opinion how he could preserve commerce; their answer, after consultation, was in three words only, *'laissez-nous faire.'*
. . . Agriculture, manufactures, and commerce, should therefore be left unfettered to the pursuit of individuals; whose pursuits will always be guided by their interest: and when they are so, they are coincident with the common interest: for a wealthy community is an aggregate of wealthy individuals who compose it; each of whom can better judge for himself, than another can for him." [50]

Jefferson realized that the ideal of laissez faire, if it could once be realized, would establish the conditions of progress. International conflicts would then be reconciled and the different nations would exchange mutual surpluses for mutual wants. "Instead of embarrassing commerce under piles of regulating laws, duties and prohibitions, could it be relieved from all its shackles in all parts of the world, could every country be employed in producing that which nature best fitted it to produce, and each be free to exchange with others mutual surpluses for mutual wants, the greatest possible would then be produced of those things which contribute to human life and human happiness; the numbers of mankind would be increased, and their condition bettered. . . . But should any nation, contrary to our wishes, suppose it may better find its advantage by continuing its system of prohibitions, duties, and regulations, it behooves us to protect our citizens, their commerce and navigation, by counter prohibitions, duties and regulations also. Free commerce and navigation are not to be given in exchange for restrictions or devestations; nor are they likely to produce a relaxation of them." [51]

From the time of Grotius onward, there had been continuous discussions of international justice and peace, but they had been found wanting under the system of mercantilism and monarchy which had set nations at each other's throats. When the new world of the enlightenment dawned, therefore, it was maintained that, with mercantilism and monarchy destroyed, a new era of universal peace and abundance would be ushered in. Jefferson referred, for example, to the Machiavellian policy that obtained between the states before the triumph of republicanism and the ideal of laissez faire. The principles of monarchy and monopoly, which mutually sustained one another, he wrote, "were legitimate principles in the dark ages which intervened between ancient and modern civilization but exploded and were held in just horror in the eighteenth century." A system of international law, which would promote international commerce, was to supplant the barbarities and injustices of mercantilism and monopoly. The law of nations, as the eighteenth century called international law, was to be an expression of fundamental covenants which were to bind all nations. It was to be derived, as Jefferson noted, from the moral law of nature, the usages of nations, and their special conventions. The law of nations had thus become equivalent to the honoring of compacts and the recognition of fundamental rights. But there were, wrote Jefferson, situations which excuse the nonperformance of contracts between man and man, just as there are also between nation and nation. Therefore, "if performance becomes self-destructive to the party, the law of self-preservation overrules the laws of obligations to others."

The ideal of laissez faire, with its obligations under the law of nations, did not therefore presuppose the destruction of the utilitarian standard. For the law of nations was to operate for the mutual advantage of nations, not for their mutual destruction. As the war of each against all had proved unworthy of civilized nations, so the extension of the social covenant to include all nations—forming a league of nations engrossed in commercial intercourse—would prove a triumph of moral science: "We make great improvements in nature," wrote Franklin; "there is one I wish to see in moral philosophy; the discovery of a plan, that would induce and oblige nations to settle their disputes without first cutting one another's throats." The project of a league of nations, of a United States of Europe, thus formed in Franklin's mind, once the example of the American states federating together was before him. Like other republican thinkers, Franklin was looking forward to harmonious international relations, the development of a law of nations, once the ideal of laissez faire had been allowed to accomplish its miracles. The interests of commerce in peace had already been established, and the interests of agriculture in stable markets had already been circumscribed, and republican thinkers were looking forward to days of peaceful international relations, so that war would not waste the fruits of labor, and peace would not be encumbered by the artificial regulations of an unnatural despotism.

5. The Free Trade in Ideas

The ideal of laissez faire had as its parallel in the intellectual world a free trade in ideas. The faith of the enlightenment—that given free opportunity to circulate, truth would carry its own evidence, and error be eliminated in the competition—was an expression of the underlying ideal of laissez faire, the ideal of free trade in ideas. The notion of a free trade in ideas was opposed, accordingly, to the system of mercantile monopoly over opinion, which implied also that no hierarchy, clerical or political, had a monopoly on the truth. With the shattering of the monopoly of opinion, and the establishment of the conditions for the free flow of knowledge, it was implied, further, that truth was a function of the market of ideas, that it had a utilitarian standard, a pragmatic sanction, an instrumental value, and that therefore it could be realized only in exchange. The young republicans were not writing propaganda, therefore, when they claimed that the condition of their existence as a class presupposed the free communication and exchange of ideas, while that of the feudal aristocracy presupposed an artificial monopoly on the truth.

The theory of republicanism demanded, and the system of private property enjoined, that to each citizen must be left the management of his own opinions and the freedom to express his wayward thoughts. It followed from the fact that the state was erected to protect each of the several citizens in the enjoyment of their lives, their liberties, and their estates, that they were to be left free also to enjoy their several opinions. Truth, however, could only be realized in exchange, as the result of the competition of each against all; and hence a free trade in ideas presupposed a market place of opinion, where truth might be the result, not of an original opinion, but of the competitive struggle of ideas. From this line of reasoning followed that truth was public, and that all the channels of communication and exchange must be left open if truth was to be determined. The young republic was to be dedicated to this new method of determining truth, and must henceforth preserve, not only the right of every man to the private property of his own opinion, but also the public means by which ideas could be exchanged and the truth determined. It was a fair claim of the natural aristocracy, and not mere propaganda, that the conditions under which republicanism could flourish were also the conditions under which mankind could be universally enlightened.

As the old governments had been founded on the suppression of opinion, the new governments would be founded on the liberation and the enlightenment of the mind. Because a republican form of government rested not on the will of the monarch but on the will of the people, it was necessary that the mind was to be unshackled and the opinion left free. Moreover, the progress of republicanism, and the continuous check upon representation for which the constitution provided, presupposed freedom of criticism, freedom to compare a principle embodied in law with a departure from it in practice. Inquiries into the science of government, to keep progress with the general advancement of mankind, required that government itself should not be left in a position to suppress a knowledge of its own errors. To the tenure of kings and magistrates succeeded the rights and liberties of the people; to monarchy and monopoly of opinion succeed the republic with its freedom of the mind. A free trade in ideas was therefore the necessary condition for the perpetuation of republican government and for the liberation of the mind of mankind.

The idea of religious freedom, or freedom of conscience, belongs with the doctrine of private right to the ideal of a free trade in ideas. The republican argument for freedom of conscience, for freedom of the soul, was simply that it belonged, like the estate of its possessor, to the sovereignty of the self, and that this sovereignty, being an inalienable right, could not be infringed. "The care of every man's soul belongs to himself," wrote Jefferson. "But what if he neglects the care of it: Well what if he neglect the care of his health or estate, which more nearly relate to the state? Will the magistrate make a law that he shall not be poor or sick? Laws provide against injury from others; but not from ourselves. God himself will not save men against their wills." [52] The will was private, sovereign, and inalienable, so that its conscience and opinions must also remain free, lest the fundamental presupposition of freedom of will, and hence of a capacity for self-government, should similarly be abridged. "If there be a government which prides itself on maintaining the inviolability of property," wrote Madison, "which provides that none shall be taken *directly* even for public use without indemnification to the owner, and yet *directly* violates the property which individuals have in their opinions, their religion, their persons, and their faculties; may more, which *indirectly* violates their property, in their actual possessions, in the labor that acquires their daily subsistence, and in the hallowed remnant of time which ought to relieve their fatigues and soothe their cares, the inference will have been anticipated, that such a government is not a pattern for the United States." [53]

6. *The Republic of Letters*

To the republic of government succeeded the republic of letters as its penman and servitor, the guardian of its values, the pressman of its thoughts. The republic of letters was now to phrase its tongue and mold its lips in silver-voiced oratory or the balanced prose of the eighteenth-century gentlemen of the middle class. To be called to this high office, to be a spokesman of the young republic, to belong to its republic of letters, required only a fit occasion and a ready pen. Born of the fruit of its first battle, Paine's formulation of the new goal of writing, of the new style of letters, was brittle and charged: "Universal empire is the prerogative of a writer," he wrote. "His concerns are with all mankind, and though he cannot command their obedience, he can assign them their duty. The Republic of Letters is more ancient than monarchy, and of far higher character in the world than the vassal court of Britain; he that rebels against reason is a real rebel, but he that in defence of reason rebels against tyranny has a better title to 'Defender of the Faith,' than George the Third."

To the monarchy of literature, with its prescriptions of style, succeeded the republic of letters, with its constitutional principles of taste. It was a succession, not of hereditary right, but of a talent for letters conferred upon the revolutionary writers by the moment whose cause they had taken up. It was believed that the republic of letters, by offering every author a worthy cause upon which to test his talents, would result in the best literary productions, and call into question the system of literary favoritism by which placemen and pensioners had been the laureates of the monarchical cause. "As the republic of letters brings forward the best literary productions," wrote Paine, "by giving to genius a fair and universal chance; so the representative system of government is calculated to produce the wisest laws, by collecting wisdom where it can be found. I smile to myself when I contemplate the ridiculous insignificance into which literature and all the sciences would sink, were they made hereditary; and I carry the same idea into governments. An hereditary governor is as inconsistent as an hereditary author." [54]

The preservation of virtue and the dispelling of vice was now to be left in large measure to the periodical press. The republic of letters must keep up its daily chant, lest the people be overcome with the importation of European vice. As the public press was the means of influencing the manners and morals of the people, and as these were manifestations either of republican or of aristocratic tastes, the republic of letters must set the style and reform the manners of its citizens. The aesthetic of the periodic movement was to be set by its needs; the press was to reform its opinions and modify its style with every mood of republican government; and by soliciting the approval of public opinion, help to set the standard of republican morals. The enlightenment had thus opened the prospect of universal progress to the republic of letters, and to it fell the task of public information, by which the wheels of the republican mechanism in government were to be kept oiled and the fundamental principles of its structure made known. It seemed a happy era that had opened up the promise of public reformation through a public press, and of universal progress through a republic of letters.

BOOK III

THE ROMANTIC MIND

"For the New World, indeed, after two grand stages of prepara-
tion-strata, I perceive that now a third stage, being ready for (and
without which the other two were useless), with unmistakable signs
appears. The First stage was the planning and putting on record
the political foundation rights of immense masses of people—indeed all people—in the organization of republican National, State,
and municipal governments, all constructed with reference to each,
and each to all. This is the American programme, not for classes,
but for universal man, and is embodied in the compacts of the
Declaration of Independence, and, as it began and has now grown,
with its amendments, the Federal Constitution—and in the state
governments, with all their interiors, and with general suffrage;
those having the sense not only of what is in themselves, but that
their certain several things started, planted, hundreds of others in
the same direction duly arise and follow. The Second stage relates
to material prosperity, wealth, produce, labor-saving machines, iron,
cotton, local, State and continental railways, intercommunication
and trade with all lands, steamships, mining, general employment,
organization of great cities, cheap appliances for comfort, number-
less technical schools, books, newspapers, a currency for money circulation, &c. The Third stage, rising out of the previous ones, to
make them and all illustrious, I, now, for one, promulge, announcing a native expression-spirit, getting into form, adult, and through
mentality, for these States, self-contain'd, different from others,
more expansive, more rich and free, to be evidenced by original
authors and poets to come, by American personalities, plenty of
them, male and female, traversing the States, none expected—and
by native superber tableaux and growths of language, songs, operas,
orations, lectures, architecture—and by a sublime and serious Religious Democracy sternly taking command, dissolving the old,
sloughing off surfaces, and from its own interior and vital principles, reconstructing, democratizing society."

Walt Whitman

CHAPTER THIRTEEN

THE TRANSCENDENTAL TEMPER

1. *The Romantic Protest*

The realm of letters had now to become a province of protest, for a previous age of reason had quite neglected the growth of the under- standing. The province of letters had now seized upon the ungainly transcendental purpose, and sought to communicate, while it harmon- ized, the divergent lisps of former ages, when in the fever of its doubt or in the high conquests of its imagination, it had whispered familiar notions or told unfamiliar truths. The age demanded, as the romantic philosophers noted, an enlightened and earnest ministry, some pastors for the new poetry, some dramatists for the new drama, and some priests to preside over the secular pulpits. It demanded of the province of let- ters that it learn from experience what formerly might have been in- ferred from fact; and that it learn, not in the uncouth and unmanly way of empiricism, but in the new way of primary experience and in- tuitive insight. Civilization and refinement, the cultivation of polite let- ters, were now thought to be not inconsistent with sensibility; and it was believed that the intellect might grow without overshadowing or ex- hausting the heart. A previous age, which had dubbed itself the age of reason, might have found the measure of things in the things them- selves, and might have accounted the values of things by the standard of a divine geometry; but the romantic age was determined to seek for its measure not without but within the soul of man, and gain by tran- scendence and intuition what a previous age of reason had neglected by way of empiricism and doubt. Individualism had thus acquired a new metaphysic, and became the representative divinity of itself; for the romantic mind became aware of its intuitive powers, while tran- scendentalism embodied the new consciousness, the new apprehension of fact.

The new consciousness was inspired in part by Coleridge's *Aids to Reflection,* which provided the transcendentalists with a critical semantic of the forms of experience; and it was borrowed imperceptibly from the romantic German philosophy, known to the transcendentalists through second-hand sources like Coleridge and Carlyle. Coleridge had discovered, meantime, that the scholastic distinction between the subjective and the objective might be useful in a critique of self-consciousness; it enabled him to distinguish *percipere* from *percipi,* and it drew a sharp line of distinction between the objects of consciousness which the self might appropriate and the form of that consciousness which belonged inalienably to the individual. The individual henceforth was declared to contain the whole range of experience in his forms of intuition, and in experience itself to participate in the private symbolism of the world. Coleridge borrowed from Schelling the new law of critical self-consciousness: "On the immediate which dwells in every man, and on the original intuition or absolute affirmation of it . . . all the certainty of our knowledge depends." Life had thus reduced itself to the province of the mind; and the transcendentalists, in their appropriation of that province, had concluded that life consists in what a man is thinking all day. That life gives birth to thought, that it culminates in thought, could hardly be doubted by the thinking man; but this private perspective, to which the world was not reduced, would prove for a Hawthorne or a Poe a burden and imprisonment of the soul. Nothing at long last was sacred but the integrity of the private mind; nothing at long last was worthy but the private and inalienable perspective of the individual. Possessing himself in his critical self-consciousness, then, Poe could with his newly found integrity declare: "My whole nature revolts at the idea there is any being in the universe superior to myself." But this newly found integrity was at long last only a romantic version of the republican doctrine of sovereignty over oneself, translated by the transcendental temper into the newly found method of critical self-consciousness.

2. *The Transcendental Method*

Some small pledge of eloquence, extracted under duress, might remain to the transcendentalist in his newly found self-consciousness. The tongue ought to express, it was said, the coincidence of the word and the thing. The transcendentalist rhetoric rested at last on the transcendentalist theory of knowledge; and that, largely taken from Coleridge, who had in turn largely taken it from Schelling, might be expressed in Coleridge's remark that: "For as philosophy is neither a science of the reason or understanding only, nor merely a science of morals, but the science of Being altogether, its primary ground can be neither merely speculative, nor merely practical, but both in one. All knowledge rests on the coincidence of an object with a subject." And Emerson wrote in "The Over-Soul": "The act of seeing and the thing seen, the seer and the spectacle, the subject and the object are one." These thoughts led the transcendentalists along the path of word origins to the realization that words in their primary signification were images and pictures of things. "Language is fossil poetry," said Emerson; for the program of reformation in literature must be to retrieve this poetry from the dross of ancient forms, to fasten words upon things. Truth henceforth must be expressed both to the senses and to the intellect, and the energy of the primitive metaphor must be repossessed. The folk image, long since faded into diction, or buried in song, must be sought again, and joined with newly coined words whose roots were deep in experience.

The language of the street, always vascular and alive, must not be contemned as vulgar. Alcott, amongst his Orphic sayings, hit off the same notion of retrieving the animal spirit which language embodied, which now frolics and prances only in the streets, in the main course of common experience. But to this desire for the energetic metaphor of the street was added the transcendental need to discover the sublime in the commonplace, the spirit behind the face of the material fact. "Nature is a symbol of the Spirit." The material image, when it is the luminous vestment of the thought, makes of brilliant writing a perpetual discourse; for the infinite, by the transcendental technique, may be apprehended in the moment of experience. Extraordinary perception, as in the poet, might render nature articulate to the eye; and make of her linked analogies a prodigal train of metaphors to body forth the thought. This was the method of Emerson in his philosophic tenses; and of Melville in his mystical gloom; it was the method common to Thoreau and to Parmenides, who might believe alike the ancient law of knowledge that: "Thought and the object of thought are but one." But with Emerson this program is vitiated by a sea-shell consciousness, in which everything is only an echo of some secret far-off sound; and his writing betrays this spiral void of the sea-shell, the reverberating intuition of a distant sound. It is faded and far off, because he liked the gnomic verse, the rule of life conveyed in an image, a philosophy summed up in a metaphor. Unhappily for the movement of transcendentalism, Emerson, its chief philosopher, was only a suburban reporter of life's main images. He had become, as he said, a transparent eyeball; but the currents of universal being did not circulate through him, nor was he a part nor a parcel of God.

He might have achieved his goal had he not taken such a godlike attitude toward experience. Not content to let each finite moment speak for itself, as Thoreau was content to do, he fastened to it the infinite truth that it expressed. The age, he said, is Swedenborg's, because it accepted the philosophy that "the soul makes its own world." Nature was to Emerson the metaphor of the divine mind; always the effect, but never the cause, of the flow of experience. His mind lay receptive, open and passive to the superincumbent spirit; his rhetoric, in consequence, was proverbial, and its tone was sacred. He was a transcendental priest caught in nervous Yankee oscillation between action and pause, living only rhythmically like the New England seasons, until a drought or a harvest descended upon his mind. "Hear what the morning says, and believe that." Constantly inundated by a new revelation, he could not compose it, could not harmonize it with his prevailing sentiments, and so lost it without an embodiment of form. "I am always insincere, always knowing there are other moods." Each thought was sentenced to solitary confinement; his paragraphs, as he said, were only "infinitely repellent particles." But in society the same repellent individualism unseated the composing muse, made of each a particle, and of none a whole. "Every man is an infinitely repellent orb, and holds his individual being on that condition." His method was revealed in his declaration that "all thinking is analogizing, and it is the use of life to learn metonymy." His thought was thus sentenced to dwell alone, unmoved even by an intense moment of literature, failing even as a sanctuary of his own intuitions.

But Emerson's method and style embody, nevertheless, the main lesson of the transcendental movement. The identity of the man and his work, at which it aimed, and the duality of the man and his thought, which it achieved, are the two poles between which literature always oscillates. Heady with the new wine of critical self-consciousness, the transcendental rhetoric attempted to identify the word with the thing; but it only issued in a brood of aphorisms, the narcotic of the moment, not the real sustenance of life. Emerson's sentences were delinquents; standing out from the convention of rhetoric, they composed their own world. His doctrine was flux, the intuition flowing with the moment; but his rhetoric was simply a transcendental reporting, not the truth of some nether world. Henceforth, as Emerson said at the outset of his career, he would utter his own thought, and dwell alone with his private truth. When rhetoric had thus become an expression of the private self, it could only be the history of private intuition; and as such, it was a reflection of the old maxim that the style is the man. But once the self-portrait of Saadi was finished, and the world dissolved in the transcendental mist, the truth left to the inquiring spirit was only the form in which, to all ages and in all climes, the harmonies of rhetoric have been cognized. Listening alone to his private intuition, then, the transcendentalist was committed to sacred literature; for he had become in his own eyes sacred, and what henceforth passed through his consciousness was to be expressed in a form appropriately his.

3. *The Intuition of Form*

When, at Walden Pond, Thoreau summed up the long brooding winter in the form of summer gladness and found each fact a release of metaphysical tension, he erred perhaps on the side of the naturalist but gained even more on the side of art. The poet and the botanist, he said, look differently at the same object; for the poet sees the seminal principle expressed in the objective fact, while the botanist can only categorize over the hearth of nature. "See not with the eye of science, which is barren, nor of youthful poetry, which is impotent. But taste the world and digest it." Nature was of interest to the transcendentalist only as it lay in the experience of a human being; her utility was to draw out and to reflect the capacities of the private man. Hidden thus away at Walden, Thoreau was a living refutation of the theories of socialism, a petty agrarian craftsman seeking again the seed of integrity which the ancient unity of the craft possessed before its rupture with industrialism. He was a borrower of ideas, quite unoriginal in his philosophy, but strangely perceptive, like a child browsing imaginatively on a forest adventure. Every leaf that stirred or tree that bowed sang the song of protest that was in his heart. The worker has time, he said, to possess only the crippled integrity of the machine; but to Thoreau at Walden the expected unexpectedness which belongs to every new work of nature and every sincere work of art reflected the long lost integrity of the craft crushed forever by the demonic machine.

These perceptions of the root of the romantic protest were of use to him in the cognizance of his art. The word, he said, is to be measured by the thing; natural phenomena are original symbols to express our thoughts and feelings. Nature stands to us in bifurcation from our own private self; we are cut off from the object of our subjective contemplation. "For an impenetrable shield, stand inside yourself." To repossess this lost and transfigured object, the self, now critically conscious of its loss, must hasten to let nature suggest the lisping notes of the inner man. Intuitions crowd in upon the self, suggested by nature, but responsive at last to the innate principles of art within. In writing, accordingly, Thoreau followed an impeccable standard: "The theme is nothing, the life is everything. All the interests of the reader lies in the depth and intensity of the life excited." Words which suggest more than they say, and perhaps say more than they suggest, were the transcendental tools; they had an atmosphere about them which only a sympathetic consciousness could excite from their mortality. The material world was thus for Thoreau, as for Emerson and Melville, only a symbol of the spiritual and more real. Perhaps at Walden Pond a momentary completeness, discovered behind the veil of phenomena, might rejoin in some esoteric juncture, the experience of the object and the subject whose unity and integrity had thus been irretrievably lost.

The intuition of form was thus the closest approach to art of which the transcendentalist was capable. It presupposes the Kantian distinction of knowledge; it suffers the artist to provide what form organic unity, the unified sensibility of artistic integrity, might require. But it is no less exacting than the organic principle in architecture, or the functional form of a full-blown phrase that sits insidiously in a paragraph defying all attempts to extract it. The sense of process, of evolvement, the transcendentalist insisted, is the basis of every intuition of form. It follows, therefore, that the forms will be fluid, will flow into one another, reincarnate one another, as the thought advances. This quality is attested by Thoreau's *Walden,* whose rhythmical movements return again and again, like the New England seasons, to the apprehension of the simple generative facts from which they start out. Art, then, is regeneration; it is the universal remedy for the universal ill, for the separation of object and subject, and for the loss of integrity. It returns to the artist the object appropriated, and privately possessed, in the symbol; it opens to him the vast panorama of all in nature to which he is secretly sympathetic and responsive, and in whose expansive themes he alone can feel at home.

The New England landscape, caught in its aboriginal settings, as at Walden Pond, overwhelmed the simply righteous man; only the artist, himself a precursor of its symbols, could seek in his intuitions the private landscapes of the imagination which the aboriginal landscapes might suggest. *Walden* stands quite by itself as the embodiment of this transcendentalist intuition of form. It is a poem of the seasons, a cyclical myth, a generous tutelage by an aboriginal landscape. But a goblin spectator is seated there in winter, musing on the lost scenes of summer, while the artist stands remote from himself, dramatically ensnared by the plot of the changing sky. Nature, unconscious in her art, becomes conscious in the artist man; her vital form, as Emerson said, "is only discovered and executed by the artist, not arbitrarily imposed on him." This artistic dictum makes the private intuition as important as the public revelation. The transcendentalist, accordingly, was content to bathe in these waters, to glide happily in the stream, so that intuition might rise to the surface with her constant breed of form.

4. The Gothic Image

The images that freight themselves upon the Goth, that surge in and out of consciousness, like the perpetual discourse of good and evil, could only publish their heroic and romantic character. One of the characters of Hawthorne's imagination was overheard to say: "Everything, you know, has its spiritual meaning, which to the literal meaning is what the soul is to the body." This may be taken as the key to the treatment of the symbol, especially in Hawthorne and Melville, which marks them off from the contemporary Emerson, Thoreau, or Whitman. The symbol expresses, not only a mysterious connection between two ideas, but even the mystic allegory of the facts; and it is the allegory, giving visible form to such a conception, that a history of redemption, a biography of morals, must inevitably represent. It was thus with Hawthorne and Melville that mysticism is given a quite material embodiment; that even realism is called upon to do service in the legions of romance. Heroes are born, not of men, but of the gods; and the artist, in his conception of his art, must remain loyal to the heritage of his birth. So it is in spiritual growth that the finite thought struggles to embrace the infinite; and in which the spirit, though dwelling "in an old moss-covered mansion," surges forward to a new faith in life.

Such a pilgrim's progress might be called a process of regeneration, if ancient Puritan words were needed; but Hawthorne, a darkling child of the romantic past, can only bring this process to fruition by calling upon the symbol, well known to New Englanders, which embodied and embraced it. Hawthorne is accordingly the master of the Gothic image, of that perpetual and mystic discourse with which the barbaric past exorcises its evil spirits; its employment as art, he noted, demands that the man of the day be idealized to himself. "I am half-convinced," he wrote, "that the reflection is indeed the reality—the real thing which Nature imperfectly images to our grosser sense." What the artist desires, like his transcendental contemporaries, is to disengage the real from the ideal, the actuality from the appearance. In this difficulty and exhausting artistic chore, only the image of the Goth will avail; only the mystical allegory of the facts, giving visible form to the conception which the symbol represents, will shadow forth the reality which lurks behind appearance. Amidst the Greek revival art, then filling the tempestuous young republic with its monstrous representations of pagan naturalism, Hawthorne alone could remark: "I am partly sensible that some unwritten rules of taste are making their way into my mind; that all this

Greek beauty has done something towards refining me, though I am still, however, a very sturdy Goth." Visiting then a medieval cathedral, the landmark of the Goth, he noted: "The cathedral showed me how earthly I was, but yet whispered deeply of immortality."

The Gothic image, appropriately considered, might also clear the question of Hawthorne's politics, that vexed question which has all the democratic and republican minds astir in behalf of the great artist. The truth is that Hawthorne expressed the heroic importance of the moment only by negating the moment in the light of Gothic truth. The philanthropist and abolitionist, directly affirming the prospect of individual reform, in ignorance of the silent working of more powerful cosmic forces, could never understand Hawthorne's seemingly pessimistic remark that "there is no instance, in all history, of the human will and intellect having perfected any great moral reform by methods which it adapted to that end." That truth is more clearly a consequence of the transcendental philosophy and the transcendental method than Emerson's more optimistic predictions or Thoreau's more dramatic civil disobedience. But a more consistent Puritan than Emerson, and a more thorough nature-mystic than Thoreau, might well understand the paradox of a democratic bureaucrat loyally attached to conservative, or at least cautious, principles. The Puritan of the seventeenth century would understand, and would no doubt applaud, Hawthorne's statement that "no human effort, on a grand scale, has ever yet resulted according to the purpose of the projectors. The advantages are always incidental. Man's accidents are God's purposes. We miss the good we sought, and do the good we little cared for." Such were the consequences of the Gothic images brought to bear on the strangely material facts of politics. That man's freedom is God's necessity, the Puritan would have understood, and understanding, would have applauded; that the present moment is but a ghostly existence compared with the mighty reality of an infinite time, the Goth would have sympathetically embraced. A mendicant, begging for time, for the passage of the several acts of the history of redemption, might well have understood that Hawthorne meditated upon "this visionary and impalpable Now, which, if you look closely at it, is nothing." With such meditations, the Gothic image became a fit symbol for life.

5. The Mantle of Tragedy

The mantle of tragedy had fallen like Maule's curse upon all the descendents of that infinitely aspiring line. From Emerson's optimistic faith in the infinitude of the private man, from the self-trust of Thoreau, it was only a step to the confident egoism of Margaret Fuller's affirmation that man is not made for society, but society is made for man. But upon this ebullient optimism, born of cosmic glorification of the individual, there fell at last the mantle of tragedy, the remembrance of sin, and the old vision of evil. For Emerson and the transcendental optimists had simply brushed these problems aside, so glorious the affirmation of goodness, that its evil necessity was hardly perceived. The absence of tragedy in the transcendental optimists was not their ignorance of the false perspectives that experience brings, but rather their intuition of the nobleness and integrity of things when surveyed in the unified sensibility of an artistic perspective. The transcendentalists had not fully perceived, in fact, that the period of capital expansion might not prove an unblessed good. The transcendental optimism had become a bigotry; the transcendental faith in the cosmic consciousness had become an American fatalism.

But this is also the note of self-consciousness, the testimony of enlightenment, of the awakening of a Gothic sensibility of the past. A certain maturity, or at least of critical self-consciousness, is required before a writer comes to the mature circle of working up the materials of his nation's past into the form required precisely by the moment through which he flows. This was the starting point, not only of that tragic brigantine, Melville, but also of the conviction of Hawthorne that the only way to endure for posterity is to live truly for your own age. A philosophy, therefore, in proportion as it detracts from the heroic ripeness of the moment, might also be said to have deceived mankind in the past. The linkages of time, fused in the work of art, were of the moment while being also inevitably of the past. Hawthorne, no less than Emerson and Thoreau, desired to live throughout the whole range of his faculties and sensibilities. The result was a renascence of the spirit, called to critical self-consciousness by the Gothic sense of heroism and romance. And if, amidst life's minor tragedies, one more tragedy reminiscent of a long-past heritage is thrown for the moment upon the universal stage, it would not be in the sense of salvation that this great act is accomplished, but in the sense of sin. It is sinfulness, intellectually comprehended, that in Hawthorne becomes sensible tragedy; but it is tragedy only because growth demands the conquering of all the dragging habits, the spiteful visage, of the declining self of the past. Hawthorne was truly a critic of the Puritan tradition, but a critic who understood it in a classic way; who had become familiar with its universal symbols, and who read in them some momentary lesson that the heroic soul might cling to in its romantic progress. Behind the ancient Puritan symbols, then, Hawthorne perceived the living truth, even for his own transcendental time. The thin white line of continuity might seem to break, the symbols to dissolve, but the artist perceived in national growth and in individual progress something which from the Puritans, "strong traits of their nature have interwined themselves with mine."

Let us then, the transcendental tragedians seem to be saying, let us open up intercourse with the world; we can at last drink down and digest the cosmopolitan world of culture, since now we have become critically self-conscious of ourselves. The artist, accordingly, must above all else possess, not delicate sensibility, but robust force, not the luster-less empty eye, but the roving ball magically surveying all things. It was a renascence of the spirit, in which the artist, for the sake of his art, kept heroically to himself; thought, when it ushered itself in, must have the stamp and introduction of its own character, must be a part and a parcel of the man. The problem of the transcendental tragedian, then, like that of the transcendental optimist, had resolved itself into the familiar tragedy of the isolated individual, or the subject forcibly torn apart from the object, in whose unphilosophical brain the unfamiliar cleavage can be bridged only by the artistic imagination. The mind was haunted, and that which haunted it was the fear of some self-alienation; it was the fear that the self might not possess its own properties, come to its completion, ripen and mature. What haunted the artist, the ghostly creatures of whose imagination aspire to material embodiment, was that, even amidst realistic detail, the work might lose the character of revelation. Hawthorne could not but live with the tragic knowledge that "the grosser life is a dream, and the spiritual life is a reality." What dreams might come then, once loose of this material garment, only the artist, secretly holding faith with himself, might symbolize to the inarticulate public, whose dreams and whose destinies he shared.

6. *The Moment of Transition*

It was for Melville and Whitman a time of transition; and for each, characteristically renouncing the past, a call for a new vision and at-titude, the unsinging of the man long silent; and a new reach, a stretch of the imagination, for a fresh and original relation to the universe. For Melville particularly it was a time of brooding renascence, of powers maturing which should soon fail; it was a moment when all the powers would be stretched to full circle, when maturing faculties would be bled of their originality, and when the warrant of life, which would soon be used up, could be renewed vitally only by the touch of creativity. For Emerson, too, it was a moment of transition, the significance of which in this brooding renascence of the intellect he fully comprehended:

"In history, the great moment is when the savage is just ceasing to be savage . . . that moment of transition,—The foam hangs but a moment on the wave; the sun himself does not pause on the meridian; literature becomes criticism, nervousness, and a gnawing when the first musical triumphant strain has waked the echoes."

Such a brooding giant, but newly awakened by the romantic echoes, was Melville. Ripening into vigor and unshackled by scepticism from a public creed, he retreated again into the vicarious anonymity of disbelief. No custom seemed strange to him then, no creed absurd; for the mind, once liberated, flies in circles above the dead corpse it has left behind, wondering and brooding, that a man might have slept so long beneath their cumbrous weight. This renascence of the liberated mind was at the same time the introduction to a tragedy, a revival of depth to the psychology of the literary artist. The material of life, wrapped up in the shroud of romance, contributed a strange and evanescent realism to the passage of time. So Melville, possessing every literary advantage of the romantic idealist, might equally stand with Hawthorne as a realist; but the realism of Melville is the realism of tragedy, which through its symbols presages the death of every finite thought and the coming into birth of each infinite one. Melville was conscious that the demonic mystery of the White Whale lay behind a sea of phenomena. His indeed was the kind of consciousness to which each new fact in nature's lexicon was a symbol of the vast reservoir of fact with which nature both embodies and betrays our ideals.

For Whitman, however, this same moment of transition was an occasion for unleashing the primitive impulse to sing of oneself. Whitman's language betrays the same experiment in self-singing; for a primitive joy in words, in naming things, seemed at once to embody and to reveal some ancient truth. But this self-singing is a particular necessity for one to whom truth lay hidden in things, which, being named, spring to life. "All truths lie waiting in all things.—They neither urge the opening of themselves nor resist it. For their birth you need not the obstetric forceps of the surgeon. They unfold to you and emit themselves more fragrant than roses from living buds, whenever you fetch the spring sunshine moistened with summer rain.—But it must be in yourself. It shall come from your soul. It shall be love." This is the primitive speaking to the primitive, expressing the loss of tribal solidarity, the vast gulf and separation of all things, which, on the philosophic plane, is nothing less than the subject astir and seeking the primitive object from which it has been severed. But things might be reunited and the cleavages healed at least in idea; and in full consciousness of this possibility, Whitman issued and openly proclaimed that "only Hegel is fit for America," for in his work, "the human soul stands at the centre, and all the universes minister to it."

Thus Whitman, by using a higher plane of contemplation, or rather by descending to more primitive levels of experience, absorbed and revitalized all the meanings of which the arguments of the earth were but the abstract conceptions. Man, standing thus once more in the open air, bereft of the sophistication of abstract idea, might then enjoy a more primitive and original relation to the universe. That seemed to the transcendentalists equally their goal as Whitman's; but Whitman, if not a real, was at least a sincere primitivist, while the philosophers of transcendentalism rose higher in the scale of abstraction in their search for the same original and primitively fresh relation to the world. Thoreau's statement gives the goal of transcendentalism: "The life of a wise man is most of all extemporaneous, for he lives out of an eternity which includes all time." To live outside space and time, to transcend them in idea if not in fact, was an open sesame to contemporaneity. This is the paradox which defines and marks out the American transcendentalist, whether poet or philosopher, from the European; and it is, moreover, an intellectual picture of the lean, tough Yankee, the rugged individual, climbing over all material obstacles in his quest of wealth. But for the transcendentalist, for the primitive, for the tragic Puritan, whether in Emerson, Thoreau, Melville, or Whitman, the whole soul was brought once more into activity. The significance of the cultural renascence lies in the fact that each of the artists of the period found his own moment of transition, by which, if not literally at least in imagination, he bridged the chasm of subject and object, and penetrated in intuition behind the screen of phenomena to the demonic agency which controlled the destiny of all things.

CHAPTER FOURTEEN

THE REALM OF NATURE

1. *The Transcendental Philosophy*

The new age was born to a new task, dedicated to a new purpose; for transcendentalism proposed no less than a revolt from the reason for the sake of understanding. The transcendental philosophy looked into physics, politics, ethics, religion, and found them to rest not on the naked fragmented facts of empiricism, but upon the facts of intuition, upon the facts derived from the speculative understanding. To reform the state, and bring society once more to a consciousness of its destiny, a new perception of fact was required among its philosophers, a new science of transcendental depth among its heroes and its young Americans. The world in its wholeness, in its organic growth and development, now appeared as the scene of individual perfection, where young heroes might grow into statured gods, and old gods regain once again the capacities of youth. Transcendentalism proposed to reform religion, ethics, politics, society, education, and morals, and amidst these great reformations, to proclaim to the world the worth and the dignity of the individual man. "The problem of the transcendental philosophy," wrote Theodore Parker, "is no less than this, to revise the experience of mankind and try its teachings by the nature of mankind; to test ethics by conscience, science by reason; to try the creeds of the churches, the constitutions of the states by the constitution of the universe; to reverse what is wrong, supply what is wanting, and command the just." [55]

The transcendental philosophy was a philosophy of emergence, and sought the novelty which should mark a stage of growth in the individual, or the reformation which should mark a stage of progress in society. Literature, politics, philosophy, and science were equally driven by the transcendental task; they were to look to the future, forget the sickly sensationalism, the agnostic positivism, and the grinding mecha-

nism of a previous age of reason, and carry the new transcendental standard in their hearts. The new philosophy proved to be more spiritual
than the rationalism and sensationalism which it displaced; it was a
philosophy of transcendental depth, which augured ill for the positivism,
empiricism, and mechanism of a previous age of reason. It was to be
founded, its disciples announced, upon a new and more generous conception of man. It was to seek its principles in the immanent spiritual
element in man, and find in the mysterious cycles of his growth the
secrets of the world. The funded meaning, the intellectual capital of
the world, was the material with which it proposed to start out, but in
a happy moment the work of Coleridge, of Cousin, and of Wordsworth
furnished a new perspective, and the classical German philosophy soon
added its confirmation that the philosophy of the Enlightenment was
doomed. The transcendental philosophy, wrote Parker, "is distinguished
by its chief metaphysical doctrine, that there is in the intellect (or consciousness), something that never was in the senses, to wit, the intellect
(or consciousness) itself; that man has faculties which transcend the
senses; faculties which give him ideas and intuitions that transcend
sensational experience; ideas whose origin is not from sensational experience; ideas whose origin is not from sensation, nor their proof
from sensation. This is the transcendental school." [56]

In the perspective of transcendental philosophy, all the singular
achievements of the age of reason stood condemned. Its fable of cause
and effect had led to the discovery of fact, and had nutured an empiricism; but the facts had fragmented themselves and lost their connection
with human history, only to lie barren and dull without the quality of
life. Positivism had given birth to agnosticism, and agnosticism to scepticism, and scepticism to atheism, until it seemed that the positivist could
not believe even in his own existence. The world machine of the age
of Newton seemed suddenly to have grown dark and cold, denying the
spiritual element in man, and the processes of germination and growth
at work in the world. From the age of reason had issued a sensationalism,
an empiricism, a positivism, and a mechanism, which the transcendental
philosophers proposed to destroy. The utilitarian standard of the age
of reason was to be replaced by the transcendental standard of the romantic age; and the natural aristocracy, which had hoped to make its reign
indefinite and the enlightenment of man universal, was to give way
before the transcendental aristocracy, which proposed to build a new
consciousness of human destiny in the mind and a new seed of divinity
in the heart. The morality of reason had proved a morality of expedi-
ence, and evil had been condemned for its mere lack of utility. The transcendental philosophers were to build a new morality, to return some

venerable and stable metaphysic, beside which the restless universe would seem an unfolding of long dreamed of forms. A new philosophy of transcendental depth was to replace the shallow metaphysics of the age of reason.

2. *The Critique of Mechanism*

In its critique of the mechanical presuppositions of Newtonian science, transcendental idealism unwittingly prepared the way for the development of an evolutionary philosophy. The qualities which Newton had banished from nature, the object, had now become the property of man, the subject. It therefore fell to the lot of the transcendental philosophers to develop the activity of the subject, of the mind, thereby producing an evolutionary philosophy of subjectivity. The same development took place in the classical German philosophy, and issued in the Hegelian dialectics. In America the romantic philosophers undertook a similar exploration of subjectivity and developed a philosophical dialectic. The way for transcendental idealism had already been prepared by the mechanical philosophy of the age of reason; for idealism found itself in the possession of all the unique qualitative wealth which Newtonian science had banished from nature. Nature was conceived as a world machine, while all its quality had been reduced to quantity, leaving quality the possession of the individual consciousness. Now as quality is uniqueness, the emergence of novelty, the transcendental philosophers were driven to develop in an evolutionary way the activity of the subjective consciousness. It remained only for a clique of transcendental nature mystics to attribute this conscious activity to the object, nature, thus giving birth to quality in the object as a parallel to the emerging quality in the subject. It followed that there was a spiritual element in man and a dialectic activity in nature which were but different manifestations of one underlying cosmic consciousness. Transcendentalism had thereby made nature a more congenial home for the soul, and had produced, as if by mutual reflexive movement, a common revolutionary activity both in nature and in man.

In the light of these developments, transcendental idealism opposed itself to mechanism, and called into question the scientific ideals of the age of reason. "The sensational philosophy has no idea of cause, except that of impirical connection in time and place," wrote Theodore Parker; "no idea of substance, only of body, or form of substance; no ontology, but phenomenology. It refers all questions—say of the planets about the sun—to an outward force; when they were made, God, standing outside, gave them a push and set them a-going; or else their motion is the result of a fortuitous concourse of atoms, a blind fate. Neither conclusion is a philosophical conclusion, each an hypothesis. Its physics are a mere materialism; hence it delights in the atomistic theory of nature and repels the dynamic theory of matter. The sensationalist's physics appear well in a celebrated book, 'The Vestiges of the Natural History of Creation.' The book has many valuable things in it, but the philosophy of its physics is an unavoidable result of sensationalism. There is nothing but materialism in his world. All is material, effects material, causes material, his God material—not surpassing the physical universe, but co-extensive therewith. In zoölogy life is the result or organization, but is an immanent life. In anthropology the mind is the result of organization, but is an immanent mind; in theology God is the result of organization, but is an immanent God. Life does not *transcend* organization, nor does mind, nor God. All is matter." [57]

The mechanical philosophy stood condemned also for its positivism. In reducing quality to quantity it had unavoidably erected a screen of phenomena behind which lurked the self-contained machinery of matter. Although the ideas of sensible experience were the source of all knowledge, it was shown that knowledge itself on this account could be no more than the flow of phenomena produced by some activity outside the mind. The ideas were associated in consciousness by the simple laws of attraction and repulsion, so that mechanism had entered by a common presupposition into subjectivity. Not only nature, but man, considered as an object, was a machine; and it was a common jest of the republican philosophers that man prefers his dinner and his girl before all other things. Mechanism had thus destroyed the conception of man inherited from less material ages, and issued in a simple utilitarian ethics in which good is the expedient and evil the unprofitable. Religion too had been reduced to a mechanical form, for in deism, although God created the world machine and imparted an initial packet of energy and motion to each of its particles, He was reduced to an abstract spectator who could not interfere with the immutable reign of law. God had thus been deleted from the universe, just as the spiritual element had been stolen from the conception of man. Positivism had therefore issued in a common scepticism, agnosticism, and doubt, which transcendental idealism, now on the verge of a romantic faith in the heroic character of divine average men, found repugnant to its ideals.

3. The Idea of Nature

The transcendental philosophy had revolted from reason for the sake of the understanding, and now it sought to return spirit to nature, so that she might seem a more congenial stimulus to the soul. The science of the day was to be dedicated to a new purpose and, by finding a new theory of nature, was to promote the truth that nature had become the residence of an immanent cosmic mind. Speculative poetry, which had seemed to a more reasonable age to be unsound and frivolous, found at last a secure home in the romantic mind, and was admired, not so much for the soundness of its discoveries, as for the proof that the mind of man could soar so high and recover in its flights the sense of perspective which the age of mechanism had destroyed. In the light of transcendental idealism, both nature and man had come to possess what the philosophers would call soul; for to nature the infinite oversoul was an adequate representation, while to man the soul was unleashed for its flight by virtue of its relation to the oversoul of which it was a part. But transcendentalism, in its more technical phases, separated the soul, or the spiritual element, from nature, which was conceived as the object set over against a common subjective consciousness, of which the soul of man as well as the spirit of nature was a part. "Philosophically considered," wrote Emerson, "the universe is composed of Nature and the soul. Strictly speaking, therefore, all that is separated from us, all which philosophy distinguishes as the Not Me, that is, both nature and art, all other men and my own body, must be ranked under this name, NATURE." [58]

Considered then as an object, nature was set over against the subjective consciousness, as mechanism opposed itself to idealism; but seen again as the incarnation of thought, as the home of the oversoul, nature was the common ground of spiritual life. The movement of ideas by which transcendentalism returned activity to nature and spirit to body culminated in the conception of the world as mind precipitated into its essences, escaping by its free activity from the hampering dross of matter. Nature precipitated ideas, was bound up with the movement of ideas, and had a dialectic activity of its own; and this activity was not essentially different from the activity of the subjective consciousness of man. Mind was not simply organization, not even a higher level of organization, but was the activity imprisoned in matter, shared in and appropriated by man. But the imprisonment of activity in matter was only a beginning state, for so soon as ideas were precipitated out of the flux, and emerged to a dialectic life of their own, spirit was thought to be free. There was indeed, as the transcendental philosophers insisted, something in the consciousness which was not first in the senses, namely, the consciousness itself, the activity of self-cognition and recognition, through which spirit was freed for its peculiar work. A cosmic consciousness thus seemed to dwell, alike in nature and in man, as the immanent dialectic principle of the universe.

Nature was the compulsory leap over the infinite globe, the power always jumping, always restless, nestling only in moments in some nook or cranny, willowing on the hilltop or absorbed in the dust; but always the cosmic force at work, the infinite regress splitting her unlinked chain, growing in society and in solitude, a burst of action or of reaction, emerging as novelty, change, motion, or the revolutionary activity of God. Nature had become a prophetic symbol of the unleashed power of the union states, of its expansive ideas, its visionary plans; it was a symbol of the salutary leap into the future which politics called manifest destiny, and which the nature mystic found in his hollow home. "Nature, true nature, and the true idea of Nature, long absent, must above all, become fully restored, enlarged, and must furnish the pervading atmosphere to poems, and the test of all high literary and esthetic compositions," Whitman had announced. The new symbol, nature taken up as cosmic destiny, as an immanent revolutionary activity, burst out of the old forms, left the ordered gardens of eighteenth-century literature withering in their artificial forms. Literature must take up the transcendental theme, discover its new mode, seek in nature its polestar and symbol. "I do not mean the smooth walks, trimm'd hedges, poseys and nightingales of the English poets," proclaimed Whitman, "but the whole orb, with its geologic history, the kosmos, carrying fire and snow, that rolls through the illimitable areas, light as a feather, though weighing billions of tons." [59]

4. *The Dialectics of Nature*

Transcendentalism had blessed the inert matter of Newton with incipient motion, had seized the scepter from the distant God, forcing him to dwell immanently as the dialectic force of matter. It had endowed matter with the processes of growth and gave it the means by which quality might be given a natural birth. It had shattered mechanism at the door of the temple of transcendentalism and had driven the countinghouse philosophy of Paley from the home of the immanent divinity. Transcendental physics started with the notion that the senses would acquaint man with the body, and that the mind would give an idea of substance comparable to the objective reality. It established the universal laws of nature *a priori,* by virtue of the immanent spiritual activity of man, whose soul, imprisoned momentarily in the body, responded to the oversoul which dwelt in the heart of nature. Facts of demonstration had proved of greater value than the facts of induction; the philosophy of transcendentalism had established that our knowledge transcends the sensible ideas of experience. Transcendentalism had confronted sensationalism in its own terms, and found it wanting; idealism had confronted mechanism, and found it dead. The transcendental physics proposed to return activity to nature, motion to matter, and the soul to the body, from which they had long since been banished by the utilitarian philosophy of the Enlightenment. The transcendental philosophers had thereby discovered an immanent dialectic principle whose activity was akin to the subjective activity of the human soul. "The world—this shadow of the soul or *other me,* lies wide around," wrote Emerson. "Its attractions are the keys which unlock my thoughts and make me acquainted with myself." [60]

To convert the raw material of experience into the wild and insurgent product of his thought, the romantic idealist took nature as an unfinished spectacle, a dream not yet rolled out, a denouement to be anticipated as a means of further enlargement, a growth of power, a maturing of his thought. Science, still wrapped up in its mechanisms, was criticized for its failure to link itself up with cosmic history, to explain the modes of motion in matter by which an immanent divine principle had brought man to the crest of the wave, with the perspective of novelty, to survey the scene. Science was to become a moral biography; it was required to whisper that man was a part and parcel of God. The nomenclature of the laboratories, the endless experiments, the counting and separating of phenomena—these were only useless labor if they did not stimulate the soul. Transcendentalism was sick of the empty cold universe of Newton; it wanted the blaze of the star, the flash of the comet, the emergence of novelty. Trancendentalism wondered where the qualitative wealth of the universe had fled, where the immanent forces of Aristotle and the eternal essences of Plato had hidden. All life was an experiment, an enlargement of experience, a means of stimulating an immanent divine activity; but science only reduced it to a barren catalogue of facts, a dry and dull recital of time and space. There was no revolutionary activity in science, no cosmic upheavals, no fit materials for the making of a hero, no storm and stress. Empirical science stood condemned for her empty mechanism; speculative science was the only remedy for a nature that had been stripped of quality and a universe that had been stripped of life.

5. *The Idea of Growth*

Amidst the endless cycle of birth and death, of construction and destruction, of generation and decay, the transcendentalist saw the emergence of higher forms of things. He was driven to an evolutionary philosophy by the activity of the subjective consciousness, by the growth of his own power to comprehend. The growth of things to higher levels of organization, and their expansion into the myriad complexity of higher forms, demonstrated to the romantic philosopher that nature was the scene of endless change. The cycles of growth betrayed levels and complexities of organization, the emergence of higher forms, seemingly out of the lower, the birth of the novel out of the familiar. The shattering of old forms in nature corresponded to the shattering of familiar customs in society, so that the transcendentalist was an incipient revolutionary, calling for a utopian march into the future. The past was determinate, swallowed down by the understanding, and placed in her old familiar categories; but the future, whose philosophy was emergence, burst all the old categories, and called for the reconstruction of experience. Transcendental idealism was the reflection of this idea of growth in nature, and in the activity of subjective consciousness; it represented an attempt to transcend the familiar round of sense experience by a penetration to higher levels of the understanding. The romantic philosophy was, accordingly, an evolutionary theory of subjectivity, whose parallel in nature was reflected in the idea of growth.

Nature had also become a symbol to the man of letters of the manifest destiny of literature; it was to throw off the old forms, destroy the ordered rationality of the eighteenth-century gardens, and grow into a wild hedge. It was to breed hungry forms, in which the thoughts of God might pause for a moment, and give itself over to a new and heroic passage into the future. The productive energies of nature were to become the nouns of an incessant metamorphosis, and the poet was to use them representatively as the symbols of some primary meaning. Philosophy was to represent pure activity, production and dissolution, the curative power of thought incarnate in matter. It was to transcend the limits of sensible experience, pierce behind the veil of phenomena, and from the phenomenology of the mind to draw an ontology of the soul. Growth was the idea of pure activity, of pure thought, either in nature or in man; and its ascent, its incipient progress, to higher forms, was to be marked by the destruction of the lower forms. The polarity of nature, the action and reaction, the mutual antagonisms and inevitable rivalries, were the source of its hungry dialectic, the symbol of its pure activity. The idea of growth meant that every thing in nature contained all the powers of nature; the dialectic activity of nature was represented in every particle of nature. An immanent divine activity, in nature and in man, struggled with the mutual antagonism of its parts, toward a premised unity, only to be dissolved at a higher level, and there to produce again the activity of mind breeding itself into matter. The universe was alive with an immanent dialectic growth, bursting out of its old forms and producing its new categories, only to emerge again to a new state of development, where thought might once more incarnate itself in matter.

6. The Metaphysics of Individualism

The transcendental quest involved the justification of the individual in the identity of himself, just as matter had revealed a mysterious thing-in-itself. Walt Whitman's search for the endless identities of divine average men was in fact not so much to demonstrate their social unity but rather to prove their democratic diversity. Democracy as a metaphysical doctrine meant diversity, men organized by their differences, each respecting differences in the other. The democratic Me of Whitman was always confronted with the alien Not Me of Hegel, as individualism was confronted by socialism in the ebullient romantic age. The progress of transcendental idealism had in the meantime provided a novel metaphysics of individualism, an ontology of the private soul, so that it might dwell in its endless identity with itself amidst the storm and stress of romantic growth. The individual was to keep to himself, to shun society, the company of friends and kindred, if these should prove barriers to his development. The idea of growth in nature had demonstrated the immanent divine activity which led to the incarnation of thought in matter. It remained only to show that the individual could grow by similar means; that he could grow out of himself and into a higher level and complexity of the self, while preserving his endless identity with himself. "The quality of BEING, in the object's self," wrote Whitman, "according to its own central idea and purpose, and of growing therefrom and thereto—no criticism by other standards, and adjustments thereto—is the lesson of Nature." [61]

The question of self-trust, of heroic manliness, was an expression of the faith of the individual in his endless identity with himself. It was a faith that through all the storm and stress of growth, in the midst of life's endless struggle, despite all odds and barriers to his development, the individual would preserve his capacity for identity. Despite the unity which transcendentalism had conferred upon nature, it was in fact a unity of diversity, a pluralism essential to the dynamic monism of the universe. Individuals were preserved amidst the advancement to higher forms, by virtue of their own capacity for growth; and for the sake of further growth, the democratic diversity of pluralism had to be premised, so that the monocratic socialism of unity could achieve a significant advance. Transcendental idealism required that individuals be preserved amidst the dissolution of the old categories, that the endless identities of divine average men should be incarnate in the new forms. "For nature wishes every thing to remain itself," wrote Emerson; "and whilst every individual strives to grow and exclude and to exclude and grow, to the extremities of the universe, and to impose the law of its being on every other creature, Nature steadily aims to protect each against every other. Each is self-defended." [62]

Society existed only as the condition of the development of individuals; its social monism was only an expression of its individual pluralism; and alike in nature and in society, the unity of the whole was preserved only through the mutual antagonism of its parts. Democracy was therefore a condition of society which should not hamper the growth of individuals; it was an ideal social state which would preserve the conditions for the fullest growth of its individual members. The utopian socialism of the romantic age was, accordingly, an expression of its fundamental individualism, of its desire to preserve the endless identities of the individual. Both in nature and in society, then, the transcendental philosophy developed a metaphysics of individualism, an ontology of the private soul. It preserved in transcendental form the goal of man's sovereignty over himself which a previous age had found to be an expression of the fundamental natural rights. Democracy as a metaphysical doctrine meant that the conditions for the growth of private property were equally the conditions for the preservation of the endless identity of the individual and for the safeguarding of his sovereignty over himself. Similarly, self-government meant the capacity of the individual for growth, the preservation of his endless identity in himself through innumerable stages and transitions in his development. Transcendentalism had thus given birth to a new metaphysics of individualism, in which the mysterious self-in-itself was preserved in romantic America with the same tenacity as the equally mysterious thing-in-itself was preserved in romantic Germany.

CHAPTER FIFTEEN

THE RELIGIOUS QUEST

1. *The Critique of Calvinism*

Calvinism lingered out a grotesque existence in New England, and preserved by tradition and habit a theology not at all in keeping with the romantic temper of the age. Its conception of the exalted power of God seemed to preclude an exalted conception of the power of man; and the predeterminism of God, by which every event was foreordained to come to pass, reduced man to the slavery of necessary connections. The philosophic necessity which was the root of the Calvinist conception of God precluded any insight on the part of Calvinism into the progressive nature of man. The critique of Calvinism had as its object the destruction of the characteristic serfdom of man as that had appeared in the heritage of feudal religion. To transcendentalism it appeared that Calvinism denied to man that which was his most characteristic trait, namely, the self-determining power of his will, without which, the romantic philosophers explained, man could have no proof of God's existence. Transcendental religion rested its belief in God on an exalted conception of the nature of man and consequently objected to the theological materialism which Calvinism represented. "The doctrine, that God is the only Substance, which is pantheism, differs little from the doctrine, that God is the only active power in the universe." Calvinism denied to man the capacity of any original power, and especially the self-determining power of his will, and so it seemed to romantic religion only mechanical materialism in religious disguise. "It is a striking fact," wrote Channing, "that the philosophy which teaches that matter is an inert substance, and that God is the force which pervades it, has led men to question, whether any such thing as God exists; whether the powers of attraction and repulsion, which are regarded as the indwelling Deity, be not the whole essence." [63]

The objection of transcendental piety to Calvinism was in its essence the same as its objection to eighteenth-century religious rationalism. Both were materialistic, the one disguising its materialism as theology, the other as a sensationalist philosophy; but the result in both was a denial of freedom of the will and the conception of the world as a machine. In both God was not the immanent divine activity of matter, but an outside motive force set over against the world and man. Calvinism represented sensationalism in theological dress, and sensationalism seemed only a Calvinism in secular form. The twin objections of the age to mechanism and the denial of free will, which both sensationalist religion and sensationalist philosophy had advocated, were a common denial of the activity of the subjective consciousness, and seemed to preclude any proof of God's existence. Calvinism had set up God as the enemy of man; it had made man a bearer of evil rather than a proof of good, and it denied any kinship between man and his creator. "This system represents the despair of man groping after God," objected Parker. "The religious element acts, but is crippled by a philosophy poor and sensual. Is man nothing but a combination of five senses, and a thinking machine to grind up and bolt sensations, and learn of God only by hearsay? The God of sensationalism is a God afar off; its religion worn-out and second hand. We cannot meet God face to face." [64]

Romantic religion, as Emerson noted, took its stand on man's capacity for virtue, while Calvinism stood on the principle of man's liability to sin. Clearly, the issue involved in the critique of Calvinism was not the government of God but the nature of man. Calvinism with its taint of hereditary sin smacked too obviously of feudal primogeniture and entail in religion; it would not allow the divinity to become the private possession of the individual man, and stood in the way of the free descent and alienation of the property of God. It happened, therefore, that the critique of Calvinism revealed that the question of man's heroic stature was the issue of that transcendent age. It fell to the lot of the romantic philosophers to challenge the grotesque doctrine descended from Calvinism for the sake of the divine average man. Christ's redemption became only an illustrious and noble example of the height to which man might attain through the study of the exemplary character of Jesus. The doctrine of original sin was denied altogether, because the hereditary succession of evil seemed not at all consonant with the cumulative and growing powers of man. The doctrine of eternal damnation, of the aristocratic election of a few saints for salvation, was put down as a hesitant and futile attempt of a more primitive age to understand that all men are elected by virtue of a common endowment of self-conscious activity; and it was opposed by the transcendental doctrine of self-trust, of faith in oneself, and in the properties of oneself. "One of the greatest of all errors," Channing wrote, "is the attempt to exalt God, by making him the sole cause, the sole agent in the universe, by denying to the creature freedom of will and moral power, by making man a mere recipient and transmitter of a foreign impulse." [65]

The idea of God descended from Calvinism was transformed into that of a personal divinity, dwelling immanently in the souls of divine average men. The measure of God's presence and proof of his existence was the self-conscious activity of man, his sovereignty over himself, and the self-determining power of his will. The sovereign and omnipotent God of Calvinism, the powerful monarch of feudalism, was transformed into a personal deity of the self, an indwelling property of the spirit, by which man exalted himself above the animals and claimed for himself a divine personality. "The idea of God," wrote Channing, "sublime and awful as it is, is the idea of our own spiritual nature, purified and enlarged to infinity. In ourselves are the elements of the Divinity." Denied his power to intervene actively in the world machine he had created, as a consequence of the philosophy of the Enlightenment, God had now been denied any existence at all outside the human consciousness, as a result of romantic religion. God was incarnate in nature because of its conscious aspiration to new forms, and in human nature, because of its self-conscious activity. "We see God around us because he dwells in us," wrote Channing. Before the divinity of the common man, the sovereign power of the Calvinist God had crumbled, so that divine average men might claim to possess a share in the qualitative wealth of the universe, and reflect in their own consciousness the benign and benevolent care which God would exercise over them.

2. The Unitarian Christianity

The Unitarian Christianity was in its own way quite a significant anticipation of transcendental religion. It criticized the trinity for the sake of unity and doubted the divinity of Christ for the sake of the divinity of man. It began its theological speculations with an exalted conception of man and reached its religious conclusions with a debased conception of God. It rested its unitarian cause, like transcendental religion, upon certain primal intuitions of human nature; it claimed the activity of the human consciousness was a symbol of the dialectic movement of the divine consciousness and, by calling into question a split infinity of being, proclaimed that God dwelt immanently in the soul of man. It proposed to rise from a conception of human nature to a conception of God, and to see God reflected in man, so that there might be no great distinction between the natural, as man's nature is natural, and the supernatural, as God's nature is supernatural. It condemned the God of eighteenth-century deism for what it truly was, a geometrical theorem, a vague shadow, a sounding name, a deity without a character, a substance without its modes, a being without attributes. For the conception of God it proposed to substitute the image of man. "The only God, whom our thought can rest on, and our hearts cling to, and our consciences recognize," wrote Channing, "is the God whose image dwells in our own souls." Here then was a conception of God which romantic religion would henceforth worship as the Great God Self.

The Unitarian Christians defended their cause by arguing against the Calvinists, that though they started their speculations from an exalted conception of man, they nevertheless had reached a benevolent and exalted conception of God. A Calvinist, armed with the artistic sensibility and philosophic insight of an Edwards, might have rejoined, however, that in reaching an exalted conception of God on the basis of an exalted conception of man they had made God's absolute sovereignty to lackey after human nature, and had consequently made the Creator dependent upon the creature. The Unitarians, however, felt that the wrathful conception of God descended from Puritanism inspired fear rather than piety and debasement rather than elevation. The question at issue, then, was whether man was really the heroic creature endowed with enormous faculties which a romantic age had proclaimed, or whether he was a debased and sinful creature, tainted by the hereditary succession of evil, and doomed to damnation, misery, and death. But the romantic age was endowed, above all other things, with a romantic faith in the individual, with a humanistic piety and a religion of man. Unitarianism, which first anticipated the romantic religion of the transcendental age, questioned the divinity of Christ for the sake of the divinity of man; and it brought in to the temple of transcendentalism a critique of the trinitarian formula which its disciples had inherited from the Puritan fathers. "We object to the doctrine of the Trinity," wrote Channing, "that, whilst acknowledging in words, it subverts in effect, the unity of God."

Without a premised unity in the objective consciousness of the cosmic mind, there could hardly be presumed a premised unity in the subjective consciousness of the human mind; and as the Kantian case for primal intuitions of human nature and for *a priori* knowledge rested on a presumed unity of the subjective consciousness, the case of the Unitarian theology rested no less on the presumed unity of the human mind. Similarly, without the supposition of a unified conscious activity in the universe, there could hardly be presumed a unified and integrated conscious activity in human nature, and the kinship between God and man could not have been defended. The Unitarian theology therefore attacked the inherited trinitarian formula, not alone for its debasing suppositions about God, but also for its debasing consequences for man. The trinitarian formula presumed a split personality in God, and thus not a unified intelligence and will; and by the same token, it struck at the unified sovereignty of man over himself, at his capacity for self-government, by making him responsible in his moral actions, not to a kindred mind which was the symbol of his own, but a triumvirate of separate sovereignties conflicting and antagonistic in themselves. The Unitarian Christianity therefore struck down the trinitarian formula for the sake of the unitarian thesis, and resulted in the conception of God as an immanent indwelling spirit, whose incarnation in nature and in man prepared the way for the evolutionary theism of transcendental religion.

3. *The Religion of Man*

When a more spiritual philosophy took hold of the New England provinces, and swept in a wide arc the staid habits of the New England churches, a romantic religion was given birth, and challenged by its dramatic individualism the narrow utilitarianism and shallow sensationalism which it proposed to replace. The romantic faith promised to be founded, not on the traditional claims of miracles and of revelations, but upon the nature of man. It gave itself over to a celebration of his powers, and was a reflection of the romantic faith in the unique dignity of the individual man. It proclaimed a spiritual element in man, an element which was established by demonstration and embodied by intuition; and it received confirmation from the importation of the writings of Coleridge, of Wordsworth, and of Victor Cousin, who had reproduced the thoughts and the dramatic insurgence of the classical German philosophy. Out of these new materials a transcendental theology was brought to fruition, and a celebration was invoked designed to lend a festival of triumph to the discovery of spiritual individualism. "So there rose a new school of metaphysical philosophy," wrote Theodore Parker, "and it agreed with the theological sects in this—*There is a spiritual element in man!*"

The revolution in religion that followed from this discovery demonstrated that man was a part and parcel of God; that there could be no religion which should hold a debasing conception of man or of the deity. The old theology of the New England churches was rejected; biblical criticism demonstrated that the Bible was not infallible, and that man was to take the good of it while rejecting the evil. Theology dropped the miraculous and took itself to spiritual anthropology, studying the roots of divinity which contributed to the manliness of the hero and the godliness of the saint. The battle between the old theology and romantic religion was joined on the issues stemming from the Calvinist heritage, which a preceding series of revolts, of the pietist, the Unitarian, and the universalist, had conveniently weakened; and out of this controversy the vital principles of romantic religion emerged triumphant. The outcome of these great battles was to establish that man possesses an element of divinity within himself, and is destined for the perfection of his humanity by virtue of the divine principle within. "Here is a revolution in theology greater than that wrought by Luther, greater than that of Jesus Himself,—for the pole is shifted from the old theology to the nature of man, wherein God permanently incarnates and reveals His truth." [66]

Thus was born a romantic religion whose theology was the study not of God but of man, and whose object was the celebration not of the omnipotence of God but of the greatness of man. It went quite beyond the early forms of revolt against Calvinism, transcended the feeble beginnings of Unitarianism, universalism, and pietism, and joined in the universal chorus to deify the spiritual element in man. This spiritual element was nothing less than the capacity for growth, and it presupposed a dialectic activity of the soul through which it was borne as in a storm safely into port. The romantic religion conceived the soul to be the aggressor, to reach out for God to supply its wants, and to grow spiritually to higher stages of perfection. Man, through the activity of his subjected consciousness, demonstrates the triumph of spirit over matter, and at the same time illustrates the incarnation of thought in nature. It followed from these premises, that wherever thought occurred, especially if the activity involved a widening of intellectual horizons, the theme of the romantic religion could be proved. Since then the activity of the subjective consciousness was a universal faculty of man, since all men possess a capacity for growth, it followed that the divinity incarnates itself in man. The romantic religion conceived the religion sense to be a universal property of man; and, although some men were more spiritual than others, although some men had a greater capacity for growth, all men shared in and appropriated the fruits of this capacity. The object of romantic religion, then, was not only to demonstrate the universal faculty of spiritual growth, but to urge upon all men that perfection of their natures which should issue in a final triumph of the religion of humanity.

4. The Critique of Religious Rationalism

The philosophers of romantic religion were now prepared to destroy the last vestiges of republican religion as it had issued from the fruitful loins of the eighteenth century. Religious rationalism, in the form of theological materialism or sensationalism, was condemned for its implicit, though not admitted, denial of the existence of God. Although the sensationalist had attempted a proof of the existence of God on the argument of design, he had actually transcended his positivist caution to do so, and this was increasingly regarded by the romantics as an illogical step. The sensationalist could not prove the existence of God on the basis of his principles, for to do so required that he transcend the limits of sensible experience, which in its turn only proved the soundness of transcendental religion. The idea of God, the romantics argued, is not an idea of sensible experience; it is rather a transcendent idea which is proved by the existence of something in the consciousness which was not first in the senses, namely, the consciousness itself. This was the basis for the romantic claim of kinship to God; it was the source of the religious sense upon which belief in God rested, but the sensationalist had completely ignored it in the impudence and shallow morality of his religion of reason.

Since the existence of a world outside the screen of phenomena must be to sensationalism only an hypothesis, the existence of God would similarly be only hypothetical. This condemned the sensationalist at best to a finite God implicit in the unity of sense experience, but was no proof, on sensationalist principles, of the existence of an infinite God. The romantics objected, accordingly, that a finite God, an imperfect God, was no God at all; and that the hypothetical caution of the sensationalist drove him naturally to atheism. Similarly, the deist was to be condemned, for his sensationalist principles could never prove the existence of an immortal soul. The positivist caution of sensationalism as a philosophy again prevented it from transcending the world of sensible experience, and precluded the possibility of self-conscious divine activity. Moreover, the sensationalist was excluded from an exalted conception of man; for the only proof of man's existence that could be derived from the ideas of sensible experience made him in the image of a machine, a mechanism of action and reaction, whose soul could be no other than material. As the sensationalist could not prove the existence or the immortality of the soul, nor the existence and infinite perfection of God, neither had he any logical reason for belief in the freedom of the will. Republican religion had developed free will as a political necessity, as the foundation of the faith in self-government; but freedom of the will would be on sensationalist principles only an hypothesis. In all these respects, then, sensationalism and its corresponding religion of reason stood condemned in the secular pulpits of transcendental idealism.

Religious rationalism and its hedonistic ethics, its cunning conscience, its virtue of the bargain, were exposed and pilloried upon the stocks of ridicule. The romantic philosophers destroyed the absurd claims of the countinghouse philosophy, and denied entrance into the temple of transcendentalism of any who admitted allegiance to the old doctrines. They proposed to examine once more into the human heart, to analyze the nature of the human soul, and find there the new basis for religion, morality, and politics. They rested themselves at last on the spiritual element in man, which was akin in its activity to the cosmic consciousness at work in nature; and they called into question any departure from the faith that man's knowledge transcends the limits of sensible experience. They avoided to the last the error of the previous age of reason—the reduction of thought to sensation; and they found in the activity of the subjective consciousness a new faith in the birth of quality, the emergence out of the night of eighteenth-century materialism of a new faith in spirit which should transcend and incarnate itself in matter. To the religion of reason, therefore, succeeded the religion of man; and to the rational, calculating ethics of the eighteenth century, succeeded the transcendental morality of the romantic age.

5. *The Transcendental Theism*

To the mathematical theism of the eighteenth century succeeded the transcendental theism of the nineteenth. It owed its prominence partly to an ennobled conception of man, and its persuasive powers to the immanent divine activity which the romantic philosophers summed up as the dialectics of God. The transcendental theism was in a way an outgrowth of the religion of nature which the eighteenth century had placed upon the agenda of history, and it owed its persuasiveness in part to the pietist theory of divine love with its lodgment of the divinity in the human heart. In Newtonian science, it will be remembered, matter was inert, incapable of motion without the supposition that God had imparted an initial packet of energy to its particles at the moment of creation. Transcendental idealism returned God to nature by supposing him to be the dialectic activity incarnate in matter; and to the human soul, by supposing him to be akin in his nature to the activity of the subjective consciousness. The result was however that the matter of the nineteenth century was just as dependent upon God, just as dead and inert without his activity, as the dead, inert matter of Newton had been. The difference, however, was significant; for in transcendentalism the motion of matter is not merely the result of obedience to abstract monistic law, but is rather the result of an evolutionary thesis revealed at the several stages of its development.

In the perspective of transcendental theism, therefore, the laws of nature, while uniform, and while always existing of necessity, were not necessarily immutable. God had thus been given once more the power to intervene actively in nature, as He had in the Puritan theory of emanations; but with the difference that His interference, which resulted in change and the emergence of novelty, was a cumulative process tending over a long period to a certain result. In brief, natural law had adjusted itself to an evolutionary theism, with the result that while the universe was still governed by law, it was a law evolved by the necessary stages of material organization. "Inanimate matter, by itself, is dependent," wrote Theodore Parker. "To assert the opposite is to make it a God. In its present state it has no will. Yet there is in it existence, motion, life. The smallest molecule in a ray of polarized light and the largest planet in the system exist and move as if possessed of a will, powerful, regular, irresistible. The powers of nature, then, that of gravitation, electricity, growth, what are they but modes of God's action?" [67]

The transcendental theism thus distinguished itself, first, from atheism, the denial of the existence of God; second, from the popular theology descended from Calvinism, which ascribed to God a finite and ferocious character; and third, from deism, which derived the existence of God from the simple unity of sense experience, without the primal intuitions of human nature. All of these derived positions of the eighteenth century seemed to lack a common character of activity, by which God becomes the principle of action in matter, and by virtue of his activity drives it to an inevitable and cumulative progress. It followed the proof of God's existence for transcendental idealism lay in the process of growth itself, in a change which could be noted, in a novelty which could be described. Whether in man or in nature, God was described in an evolutionary way; he differed from the God of the eighteenth century in being a quality rather than a quantity. It might be said, therefore, that while the religion of reason led to quantitative theism and mechanistic metaphysics, the romantic religion led to a qualitative theism and an evolutionary metaphysics. This result, indeed, was more or less inevitable, once the transcendentalist had resolved to rest religion on certain primal intuitions of human nature. In brief, the existence of God was proved by the consciousness of man.

The God of transcendental theology is thus the Great God Self. The transition which the idea of God had undergone since the days of the Puritans, when he was accorded every sovereign power, every divine right, was a measure of the development of the American ideology. Stripped first by the eighteenth-century rationalist of his power to interfere in the operations of the world machine, bound by his own constitutional law, God was at last transformed by the transcendentalist into the divinity of the individual man, and thereby individualism caught an adequate metaphysic. God came at last to dwell in the individual man, in the divine average man, so that He might establish the heroic qualities of the divine average, and proclaim democratic diversity as the means of his progressive reign. God came at last to dwell in man, immanently of his spirit; for the transcendental God is the Great God Self, and transcendental divinity is an exercise in the metaphysics of individualism. God was the power of growth in the individual, his spiritual capacity, his subjective conscious activity, enlarged by an infinite image, and made familiar by an exalted conception. Stripped of his antique powers, God had revealed himself in the powers of man; He existed only as a faculty of human nature, only as a quality of human life. Dwelling immanently in nature and in man, God revealed himself as the active relation of the ideal and the real, the quality of existence which gave it life and motion and change. God was the idealistic thesis of transcendentalism, made of necessity out of its faith in the perfection of the moral and intellectual powers of man. The Great God Self was a perfect image of the common man enlarged by a transcendent conception of himself into the stature of a hero and the proportion of a god.

6. *The Dialectics of God*

The transcendental gospel must sooner or later touch the fringes of God's cloak; for the simplest lessons of transcendentalism disclosed a God different in conception from the God of the eighteenth-century rationalists. The disciples of reason, it will be remembered, had been driven by the progress of Newtonian science to establish God as a mathematical theorem; He was a supposition necessary, as we have seen, to the metaphysical assumptions of Newtonian science. The religion of reason was in fact nothing less than a mathematical theism, in which God was the first integer of a series, whose existence could be proved either by descent from the First Cause or ascent from the Last Effect. God had in the meantime been deleted from nature and established at an infinite remove from the world machine. God had created the universal machine and had set it in motion, but thereafter could not really interfere with its operation. This conclusion, essential to eighteenth-century deism, had the uncomfortable result that man might do entirely without the conception of the Creator; for the created machine operated so perfectly without divine interference that the conception of God and the piety of man began to occupy less importance in the philosophy of the Enlightenment. The inescapable conclusion of the age of reason was that, while God was a necessary assumption for any scientific hypothesis, His role in the operation of the universe and the necessity for faith in Him became less and less apparent. Thus directed by the common positivism of its philosophy, the religious rationalist had drifted easily into atheism, scepticism, deism, and doubt.

The facts of transcendentalism, however, establish the truth of intuition, and the *a priori* validity of certain primary conceptions. To Theodore Parker the chief lesson to be drawn from transcendentalism was that the ideas of God, immortality, and freedom have, in the manner of the Kantian analysis, an *a priori* foundation in human nature itself. The foundations of the transcendental religion Parker had found in the critical philosophy of Immanuel Kant, who "gave me the true method, and put me on the right road." In Kant, Parker found an unassailable foundation for transcendental piety; he found certain primal intuitions of human nature, which depended upon no logical process of demonstration, but were rather facts of consciousness established by its subjective activity. In the activity of the subjective consciousness, then, Parker found an instinctive intuition of the divine, an ethics of intuition, a foundation for the belief in the immortality of the soul. All these essentials of transcendental piety were based on the study of man; a religious anthropology was established, and the foundation of religion was laid in human nature. Belief in God, accordingly, came from faith in man; and consciousness of the existence of God rested on the self-conscious existence of man.

It followed that man's consciousness of God must be an "affectional fact" of his nature, that a transcendental piety is the fruit of the religious faculty. God is therefore infinite, and perfect because of His infinity. But it happened, since divinity was founded on human nature, that this was a clever transcendental way of revealing the divinity that dwells in every man; and it was a considerable anticipation of evolutionary theism, because by the transcendental premise and the Kantian criticism God had become an immanent indwelling spirit. God was in fact the dialectic activity of the universe, revealed in nature, as thought incarnate in nature, and revealed in man, as the activity of the subjective consciousness. The affirmation of all Being in unity, as an affirmative conquering a negative, or dissolving a mutual antagonism for an emerging novelty, was the activity of God. The dialectical thesis of affirmative unity as it emerges from the struggle and interpenetration of myriads of warring opposites was the essence of God. Transcendental theism was, in final analysis, a faith in the progressive character of the dialectic activity of the universe. "Essence, or God," wrote Emerson, "is not a relation or a part, but the whole. Being is the vast affirmative, excluding negation, self-balanced, and swallowing up all relations, parts and times within itself."

Now this same activity of subjective consciousness, tending always toward unity and synthesis, was observed to be the distinct element of man, the basis of his spirituality, and the divine element within him. Hence the romantic philosophers based religion upon human nature, the existence of God upon the consciousness of man. God was incarnate in matter because He was the basis for the dialectic activity of matter, which the transcendentalists called consciousness or mind. God was also consciously evolving matter toward novelty, the emergence of the divine thesis out of the antithesis of preceding stages of material organization. In man, therefore, the same processes of growth were at work, and the activity of the subjective consciousness was taken to be an instance of the dialectics of God. It followed that God was an indwelling divine activity, revealing Himself in the facts of growth, incarnating Himself as spirit in matter and as mind in body. But it also followed from this reasoning that there was a genuine basis for the kinship between man and God, as there was also for the kinship between man and nature. God was, in the last analysis, the immanent dialectic process of the universe, without which there could be no creation, no growth, and no manifest destiny in the world.

CHAPTER SIXTEEN

THE DEMOCRATIC FAITH

1. *The Transcendental Politics*

The significance of the transcendental revolt against the age of reason will hardly be borne in upon the observer unless it is remembered that republicanism was a metaphysical doctrine as well as the structure of an actual government. The romantic philosophers transformed the fundamental documents of the American revolution into mere expressions of the transcendental dogma, and concurred with the age of Jackson in politics that its fundamental ideas were now to be put to a test. They supposed the American Revolution to be an expression of the primal intuitions of human nature and an example of its inevitable struggle to reach a higher level of self-conscious freedom. "The American Revolution, with American history since," wrote Theodore Parker, "is an attempt to prove by experience this transcendental proposition, to organize the transcendental idea of politics." The romantic philosophers took the Declaration of Independence to be one expression of this primal urge in human nature to self-conscious freedom; they discovered that it had embodied in political form the critical idealism of Kant, and aimed to transcend the level of sensible experience like the philosophies of Fichte and Schelling. They found the idea of natural rights congenial to their faith in the primary rights of private consciousness, and discovered the proof of democratic diversity in the supposition that all men are born equally with this claim to self-conscious freedom. The role of government was to encourage this growth by protecting the primary rights of human nature, and guarding from alien and hampering influences its primary urge towards growth. The transcendental politics, in brief, was a reflection of the need of native industry for the protection and encouragement of government, and only represented in a literary way the fundamental romantic faith in the growing powers of the individual.

The romantic effort to confer upon man a transcendental dignity soon coalesced with the expansion of native industry, and brought into the temple of belief a new political metaphysic. By this strategy the fundamental rights of man were transformed into a cosmic constitution, so that life, liberty, and property, the fundamental tenets of republicanism, were given a quite immaterial embodiment in the consciousness of God. "The idea demands for its organization a democracy—a government of all, for all, and by all," wrote Parker; "a government by natural justice, by legislation that is divine as much as a true astronomy is divine, legislation which enacts laws representing a fact of the universe, a resolution of God." By virtue of this development of political theory the natural rights were transformed into divine rights, and the privileges and immunities of kings were proclaimed as the testament of divine average men. Such was the meaning of that romantic democracy of which the transcendental philosophers spoke, of that religious democracy which Whitman proclaimed, of that mighty self-trust which Emerson unveiled. The transcendental politician had proclaimed a new religious democracy, a democracy of divine average men, whose brotherhood was spiritual, and whose natural rights were divine. Compared with the divine rights of average men, the primal intuitions of whose subjective consciousness were embodied as cosmic law, the claims and allegiances of government were but a spurious depotism, the anarchy and atheism of a tyrant.

2. The Critique of Republicanism

What the new religious democracy found to criticize in the theory of republicanism which had descended into its hands from the age of reason was not so much the structure of its government but the metaphysical assumptions of its thought. Republicanism—in its eighteenth-century form—was declared to be a species of the sensational philosophy revealing itself in politics; it was a mechanical materialism in its metaphysical assumptions, and a practical atheism in its wordly effects. It had appealed to human history, but not to human nature; it had declared natural rights but not divine rights. Its conception of political justice was political expediency, and its moral inquiries were nothing but a division of political economy, a reckoning of the cost of adopting any principle. Republicanism had based its claims to recognition on historical precedents, assumed originals in nature, or musty old parchments lost to human dignity. Republicanism was the political philosophy of sensationalism; it was the political dimension of mechanical materialism, a mere philosophy of power, whose conception of ethics was selfish-

ness and whose conception of truth was the expedient. Republicanism
was a mere political utilitarianism. "The aim of sensationalist politics,"
wrote Parker, "is the greatest good of the greatest number; this may
be obtained by sacrificing the greatest good of the lesser number,——by
sacrificing the individual,—or sacrificing the absolute good." The aim
of republicanism was identical with the aim of political economy, the
wealth of nations, and it was a philosophy of expediency and power.
It was political atheism: "Political morality is impossible in the atheistic
state; there can be only political economy, which aims to provide merely
for the selfishness of men."

Whether the form of government is monarchical, aristocratical, or
democratical, it is all the same selfishness that supports these political
forms of the sensational philosophy; and whether the republican form
of government be tethered to one or another of these three-headed
sources of evil power, the result is the same for the divine average men
who are to make up the new religious democracy. Republicanism, however it may embody more or less of the monarchical, aristocratical, or
democratical element in its structure, is nothing more than a mechanism
of expediency, a political atheism, a moral anarchy: "But the politics of
practical atheism must be based on selfishness. As selfishness obtains in
the individual, establishing a personal anarchy of desires; in the family,
establishing a domestic anarchy of its members; in the community, establishing a social anarchy in the classes thereof; so it must prevail in
the State, establishing a national anarchy of its various parts." Republicanism rests on the metaphysical assumption that the world is a
machine; it is a political expression of mechanical materialism, and
knows only action and reaction, attraction and repulsion. "Men will be
consciously held together, in a negative manner, by the mutual and
universal repulsion of selfishness, not at all, positively, by the mutual
and universal attraction of justice. All men will be natural enemies,
joined by mutual hatred, huddled together by want and fear." The
prophet of such a political science, wrote Parker, was Thomas Hobbes,
whose description of the war of each against all is a perfect reflection of
a society based upon the political philosophy of sensationalism.[68]

3. The Young Americans

When the significance of the hour penetrated into the councils of the
young Americans, they proclaimed that a new epoch had been reached
in the practice of government, and that a new vision had been enter-
tained for the destiny of the nation. Manifest destiny had become, not
only the destiny of the nation, but of the young Americans who filled

the expansive hour with their hopes and practised in their manliness the awkward vigor of the adolescent nation. A country unencumbered by the remnants of feudalism stretched from ocean to ocean, while a heterogeneous population stirred with the freedom which was its newly won right. America then seemed the country of the future, a nation of equal laws and happy men, which had no other destiny than the perfecting of liberty, no other hope than the extension of its freedom. It inspired the mind with its illimitable prospect; it aroused the emotions with its imprescribable rights. It was healthy and strong, the land of the laborer, of the democrat, of the philanthropist, and of the reformer, each in his own way the heir of its virile future and the happy possessor of its noble past. The young Americans saw the experiment of free government coming to a new fruition; saw divine average men rising to their majority and claiming for themselves a share in the beneficent destiny of the American nation. It was a happy hour, through all the cities and states and territories; it was, as Emerson noted, a country of beginnings, or projects, of designs, and of great expectations, for mechanism in government was now to be laid aside.

The age was nothing if not heroic, and the secret of its heroism, the secret of its youthful Americanism, lay in the immense possibilities the adolescent nation possessed. The nation prided itself on its manifest destiny, and the young Americans proclaimed it as the native liberty of the individual man. The nation prided itself on its productive energy, and the young Americans proclaimed it as the manifestation of the heroic man. The future of America as a nation and of the young American as an heroic individual were thus intertwined; the resources of the nation were the resources of the individual, and the industry of the nation was matched by the rugged power of the divine average man. "There is a moment in the history of every nation, when, proceeding out of this brute youth, the perceptive powers reach their ripeness and have not yet become microscopic: so that man, at that instant, extends across the entire scale, and, with his feet still planted on the immense forces of night, converses by his eyes and brain with solar and stellar creation. That is the moment of adult health, the culmination of power." [69]

In letters and in politics, in industry and in life, the age beckoned toward immense possibilities, opened up its promise to the fruition of every hope and the fulfillment of every desire. The promise of democracy, of capitalism, of letters, and of science, lay in the future, whose emerging ideals had already made their appearance in the age of the young Americans. They were to gather to themselves a new standard, laugh at the follies of a decimated feudal aristocracy, and betake themselves with vigor to the new program. The young Americans were to form a transcendental aristocracy whose office was to teach the young nation, to minister to the new wants, to proclaim the new destiny. The natural aristocracy of the eighteenth century, with its narrow conception of reason, and its limited conception of truth, was to appear as a scant beginning, a mere shadow, of the giant statured heroes who formed the transcendental aristocracy. They were to compose for themselves a poetic conception of the nation's destiny, to sing of it and of themselves, and to reflect every facet of the national life as a revelation of the transcendental dream. Life had grown insurgent beneath her old forms; truth had grown restless behind her formal code. The young Americans were to release the national life to a new and greater growth, and to bring forward the nobler truth which the dream enjoined.

4. *The Democratic Temper*

For one who saw the endless pronouncements, the universal greetings, which Hegel might confer upon the divine average man, the main question of the romantic age had now issued from German romantic philosophy. Walt Whitman knew that the whole problem of the universe had now unraveled itself in Hegel; and the lesson that Whitman drew from it was one that all men, in the full romantic glory of their new individualism, might clearly comprehend. To the individual man, a single question; to the divine average, a cosmic answer: "What is the fusing explanation and tie—what the relations between the (radical, democratic) Me, the human identity of understanding, emotions, spirits, etc., on the one side, of and with the (conservative) Not Me, the whole of the material objective universe and laws, with what is behind them in time and space, on the other side?" To understand why the age both began and ended with this question, we must take ourselves behind the scene of endless pronouncements, behind the universal greetings, to the question, bred in America, of the place and rank of the individual man in the cosmos of being. The ferment had produced the idea; and the flux had called for the question. It remained only to establish that the individual man, the divine average man, had sparks of the divinity in his soul, and the future of the cosmos in his heart. The radical democratic Me exists by disjunction, a syllogism on the wave of flux; the conservative Not Me is the peripatetic conclusion, the philosophic necessity of endless identities.

Without the radical, democratic Me, there could be no individuals, no heroes; without the conservative Not Me, there could be no divine average, no folk democracy. This revelation meant, among other things, that politically the romantic could not be satisfied; for the radical democratic Me will not be governed by any but himself. "Not any one party, or any one form of government, is absolutely and exclusively true." Nothing will serve the divine average man but his own divinity; no one can prophesy for him; no one can count the tragedy of his hours. He alone, a hero against the cosmos, bears his own standard of optimism, his own conception of his cosmic destiny: "In short, (to put it in our own form, or summing up,) that thinker or analyzer or overlooker who by an inscrutable combination of train'd wisdom and natural intuition most fully accepts in perfect faith the moral unity and sanity of the creative scheme, in history, science, and all life and time, present and future, is both the truest cosmical devotee or religioso, and the profoundest philosopher. While he who, by the spell of himself and his circumstance, seeks darkness and despair in the sum of the workings of God's providence, and who, in that denies or prevaricates, is, no matter how much piety plays on his lips, the most radical sinner and infidel." [70]

The sinner and the infidel have never lasted in America, where optimism is indigenous and hope is boundless. No German pessimism, no French cynicism, no Carlylean world decadence, could be drawn by an American thinker from the pages of Hegel. For he was the confirmation of her hope, the philosophy of her optimism. Whitman tells us, in a footnote to his interpretation, how he drew from Hegel a confirmation of all the hopes of the New World democracy: "I have deliberately repeated it all, not only to offset Carlyle's everlurking pessimism and world-decadence, but as presenting the most thoroughly American points of view I know. In my opinion the above formulas of Hegel are an essential and crowning justification of New World democracy in the creative realms of time and space. There is that about them which only the vastness, and multiplicity and the vitality of America would seem able to comprehend; to give scope and illustration to, or to be fit for, or even originate. It is strange to me that they were born in Germany, or in the old world at all. While a Carlyle, I should say, is quite the legitimate European product to be expected."

The romantic German philosophy had thus come to an American fruition, which existed quite apart from the original texts. If then Hegel's moments of history seemed to the Americans a recipe for manifest destiny, or if Hegel's deification of the state meant for the Americans that law is king, it should not surprise us that Hegel's elaborate formulas for the dialectic of history became in America a prescription for the divine right of individuals. An empiricist twist was given to the syllogisms of the old German fakir; a nominalist hope was drawn from between the lines of the rationalist text. Hegel could be made to serve equally the right or the left, the radical democratic Me or the conservative, alien Not Me, the democratic individualist or the monocratic socialist. What the individualist drew from Hegel, in the harassed moments of his own heroic storm and stress, was that experience must be its own judge, that the hero must realize himself during each moment of his history, and throw his own dialectic growth against the unpaged texts of a manifest cosmic destiny.

The romantic philosophers had thus contributed a self-consciousness to the bold experiment of transcendental democracy and Darwin had embodied their favorite idea in strictly scientific form, and yet there was missing from all of them the dramatic insurgence of manifest destiny, whether in the individual or in the nation. Hegel, of course, had expressed the language of the absolute, and had incarnated it in the state; but the absolute state would in the long run prove hostile to the absolute individual, and seemed rather to require an absolute obedience in him. The transcendental hero existed by an absolute right, and the character of his claim to divinity precluded a new lease for it on the house of state. To Hegel, therefore, and to all the romantic philosophers, all the ensemblists, a warm greeting for a heightened self-consciousness; but to the romantic democracy, to the society of heroes and divine average men, the beckoning westward of manifest destiny, and the call to establish a society of equal laws and happy men. Romantic democracy was interested to the last in the fundamental problem which the German classical philosophers had set for it, the relation between the radical, democratic Me, the human identity of understanding, emotions, and spirit, on the one hand, of and with the conservative Not Me, the whole material objective universe and laws, with what was behind them in time and space, on the other. This was the fundamental problem of romantic America, to which the German philosophers might contribute by way of erudition, but which at long last the transcendental generation was to transform into a problem of its own.

5. *The Great God Self*

It was an age of heroes, of endless pronouncements in Yankee streets, and of strange, small men enlarged by history to the stature of gods. But it was an age, also, of those endless identities, the divine average of the democrat, which multiplied by themselves and geometrized by the spirit had plucked the image of God in order that it might serve in the image of men. There existed a native hero, the small farmer, who had apprenticed himself to servitude long enough to gain his capital independence; who then set himself up in a self-sufficient manorial, the lord of his estate, the historian of his destiny, the serene child of his own images and fruitions. Such was the conclusion of the romantic age, that the small man, writ large, was the independent hero of us all; and when the petty producer had raised himself into the common councils, conversing with men who likewise languaged an independent spirit, he had become the hero and the representative of all other men. The hero was the divine average writ large by history, conceived and dedicated to the task of preserving the opportunities by which other small men might rise. Of such materials was the democratic god constructed; of such proportions was the divine average fulfilled. The romantic age had called for its heroes, which now the poet and the prophet voiced to the common men about him, speaking in accents roomed and spectered with the knowledge that the hero was only the common man multiplied by himself.

Whitman had caught the vision, and heard the call of average men; so he set out to heed the common call, to speak of those endless identities, of that divine average. The generosity of nature and the largeness of the nation called for some symbol, for some representative of itself. "Not nature nor swarming states nor streets and steamships nor prosperous business nor farms nor capital nor learning may suffice for the ideal of man . . . nor suffice the poet." The pride of wealth and cities, all the returns of commerce and agriculture, even the symbolic magnitude of native geography, would not suffice the poet without his happy breed of men. Whitman had set out in verse what the divine average might seek in the street, "to enjoy the breed of full-sized men or one full-sized man unconquerable and simple." He sought his ideal man, as Lincoln had, in the creation of a large, independent, democratic class of small owners; the hero of such a swarm of freeholders was simply the dominating individualism of this class dramatized in the light of the history of their surge to freedom. The democratic temper of the age, which combined its hero worship with its love of the common man, of the divine average, is the protest of this imaged god, that he should find obstacles put in his path to the realization of his own destiny, to the fruition of his own character. The hero is above all else an individualist, dominating by the force of his character a reluctant environment, creating as a result of his work the means of further enlargements, opportunities for the making of more heroes, democratic vistas for the multiplication of the divine average.

A heroic age demands a primitive metaphysic to accompany it in its retreats and alarums; and it requires obedience, not to its own simple whims and caprices, but to a cosmic tug and pull, in answer to powers greater than itself. The hero was not simply the divine average, not a mere addition of the simple features of the common man, but an enlarged image of the best features which the best men display. The hero was a cosmic figure, a Greek god descended into Yankee streets, to whisper the old truths and sing again the old familiar songs. The hero was the godlike image of a divine average man as such a man would appear in a cosmic republic, full-blown and free, governed and protected by immutable law. The cosmic republican was indeed a suitable background for our hero, a government adapted to the immensity of his will and the creative plummet of his understanding. The hero worshipers supposed that a government founded on law and not on men must find some heavenly repository for its sacred documents; it must seek the law not in the face of nature but on the tablets of God. The true democracy of heroes, like the spiritual socialism of the utopian philanthropists, existed only in the imagination of the hero worshipers, as an extension of the ideal existence of divine average men. But it expressed what all the rugged individualists of that heroic age aspired to—a natural home for the hero, where the law of individual liberty should not conflict with the immutable law of the universe. There, in the cosmic republic, the heroic liberty of the individual was identical with obedience to the laws of nature.

In every field of human endeavor and inquiry the romantic mind had discovered a new divinity; and the lesson which the new divinity taught—which the transcendental priests preached in the sanctity of their secular pulpits—was that each human being is a revelation to himself and to others, the fruit of immanent spiritual processes generated in the soul of man. There was a great god loose among the transcendental categories, the Great God Self—that is the secret and essence of the transcendental movement. Nature, books, friends, history—all were to serve the new god, all were to be placed upon his altar; so that a threatened wrath, a sin as it were, the failure to achieve critical self-consciousness, was the punishment exacted upon the fallen by the new divinity. When translated into secular terms, this new theology of Selfhood, this new religion of individualism, meant that experience was to be its own judge, was to bear its own fruit; man was henceforth to be his own master, judging by that eternal principle of his own Selfhood the whole body of experience which should be its destiny. "The very time sees for us, thinks for us," wrote Emerson; "it is a microscope such as philosophy never had." Each moment was to be drained of its significance, sucked dry of its homely sapience, and tapped for its oracular wisdom; for the transcendentalist intended to represent the genius of his age, to write the spiritual history of his day, "standing in this great cleft of Past and Future." He had learned his technique among the poets, and he drew his philosophy from their heady wine. "The invariable mark of wisdom is to see the miraculous in the common." It is to see the significance of things, not as they are in themselves, but as they are to the intuition of the perceiver, as an image of himself. That indeed had been the lesson of Kantianism, in the dark whirlpools of the critical philosophy, when German romantic philosophy was budding in the spring of German nationalism. Now it was to be the lesson of transcendentalism, also; it was to be the lesson of the new gospel of individualism, when that principle took up its transcendentalist robes to preach in the new secular pulpits, the rostrums of the street and market place. "Every spirit builds itself a house; and beyond its house a world; and beyond its world a heaven. Know, then, that the world exists for you. For you the phenomenon is perfect." Thus had Emerson said it; thus had the seer set it down.

That sometimes this transcendental individualism might dwell in society rather than in solitude need not surprise us. Spiritual association, the dwelling together in rough companionship of all these manly individuals, was the logical fruit of the transcendental philosophy. Brook Farm and Fruitlands, the retreats of these seventy jarring sects, were tracts for troubled utopians, primitive gardens of Eden where a friend was another "I." These retreats of transcendental socialism, utopian and fantastic in their way, were cloisters of the new transcendental priesthood, fortresses of the new theology, where respect for oneself was the common principle of spiritual association. But the principle of primitive communism, of original Christianity, which was the object of spiritual socialism, could not in these crude utopias repeat the aboriginal life of the spirit. Alcott with his Orphic sayings, Emerson with his prophetic sentences, could only reveal himself, could only communicate with himself; for the only common bond of these egoists assembled to perpetuate the ideals of aboriginal communism was that the world belongs to every man, that every man is an inlet and outlet to the same. The Great God Self could not dwell at last with other gods, for his first commandment was: Thou shall have no other gods before me. "Build, therefore, your own world. As fast as you conform your life to the pure idea in your mind, that will unfold its great proportions. A corresponding revolution in things will attend the influx of the spirit. . . ."

What is the secret of this transcendental method? What is the formula for this Orphic saying? It is that the individual is a revelation of cosmic truth, that God puts His wisdom into that earthly receptacle, that divinity dwells in the soul of every man. Truth has become the private possession of individuals; the Yankee transcendentalist has minted his coin out of the private revelations of the spirit, and has listened to the voice only of the Great God Self that dwells within. The transcendental seer had undertaken to accumulate the funded meanings, the intellectual capital, of the entire world. The immanence of this process by which he converted everything his experience touched into intellectual capital led him to conceive of divinity in terms of immanence, in terms of the process of accumulation by which he grew in spiritual riches and bathed in spiritual truth. His pathetic attempt at spiritual association with his fellow transcendentalists was therefore doomed to failure; for each of these transcendental egoists was thrown by the spirit within into a chaos of competition, into an anarchy of rude bickering and the rubble of crude strife. Spiritual association was literally impossible so long as the Great God Self stuck close to his first commandment: Thou shalt have no other gods before me. It happened, accordingly, that spiritual social-ism failed; while each of the transcendentalists went his own way, uttering his own Orphic sayings, yielding only to the impromptu voice of the divinity of himself, driven at last to some wayward retreat of his own—a library in a mossy house in Concord, a tent pitched along the Merrimack River, or even at sea, on the whale's road, where the white foam sprays and the horological soul dreams of its chronometrical truth.

CHAPTER SEVENTEEN

THE GREAT AWAKENING

1. *The Transcendental Education*

The effort to reform society, morals, politics, and religion now fell upon education, and the pedagogical task was conceived to be the making of heroes; for unless the divine average man is given an heroic stature, the enterprise of reform will lack a reliance on the individual. The transcendental education has for its chief theme, accordingly, the development of self-trust, which is also conceived to be a cult of self-cultivation. The cultivation of all the emerging powers of the individual, a renascence of the faith in humanism, also accompanies the gothic mysticism and romance of the age. It brings itself to focus on the ripening powers of the individual mind and proposes to plant there a seed of virtue which might grow into a cosmic morality. The world was a school of character, a match for the emerging powers which it would set to work, and consequently the scene where the primal intuitions of human nature might be brought to their fruition. But education was to rest, first of all, upon the facts of human consciousness; it was to be the means of unfolding innate powers, of bringing to perfection, as if by reminiscence, the primary faculties of the human mind. A former age, which thought of enlightenment in terms of the association of the ideas of sensible experience, was to discover that its culture was shallow and its education a mere discipline of the senses. It was to discover that a succeeding romantic age had uncovered a new lesson and learned an old truth, for the last victory of intelligence was the discovery that the world terminates in the consciousness of man.

This faith in the heroic character of man was the great awakening of the romantic age; it was a new evaluation of the self-conscious activity of the mind by which it grew enlightened, and from whose enlightenment the symbol of the transcendental education was to grow. Now, by various secrets of the transcendental method, the world has suddenly opened its lessons to the individual man; it stood to him in the relation of tutor or teacher, and its immanent dialectic activity was to be the parallel secret of his inner growth. Education was now to be seen, not as a narrow round of duties and prescriptions in a schoolhouse, but as the generous tutelage of the world; it was to be as wide as the horizon of self-conscious activity, and was to take its lessons under a universal master. Education was a salutary embrace of a momentary reflection caught as the froth of a wave in the flowing sea of primal intuitions, and it came in snatches, the idle lesson of a casual hour. "The regular course of studies of the years of academical education have not yielded me better facts than some idle books under the bench at the Latin school," wrote Emerson. "What we do not call education is more precious than that which we call so. We form no guess, at the time of receiving a thought, of its comparative value. And education often wastes its effort in attempts to thwart and balk this natural magnetism, which is sure to select what belongs to it." [71]

The lesson of transcendentalism was that the individual should keep to his own course, open up only those books which evoked a sympathetic response in his soul, and carry into the world the generous process of his own tuition. The outcome of the transcendental education was that, in the generous tutelage of the world, the individual was the selective principle. He was the focus and center of subjectivity and quality, of the properties which Newtonian science had banished from the world. He must, therefore, keep to himself, follow his own course, rejecting as spurious the claim of any study over him which did not contribute to his personal growth and minister to his personal needs. The result was that education was transformed into a school of individualism, where character could grow and personality expand in proportion as the world of experience revealed itself as the realm of exclusive property. This result, already noted in society, politics, and religion, was also inevitable in education; for in transcendental idealism, the subject is separated from the object, which exists only by virtue of the subject's self-conscious activity. The parallel activity in nature, its dialectic activity, the subject responds to only as another "I," as a symbol of the divine idea which each individual represents.

The same reality was present in all teaching. The teacher could teach and the learner learn only as each expressed the endless identities of divine average men, the fulfillment of some promise of growth in each of them. The benefit which accrued to the teacher was therefore no less than that which accrued to the learner in his learning. When the two selves met in the endless identity of some lesson, the magnetism of growth sent up her shower of sparks, electrifying the will and engaging the understanding in a common lesson of self-conscious activity. The lesson of transcendentalism for education was that a self must meet another self and join on some transcendent plane into common identity. Growth was dependent upon the assimilation of a lesson in the primary forms of experience; and the Kantian critical idealism had made familiar to the romantic philosophers the transformation of experience into self-conscious activity. It followed that a common self-consciousness, as in teaching, might breed an endless identity, and the two consciousnesses be wrapped up in a common self. "There is no teaching," wrote Emerson, "until the pupil is brought into the same state or principle in which you are; a transfusion takes place; he is you and you are he; then is teaching, and by no unfriendly chance or bad company can he ever quite lose the benefit." [72]

2. *The School of Experience*

The school of experience into which the transcendental education proposed to plunge was above all other things progressive. The theory presupposed an order of development in the individual, but also an evolutionary force in nature, between which, for the sake of self-conscious activity, the school of experience continually oscillated. The teachers of the school of experience were not indeed teachers at all in any official sense; neither parent nor state-appointed teacher was the tutor of the child. If experience was the school, then the self-conscious activity of the child, the progressive unraveling of his web of growth, was his real tutor. Nature, society, individuals, all existences and events, were for transcendental idealism the means of growth, the materials of self-conscious activity. This position, it was thought, would justify the individual in the stature of a hero and in the proportions of a god. For the romantic age was dedicated, alike in religion, politics, philosophy, and education, to the cult of hero worship, and more importantly, to the production of the heroic American. In accordance with this ideal, then, the school of experience was progressive, adjusting itself to the needs of its pupils, responding only to his insights and to the self-conscious activity of his growth. "The child is not put into the hands of parents alone," wrote Channing. "It is not born to hear but a few voices. It is brought at birth into a vast, we may say, an infinite school. The Universe is charged with the office of its education." [73]

The appeal to a school of experience, the emphasis on the generous tutelage of the world, was for transcendental idealism a way of expressing its basic interest in individualism, in pluralism, in democratic diversity. The individual had become the focus of subjectivity and quality, where strange forces of qualitative uniqueness continually emerged as the result of the individual's self-conscious activity. To transcendentalism, accordingly, the school of experience was a school of individualism; its lessons were designed for the individual and could only be learned individually. The whole secret of education thus appeared to be respect for the transcendental secrets of individual growth, the recognition of the privacy of experience and the personal quality of action. It followed that the child could learn when he would learn; that his willingness to absorb a lesson was only an expression of his readiness to assimilate a new experience. "I believe that our own experience instructs us that the secret of Education lies in respecting the pupil," wrote Emerson. "It is not for you to choose what he shall know, what he shall do. It is chosen and foreordained, and he only holds the key to his own secret. By your tampering and thwarting and too much governing he may be hindered from his end and kept out of his own. Respect the child. Wait and see the new product of Nature. Nature loves analogies, but not repetitions. Respect the child. Be not too much his parent. Trespass not on his solitude." [74]

3. *The Democratic Learning*

The interest of transcendental idealism in democratic diversity produced in time a parallel interest in democratic learning. The ordinary tutelage of nature, friends, society, though an essential part of the transcendental education, was not without its implications for the new democracy. The whole enterprise of educational reform, indeed, presupposed the native equality of the human particles that were to be educated; not indeed an equality that precluded diversity and a commonness that prevented the birth of genius, but rather that an equal fund of native liberty might breed a wild insurgence and lend itself to transcendental diversity. The interest of the age in heroes, its piety before the natural genius, and its hero worship, were but expressions of this underlying faith that men were equal in native liberties even where they might not be equal in ultimate talents. The democratic learning proposed, therefore, that education be based on the native liberty, the self-conscious insurgence, which it thought was the common property of each child. Education, then, was to be founded on democratic diversity and, by the encouragement of this growth, was to produce a nation of heroic individuals.

The transcendental idealist had therefore stumbled upon an old contradiction, recognized in the pages of Jean Jacques Rousseau, that one must choose between making the man and making the citizen, that one cannot make both. This contradiction underlay the appeals of the transcendental philosophers in behalf of the schools, though they themselves, in the expansiveness of their doctrine, were hardly aware of it. For on the one hand, the schools had become a national necessity, a public need of the state, and were to be supported out of public revenues; but on the other hand, the goal of education, at least as the transcendentalist conceived it, was to manufacture pluralisms and increase democratic diversities. The contradiction that the public school should produce a romantic rebel, for whom truth is the warrant of private experience, and heroic character the measure of his departure from public standards, was one into which, not only the transcendental educators, but the progressive educators of a later day fell. For the moment, however, the transcendental educators paid scant attention to their own contradiction, because to them society was no more than an aggregate of individuals, whose very diversity was the means of a better and more cultured society. The problems of society were therefore preëminently the problems of education, to be solved by the reformation of man, by the multiplication of his powers, while the social aggregate grew cohesive amidst the mutual antagonism of its parts.

Democratic diversity, by multiplying the needs and powers of individuals, was to cohere through a mutual demand and common supply. The progress of society was to be dependent upon the progress of individuals, and these could only become progressive if human nature was understood and education based on the cultivation of human powers. The cultivation of the human faculties, of diversity among individuals, may be said to be the goal of the democratic learning. Divine average men, going to school for the sake of the diversities which made them divine, were to emerge as heroes and to cultivate by their presence every worthy science and every good art. The leaders of democratic society were to supply by their example the shortcomings of the more ordinary mass, and by their presence to lend enchantment to a self-conscious cultivation of all human powers. "Let us make our education brave and preventive," wrote Emerson. "Politics is an afterwork, a poor patching. We are always a little late. The evil is done, the law is passed, and we begin the uphill agitation for repeal of that which we ought to have prevented the enacting. We shall one day learn to supersede politics by education. What we call our root-and-branch reforms, of slavery, war, gambling, intemperance, is only medicating the symptoms. We must begin higher up, namely in Education." [75]

The education of everyman was therefore the concern of every man; it was as if no man could be educated until all were raised above the level of apathy, ignorance, and indifference. As all men had equally a native liberty, all men were to be cultivated in their native insurgence, so that the national literature would speak the national mind, and the arts represent the part and parcel of divinity in which each shared. Politics was patchwork and compromise; education was primal, primitive, and was based upon the primary intuitions and faculties of human nature. Romantic education, then, rested upon the same democratic diversity that romantic religion and romantic politics had established as the primary material of national culture. The object of education was said not to be narrow, mean, or provincial, not an education of a sect or party, but in the transcendental spirit, the education of generic man. It was generic man, in his individuality, in the pluralism of his existence, formerly neglected in theocracies and aristocracies, that was now to become the exclusive goal of transcendental education. Democracy meant, not the sharing of a common goal, but the possession of a common nature; and education meant, not the citizenship of men as a class, party, or nation, but the diversity of their development through a common and manifest destiny. The democratic learning was a symbol of the educational ideal of a generation of divine average men who had come to believe themselves no longer ordinary, and in some sense no longer mortal. It was to generate among the diversity of men an evolutionary unity, and express by way of an heroic symbol the common synthesis to which each aspired.

4. *The Cult of Culture*

It now appeared that American schools could fulfill their mission, and the American nation its historic goals, only if a new, independent, and democratic culture could be built to represent American character. The call for cultural independence was in its way as significant a step as the Declaration of Independence had been to a preceding generation; for it represented an end to that long apprenticeship to the literatures of other nations, and a declaration that a novel and unique culture had emerged. It was a culture which identified itself with the future rather than the past, which looked not to historic monuments and syllables long ago expressed, but to a prophetic literature which would express the unlimited progress and imprescribable rights of a young and adolescent independence. The cult of culture was therefore not a worship of the past, not a recalling of a long-lost but nobly celebrated genius in the nation, but an anticipation of the pregnancy to which all the signs of the time pointed. The romantic age was in its way a cultural renascence fed by the realization that there were few great traditions upon which literature could build, and little in the foreshortened perspective of the past to celebrate; that therefore the new age was free to build a great tradition on the meager beginnings, freer than any age in any country because it was itself so new. The cult of culture arose, accordingly, to celebrate the new ideals, to proclaim the new independence, and to issue the call for a new way of life.

The primary task in the cultural renascence fell upon the national literature, because the other arts were at the moment lagging in the old forms, hesitant under the influence of older and foreign traditions. Literature, on the contrary, felt the national growth as its own and appropriated the insurgency of native liberty as a literary form. By literature, therefore, the age invariably meant the expression of the national mind in writing, the celebration of its ideals in the form made congenial by the artist's taste. But it was not only to celebrate the national mind and to represent it in the parliament of letters, but also to liberate it, to free it from the old form so that it could create a new; and it intended that literature should not be limited to the conventional types, but should embrace philosophy, science, education, morals, and become a lyceum of good taste, a secular pulpit for the transcendental priest. As the age had proclaimed the manifest political destiny of the nation, so the men of letters were to proclaim the destiny of its literature, and the growth of its mind. The destiny, as the transcendentalist saw it, was that the nation should take its place, through its authors and artists, among the great nations of the world. The renaissance of culture corresponded, therefore, to the renascence, or rather the beginnings, of native industry, and had as its object to stop the importation of foreign products, whether industrial or artistic, so that a native literature might grow up without the competition of alien ideals.

"A people, into whose minds the thoughts of foreigners are poured perpetually," wrote Channing, "needs an energy within itself to resist, to modify this mighty influence, and, without it, will inevitably sink under the worse bondage, will become intellectually tame and enslaved. We have certainly no desire to complete our restrictive system, by adding to it a literary non-intercourse law. We rejoice in the increasing intellectual connexion between this country and the old world. But sooner would we rupture it, than see our country sitting passively at the feet of foreign teachers. It were better to have no literature, than form ourselves unresistingly on a foreign one. The true sovereigns of a country are those who determine its mind, its modes of thinking, its tastes, its principles; and we cannot consent to lodge this sovereignty in the hands of strangers. A country, like an individual, has dignity and power only in proportion as it is self-formed. There is a great stir to secure to ourselves the manufacturing of our own clothing. We say, let others spin and weave for us, but let them not think for us. A people, whose government and laws are nothing but the embodying of public opinion, should jealously guard this opinion against foreign dictation. We need a literature to counteract, and use wisely the literature which we import." [76]

The transcendental renascence had therefore come to express a theme which had proved congenial to America; it gave rise to an attempt to understand human nature as a national concept, to see in the varieties of national experience and in the diversities of national character a perennial theme which might lend itself to definition. The first proposition of cultural independence was that in America human nature is self-formed, self-cultivated, and self-governed. Hence, the cult of national culture was also a cult of self-culture; it presupposed that the means of culture were to be diffused; that the lyceum, the pulpit, the school, the press, the library, were to be the common means placed in common hands to attain an uncommon result. The responsibility of the state was conceived to be limited to the establishment and support of the means of culture, while the actual cultivation was to be left in private hands. That is why the celebration of our ideals and the study of our character, whether in poetry, philosophy, or the arts, has always taken the form of individual expression, and seemed the product of an original mind. In brief, while the means of culture have always been public, the ends have always been private; the means having been provided by the benefactions of the state, it was left to the native industry and genius of the individual to convert the public means into a private appropriation, and to grow by the very diversity and individuality of the form of his self-cultivation into a symbol and representative of the nation. The peculiar result has been that even the sophisticates who fled to other lands there to denounce the shallowness of American culture and the economic motives of American life have themselves been among the most representative Americans, expressing by way of contempt for the things which made their revolt possible, the democratic diversity and cultural individualism which all along it was the goal to create. That is why, also, when this insight is gained, the repatriate returns to native shores, and, like Bacon's atheist, becomes an older and wiser man.

5. *Education as Growth*

All the forces of the romantic age combined to produce the conception of education as growth. The literature of education, descended from Rousseau and Pestalozzi, spoke of the unfolding of the native powers, of an order of development in the individual. This conception in its turn owed its form to the idea of the self-regulating powers of nature, which, having proved congenial to the forming of republics, was now to be mirrored in the conception of man. The transcendental conception of an immanent conscious activity in the individual, by which the qualities of the world might be appropriated in private form, was also friendly to the conception of education as growth. Education now appeared as an unfolding of native talents in the presence of native liberties, and its substantive rule had become: respect the pupil, do not interfere in the normal processes by which his powers are unfolded. "Man is endogenous, and education is his unfolding," wrote Emerson. "The aid we have from others is mechanical compared with the discoveries of nature in us. What is thus learned is delightful in the doing, and the effect remains. Right ethics are central and go from the soul outward. Gift is contrary to the law of the universe. Serving others is serving us. I must absolve me to myself." [77]

The secret of the transcendental method—to appropriate the funded meanings, the intellectual capital, of the world in private form—thus revealed itself also as the principal method of education. Transcendental idealism had argued that nothing was to be understood aside from its revelation of the self, that the Socratic doctrine of self-knowledge was after all the only form of knowledge which could be tested by the understanding. It thus appeared that the method of education ought to adjust itself to these transcendental premises; that education ought to follow the natural order of development in the individual, respecting the pupil's immanent self-conscious activity, and offering its materials only in the form of his private understanding. When education was conceived as growth, the secret of method lay in respecting the native powers of the student, and in engaging his self-conscious activity as a subject. Following out the preconceptions of romantic philosophy, the transcendental educators believed the object could not be known except in the self-conscious form of the subject, and hence that the learner could not learn nor the teacher teach without the appropriation of the curriculum in private form. Respect for the student meant respect for individualism, the principle of native liberty and native power by which the nation would grow to be a realization of its manifest destiny.

The transcendental educator therefore used the strongest language to advise paternalistic legislators not to interfere with native industry, but rather to encourage and protect the normal processes of growth. It was the program of Hamilton and of Whiggism applied to education, and it had as its object the development of a native product which should rival and transcend competitive foreign ideals. The outcome for education was a constant insistence upon the encouragement of the natural powers of the individual, so that his native industry might be rewarded and his individual talents ripen. The transcendental educator had proclaimed that education was to be based upon human nature, and like the romantic philosophy transcend by intuition the limitations of merely sensible experience. It followed that discipline was not to be imposed as an alien structure upon the native genius of the child, but was rather to be an outgrowth of his ripening powers, the fruit of his immanent self-conscious activity. Freedom to develop naturally was therefore the slogan of the romantic educator, and a program of noninterference was his legislative wisdom. Education, like legislation, should be designed to encourage native industry, develop the native faculties, while protecting them from outside rivalries and the distortion of the normal order of their growth.

6. *The Hegelian Education*

The transcendental educator had learned from Hegel that self-conscious activity was the only form in which a genuine maturing of the native powers could be produced. Educational psychology discovered the method of introspection and proposed to demonstrate how the mind might arrive at a higher stage of consciousness. The educator was henceforth to investigate the forms of mental activity and their development or evolution, and he was expected to convert the raw materials of education, the materials of the curriculum, into a higher form of consciousness. Romantic idealism, following out the method of Hegel, traced the development of mental activity through its three fundamental stages, and proposed to build a method of education out of this evolutionary mental process. From the first stage of mental perception the mind conceived its objects as having an independent being and existence, apart from their relation to other things. In a second stage it saw everything as dependent upon the environment, so that everything was seen to be relative, and not to exist apart from its relations to other things. At a final stage the mind discovered a new absolute unity in all things, an organic integration, in which the relativity of phenomenal things was seen as but a manifestation of the absolute unity of self-conscious Being.

The two first stages of thought were identified with the age of reason, with its sensationalism, its empiricism, and its positivism; and were considered inferior, although perhaps necessary, stages in the light of the third and final stage of thought. The romantic age naturally identified itself with the third stage, and called into question the presuppositions of the first two stages of thought; it questioned the environmentalism of the age of reason, the sensationalism of the philosophy of the Enlightenment, the utilitarian standard of the eighteenth century. The outcome of this critique of rationalism was, however, congenial to the building of new goals for education, for the conception of learning as the self-conscious activity of the learner. The Hegelian contribution was to reinforce the conception that things can be known in the only form in which the knower can know them, namely, as the self-conscious activity of the knower, as the product of his private appropriation of the qualities and properties of the thing that is known. From Kant and Fichte and Schelling, transcendental idealism had already come to possess this insight, but with Hegel a new dimension was added, namely, the conception of the Absolute. In the final stage of thought, therefore, in the stage at which the romantic age believed itself to have arrived, the absolute unity of all things, a transcendental unity which rose above the sensationalism of the first stage and the relativism of the second, was conceived as a stage of true being.

The transcendental program in education rested upon this Hegelian insight and bred a hungry introspection of the self for the sake of understanding. As the absolute unity of self-conscious being was a program of growth leading to the integration of all the powers, the Hegelian education aimed, first, at the self-conscious unity of the human being, at the ripening and maturing and integration of his powers. Moreover, this program was conceived to be directed toward the freedom of the subject, not only in the sense of liberating his native powers, but also as the only freedom that was meaningful to Hegelians, namely, the freedom of self-conscious unity. This freedom could only be realized in the form of unity, achieved by an adaptation of ends to means, and actualized in the form of a realization of purpose. In this form, the achievement of freedom on the part of the individual was supposed to parallel an analogous development in nature, whose dialectic activity actualized its evolutionary thesis in the form of a realization of self-conscious unity. The Hegelian education attempted to encourage an evolution of the powers of the individual to achieve the unity and freedom of self-conscious realization at various stages of his growth. The evolutionary thesis of transcendental idealism had therefore been given a Hegelian absolute dimension which lent itself to transcendental piety and contributed a new method to romantic education.

"The evolutionary theory recognizes introspection as existing in the objective world," wrote Harris. "—it sees in nature a tendency to develop such beings as possess internality and energize and realize their ideals. It is curious to note that this movement in science begins by the utter repudiation of what is called teleology; i.e., it sets aside the old doctrine of design which looked for marks of external adaptation of nature to ulterior spiritual uses—such external design as one finds in a watch, where various parts are artificially adapted to produce what they never would have produced naturally. Such external teleology ignored the immanent teleology of nature. By rejecting the old mechanical teleology, which makes nature a machine in the hand of God, evolution has come to see the teleology which God has breathed into nature—to see, in short, that nature is through and through teleological. Nature is, in every part of it, governed by ideals." [78]

This contribution of Hegelian education helped the transcendentalist to penetrate to deeper levels of the meaning of self-conscious activity. It was discovered that the concept of self-activity was indispensable to the study of the self as an object, to that unity of subject and object, by which the mind could grow in the power to realize its purposes. Thinking thereby became the activity of the understanding, and rested upon recognition, upon a knowing of universals. The pluralism, the nominalism, of the age of reason was destroyed, and the method of empiricism called into doubt, by this new enthusiasm for evolutionary realism. Education henceforth was to devote itself to the development of the power of recognition, whose cumulative and growing faculty of apperception, would contribute to the absolute unity of experience. In the perspective of the Hegelian education, then, the ideal of democratic diversity, which had been the essence of the democratic learning, was shattered in the attempt to realize an absolute unity of experience. While the democratic diversity of transcendental education was presupposed as a condition for the beginning of self-conscious activity, still its ultimate outcome was to prove hostile to transcendental individualism. For the Hegelian educator began at once to speak—as Hegel had done—of the state as the historic embodiment of the Absolute, whose absolute obligations might transcend the relative rights of individuals. Henceforth, for the Hegelian disciple, there could be no realization of individuality, no prospect of growth, outside the absolute unity of the state. At this stage, therefore, the democratic diversity of transcendentalism had been challenged by the absolute alien Not Me, and proved in the end hostile to the transcendental program of education. Romantic philosophy had thus destroyed itself in the pursuit of the very ideal which had driven it on; but in the meantime, transcendentalism was discovering other variations on its traditional themes, and looked forward to an era in which the radical, democratic Me might once more come to terms with the alien, absolute, Not Me.

CHAPTER EIGHTEEN

THE QUEST OF TRUTH

1. *The Romantic Philosophy in America*

The world insurgence of the classical German philosophy communicated to America a romantic self-consciousness, which now by the various secrets of the transcendental method could be viewed appropriately from the private perspective of the individual. This consciousness of the self, which was the central dogma of transcendentalism, became in America a consciousness both of nature, in which a cosmic self was revealing itself, and of human nature, in which a parallel human self was achieving various stages of its growth. To follow out the progression of thought by which these amazing deductions were reached, it must be borne in mind that Locke, tracing out the mechanical view of nature presented in Newtonian science, had conceived the life of consciousness in a thoroughly mechanical way, so that consciousness had become the mere reflection or reproduction of sense impressions. The content of consciousness was thus limited to sensible ideas, which, associating by similarity or contiguity—that is, in space or time—merely reproduced in a more or less predetermined way the objective train of sensible associations. Thus arose the central problem of modern philosophy, the problem of knowledge which the age of reason was incapable of solving. For the mechanical view of human nature contradicts the most fundamental tenet of republican freedom, the presupposition that man possesses freedom of the will, and hence is capable of self-government.

Thus it happened that the philosophic disputes that follow Locke have as their substance the problem of consciousness, the mechanism of which seemed to preclude the freedom of the will. The philosophies of Berkeley, Hume, and Kant, which have as their principal subject matter an analysis of human experience, are in fact but several stages in which the subject is cut loose from the object. The tendency of all these early philosophies was clearly in the direction of empirical idealism, and the typical problem which they confronted, as with Kant, was an analysis of experience from the standpoint of critical idealism, so that the private freedom and the creativity of the subject is preserved, despite the more or less predetermined empirical content of the knowing mind. Kant, Fichte, Schelling, represent various stages of this process, which culminates in Hegel. The self-conscious activity of the subject reaches its fullest development in Hegel; and having become Absolute, having been embodied in nature and in history, passes into its opposite, objective necessity, and vanishes from the living scene of philosophy, only to reappear in more or less attentuated form in later idealism and positivism. Philosophy more and more tended after Locke, then, to be occupied with a single problem, the problem of consciousness; but in developing this principle of individualism through a series of contradictions to its highest level, to its self-conscious level, it had become embodied, as in Hegel, as social consciousness. It had in fact ceased to be a principle of individualism, and had become a principle of collectivism. The whole of subsequent American philosophy may be said to have become various recipes for avoiding the ultimate assumption of romantic idealism, while deriving from it all that it would lend to the cause of democratic diversity.

The fact is that American philosophy did not object to having the Absolute of Hegel embodied in nature and history as a cosmic consciousness, as the dialectics of God; and in the days of heroes and manifest destiny this was indeed what the Absolute seemed to be. The chief concern of American philosophy was that the Absolute, in which transcendental idealism culminated, should be embodied in nature, in society, and in human nature, as a cosmic consciousness, as the consciousness of God, which was only a reflection of the self-conscious activity of the individual man. When however the disciples of Hegel began to speak of the Absolute in terms of objective necessity, the embodiment in nature and in history of dialectic necessity, the native philosophers of course recoiled from a doctrine which denied freedom of the will, the value of democratic diversity, the capacity of man for self-government. Such an outcome, indeed, seemed not a solution of the problem, but merely a return to the materialism of the age of reason, from which transcendental idealism had taken its start. It happened, therefore, that while the romantic philosophers in America shared in and appropriated the results of transcendental idealism, they scrupulously avoided some of the outcomes of the Hegelian stage of it, which they saw would transform it into its opposite. Hegel, therefore, is the dividing line of modern philosophy, the father of both right and left, of absolute idealism and absolute materialism, in which American transcendentalism represents a preparatory stage. The origin of transcendental idealism, accordingly, may be looked for in the problem of Kant, whose critical idealism became a transcendental philosophy in Fichte and Schelling, and culminated in the Absolute idealism of Hegel.

"These men are the illustrious four who have originated and carried out, with epic succession and completeness, the modern systems of critical and transcendental philosophy," wrote Whitman. "The critical is represented by Kant, who begins and ends it. The transcendental rises out of and is founded upon the critical and could have had no beginning or growth except from its previous existence. There is a close relative-connection, sequence, etc., between all the four even in time. They fit into each other like a nest of boxes—and Hegel encloses them all. Taking their whole philosophy, it is the most important emanation of the mind of modern ages and of all ages, leaving even the wonderful inventions, discoveries of science, political programs, great engineering works, utilitarian comforts, etc., of the last hundred years in a comparatively inferior rank of importance—outstripping them all. Because it assumes to answer and does answer, as far as they can be answered, the deepest questions of the soul, of identity, of purposes worthy of the world and of the relation between man and the material nature and workings of the external universes, not depreciating them but elevating man to the spiritual plane where he belongs, and where after all that physical comfort and luxury, with mental culture, and political freedom, can accomplish, he at last finds, and there only finds, a satisfaction worthy of his highest self, and achieves happiness." [79]

2. *The Origin of Transcendentalism*

The problem bequeathed to Kant by Newtonian science and by the psychology of Locke, though he himself nowhere explicitly states it, was in its essence the contradiction between the mechanical view of nature and the republican conception of freedom. The world of Newton had allowed a certain freedom to the individual particles which made up the universe, it will be remembered; God contributed an initial charge of energy to the particles which proceed on their ideal course, influenced only by the mysterious force of gravity. In this scheme of universal relations, it would be difficult for any one particle to know the spatial and temporal connections of other particles unless it could sit outside this framework and view the events as a divine spectator—as God. Thus arose the problem of consciousness; for how could a single particle have knowledge of other particles, and also how could it become conscious of its own unique path without a knowledge of the particles with which it was associated? But as a matter of fact man was included within the scope of the Newtonian world; it must be so constituted, then, that the individual particles all carry space and time and other categories in their heads, reproducing on a small scale God's boundless sensorium. Experience would then seem to fill in the categories already arranged in consciousness. This was the conclusion to which Kant was driven in his attempt to solve the contradiction bequeathed by Newtonian science and the psychology of Locke. He solved the problem by making the universal determinism of the Newtonian world subjective; he simply set up space, time, and the other categories as the *a priori* conditions of human knowledge, as the predetermining forms of the knowing mind.

It happened, accordingly, that the transcendentalist stressed, in opposition to the sensationalist philosophy of the age of reason, that there was something in the consciousness which was not first in the senses, namely, the consciousness itself, the *a priori* condition of all human experience. The experiences of separate individuals have therefore a unity of apperception derived from the *a priori* forms of consciousness. This however led to a further contradiction, but it was overcome by the same device. The subject can only know what he can experience, the fundamental tenet of empiricism, and can never transcend the limits of possible experience. But Kant showed that in every assertion the knower transcends the limits of experience, and that he was justified in this transcendence of the limits of sensible experience by the fact that the forms of consciousness will be always the same. However, Kant added, the knower cannot know the thing-in-itself; for we experience nature phenomenally, and of the experienced phenomena only the fittest will survive. Thus a screen of phenomena intervenes between the knower and the known, while yet the categories of the consciousness give a unity of experience. Hence, for philosophy the nature of the knowing self and the conditions of experience were, so to speak, the transcendent considerations.

"Kant analyses, dissects, dissipates, the vast suffocating miasma that had so long spread impediments to philosophy," wrote Whitman, "—clears away, removes, sometimes like a surgeon's knife—yet in fact and after all decides little or nothing—is of indescribable value—denies the possibility of absolute knowledge of the external world—begins with Hume—admits that we receive all the materials of our knowledge through the senses—but immediately rises above that admission. Long before, the speculations of Locke and the other materialists, had reached the formula that 'there is nothing in the understanding which was not arrived there through the senses.' Leibnitz had replied, 'Yes, there is the understanding itself.' Kant's entire speculations are but a splendid amplification of this reply. He endeavors to get at and state the philosophy of the understanding. The problem of the relation between the understanding and the universe of material nature, he did not attempt to solve." [80]

In this development of his thought, however, Kant had only transformed the predeterminism of the Newtonian world into a predeterminism of the mind. Our experience turns out to be unified, connected, integrated, capable of entering into and explaining the experience of another in its common terms. The unity of apperception, the integration of sensible experience, was therefore attributed to the subjective consciousness and its predetermined categories. The conditions of experience cannot be alienated from the experiencing self, because that is what the self in its consciousness is. Now Kant did not deny the existence of a reality, a thing-it-itself, behind phenomena; he only asserted that reality could be known to us only phenomenally, as a private property of the categories of consciousness. Even the self of ourselves, the self-in-itself, is unknowable. Our true self must therefore be, not our phenomenal self, which only partially reveals to us the true self, but a self-in-itself lying behind the phenomenal self which screens and hides it from us. Therefore, while phenomenally the will may not seem to be free, the true self-will, the will of the self-in-itself, must be free. Kant explicitly stated that in these matters we must rest on faith that the will is free; we must transcend the phenomenal self to the true freedom of the self-in-itself. Kant makes it clear, moreover, that we can know only such phenomena as are fit to be known; that our form of consciousness makes it certain that only a phenomenal manifestation of an underlying reality will be known to us.

The outcome for transcendentalism was the realization that institutions and individuals exist only to be transcended, only to realize their higher selves. The church, the state, the individual, were all only phenomenal identities—not the divine average which would grow out of them, not the higher identity, or organic unity, which was already contained in them as a seed, and would one day sprout into perfection. This thought meant, among other things, that everything, not just the American nation, contained its manifest destiny, its cosmic goal. The result was favorable to transcendental piety, and gave the programs of philanthropic reform a mighty metaphysic; for it was believed that the hero was essentially a reformer, carrying out by the strict determination of his will, what the will of each when combined as the will of all, would have demanded had it articulated itself. Hence the age was interested in its heroes and in its gods, and each man in seeking to transcend his phenomenal self, to attain to a higher self-consciousness and virtue, was presumed to have entered into an heroic course. The Kantian critical idealism had set forward the movement which was to lead to the discovery of the self, but it remained for Schelling to contribute a transcendental method for the attainment of this higher realization of the self.

3. *The Discovery of the Self*

In seeking a solution of his own problem, Kant had left the self as a knower incapable of knowing itself except phenomenally as object, as the known. The mysterious thing-in-itself, nature, was thus left in the same state as the mysterious self-in-itself, man. The subject–object relation had generated apparently an insufferable antinomy. It remained for Schelling to discover the true self, as distinct from the empirical ego or phenomenal self, in the light of transcendentalism and by means of the dialectic method. He begins with the problem as it had been left by Kant: The self can be known to us only as object, only phenomenally; therefore we can never know the true self, the self-in-itself, the principle of its individuality, which lurks behind this phenomenal screen. It was clear then that the main problem left by Kant came down to the achievement of self-consciousness. The self, mysteriously embodied but not revealed in the processes of experience, must now discover itself. More technically stated, the problem was to bridge the causal, mutually determining relation of knowing, to transcend it, as it were, so that the self in its discovery might remain free.

"Meantime, Fichte had begun by declaring for Kant," wrote Walt Whitman. "He founds and builds largely on the distinction between the *I* and the *not I*. Upon the fact that a man can only realize anything in its relations to himself, and from the capacities and measurements that constitute himself, he lays so much stress, that the whole universe becomes, in brief, the *I* as that is the only thinking subject, active principle and consciousness. . . . Fichte, as will be seen, grows out of and is closely related to Kant. . . . *Subjectiveness* is his principle, explaining all. Strongly stated nothing exists but the *I*. And in this central fact is every moral obligation, duty, conscience, giving vitality to all. Then comes Schelling who professes largely to answer the questions left open by Kant with a doctrine of 'spontaneous intuition'—in other words to solve the problem left open by Kant with the theory that the human mind and external nature are essentially *one*. That that which exists in concrete forms, etc., in Nature, exists morally and mentally in the human spirit. The difference between him and Fichte is that Schelling's philosophy is more largely *objective*. The chief forte of it— seeking to counterbalance and restrain Fichte's all-devouring egotism— is *the essential identity of the subjective and objective worlds,* or, in other terms, that which exists as mentality, intelligence, consciousness in man, exists in equal strength and absoluteness in concrete forms, shows and practical laws in material nature—making the latter one with man's sane intuitions. The same universal spirit manifests itself in the individual Man, in aggregates, in concrete Nature, and in Historic progress." [81]

In the posing of this problem, Schelling had taken for granted that the true self, or principle of individuality, was perfectly free and un- determined. The self as knower is perfectly free, while as known it is predetermined to have a definite constitution and structure. To know itself, however, it would have to take itself as the object, as determinate. This suggested that the self might have a dual constitution; for, on the one hand, the self is ideal, limitless, as long as it remains the subject; but in practical life, in action, it is drawn into the mutually determining causal relation of knowing, and hence the real or practical self has be- come limited and determinate. The free subject, then, can express itself only in a self-conscious limitation. Now this situation in which the self is ideally free but practically limited admirably sums up the position of German nationalism of the time; its revolutionary aspirations are limit- less, but it has a series of practical failures which embody in history the record of its self-conscious limitations. But to become self-conscious, through penetration of the self as object, is to know its own constitutional limitations. However high the revolutionary aspirations might soar, they must express themselves practically through self-conscious limita- tion. Still, this process itself embodies an elemental dialectic; for in pass- ing to a higher stage of consciousness, the self has only become more conscious of the principle of individuality which it embodies.

Schelling had thus come to express the most elementary principle of spiritual life, that the self must possess itself, view even itself as private property, and possess itself as object if it is yet to remain free. The ob- ject can thus be known to the knower only as self-knowledge, as a private possession; and this must be true, also of the self-in-itself. The self must then possess itself in order to reach a higher stage of self-consciousness. Until its self-consciousness is its own, it is not really self-conscious at all, and hence hardly to be thought of as a free self-determining subject. Now the stage of dialectic history which for the moment had ushered itself in, posited truth as the outcome of a process, and of one which was essentially dialectical by virtue of the fact that contradictions, self-conscious limitations, must be overcome. The will of man, nominally free, is also forced to express itself in a series of self-conscious limitations; but in overcoming these, it spirals up the dialectic series to its absolute freedom. The problem thus posed was how the self becomes conscious of itself by passing through a series of contradictions until it reaches a higher stage of consciousness, a stage at which it is truly self-conscious.

For Schelling, however, the dialectic suggested by the categories is not only the dialectic of the self, but also that of nature. When nature is viewed as a process, therefore, its dialectic becomes objectified; everything in nature seeks its opposite and transcends its isolation, for every object is a polarity of mutually opposing tendencies. On the other hand, nature displays an integrated series of levels, which reach to the highest stage in man, in the principle of individuality. Thus if one abstracts from the subject in order to study the object, one has soon described a subject; while if one abstracts from the object in order to study the subject, one has soon described an object. Nature has thus become the self described as an object. Just as the objective view has led us to regard nature as a process of unconscious dialectic out of which the conscious self is evolved; so too, the subjective view leads us to nature as that which the self necessarily, though unconsciously, constructs. The mind strives to realize itself in nature, and nature wishes to embody itself in mind. The conclusion of this whole line of reasoning, then, is that thought and being are one.

Now the self is a knower of phenomena, so that, to be conscious of this self, the self must be capable of a type of thinking which becomes immediately its own object. To know the knower, then, is a dialectical process; for in self-knowledge the self becomes the object in so far as it is the knowing self. The existence of the self thus becomes for Schelling an act of self-consciousness. In brief, the self exists only for itself, and can know itself only as it comes to know itself in an act of self-consciousness. In a higher stage of self-consciousness, therefore, the self has become conscious of itself both as subject and object, and thought and being have become one. The destiny of this self is to express itself in objective form as moments of self-knowledge, but at the same time it is continuously learning of itself both as knowing subject and as known object. The same result is obtained when a number of selves become conscious of each other as objects, and then through this consciousness rise to a consciousness of themselves as subjects. When the act of one becomes significant for another, not only phenomenally significant, but self-consciously significant, social consciousness has emerged. It follows from this social consciousness that a moral sense could arise, defining the ideal of ideals which all self-conscious selves will hold, namely, the ideal of complete self-expression. In brief, the romantic self has been trying to be the Absolute, to transcend its finite, limited self expression in this world in order to reach a higher stage of self-consciousness and individuality by transcending all natural limitations. The transcendental idealism of Schelling is thus an ideal expression of the very real goal of romantic freedom, which it transcends through the ignorance of the necessity which had made it desire to be free. The goal of romantic freedom, for the moment unattainable in backward Germany, had turned inward upon itself, expressing itself in a series of contradictions by which it has attained the absolute freedom which it had always secretly sought.

4. *The Dialectic of History*

The transcendental dialectic has now culminated in Schelling. The self has possessed itself by transcending itself; it has gained self-knowledge by knowing itself both as knower and known, both as subject and object; for at this stage, thought and being are identical. In a degree this achievement has disrupted Schelling's original goal, for nature has emerged to subjectivity, and mind to objectivity, or rather to a higher stage of self-consciousness. Once this goal had been reached, however, nothing remained but to embody the dialectic in history, in the struggles of men, of classes, of nations, for a self-conscious unity of apperception. At the same time, the steps taken by Schelling made it inevitable that logic and history should be united in one supreme dialectic of thought. Henceforth it would be possible to speak, not only of the dialectic of nature and of the self, but also of the dialectic of history. In this inevitable dialectic the world spirit realizes itself through various discrete stages which are nevertheless pregnant with the becoming of the future. In brief, Hegel planned a biography of the world spirit to illustrate the social history of the Absolute, the world spirit revealing itself to men and nations at various moments of its development.

The world spirit in its discrete incarnations in different peoples and nations, in its flights and transmigrations, is essentially progressive; for amidst the contradictions of present life it always moves on to a higher stage. These various moments of its history express an attitude, a philosophy of life, which realizes itself in modes of behavior peculiar to the time. Each stage of social consciousness, taken by itself, is perfectly rational; yet in the course of time it develops contradictions within itself which lead on to the next stage of social consciousness. Hence each stage of history must reconstruct the categories and intellectual materials handed from the past, and continue in them that thread of continuity which the dialectic has unwittingly revealed at each stage. In the Absolute the truth is fully revealed, because the temporal diversities which separate the various moments of its revelation are eternally present to itself. In other words, the Absolute defines the kind of self-consciousness which transcendentalism thirsted to attain. The Absolute is the conception of individuality, of transcendental freedom, taken in its absolute unity of apperception. History was henceforth nothing but the history of ideas, each of which, for its moment or stage was rational and true, but which, surveyed by the Absolute, proved itself to be a finite error, only a contradiction by which the dialectic moves on to the next higher stage.

The meaning of the dialectic for the transcendentalist, however, was that the seed of individuality would flower if once the steps were taken to possess, on its own higher level, all the forms and categories of consciousness which the dialectic had revealed. The world had become the province of the transcendentalist; it only remained to appropriate its intellectual riches, to reconstruct philosophy, and to pour the elemental truth of the lower stages of history into the higher stage of transcendental truth. Unless, however, self-consciousness has reached the stage of social consciousness, the self is hardly prepared to carry out this program. Hegel devotes himself, accordingly, to an analysis of how history comes to embody a social consciousness. If therefore the transcendentalists were to recover at their higher stage of history the intellect and the culture of the lower stages, they must be prepared to read the chapters in the biography of the world spirit already written down, and then to transform these into their own peculiar romantic mode of consciousness. They would then attain the highest stage of social consciousness possible for their epoch, and would inevitably carry out the dialectic progression which the world spirit has determined for them. For its own stage of development, then, the transcendental mode of conscious is the only possible and also the only rational way of conceiving things.

This analysis would seem to make the romantic mind conscious that its own days were numbered; but Germany's backward state politically had not yet permitted full individual freedom to flower. On the other hand, Hegel defines a stage of philosophical consciousness by virtue of which it is possible to survey the various stages of consciousness in their continuity and development, so that a world of reason is revealed to the organized self-consciousness. In this stage individuals should devote themselves to a finite realization of the Absolute. Truth is therefore a process which necessarily involves finite error as an ingredient of its development; and, as a matter of fact, truth only reveals itself in finite error. The self is likewise the union of mutually exclusive and contradictory tendencies, but it grows by overcoming its own contradictions, by transcending itself. Moreover, since every finite thing, taken alone, contradicts itself, the finite self realizes itself only in social consciousness, but this in turn realizes itself only in the self-conscious determination of the Absolute. The world spirit, then, while revealing itself in the individual and social consciousness, in peoples and nations, is an incarnation of the divine.

It follows from this incarnation of the divine, of the Absolute, in peoples and nations, that the individual will be stirred up to surge against a sea of troubles, that nations will become conscious of their manifest destiny, and that history will henceforth be nothing more than an inevitable dialectic and clash of contradiction from which truth, progress, and freedom will be realized in the end. Once the dialectic had been embodied, not only in social consciousness, but also in the various stages of historical consciousness, man became, as it were, the latest and most perfect incarnation of the divine. While this teaching was a momentary revelation to the transcendental philosophers, it also spelled their doom and discomfort; for no one could prevent the inevitable dialectic from crushing out of existence the very philosophers who had become conscious of it. The problem thus posed to future philosophers was whether humanity, having reached an appropriate level of social consciousness, could make history after its own fashion. Philosophers who were unable to give a straightforward answer to this problem would at least confess that the contribution of the dialectical method and the analysis of stages of social consciousness makes it imperative that, in the words of the romantic philosophers, the objective should become subjective, and the subjective should become objective; so that the subject, man, returning to his self-consciousness from his penetration of nature, the object, should embody in the form of his consciousness and subjectivity those very laws which nature, in revealing herself to the subject, makes an inevitable ingredient of the higher stage of social consciousness for which he strives. But once Hegel had embodied the dialectic in history, it only seemed that the dream of transcendental freedom, however revealed at some moment of history, would henceforth be forever unattainable; because freedom could only reveal herself in some finite and disruptive moment of a pregnant necessity.

"Only Hegel is fit for America—is large enough and free enough," wrote Whitman. "Absorbing his speculations and imbued by his letter and spirit, we bring to the study of life here and the thought of hereafter, in all its mystery and vastness, an expansion and clearness of sense before unknown. As a face in a mirror we see the world of materials, nature with all its objects, processes, shows, reflecting the human spirit and by such reflection formulating, identifying, developing and proving it. Body and mind are one; an inexplicable paradox, yet no truth truer. The human soul stands in the centre, and all the universes minister to it, and serve it and revolve around it. They are one side of the whole and it is the other side. It escapes utterly from all limits, dogmatic standards and measurements and adjusts itself to the ideas of God, of space, and to eternity, and sails them at will as oceans, and fills them as beds of oceans." [82]

5. The Idealist Mind

Transcendental idealism had thus discovered the creative activity of the subject at work in the universe, and to that alone, as a condition of its growth, would it respond. "Thus inevitably does the universe wear our color, and every object falls successively into the subject itself," wrote Emerson. "The subject exists, the subject enlarges; all things sooner or later fall into place." In terms of the traditional subject–object antinomy of philosophy, transcendentalism sought to express the creative activity of the subject, the dependence of the known on being known; but in the course of its somewhat singular development, it had incarnated the activity of the subjective consciousness into nature, so that the creative universe might be explained in the same terms as the creative individual. The outcome of the romantic philosophy, therefore, lent itself to the metaphysics of individualism, and seemed to prove that the subject was the condition for the existence of the object. It happened, accordingly, that the transcendental philosophers found the universe responded to the creative growth of individuals, that it was a suitable home for the development of transcendental optimism. The world existed for the sake of the individual, growth was its character, and expansion its necessity; hence the transcendental hero seemed to enclose the object, as a revelation of his self-conscious activity. The subject had thus grown to heroic proportions, while the object had become the province of his mind.

"Perhaps these subject-lenses have a creative power; perhaps there are no objects," wrote Emerson. "Once we lived in what we say; now, the rapaciousness of this new power, which threatens to absorb all things, engages us. Nature, art, persons, letters, religions, objects, successively tumble in, and God is but one of its ideas. Nature and literature are subjective phenomena; every evil and every good thing is a shadow which we cast. . . . The great and creative self, rooted in absolute nature, supplants all relative existence and ruins the kingdom of mortal friendship and love. Marriage (in what is called the spiritual world) is impossible because of the inequality between every subject and every object. The subject is the receiver of Godhead, and at every comparison must feel his being enhanced by that cryptic might. Though not in energy, yet in presence, this magazine of substance cannot be otherwise than felt; nor can any force of intellect attribute to the object the proper deity which sleeps or wakes forever in every subject. Never can love make consciousness and ascription equal to force. There will be the same gulf between every me and thee as between the original and the picture. The universe is the bride of the soul." [83]

This discovery meant, among other things, that the world proceeds from the same cosmic mind as man, that a common spirit incarnates itself in nature and human nature, and the two are drawn as one through the same spawning activity. But nature seemed a remoter and inferior sort of incarnation, and the dialectics of nature on a lower divine plane than the gymnastics of the soul. Matter was a Proteus of many shapes and colors, escaping from the net of philosophy when she seemed closest to an embrace. But while matter was mysterious, her dialectic activity seemed a demonstration of an immanent divine consciousness, an over-soul to which the undersoul responded as a child to its parent. Of the two methods of philosophizing, between the externality of the materialist and the internality of the idealist, transcendentalism had already made its choice. It comprehended the familiar American antithesis between mechanism and idealism, and because it could conceive of matter in no other than a mechanist disguise, it chose without hesitation the creative activity of idealism. Matter existed as a revelation of a cosmic mind whose activity was akin to that of the human mind; and because matter could not exist without the supposition of subjective self-conscious activity, mind seemed the only reality.

Out of the dialectic idealism of Hegel, then, the only progress seemed to lie in dialectical materialism; but its dialectic movement toward the Absolute swallowed down all relative differences, and hence precluded the democratic diversity for which American philosophy was striving. In the Hegelian dialectic, individual differences exist only to be transcended, and are only relative and expendable means for an absolute end. But this outcome of the dialectic method precluded any metaphysics of individualism in which individuality would be the end rather than a means. While admitting a dialectic activity in nature, therefore, and even a corresponding dialectic activity in human consciousness, the American philosophers were loathe to destroy the traditional principle of individualism upon which rested the presupposition of freedom of will; for freedom of the will was the necessary metaphysical assumption both of the republican doctrine of self-government and the transcendental doctrine of democratic diversity. Both doctrines were forms of the prevailing American metaphysics of individualism, upon which rested the favored conceptions of God, freedom, and immortality.

The Hegelian method had therefore reinstated an absolute monism, which, if it took a materialistic direction, would prove hostile to the pluralistic universe of individualism. The only safeguard of the traditional metaphysics of individualism lay, therefore, either in the resurrection of eighteenth-century positivism in a modern sophisticated form, or else in the development of a new doctrine in which the outcome of the dialectic activity of the universe is the creation of new individuals, the perpetuation of a pluralistic world, as the very condition of its having any monistic unity. "Pluralistic empiricism knows that everything is in an environment, a surrounding world of other things," wrote William James, "and that if you leave it to work there it will inevitably meet with friction and opposition from its neighbors. Its rivals and enemies will destroy it unless it can buy them off by compromising some part of its original pretensions." All subsequent American philosophy has become dominated by the outcome of the Hegelian dialectic, and the traditional principle of individualism has survived only on the condition of sacrificing some part of its original pretensions. The succeeding age of Darwinian biology and Einsteinian physics, using the new empirical content of experimental science, is very largely the story of the philosophic sacrifices which traditional individualism was forced to make as a condition of its persistence in the new era.

BOOK IV

THE MODERN TEMPER

"In the sciences which lie farther afield from the technological domain, and which, therefore, in point of habituation, are remoter from the center of disturbance, the effect of the machine discipline may even yet be scarcely appreciable. In such lore as ethics, e.g., or political theory, or even economics, much of the norms of the regime of handicraft still stands over; and very much of the institutional preconceptions of natural rights, associated with the regime of handicraft in point of genesis, growth and content, is not only still intact in this field of inquiry, but it can scarcely even be claimed that there is ground for serious apprehension of its prospective obsolescence. Indeed, something even more ancient than handicraft and natural rights may be found surviving in good vigor in this 'moral' field of inquiry, where tests of authenticity and reality are still sought and found by those who cultivate these lines of inquiry that lie beyond the immediate sweep of the machine's discipline. Even the evolutionary process of cumulative causation as conceived by the adepts of those sciences is infused with a preternatural, beneficent trend; so that 'evolution' is conceived to mean amelioration or 'improvement.' The metaphysics of the machine technology has not yet wholly, perhaps not mainly, superseded the metaphysics of the code of honor in those lines of inquiry that have to do with human initiative and aspiration. Whether such a shifting of the point of view in these sciences shall ever be effected is still an open question."

Thorstein Veblen

CHAPTER NINETEEN

THE WORLD OF DARWIN

1. *The Age of Darwin*

The way had been prepared for evolutionary science by the development of transcendental idealism; but the general ideas which had come to the romantic philosophers by way of speculation and intuition were now given a scientific warrant in the epoch-making work of Darwin. Though at first Darwinian science seemed hostile to traditional religion, the age had already been prepared for the dynamic ideas of growth, change, and process which Darwin established as the categories of biological science. Religion had been taught that piety might be rejuvenated by the idea of an immanent divine activity incarnate in matter. Psychology had learned its method of introspection from the romantic philosophers, and was about to analyze the structure of the mind in its various acts of apperception and assimilation. Politics had learned that not any one political system is absolutely true, and that democratic diversity might lead to a dynamic growth of political forms. Literature had come to a renewed self-consciousness by learning that its sentences must express the waywardness of its thoughts, and its thoughts the hazard of its immanent artistic process. Education had discovered a method of learning, through which the knower and the known might become united. The romantic age had uncovered the idea of growth in the intellectual world, and with its speculative expansiveness had concluded that it must pervade the natural world as well. But it remained for Darwin to give the transcendental intuition a scientific embodiment, and to discover in the realm of biology a dynamic impulse to transcend and destroy its old worn-out forms.

There followed, among educated persons, a new critical awareness of man as a biological creature. All the creations of man seemed to reflect an aboriginal force working itself out in his mind and his institutions for the sake of setting up a better in their place. Cosmic philosophies were born which sought to give the title of God to the mysterious dynamic forces at work in the universe, and upon which man so obviously depended for the success of his enterprise. Nature became the scene of a struggle for existence, a battle of the hungry forms, in which triumph emerged for the sake of the continuance of life. The vast economy of nature once more took on a resemblance to the Puritan cosmos, where men were predestined either to success or to failure, in a way of providential wisdom. Adjustment became the watchword of success, and compromise with a reluctant environment the only means of staying alive. Man seemed a highly successful though imperfect form, destined to be succeeded by a superman, whose philosophy of power knew no other criterion than biological survival. Knowledge became an instrument of action, and philosophy a tool for solving problems. Education was to give the student the tools of survival and to practice him in the art of solving problems, and traditional subject matter was condemned when it did not lend itself to the struggle for life. Literature took on a crude naturalism and tried to reflect in its rough pages the struggle for life, which it thought was the embodiment of art. Literature tried to surpass its old forms, leap over the boundaries of restraint and good taste, in an effort to anticipate a new epoch in the war of *belles lettres*. Previous standards and previous epochs, whether of letters, politics, education, or morals, seemed childish indeed when confronted with the new criterion of survival, and tradition was dissolved with a chorus of celebration among the sophisticated.

The doctrine of evolution had thus given rise to a habit of viewing things dynamically, of seeing them in their growth, their development, their emergence; and in this perspective everything took on an air of historic relativity. Old institutions were doomed because they were old; new truths would soon be supplanted by newer ones; man himself was relative to his epoch and only successful as he adjusted to it. The age had discovered all the pretenses of absolutism, and would not yield to truth in any permanent disguise. The age of reason had destroyed the absolutism of the feudal ages, only to fall into the fallacy of an absolute mechanism. The age of romance had destroyed the fallacy of an absolute mechanism, only to fall into the more serious error of regarding the private intuition as absolute truth. The age of Darwin would banish all absolutes and, avoiding the errors of previous generations, would present itself as the first genuinely scientific epoch in the history of mankind. But nature had bred the same systematic illusion, so that the age of Darwin, in banishing all absolutes, only established the relativity of all absolutes as its absolute fallacy. The age of Darwin was brought to completion in the development of new philosophies of positivism and empiricism, which proposed to banish all metaphysics from its theories and all absolute conceptions from its cautious undertakings. The scientific work of Darwin was brought to completion by the scientific work of Einstein, who gave to the philosophers of his day an absolute warrant for believing in relativity, and embodied the dynamical process of biology in the realm of physics; thus bringing to completion, with the modifications of Planck, the line of thought which stretched back into the nineteenth century.

2. *The Struggle for Existence*

Nature had bred a systematic illusion, because the categories of thought and the forms of life were equally doomed by the struggle for existence either to a justification in the service of life or to an ignominious death when they were no longer the instruments of survival. The war of nature is incessant, wrote Darwin, and her fluid categories flow into one another, giving birth to small gradations which equip some species for the struggle of life and just as surely doom others less adequately equipped. The fertility of the species exceeds the available food supply, bringing the Malthusian law of geometrical progression into prominence and precipitating a struggle of each against all. "A struggle for existence inevitably follows from the high rate at which all organic beings tend to increase," wrote Darwin. "Every being, which during its natural lifetime produces several eggs or seeds, must suffer destruction during some period of its life, and during some season or occasional year, otherwise, on the principle of geometrical increase, its numbers would quickly become so inordinately great that no country could support the product. Hence, as more individuals are produced than can possibly survive, there must in every case be a struggle for existence, either one individual with another of the same species, or with individuals of distant species, or with the physical conditions of life. It is the doctrine of Malthus applied with manifold force to the whole animal and vegetable kingdom; for in this case there can be no artificial increase of food, and no prudential restraint from marriage. Although some species may be now increasing, more or less rapidly, in numbers, all can not do so, for the world would not hold them." [84]

Now at long last the Puritan economy of redemption and the balanced and harmonious economy of the eighteenth century had given way to a more radical evolutionary conception of the economy of nature. The fluid categories of evolutionary science corresponded to the fluid categories of evolutionary capitalism in its period of most rapid expansion, giving rise to a conception of nature whose components are not equal and balanced particles, but to the conception of hierarchic domain systems in which some groups and species are subordinate to others, and in which dominant groups and classes precipitate variations in form in order to maintain their dominance. The immutable laws of nature which the eighteenth-century philosophers had supposed was the chief characteristic of nature's invariable economy had now given way before an evolutionary expansion, in which the different forms of capital and the different classes of men struggle to precipitate themselves into the new forms. The ideal of laissez-faire, self-regulating capitalism was shattered on the discovery of evolutionary science, and the disintegrating forms which were doomed by this evolutionary rupture of society began calling for a return to the old days of a harmoniously balanced economy. The theory arose, not that government should stay out of economic affairs, but that it should intervene to protect the forms that were momentarily suffering a disadvantage; and by a direct experimental rupture of the economy of nature should modify the struggle for existence. These developments, however, were still in the lap of time, though their intellectual roots were deep in the soil of Darwin's economy of nature.

The economy of nature, which, in the idyllic picture of the eighteenth century had seemed so peaceful and harmonious, now broke out in all her wrath, revealing her irony and her cruelty in an evolutionary destruction of all the old forms. Nature was a scene of the struggle for existence, and man was the dominant animal because of his cunning, his intelligence, and his scientific culture. But even the animal man, broken up into groups, hierarchies, and domain systems, was struggling to maintain his dominance over other men; he was plunged into the war of survival, and would sacrifice to the cash value of success his honor, his truth, and his integrity. Even God was seen to be transformed by the successive generations which had worshiped Him, and religion experimented with new conceptions of God to see whether they might not be more adequate to survive. Politics was invaded by bribery, graft, and corruption, and none of its methods proved too dishonorable so long as they should succeed. Literature portrayed the fierce struggle, and letters were considered unmanly without the tragic triumph of its hero. Main Street seemed the embodiment of the war of flesh in middle-class society, and while success was wrung from a reluctant environment, its characters crushed one another beneath the weight of their will to live. The art of education was reduced to the art of practice, and the mind refused to hold any content except that which lent itself to an instrumental realization of its goals. Ethics was reduced to a principle of expediency, and morals became the common creed of selfishness. The struggle for existence was thus seen to be the common denominating principle of all life, and an eager generation took it up as a justification of the cash-value of its newly discovered god.

3. The Principle of Natural Selection

The principle of natural selection seemed a law of the biological world, the mechanism for the transformation or preservation of the species, and no doubt Darwin intended it to be as deterministic in its action as any natural law. But he clearly did not mean by natural selection any conscious choice on the part of nature; he did not intend to give theologians any room for reading design or conscious intelligence into the mechanism of biological events. The economy of nature was to Darwin a flux of life, the appearance and disappearance of biological forms, in which the principle of natural selection seemed to assert itself. This was sufficient clue, however, for the army of theologians and philosophers who wished to convert natural selection into a beneficent principle, to read a cosmic design in the survival of the fittest, and find room for a generous hypothesis of universal progress. In the course of its somewhat singular history, the principle of natural selection served in many disguises as a scientific warrant for the most fantastic speculations, and carried a succeeding generation of thinkers into a wild frenzy of hypothesis. While for Darwin the principle had the status of a hypothesis, of a theory large enough to contain all the facts which his biological studies had uncovered, speculative men were soon erecting cosmic philosophies on it, and a generation of sociologists carried it into the construction of a science of society.

"The preservation, during the battle for life, of varieties which possess any advantage in structure, constitution or instinct," Darwin wrote, "I have called Natural Selection; and Mr. Herbert Spencer has well expressed the same idea by the Survival of the Fittest. The term 'natural selection' is in some respects a bad one, as it seems to imply conscious choice; but this will be disregarded after a little familiarity. No one objects to chemists speaking of 'elective affinity'; and certainly an acid has no more choice in combining with a base than the conditions of life have in determining whether or not a new form be selected or preserved. The term is so far a good one as it brings into connection the production of domestic races by man's power of selection and the natural preservation of varieties and species in a state of nature. For brevity's sake I sometimes speak of natural selection as an intelligent power; in the same way as astronomers speak of the attraction of gravity as ruling the movements of the planets, or as agriculturalists speak of man making domestic races by his power of selection. In the one case, as in the other, selection does nothing without variability, and this depends in some manner on the action of the surrounding circumstances in the organism. I have, also, often personified the world of Nature; for I have found it difficult to avoid this ambiguity; but I mean by nature only the aggregate action and product of many natural laws, and by laws only the ascertained sequence of events." [85]

American philosophers were soon building a principle of continuity out of the materials furnished by Darwin's principle of natural selection. The facts of biology appeared to establish an inherent capacity for adaptation on the part of organisms, and the capacity to be adapted on the part of the environment. A theory thus arose that would account for the balance between the capacity of the organism and the adjustment of its environment. The organism was conceived to be maintaining a state of equilibrium, both internally with the forces within itself, and externally with the forces of the environment. Adaptability, therefore, appeared the mark of the highest organisms, and adjustment to an environment partly friendly and partly hostile was thought to be their goal. This double adaptation, both of its own internal forces and of external forces to one another, gave rise to the seminal principle of continuity as a philosophic expression of adaptation and growth. The processes whose seemingly fortuitous coöperation brought about the evolution of organisms were all such that could be included under the concept of equilibration and adjustment. The characteristic of a high level of adaptability was therefore attained when every condition of the distribution of external forces was met by a corresponding distribution of internal forces. Life had become a marvelous balance amidst the general flux, a dangerous equilibrium attained in a world partly stable and partly precarious. Darwin's principle of natural selection had thus become the philosopher's concept of a continuous equilibration. Life was a moving equilibrium precariously balanced on the flux.

4. *The Meaning of Evolution*

The controversy over natural selection betrayed the simple fact that hopes spring eternal in the human breast; for unless evolution is interpreted as working itself out to a definite end, there is little room for intelligence in the cosmos and no room for God in the human heart. The evolutionary theology had apparently settled the problem for the faithful; for they, in the first moment of their enthusiasm, had seen evolution working itself out to a determinate end, an end they could safely identify with God. The universe was a constant revelation, a bible of factual piety, revealing an immanent teleology, or the security of a benevolent God. The old Aristotelian categories with their immanent biological explanation of the universal mechanism seemed the safest repository for the new facts of evolution. It was strongly suspected, wrote an observer, that the law of evolution, the teleological explanation for the facts of evolution, would not be found in phenomena not connected with the life of the individual organism, with the hopes that spring eternally in the human breast: "We strongly suspect that the law of 'evolution' will fail to appear in phenomena not connected, either directly or remotely, with the life of the individual organism, or the growth of which this law is an abstract description. And, heterodox though the opinion be, we are inclined to accept as the soundest and most catholic assumption, on grounds of scientific method, the too little regarded doctrine of Aristotle, which banishes cosmology from the realm of scientific inquiry, reducing natural phenomena in their cosmical relations to an infinite variety of manifestations (without discoverable tendency on the whole) of causes and laws which are simple and constant in their ultimate elements." [86]

For Charles Peirce, however, evolution meant growth, and growth meant that a principle of continuity was at work in the universe. Evolution implied above all other things that though the universe was not necessarily guided by a divine mind, it might indeed be invested with divine purpose, governed by an immanent teleology of its own. The facts of evolution and diversification pointed to the sporting tendency of nature, by which novelty was produced and genuine newness emerged. "Once you embrace the principle of continuity," he wrote, "no kind of explanation of things will satisfy you except that they grew." The idea of growth involves of necessity the principle of continuity, and that in its turn presupposes that nature can assume habits, regulating itself by its own immanently developed law. Natural law was thus a result of evolution, and the whole universe was developing according to purpose. Mind and matter were to be regarded as fundamental manifestations of an underlying law, the cosmic constitution of nature and the mental habits of man being instances of a single evolutionary law. Peirce had thus resurrected an old American doctrine of constitutional law, and had given it an evolutionary expression. But while the eighteenth century had built its conception on the immutable reign of law, Peirce had transformed its stable constitution into an evolutionary document. The outcome, however, was the same in both eighteenth and nineteenth century doctrines; for the universe was governed by cosmic law, and was becoming increasingly regulated by its immanent constitution.

The controversy over evolution thus concerned the method of evolution. If evolution produced new organic unities and ends were realized in nature, then genuine newness, qualitative uniqueness, or what Peirce called "sports," would reveal themselves to be the essence of the evolutionary process. But if, on the other hand, evolution is conceived to be the result of mechanical necessity, the reproduction at a higher and more valuable level of characters already contained as a seed in more primary forms, then evolution must be a very gradual process, slight changes multiplying over long periods of time to produce insensible variations of form. Peirce unhesitatingly chose the method of sporting because it presupposed a saltative leap in nature, a genuine rupture of her complex web, and the doctrine of chances. The doctrine of chances was in its turn a necessary preconception for Peirce's statistical interpretation of nature. The doctrine of chances simply expressed the mathematical law of induction, reasoning from a sample taken at random to the whole universe to be sampled. The random nature of the sample insured that the law of sporting was an absolute law of nature, and consequently lent support to the interpretation of the evolutionary process in terms of revolutionary ruptures and saltative leaps. The principle of natural selection was thus to Peirce only a biological expression of the random sample, and one toward which the use of the inductive method would always tend. He therefore assumed that natural selection had favored animals which learned to reason inductively; and by that development evolution had led to man with his abstract conceptions of time, space, and force.

5. *The Birth of Intelligence*

Meantime, however, amidst the violent conflict of the struggle for existence, growth had her endless perspectives and wished to give birth to a new form of democracy. Although in the evolution of life individuals are sacrificed to species, and the species to more dominant forms and characteristics, until at last no species is final, no category is absolute, it was nevertheless true that progress, change, and growth were indigenous to the whole process and could not be erased. Individuals might die while they were breeding new forms, but the forms themselves, retreating from the likeness of their parents, would persist in continuity, embodying some elements of the lower in the higher, and beginning again with an inevitable progress to ascend to higher forms. The age of Darwin therefore looked forward with increasing faith in the future, even while about it transitory forms were perishing and cherished ideals were being destroyed. The idea of growth, which made progress a necessary ingredient of reality, had bred a new optimism amidst the general wreckage of survival; and while the rubble of former ages was swept away, the new lines of ascent began to make their appearance. Mind had emerged amidst the flux, and promised the continued dominance of the higher forms of life.

"Man in the rudest state in which he now exists is the most dominant animal that has ever appeared on this earth," wrote Darwin. "He has spread more widely than any other highly organized form; and all others have yielded before him. He manifestly owed this immense superiority to his intellectual faculties, to his social habits, which lead him to aid and defend his fellows, and to his corporeal structure. The supreme importance of these characters has been proved by the final arbitrament of the battle for life. Through his powers of intellect, articulate language has been evolved; and on this his wonderful advancement has mainly depended. As Mr. Chauncy Wright remarks: 'A psychological analysis of the faculty of language shows that even the smallest proficiency in it might require more brain-power than the greatest proficiency in any other direction.' He had invented and is able to use various weapons, tools, traps, etc., with which he defends himself, kills or catches his prey, and otherwise obtains food. He had made rafts or canoes for fishing or crossing over to neighboring fertile islands. He has discovered the art of making fire, by which hard and stringy roots can be rendered digestible, and poisonous roots or herbs innocuous. This discovery of fire, probably the greatest ever made by man, excepting language, dates from before the dawn of history. These several inventions, by which man in the rudest state has become so pre-eminent, are the direct results of the development of his powers of observation, memory, curiosity, imagination, and reason." [87]

Darwin had thus made clear that intelligence emerges in the service of life. This was immediately taken to be a footnote to progress, for the functional theory of mind seemed to prove that intelligence had been given birth out of the womb of social activity. It followed that with each advance of society, with the increasing complexity of its organization and the specialization of its division of labor, higher types of intelligence should develop. The birth of intelligence out of the occupations of mankind seemed to suggest that life might grow heroic amidst the struggle for existence, and decline to be replaced by a higher form because of the development of a superior intelligence. When carried out to completion, the theory envisaged the experimental intervention of man in the economy of nature, to turn its forces to his purposes, to extend the term of his duration, and to make the environment a more congenial stimulus to longevity. If intelligence had been born out of a group struggle for existence, in the performance of the normal round of occupations, it seemed to follow that the group could be made secure by an incarnation of its lessons in some instrumental realization of its ends. Following upon this discovery, a technological theory of the birth of language and mind made its appearance, and promised, by investing in intelligence, by the perfecting of technique, that the flux of matter might be mastered and nature guided in her blind creativity. All the problems of the age thus seemed to be problems of technique, of mastering the means to better ends, and technological progress appeared as the solution of man's most pressing problems.

This happy conception bred a new optimism and generated a new piety before the empirical facts. Empiricism was restored as the sure guide to nature, and experience in its primary forms was found to be better than the intuitions of transcendentalism. Thus succeeded an age of pragmatism, which, while it did not deny the Darwinian hypothesis of a struggle for existence, had come to believe that the struggle was primarily intellectual at the higher stage to which man had evolved. It proposed to let loose a creative intelligence which would seek for better means for the embodiment of its ends; and it refused to let its theory stray from its practice, by insisting that theory had emerged in the service of practice, and was instrumental to the realization of some biological end. Technique, or know-how, thus made its appearance again in the form of a Baconian conception of knowledge. Inquiry was reduced to a mechanism of doubt, while a problem was said to be solved when the doubt had passed away. Science began to seem a method for banishing doubt from the sceptical mind, and truth was conceived as the fruition of some experimental or practical test. As intelligence had come to its birth on the basis of a technical decision or practice, truth was seen to be evolved from practice, the lingering intellectual habit or mode of conception of some former practical achievement. A philosophy of technology was bred out of the biological conceptions of Darwin, and utility was counted, as in the age of Jefferson, the standard and test of virtue.

CHAPTER TWENTY

THE EVOLUTIONARY THEOLOGY

1. *The Creative Cosmos*

A generation of men who had grown up under the fixed and orderly universe of Newton was now ushered in upon a scene of inexplicable grandeur; for evolutionary science seemed to proclaim a world of endless variety and creativity, a world of growth and development and change, in which there were no fixed and unalterable forms or species, no stable perspectives and fixed points of reference. It was an age of cosmic philosophies, of epics written to embody the design of the universe; and just because the creative process alone seemed real, all the stable concepts and inherited notions of older generations no longer satisfied. The cosmic philosophers were searching for a universal law which at once would explain natural history and human progress, a law which would illustrate the inevitable triumph of the human spirit. In a moment of change, of eruption in consciousness, the mind is most creative and most alive; and so it was easy for the cosmic philosophers to stagger a hypothesis that would identify the creativity of consciousness with the creativity of God. In brief, a cosmic creativity suggested a God surprisingly like the authors of the cosmic philosophies, progressively working toward the realization of their purposes in the mirrored text of history. "The infinite and eternal Energy from which all things proceed, and which is the same power that in ourselves wells up under the form of consciousness, is certainly the power which is here recognized as God." [88]

But the quest for certainty amidst the endless perspectives of growth, to which evolutionary science had thus given birth, illustrated the need of the cosmic philosophers for some notice of saving grace; and most of the philosophic epics written under the influence of that need amounted to what Jonathan Edwards would have called a history of redemption. What notice might come among these endless perspectives that man was a creature to be saved, that he might be favored as a species in the universally creative chaos? The identification of consciousness in man with intelligence in God was a generous hypothesis thrown up by this need of cosmic security and redemption. It placed man in a cosmic setting and favored him with the characteristic which at long last ruled the universe. To what ends the universe was tending, or from what purposes it had been derived, remained unanswerable questions; but the realization dawned that man and nature shared a common destiny and were pervaded by a common hope. "The universe as a whole is thrilling in every fibre with Life,—not, indeed, life in the usual restricted sense, but life in a general sense. The distinction, once deemed absolute, between the living and the not-living is converted into a relative distinction; and life as manifested in the organism is seen to be only a specialized form of the Universal Life." A creative cosmos had been discovered, and man had been placed among the endless perspectives of its growth, a child both of nature and of the creative intelligence which ruled the universe.

The progress of science had in the meantime succumbed to a natural piety, and if it was felt that all that is human must learn from experience, it was also realized that nature is the inexplicably marvelous theatre of the human act. Scepticism and despair and doubt, confronted by nature's vastness and her sublimity, now vanished with the night; and a new naturalism, pious before the facts, was given once again to the chastened world. Nature might be impartial and free from the taint of superstition, but she was also in her jovial moods the friend and benefactor of mankind. Morality was at once renewed and science confirmed by this new faith of naturalism. When at long last a sophisticated, disillusioned, and disenchanted generation had resolved to set its house in order, it discovered again the childlike wonder of the first philosophers, hoping, in that discovery, that a renewed wisdom and winnowed piety might flourish again among us. When natural philosophy had thus purged itself of all taint of the genteel tradition, it found itself in possession of another religion of nature and a happier metaphysic.

Science was thus recovered beneath the gloss of cosmic commentators and refused to bear service in the name of orthodox religion. A common faith was generated out of a common hope, and discovered itself to have a naturalistic origin and a humanistic end. Meantime, lest the religious in experience be strangled by the seventy jarring sects with their seventy conflicting opinions, it was asked that natural piety be not confused with the absolute dogmas of traditional religion. The pursuit of happiness was seen to be a desirable goal, and the discipline of asceticism was regarded as suitable only to barbarism, mysticism, and romance. Naturalism found the pursuit of happiness to be a demonstration of a divine goal; that in pursuing something so human, man was after all demonstratively and pathetically divine. To know nature, and to pursue happiness amidst competing impulses which reason harmonizes, was henceforth the chief end of man; and it gave rise, in due course, to a pragmatic conception of God. The creative cosmos had thus once more generated conceptions suitable to her evolving needs, and naturalism concurred with humanism that science and experiment were the only inlets to the truth. The faith of naturalism had therefore bred a new religion, a factual piety. It remained only to harmonize the new faith with the ancient hope of regeneration, to bring into the temple of naturalism a creed which should be at once naturalistic and humane. It happened, accordingly, that the new creed emphasized the intellectual capacity of man, the froth blown from the towering cosmic waves, which sometimes took up a human habitation and discovered an earthly home.

2. The Passing of the Genteel Tradition

Moral orthodoxy, when it was confronted by the faith of naturalism in facts, must either succumb to a natural piety, or harden its old shell in the hope of persisting uninterrupted in an aged blindness. Then it will become the possession only of the privileged, whose possessions give it title and propriety to the old faith. But while this is persistence of a sort, it is persistence in passing; for the old faith, having become the possession of the privileged, is maintained only by tradition, and will vanish when that falls. Among the orthodox a new Platonism was espoused to enable absolute morality to survive in a world of fact. But while this absolutism takes the cosmos for its object, it must reaffirm the particulate conception of morality, because it was in the individual that the moral heritage had come to absolute fruition. The moral tradition which in giving up its life had become the possession only of the privileged had thus come to reside among the genteel. Beneath the encased jargon of this genteel faith, however, hid a moral anarchy which Plato would have blushed to own. Meantime the facts increasingly confirmed that nature has no good and bad in its lexicon, and it was suspected even among the orthodox that the old morality might after all be no more than a projection out of human experience. When the life has gone out of an old doctrine, however, it persists in memory and tradition as the end of that loyalty which characterizes a ruling class. It happened, therefore, that the genteel tradition persisted, even while passing into the hands of nature from whence it had come.

Even the philosophers of nature who had set out to undermine the cosmic pretense found themselves imprisoned behind their own logic. If a philosopher trained in Germany comes to tell the American people that they must be loyal to loyalty, he has only entered into the genteel tradition by a back door. But this effort to be loyal to absolute morality by being loyal in the name of her most human manifestation is only another way of preaching duty. The truth is the natural man has always hated a morality which preaches duty; but since that is the essence of morality, only a cosmic hypocrisy could hide the anarchy of pretense. The unregenerate natural man who rebelled against the false tyranny of the Roman symbol has now in his aged blindness taken up some equally fraudulent protestation of sin. So a moral absolutism reigned as the privilege of the ruling class, while the brilliant young intellectuals renewed their Platonism and humanism in an effort to preserve the genteel tradition. But the facts of nature declared war on its cosmic pretense, and the rising young naturalists proclaimed that nature knows neither good nor bad. Meantime, certain radicals, lately dismissed from the universities, had discovered that the metaphysical hypocrisy of a privileged older generation had as its source, not so much a pretense, as a view of reality falsified by a strange perspective on the facts. In brief, the radicals discovered that what the possessors of the genteel tradition found confirmed by the experience of the day, while marketing their wares according to the rule of chance, was given a supernatural extension, so that a cosmic mind was but a purged and chastened world exchange. It happened, accordingly, that these ideas were soon bruited about the streets, and that every pulsating youth set out to prove that morality was a delusion and religion a fraud.

This conclusion was perhaps an uncommon extension of the Darwinian hypothesis of the evolution of morals, but it did a great deal to dispel the genteel tradition; while it bred a renewed search for a natural morality and a humane ethical wisdom which had not made their appearance since the days of Aristotle. If then it should be held that ethical rules and moral injunctions evolve with the species and correspond to its development, and if, on the other hand, the moral standards of society evolve with the political group and correspond to its stage of social consciousness, the pragmatic morality of the streets, with its ethics of action, was more nearly correct in its approach to the problem than the genteel absolutism which it displaced. With a Darwinian morality, enjoined by the struggle for existence, it could never happen that the socially conscious moral altruism of man should rise higher than the motives of self-preservation with which the species had endowed him. In brief, the disciples of Darwin could envisage no higher stage in the evolution of ethics than one of equilibrium reached by a balance between social morality and personal, pragmatic ethics. At this stage of their thinking they presupposed a disjunction and eternal conflict between the individual and society; they presupposed, in brief, a competitive capitalism which would express eternally the antagonisms and contradictions at its base. "The organized moral qualities can not normally transcend in power, as motives of human action, those which secure man's physical preservation," wrote a disciple of Darwinism. "Lines of men in whom the sympathetic and generous qualities predominate over the self-preservative, must inevitably become extinct. Evolution can produce no higher development of the race (whatever may sometimes appear in individuals) than an equivalency of these two classes of forces. Beyond this the organization of the social faculties of the brain must always be repressed in the race, so that we can only expect to attain an equilibrium between them and the more purely selfish ones, as the very highest result of unassisted evolution." [89]

The evolutionary ethics was an outcome of the struggle for survival and reflected the fierce competition among species and individuals in the vast economy of nature. It was the first fruit of Darwinism, and though it revealed nothing better than a utilitarian standard, it had at least escaped from the monumental hypocrisy and cosmic pretense of moral absolutism. The genteel faith of the fathers, which had built upon an absolute morality, was thus passing; and a new generation raised on Darwinian conceptions set out to apply their laws of nature to the life of society, laughing as they went at the fraud with which the fathers had covered up their cosmic pretense. It therefore fell to the lot of a succeeding generation of philosophers to build an evolutionary theology out of an evolutionary science, and seek once again some absolute claim on the actions of individuals which would act as a counterpoise to the ethics of expediency toward which Darwinism seemed to be leading. Yet there was no hope of returning to transcendentalism, absolutism, or the genteel tradition, for these had been banished by the new science, and stood condemned by the new life. The evolutionary philosophers therefore sought in human experience itself some confirmation of the hope that there were moral obligations transcending finite selves, so that the law of the jungle, the survival of the fittest, might not breed contempt for the law of God, the survival of the good.

3. *Scepticism and Animal Faith*

In a moment of happy intuition Professor Santayana had struck off an appropriate title for the intellectual drama of modern times. It be-

248 THE MODERN TEMPER

gins in scepticism and it issues in animal faith. It may be a tale told by an idiot, but it has the idiot's delight about it, and it smacks of that romantic chagrin with which the ego of Fichte had posited an external world. The forces of nature, seemingly impervious to human designs and pretense, had cast all things in episodes of evolution; but these, while they are distinguishable by the mind, offer us no first principles of criticism. The empiricist's criticism of knowledge issued in a reduction of meanings to matters of fact, as they are caught up in human action and substantiated by human knowledge. In the meantime, transcendentalist critique had worked toward the same result while starting out from a different perspective, and all the beliefs to which man had fallen heir were found to contain subjective principles of interpretation. It happened, accordingly, that all honest philosophers had come by one route or another to realize that there is no first principle of criticism, so that philosophy had increasingly to be regarded as a critical method of developing methods of criticism.

When therefore the philosophic mind had purged itself of those vast panoramas of preconception from which it had always started out, it was left with nothing but a critical method with which to confront the sublime realm of experience and nature to which, as in all efforts at reconstruction, it had inevitably fallen heir. The first discovery that this chastened philosophy chanced upon was that scepticism is itself a form of belief, that a man bears ideas as a tree bears fruit. Happily for an age of criticism, then, scepticism, it was found, merely gave up all refined dogma for a dogmatic critical attitude; while man, for his part, always lived under the brute necessity of believing something, as a condition, so to speak, of his contingency, and without which he could neither live nor act. The discovery that man should believe something was evidently a step forward; but in the moment of congratulating themselves on this achievement of their arts, the sceptics realized that their discovery did not justify any particular belief.

The transcendentalists had already considered this problem and had fallen—as the transcendentalist critic always does—into a romantic solipsism. The romantic philosophers, in their critique of experience, had delivered dogma, which has always been communal property, over into the private possession of individuals. Meantime, the modern sceptics had accounted the postulates of empirical science as gratuitous dogmas, granting only that they might have a certain methodological value as principles of economy or as the hidden axioms of experimental procedure. The sceptics claimed they were not hostile to ideas, which they insisted in holding in a state of doubt and suspension, but merely refused to assign them the title of truth. At this moment, however, the pragmatists discovered that ideas become beliefs when they precipitate action, so that a world which had been supposed so entirely free was filled with a surreptitious mechanism. Confronted by this bold piece of pragmatic strategy, which had introduced a mechanical ground or genesis of ideas, suggesting thereby that this ground or genesis might also be their adequate justification, the sceptics retreated to a philosophic stronghold long before prepared by sceptics for just such an occasion. It happened, accordingly, that scepticism found its last refuge in an analysis of the immediate. But all attempt to be absorbed only in the present moment, which for solipsism and radical empiricism alone is real, proves that a present can exist only for past or future, and that every attempt to capture immediacy posits history and time, the ground and cause and motion of all things.

Scepticism was thereby put to rout, and the natural philosophers turned their own naturalistic critique of belief on scepticism itself. The distinctions made in discourse, with which knowledge deals, were taken by natural philosophy as genuine distinctions in nature. The sceptics had taken pure experience in its immediacy as their starting point, and had accepted that alone as real. But natural philosophy insisted that experience, taken by itself in its purest immediacy, is groundless; it is the subject experiencing without positing the object. The sceptics were unmasked as philosophic solipsists, whose positivism was betrayed as a subtle form of idealism. Once natural philosophy had unmasked the positivists and sceptics, it realized that mysticism was after all only an ultimate form of scepticism, and that the whole movement of critical epistemology was falling into a double decadence of mysticism and positivism. The mystic, lacking faith in the natural world and in mortal life, projects his quest for security into the remoter objects of intuition; and so the mystic, who hates the illusion mortal things are heir to, becomes himself the victim of a Grand Illusion. Similarly, the positivist, taking data singly and without a ground, can never prove their existence; but for the sake of system in his philosophy, he slips in the back door of his view various principles of economy and procedural axioms which are implicit in the discovered datum. Thus it happened that mysticism and positivism were found to be the religious and scientific sides, respectively, of a common solipsism and idealism.

Natural philosophy had thus come to dispense with scepticism by means of the tools which the sceptics had placed in her hands. Knowledge was henceforth animal faith, such as the hazard of all vital existence might deliver; but the fallacy of the sceptic was avoided. For the sceptic had taken each datum separately as it appears, rather than consequentially as it precipitates action and underground connections. But while an ultimate scepticism had been rejected, natural philosophy had learned that to live intensely the life of thought, animal concern must be suspended, the will deflected from its course, and the intuition captured in the moment of its flight. Thus purged of animal heat and hunger, the philosopher discovered himself to be in the presence of more luminous and less equivocal objects than animal hazard might have delivered to him. It happened, accordingly, that by means of the tools fashioned in the sceptic's workshop, natural philosophy had chanced upon the realm of essence. While this discovery was mainly Platonic, it was a Platonism purged of the taint of superstition, in which the Socratic criticism of knowledge was reinstated. For essences were shown to be indispensable terms in the perception of matters of fact. But whereas in orthodox Platonism the essences or ideas have a special metaphysical status and are, so to speak, communal property in the universal ferment of being, the purged Platonism to which natural philosophy returned gave to the philosopher an inalienable and infinite private property in the universal realms of being.

4. *The Evolutionary Theism*

Darwin himself, although at times he seems carefully to guard himself against it, had lent a helping hand to the theologians in their argument for conscious intelligence pervading the universe. With Darwin, however, the argument is based on evolutionary law, the principle of natural selection, which is closely identified in his mind with the idea of God; for he distinguishes clearly between the Aristotelian purpose implicit in Greek science, and the mechanism of variability and transformation in the species: "I am aware that the conclusions arrived at in this work will be denounced by some as highly irreligious; but he who denounces them is bound to show why it is more irreligious to explain the origin of man as a distinct species by descent from some lower form, through the laws of variation and natural selection, than to explain the birth of the individual through the laws of ordinary reproduction. The birth both of the species and of the individual are equally parts of that grand sequence of events, which our minds refuse to accept as the result of blind chance. The understanding revolts at such a conclusion, whether or not we are able to believe that every slight variation of structure—the union of each pair in marriage—the dissemination of each seed—and other such events, have all been ordained for some special purpose." [90]

A succeeding generation of cosmic commentators lost Darwin's caution and plunged without remorse into a sea of speculation. The result of their labors was the development of an evolutionary theism; but it ought to be noted that the new evolutionary theism differed from the theism or the deism of the eighteenth century as an immanent god differs from an external one. The evolutionary theism was a form of revolt against the mathematical theism of the eighteenth century, and refused to think of the creator as an outside external force communicating with the universe only by fixed and immutable law. "Just as the early Christians persisted in calling themselves theists while asserting that God dwells in a temple not made with hands," explained Fiske, "so may the modern philosopher persist in calling himself a theist while rejecting the arguments by which Voltaire and Paley have sought to limit and localize the Deity." In brief, evolutionary theism represented a rejection of both the transcendental theism of the romantic age and the mathematical theism of the age of reason. The former, while positing God as an immanent divine activity, had abstracted too much from the incarnation and had represented God as an idea; the latter had erected a mechanical deity who was external to the universe, ruling only at an infinite remove from the world machine. In both cases, evolutionary theism objected to the anthropomorphic conceptions of the deity, to the attribution of human qualities and likenesses to him. For evolutionary theism, God was neither anthropomorphic nor an abstract idea, but rather the conjunction of forces in the universe by which its dynamic equilibrium was produced. The idea of God represented the combination of the twin hypotheses of an evolutionary age, the persistence of force and the relativity of knowledge; and the cosmic philosophers were driven to a conclusion that, "There exists a Power, to which no limit in time or space is conceivable, of which all phenomena, as presented in consciousness, are manifestations, but which we can know only through these manifestations." [91]

The evolutionary thesis of the age was the persistence of force, of change, and of motion; but this was conceived in the light of the relativity of human knowledge, and grew out of the subject-object antimony of philosophy as the third term which united the other two. This third term which unites the subject and object was mind or consciousness, the relation, law, or generality, which joined problematic and determinate characters in the universe to produce novelty, emergence, and growth. Thus it happened that out of the revival of naturalism, a new empirical idealism was developed, and this in its turn soon degenerated into positivism. The cosmic commentators, like their transcendental predecessors, had discovered the subject-object relation, but whereas for transcendentalism the subject alone is real, and while for republicanism the object alone is real, for the cosmic philosophers, and for the positivists of a later epoch, the relation which unites the two terms is the only reality. This development marked a significant advance over both republicanism and transcendentalism, however, because the evolutionary God was conceived to exist only in change, when the subject and object were united for the production of novelty. Unlike the God of the eighteenth century, who was a mechanism for the production of effects, the evolutionary God was the teleology which desired them. Hence there was a return to the naturalism of Aristotle, but with a modern positivist caution; for whereas in Aristotle the ends of the universe are more or less permanent and fixed, the purposes of the evolutionary God were continually changing, rupturing the fabric of the universe for the revelation of some novel end, while uniting the subject and object as a condition of the reality of consciousness in the growth of the universe.

The third term, the relation of knowing which unites subject and object, Peirce developed as an ingredient of evolution; the active causal relation of knowing was to him the necessary condition for the existence of a creative universe. "The starting point of the universe, God the Creator, is the Absolute First; the terminus of the universe, God completely revealed, is the Absolute Second; every state of the universe at a measurable point of time is the third," he wrote. "If you think the measurable is all there is, and deny it any definite tendency whence or whither, then you are considering the pair of points that make the absolute to be imaginary and are an Epicurean. If you hold that there is a definite drift to the course of nature as a whole, but yet believe its absolute end is nothing but the Nirvana from which it set out, you make the two points of the absolute to be coincident, and are a pessimist. But if your creed is that the whole universe is approaching in the infinitely distant future a state having a general character different from that toward which we look back in the infinitely distant past, you make the absolute to consist in two distinct real points and are an evolutionist." [92]

5. *The Experimental Religion*

There followed an attempt to construct religion along the lines of experiment, and to speak, not of abstract theology and supernatural religion, but of the religious in experience. This development meant that all men were equally to claim insight into the manifestations of the deity; that they all possessed the religious faculty as a common ingredient of human nature, and that therefore there would be a kind of democracy in the redemption of men. The church was thought to exist for the purpose of inviting men, through their own personal experience, to the enlarged perspective and cosmic dignity of the theme of which the religious quality of experience made them aware. The prayers, the incantations, the ceremonies, were thought mere external forms, useless if taken by themselves, but perhaps an aid in precipitating the religious emotion and preparing the mind for the reception of some new truth. The experiences to which the ministers of the church appealed were the common possession of all men, so that all might be united on the basis of a common faith. Thus arose an experimental religion, which sought to gain insight into the cosmic perspective of the evolutionary God, by projecting the self in imagination to the ideal of organic wholeness which might lend a new dynamics to human life.

"The connection between imagination and the harmonizing of the self is closer than is usually thought," wrote Dewey. "The idea of a whole, whether of the whole personal being or of the world, is an imaginative, not a literal idea. The limited world of our observation and reflection becomes the Universe only through imaginative extension. It cannot be apprehended in knowledge nor realized in reflection. Neither observation, thought, nor practical activity can attain that complete unification of the self which is called a whole. The *whole* self is an ideal, an imaginative projection. Hence the idea of a thoroughgoing and deepseated harmonizing of the self with the Universe (as a name for totality of conditions with which the self is connected) operates only through imagination—which is one reason why this composing of the self is not voluntary in the sense of an act of special volition or resolution. An 'adjustment' possesses the will rather than is its express product. Religionists have been right in thinking of it as an influx from sources beyond conscious deliberation and purpose—a fact that helps explain, psychologically, why it has so generally been attributed to a supernatural source and that, perhaps, throws some light upon the reference of William James to unconscious factors. And it is pertinent to note that the unification of the self throughout the ceaseless flux of what it does, suffers, and achieves, cannot be attained in terms of itself. The self is always directed toward something beyond itself and so its own unification depends upon the idea of the integration of the shifting scenes of the world into that imaginative totality we call the Universe." [93]

Here then was a significant advance in religion—a recognition of its human origin without a detraction from its divine power. The external deity of the eighteenth century had entered like the transcendental god directly into human experience. The movement which began with the critical idealism of Kant, and which inspired the revolt of the romantic philosophers against the mathematical and abstract God of republicanism, here comes to a new fruition. The idea of God transcends the limits of possible experience, and yet is not allowed to depart from human experience. Religion is conceived as an imaginative projection of the self into the unity and oneness of the universe, and like transcendentalism represents the attainment of a higher level of self-consciousness than mere sense experience permits. Yet God must be an immanent divinity because the ideal, which is the fruit of the imaginative projection of the self into the unity of the cosmos, while no less ideal, is still the fruit of experience, the conscious labor of the human intellect. This experiment in godliness, then, was the outcome of the new religion, and like the experimental Christianity of Jonathan Edwards, it presupposed that an experimental rupture of the course of events was the process in which the individual seeks for his God. It differed from Puritanism, however, by a republican presupposition of free will, and it was similar to transcendentalism in its admiration of the Great God Self. The experimental religion embodied in new form the preceding stages of American religious experience, and demonstrated once again its deepseated faith in the promise of individualism.

Religion was experimental whenever it became an activity pursued in behalf of an ideal. The religious in experience was thereby identified with the artistic in experience, and the creativity of the universe was married to the creativity of the individual man. The union of problematic and determinate characters in existence made every activity pursued with conscious purpose religious in quality, because all possibilities seemed ideal in nature, while their realization lent the power of religious emotion to the ideal pursuit. Here then was an experimentalist's faith in the future, which at the same time was a faith in the reality of the ideal. The past was determinate but the future was problematic, and the experimental religion entered at this juncture into the temple of the gods. It did not neglect the historic and evolutionary factor in present existence, and yet refused to issue a dogmatic prediction on the outcome. All it could say, to the thin voices that rallied around it, was an attenuated transcendentalism, calling upon man to have an heroic self-trust, and to realize in this life the higher and better self to which immortality pertained. The genuinely new element introduced was the scientific; for experimental religion considered intervention in the course of nature to be its duty, and the fulfillment of its ideal obligations to be required by its chief god. Unless experience is filled with a scientific content, the platform for the imaginative projection of the self into the totality of conditions which the self confronts would indeed be shaky; without science, all the efforts of experimental religion would seem as obscure and mystical as those of more primitive and barbarous ages. Not with prayer, not with incantations, not with ceremonies, but by a steady pursuit of the ideal was the aid and comfort of the experimental divinity to be invoked; and only on the assumption that all men possess equally the capacity for this endeavor, could the new god lend its power to the democratic redemption and salvation of all men.

But the experimental religion laid aside the stable and orderly categories of the Newtonian world and took up the fluid categories of the world of Darwin. God was conceived, not as an abstract spectator of the world machine, but as the activity by which an experimental rupture broke through the fabric of nature and society. Thus conceived, God was no longer the laissez-faire spectator of the eighteenth century, but was in fact the experimental method of evolutionary novelty, continually interfering in the order of nature to introduce new cumulative sequences of causation. This development in religion was a reflection of the growing distrust of the laissez-faire, self-regulating economy of nature which Newton had established in scientific terms for the eighteenth century; and it represented the desire to intervene in the natural economy for the sake of restoring stability to the anarchy of its precariously balanced flux. The restoration of economic equilibrium, out of crises and depressions, was seen to depend more and more upon the intervention of man; and hence it called for a theory in which man intervenes actively in nature to establish the conditions of stable equilibrium without which his life would constantly be threatened by the hostile forces of nature. In religion, this development meant the growing distrust of the laissez-faire doctrines of the eighteenth century, and in that form was a religious reflection of a weakened faith in the self-regulating powers of a capitalist economy.

"There is a strong reaction in some religious circles today against the idea of mere individual salvation of individual souls," wrote Dewey. "There is also a reaction in politics and economics against the idea of *laissez-faire*. Both of these movements reflect a common tendency. Both of them are signs of the growing awareness of the emptiness of individuality in isolation. But the fundamental root of the *laissez-faire* idea is denial (more often implicit than expressed) of the possibility of radical intervention of intelligence in the conduct of human life. Now appeal for supernatural intervention in the improvement of social matters is also the expression of a deep-seated *laissez-faireism;* it is the acknowledgment of the desperate situation into which we are driven by the idea of the irrelevance and futility of human intervention in social events and interests. Those contemporary theologians who are interested in social change and who at the same time deprecate human intelligence and effort in behalf of the supernatural, are riding two horses that are going in opposite directions. The old-fashioned ideas of doing something to make the will of God prevail in the world, and of assuming the responsibility of doing the job ourselves, have more to be said for them, logically and practically." [94]

6. *The Pragmatic God*

The tendency of the age was to find out in a pragmatic way whether the God of traditional religion could meet the test and answer the demands of human experience, and then to transform the conception of God in the light of the results of this experiment in godliness. It followed that God must prove his worth in human experience, or be rejected as a false deity. The cash value of the idea of God, to use James's unfortunate expression, had to be established, so that a sophisticated generation might not fall into idolatry. "We and God have business with each other," wrote James; "and in opening ourselves to his influence our deepest destiny is fulfilled." The business of God with man was to prove the worth of His conception, and the business of man with God was to seek the cash value of His existence. The meaning of God in human experience was thus taken by pragmatic religion as something to be realized in human experience, an hypothesis to which earlier generations had succumbed but which a pragmatic generation would test in practice. The result was that the conception of God was altered to fit the pragmatic test, and became in fact a pragmatic God. To the theologians who had been reared on God's absolutism, especially to those who had any trace of Calvinism in their religious heritage, the pragmatic generation seemed to have reduced God to a mere utility, and the conception of God to a pragmatic hypothesis. "On pragmatistic principles, if the hypothesis of God works satisfactorily in the widest sense of the word, it is true," wrote James. [95]

By God, then, the pragmatist ordinarily meant a mind, or generalized existence, which was analogous to the mind of man, and to which the mind of man, in the moments of its highest aspiration, no doubt corresponded. A general law discovered by science, and acted upon by the pragmatic philosopher, gave rise to the conception of a God, the general embodiment of law or order in the universe. Without the presupposition of such a general law, the pragmatist argued, no action could be intelligent; and conscious choice, and hence morality, would be interdicted. Building, then, upon the function of mind in human experience, the pragmatists added it as a dimension of the universe, without which the universe would be unintelligible to man. The cash value criterion, however much it might have been suggested by the economic categories, was meant to establish the active relation between the real and the ideal without which the latter could not exist. Any idea seemed to remain only an idea, only a possibility or hypothesis, until it was tested out in action; and from this simple fact arose the notion that ideals reconstructed in the light of action would bring to the test of universal law or mind the appeal of action before the court of experiment. It followed that God could be reached, and also that He could be worshiped, only pragmatically; that He was in fact a pragmatic God. Man was a fragment of the flux, poised upon the crest of the wave, and his salvation depended upon a plan of action which anticipated and predicted the next pause or flux of existence in which a fragment of God's thought had momentarily been suspended.

CHAPTER TWENTY-ONE

THE SCIENCE OF SOCIETY

1. *The Machine Age*

The forces which had produced Darwinian science, the revolutionary insurgence of native industry, now produced an interest in technology as the fruit of modern science and the rebellious element in modern life. A science of society was at the moment being built, and students of society were looking for the powerful forces of change in society, seeking to discover a Darwinian movement by which societies come into being, flower momentarily in their characteristic forms, only to perish and pass away. The students of Darwin had traced the birth of intelligence to the use of tools and the mastery of techniques by which the economic life of primitive communities had been carried on. Following out this thesis, sociologists seized upon technology as the genuinely revolutionary element in modern society. The invention and use of tools, by driving occupational life into certain channels, had given birth to certain faculties of the mind and certain facets of the character, which in modern society might be summed up as the modern temper. In America the machine age had produced an uncommon interest in technology and science, while the success of Darwinian science had concentrated the interests of social scientists on the laws of motion in society by which social formations and transformations have given rise to modern society. The union of these two interests, of America's tremendous technological achievements and of social Darwinism, led eventually to the building of a philosophy of technology, which was the basis both of an evolutionary social science and an experimental temper of the mind. This philosophy of technology constitutes the unique contribution of America to twentieth-century thought.

It was not alone that a school of pragmatic philosophers arose who turned their attention toward the practical issue of theory and the experimental method of inquiry; for these developments were rather the reflection in theory of more primary things. It was not even that pragmatists studied the canons of scientific research as applied in the work of the pure scientist, only to generalize these procedures as an experimental philosophy. It was rather that scientific research had itself been shaped by the canons of the machine age, so that however pure and disinterested the work of a scientist, his theories had immediate practical bearing. Practical applications of scientific theory were from the point of view of the scientist quite incidental to his work; but because he worked under canons of inquiry shaped in a machine age, and dominated for the most part by a mechanistic conception of natural processes, he inevitably produced the knowledge that is power of the Baconian maxim. The whole scene of American life had in fact been shaped by machine technology, and increasingly in the twentieth century was dominated by its instrumental purposes. The scientist was caught up in these powerful currents, producing knowledge as a machine stamps material forms in its own image. In fact, the scientist himself was increasingly regarded as a machine for producing scientific research, and his so-called cautious scientific temper of mind was the means of imprisoning his personality in the common mechanism of the age. His rules of method became the means of his own enslavement to machine processes, with the unusual consequence that the scientist who considered himself most pure in his theoretical pursuits was in fact the most instrumental agent of the machine age.

In truth the age was more and more stamped in the image of the machine, and for the producing classes, the worker, the scientist, the engineer, it more and more seemed an object of necessity, driving humanity on with its impersonal forces, reducing human relationships to a cold cash-valued utility, and bringing every form of quality and property into the market of its purposes. The philosophy, science, literature, education, and morals of the modern period are a reflection of this fact, and exist either as an exploration of it or as a speculative and imaginative reaction against it. Habit and custom conform to the machine; thought and action are molded by its mechanical sequences. The machine compels adaptation to its operations, compels thought to follow out its processes, and requires that habit be fashioned in its image. "Within the ranges of this machine-guided work," wrote Veblen, "and within the range of modern life so far as it is guided by the machine process, the course of things is given mechanically, impersonally, and the resultant discipline is a discipline in the handling of impersonal facts for mechanical effect." The cause thus seemed to be mechanical, and the effect its inevitable outcome, so that the machine age lost the whole lesson of the transcendental movement as it submitted to machine domination. The revolt from the speculative vagaries of romanticism only produced an enslavement to the speculative limits of mechanism, and the machine age dominated, alike in its empiricism, its positivism, its naturalism, and its instrumentalism, the whole temper and character of modern times.

The philosophers of the new epoch, the sociologists, the scientists, the theoreticians, were thus caught up in an inevitable contradiction. On the one hand, they had to demonstrate, as disciples of Darwin, that the world was a scene of endless growth, development, and change; but on the other hand, as children of the machine age, they were predisposed to view the world as a mechanism, to see it as an inevitable sequence of cause and effect, production and reproduction, a fable of ends and means. These twin requirements of the age, together with the diverse materials handed down by previous generations and more or less honored because of their native commitments of value, set the problem for American thinkers in the twentieth century. They were all driven on by the contradiction between mechanism and evolutionism, while their solutions of the problem lay somewhere between these two poles of their thought. The characteristic of the modern temper, therefore, may be summed up as a philosophy of technology, especially when, with some of the ingenious thinkers, technology is taken to mean not simply mechanism, but mechanism of change. When it was discovered that technology might mean not only a mechanical reproduction of cause and effect, but also a variation upon the sequence by which slight novelties were produced, the American thinkers had found not only a unique but a characteristic, indigenous, and native mode of thought. With this clue, the modern temper developed an American world view, and in politics, economics, education, and morals erected a philosophy of technology.

2. *The Social Darwinism*

When the attempt was made to apply the doctrines of Darwinian science to society, it had to be conceived as a social organism, with all the powers of reproduction, sensitivity, and adaptation to its environment. The idea of progress, descended from the eighteenth century, was first of all transformed from a serial or uniform progress into a mechanism of variation by which slight changes accumulated to produce larger transformations. Progress, therefore, seemed not necessary and universal but partial and contingent, depending upon the conjunction of diverse and often conflicting forces in society. Progress was only the reverse side of declension, and the advance or decline was supposed to depend on cycles of growth or stagnation through which society passed. The environment was conceived to include physical and psychical factors, so that it was thought that as psychical factors come to predominate in the modes of adjustment of society, it would be not so much subjected to the alternation of generation and decay. Thus arose a social positivism, which followed in the wake of Comtean social science, and presupposed that adaptation could be reduced to a mechanism. It rested on the assumption of ameliorating forces at work in society, by which in time society would come to incorporate in itself compensating mechanisms of adjustment and adaptation. It imagined there would be a gradual approach to equilibration, a mutual adjustment of internal and external forces, and failed to see that perfect equilibrium would be stagnation and death.

The social Darwinists were thinking in terms of a mechanism of adjustment, and rested their case on an economy of nature in which supply and demand constantly tend toward a balance. This in its turn was derived from the conception of a laissez-faire, self-regulating, capitalism, and presupposed a free market. The antagonistic motives of egoism and altruism, which the social positivists imagined to be the rivals of progress, entered into the adjustment of society to its environment, and soon suggested that psychical factors, that is, foresight and intelligence, would be roused to activity. Thus arose the utopian hope that with altruistic motives brought more and more into play, with intelligence and foresight incorporated into the social mechanism, there would be a lessening of selfishness and egoism in the face of the need for a common adaptation of the social organism to its environment. The conception of a mechanism of adjustment which had arisen on the presupposition of a laissez-faire order of nature was soon turned upon its foundations, and led to an outcry against the wasteful method of competition. Lester Ward, among others, saw the economy of nature to be practical but uneconomical, and urged upon society a more intelligent system of supplying its wants. His distinction between a coöperative and a competitive society occupies the same ground that previous thinkers had discussed as the distinction between egoism and altruism. "Cooperation is an artificial principle, the result of superior intelligence," he wrote. "Competition is a natural law, and involves no thought. Hence those who cooperate thrive at the expense of those who compete." [96]

3. The Development of Man

In following out the Darwinian premises, students of society had thus been forced to concede that a competitive society had produced a competitive man; that the struggle for existence between men, species, and nations had bred an aggressive and acquisitive instinct, habits of warfare and the custom of attack and defense. This conclusion, as inevitable as it seemed, hardly squared with the ennobling conceptions of the transcendentalists and completely dissipated the assumptions of Christian morality. The problem thus arose of how man ought to be conceived in the light of the presuppositions of Darwinism, whether there was any ground to hope that man might develop into a coöperative and peaceful species. Everything the students of society might hope for, however grounded on Darwinian suppositions, was in the nature of utopian speculation; for it momentarily seemed that man might be the most intelligent, cunning, and aggressive of the animal kingdom, dominating by the force of his intelligence not only inferior species but other men. This view of man, which was a legitimate product of Darwin's conception of an economy of nature, really assumed that the principle of natural selection would operate in society as well as in the biological world; it assumed that a struggle for existence and the survival of the fittest, whether of nations, classes, and individuals, would produce dominant types. In this form social Darwinism left much to be desired, and the age revolted from too literal an application of Darwinian principles to society; for the inevitable outcome was a conception of man as an aggressive, ruthless, cunning creature, whose only ethics could be expediency, and whose only allegiance would be to the perpetuation of himself.

There remained for the age another course of interpretation, however, in which it would be assumed that society, by the very necessity of its survival, would gradually modify the aggressiveness of individuals and ameliorate their selfish instincts. But in this alternative the speculation militated against the deep-seated individualism and the competitive capitalism which was its root. Here then, in the interpretation of man, the sociologists broke into two camps. The strict Darwinists refused to be led aside by speculations on the moral improvement of man, and insisted that struggle, competition, and warfare were the inevitable ingredients of progress, the condition of the survival of the fittest, and in that sense also the condition of the survival of society. The liberal Darwinists followed out Darwin's own suggestion that in the course of his history man would develop a moral instinct and society would be increasingly integrated by the bonds of sympathy, altruism, and brotherly love. In both cases competitive capitalism was to be left untouched; on the one hand, because it was the necessary condition of social progress, on the other hand, because its competition would be the means of developing coöperation. In this form social mythology flowered on the roots of Darwinian science, and refused to speculate on any change from the capitalist system. Though a succeeding generation cultivated an evolutionary economics, criticized the dogma of laissez-faire, and called into question the wastefulness of competition, the first generation of social scientists left the capitalist system untouched in their speculations, and in fact presumed it as the fundamental background of their inquiries.

4. The Domain of Ideology

It was an easy conclusion from evolutionary theory that the forms of thought (ideas) and the systems of thought (ideologies) had a natural history of their own; not indeed as separate from the life of the body, whether of man or of society, of which they were the flowering superstructure of consciousness, but as forming a kind of biography of the spirit. It followed that the history of ideas might be studied in the form of a spiritual biography, and that the character and intelligence of peoples and nations might be discovered in their intellectual history. But it followed also—and this was a moment of distaste and aberration—that at certain stages in their development the ideas would have become barriers to the progress of a nation, stopping up and clogging the natural flow of national consciousness, like arteries hardened against the flow of blood. In brief, it was discovered that a system of effective truth, the product of a particular stage of consciousness, might indeed at a later stage harden into dogma, limiting the horizon of every original mind, blocking the evolution of an appropriate ideology suited to higher and more complex forms of existence.

The life of thought, which formerly occupied only the saints in their contemplation, had now become the province of the sociologist, who looked upon its forms and saw in the evolution of its ideologies the conditions which favored the survival of societies. The realm of the mind, which had seemed to possess a sanctity of its own, uninterrupted by the conflicts and adjustments of societies, was now seen to be a reflection of social problems. The meeting of the subject and object in thought seemed to betray the adjustment of external and internal conditions between the organism and its environment, and speak of that vital juncture as a means of reaching intended ends. Thought was conceived to embody the connected sequences involved in attaining a desired equilibrium, and was merely the product of a biological adjustment. Ideas, whether in individuals or societies, whether in single organisms or in social organisms, merely served the purposes of life, and were instrumental to the satisfaction of biological needs. The former glory and divinity of thought, found in the contemplation of the saint, was reduced to the satisfaction of desires, the adjustment of the organism to the environment. Similarly, a biological interpretation was given to systems of thought, to ideologies, and these were conceived to mirror the adjustment of the social organism to its myriad problems, its attempt to seek a theoretical equilibration between the resources of the environment and the needs of society. All the sanctity of the philosopher in his ivory tower was driven by the vulgar into the street, and he was seen to be no more noble a creature than a decapitated frog responding to the stimulation of an experimentalist.

The capacity of responding to the environment, which at the lower levels of life is quite limited, mainly physical or biological, becomes in the higher forms psychological. Mind emerges from the flux of adjustments, and adaptation is achieved by foresight and intelligence, by a response in anticipation of the known actions and reactions of existence. Science, technology, and the arts all evolve in the service of life; though in higher and more complex societies, they may take on specialized functions seemingly remote from their original practical service. The domain of ideology, of mind, of systems of ideas and the culture of peoples, is thus merely the product of a long period of adjustment of the social organism, either internally to forces within itself or externally to forces in its environment. Matter, life, and mind, the three levels in nature, were differentiated out of one another over a long period of evolution, and indicate different degrees of organization, different capacities to organize and adjust internal and external forces. The differentiated products of mind, the culture and ideologies of society, are all of this humble origin, though in the course of a high level of their specialization they may have drifted from their original practical bearings.

This insight led the social Darwinists to suggest that culture and ideology be returned to the service of their biological needs, that theory be reunited with practice, and the whole realm of mind be reduced to a process of adjustment; and it had the unfortunate result that any idea might be justified as truth, and any ideology claim a monopoly on the opinion of mankind, if only it could be shown to serve some biological or social need. As social organisms had developed their ideologies in the long course of their struggles for survival, it was a fair deduction of social Darwinism that any distortion of truth might be made to serve an instrumental need. "The true, to put it very briefly, is only the expedient in the way of our thinking," wrote James, "just as the right is only the expedient in the way of our behaving." Such a return to the sensationalism, the positivism, and the mechanism of the eighteenth century was inevitable to a generation of thinkers who applied Darwinism without hesitation to the realm of the mind, and reduced the domain of ideology to the status of a biological function. Henceforth, nothing could claim the allegiance of mankind except survival, and ethics was reduced to a philosophy of selfishness, while the flowering of ideology was delayed until it had discovered for itself some service it could render to the dynamics of life.

5. The Evolutionary Economics

The disciples of Darwinism now turned to the task of developing an evolutionary economics. Its purpose was to advance beyond the common sense deliverances of classical economics, and it proposed to call into question the theory of value as represented in Adam Smith and the agrarian theory as represented by the physiocrats. Both phases of the attack were really critiques of the laissez-faire economics of the eighteenth century, as both had rested on sensationalism in philosophy and hedonism in ethics. The evolutionary economics represented a rejection of the mechanical conception of human nature; and in fact, as Adam Smith had made his inquiries under the title of moral philosophy, was as much an ethical inquiry as an economic one. It was sometimes called, accordingly, institutional economics, and it stressed the role of evolving cultures, institutions, and ideologies in shaping man's conduct and ethical conceptions. The evolutionary economics argued that the cumulative growth of habits, the inevitable shaping of human character, had undermined and called into question the preconceptions of eighteenth-century theory; that classical economics ought to be replaced by an economic theory which would recognize the active role of man in changing the institutions under which he lived. As the laissez-faire preconceptions of eighteenth-century theory had by its very title claimed the non-interference of human agencies in the settled, bountiful, and orderly course of nature, so the evolutionary economics rested on the assumption that man could intervene actively in nature, control and alter its course through institutional means. In this form, of course, the evolutionary economics was actually a critique of unregulated capitalism; and on the theory that the state was a neutral agency in the service of man, it urged the intervention of the state in economic affairs.

Adam Smith came in for the brunt of the attack. The invisible hand of providence which Smith felt would happily guide economic affairs was after all only a theological guise for mechanism; and it was mechanism in economics that the new evolutionary economics proposed to destroy. In common with other philosophers of his age, Adam Smith had conceived the creator as wisely not interfering in the settled course and order of nature. This conception of the world machine, as we have seen, had the happy outcome that the selfishness of men, a basic conception of republican theory, was an essential part in the creator's plan, so that the public good was best served by non interference in the economy of nature. Darwin's example of man's intervention in the course of evolution to produce new animal stocks and breeds, however, was too pressing an illustration to be unnoticed. The institutional economics took it up, supposing that in the evolution of humanity new types of men might be bred whose predatory acquisitiveness and selfishness might not be the dominant characteristics of their nature. The new science imagined also that human welfare was not to be promoted by the unregulated operation of the economy of nature, but that on the contrary, the state and other institutions of society were to intervene actively in its operation. This conception, in its turn, presupposed the spread of enlightenment and the gradual emancipation of the public from the prejudices of classical theory. The declared object of evolutionary economics was the public welfare, and its principles were soon combined in what came to be known as welfare economics. The evolution of welfare economics into the present conceptions of a welfare state would bring the history of the new science up to date.

There was an undeniable idealistic element in evolutionary economics. It opposed itself to the mechanism of classical economic theory in the only form in which American thinkers have opposed mechanism, namely, idealism. In this form it was a kind of transcendental protest against the narrow and shallow conceptions of human nature descended from the eighteenth century. The hedonistic conceptions of the classical school, expounded by John Adams in the famous remark that the first concern of man is his dinner and the second is his girl, appeared to the disciples of the new science of institutional economics to leave out of consideration what Veblen called a quasi-spiritual or non-causal element in human conduct. This additional element of continuity arose, first, when events brought about consequences that were not intended, and second, when active interference in the course of nature introduced additional sequences which would not have occurred if the original causal mechanism had been uninterrupted. There were, argued Veblen, bridges and ruptures in the causal sequence, whose outcome, even where intended, was different from what one would expect from a perfect mechanism. In brief, the disciples of evolutionary economics were calling into question the mechanical presuppositions of classical economics, and trying to establish that nature is not a perpetual machine endlessly repeating her cycles of design and fulfillment, but rather an organism whose growth precluded the possibility of one day's success being repeated on another. The outcome of the new science was, accordingly, that the laissez-faire principle of classical economics was found wanting for the very real need of active intervention in the economic processes of society. The public welfare was presumed to be the end of the state, and institutional means for regulating and controlling its economic processes were considered a necessity, so that the new science was designed to produce not only a welfare economics but also a welfare state.

6. The Theory of History

The nineteenth century was not only an age of evolution, of cumulative causal sequences which marked the birth of new forms and the death of the old, it was also a century of force, of energy, of primary motive power applied to the machinery of industry. Along with the evolutionary theory, therefore, arose a corresponding note from physics on the accumulation and dissipation of energy, and these two entered by a happy combination into a new theory of historical change. The house of Adams was busy in this field; for it attempted to apply physical and biological concepts to the study of history, speaking of its change in terms of force, mass, and motion. The carrying over of these physical and biological conceptions into social science, however fantastic the resulting theories, represents a significant advance over the classical history of cycles. Polybius and Spengler and Toynbee represent the old school; theirs is a history of cyclical change, and carries a common preconception of either classical or eighteenth-century mechanism. The house of Adams, on the other hand, was interested in the chief contribution of nineteenth-century thought, namely, the idea of growth, and saw clearly that both biology and physics had undermined the mechanical conceptions of preceding ages. It therefore fell to their lot to hazard the first awkward theory of historical change based on the conception of growth, in which social formations and transformations, dressed up in the language of physics and biology, are seen as cumulative causal sequences, continuously giving rise to the birth of new social forms and the dissolution of old ones. This evolutionary theory had the uncomfortable result of reminding a smug generation that the form of their society and their way of life was neither the latest nor the best that had been placed upon the agenda of history.

"As the universe, which at once creates and destroys life, is a complex of infinitely varying forces," wrote Brooks Adams, "history can never repeat itself. It is vain, therefore, to look in the future for some paraphrase of the past. Yet if society be, as I assume it to be, an organism operating on mechanical principles, we may perhaps, by pondering upon history, learn enough of those principles to enable us to view, more intelligently than we otherwise should, the social phenomena about us. What we call civilization is, I suspect, only, in proportion to its

perfection, a more or less thorough social centralization, while centralization, very clearly, is an effect of applied science. Civilization is accordingly nearly synonymous with centralization, and is caused by
mechanical discoveries, which are applications of scientific knowledge,
like the discovery of how to kindle fire, how to build and sail ships, how
to smelt metals, how to prepare explosives, how to make paper and
print books, and the like. And we perceive on a little consideration that
from the first great and fundamental discovery of how to kindle fire,
every advance in applied science has accelerated the social movement,
until the discovery of steam and electricity in the eighteenth and nineteenth centuries quickened the movement as movement has never been
quickened before." [97]

Here then was a technological theory of history in which the predominating terms were to be force, mass, and motion. The accumulation of forces, the concentration of energy, the application of science,
leads to a transformation of the environment, sets up a different equilibrium of external and internal forces, explodes where the stress is too
great, or settles where the combined forces congeal into solidity. These
forces of historical change seemed to be directly calculable, so that history was to become as much the province of the physicist and mathe-
matician as of the conventional historian, who at the time could only
mumble something about the mystery of repeated cycles. In this new
form, then, the science of history lay, as Adams declared, in the hands
of the physicists, and the future historian must seek his education in the
world of mathematical physics. Nothing can be expected from study on
the old proposition of all historical inquiry, which the classical theories
had apparently overlooked, namely, that time is real, that there can be
no return to the past. The intersection of events, the massing and accumulation of forces, the concentration of energy, were all the manifestation of an exploding energy diffusing itself within the bosom of
society and multiplying its concentrated force with every historical
change.

There could not be a return, accordingly, to the mechanical theory
of history nor to the mechanistic presuppositions upon which society
had heretofore rested. As the disciples of nineteenth-century science began their summing up in the opening decades of the twentieth century,
they realized that they had been ushered into an age of inexplicable
grandeur whose full dimensions their traditional minds could hardly
comprehend. They knew only that all past assumptions, all comfortable
dogmas, all the prejudices of preceding ages, were doomed before the
mighty rushing of force and the tremendous exploding of energy which
the new epoch had discovered. The house of Adams was of the old

school, but it foresaw enough of the future to cause it to doubt the time-honored symbols of American life. Science had shattered the old categories of thought, and its new forms had not emerged with sufficient clarity to justify complacency. The house of Adams in history, Veblen and Marshall in economics, Peirce, James, and Dewey in philosophy, were all trying to assimilate the significance of nineteenth-century thought, all trying to find new categories with which to deposit the ruptured empirical content of science. America once more was a land of beginnings, of projects, of designs, but its hopes and preconceptions, its time-honored symbols and traditional ways of thought, were shattered forever. For upon the common ground of mechanical conceptions had rested, not only the science of previous ages, but also the American republic. Henceforth, any theoretical justification for republicanism would have to rest, not on the shattered categories of eighteenth-century thought, but on some newly found conception into which both the empirical content of science and the practical import of values could be judiciously assimilated.

CHAPTER TWENTY-TWO

THE STATE OF THE UNION

1. *The Evolutionary Politics*

The social theorists, in their general revolt from eighteenth-century mechanism, had now to consider the outcome of Darwinism in the realm of politics, and to discover among its evolutionary principles the materials for a critique of eighteenth-century republicanism. The theory of government established in the age of reason, it will be remembered, presupposed the sovereignty of man over his life, liberty, and property, and established certain safeguards by virtue of which man could not be deprived of his inalienable rights. In considering the objects of government, the age of reason had come to a common conclusion that the purpose of legislation was to protect man in the enjoyment of these inalienable natural rights. These rights were considered inalienable on the grounds of a metaphysical assumption which had been more or less justified by the Newtonian scheme of world mechanism. In Newtonian science, the individual particles are granted an initial charge of energy in the beginning, so that they proceed on their ideal paths undisturbed by any outside forces, excepting for their collisions and the mysterious omnipresent force of gravity. Gravity occupied in the Newtonian scheme the force of monistic law, so that the individual particles, in proceeding according to the inner determination of their will, only intersected other particles and were deflected from their course by gravitational attraction or repulsion. This conception, however, gave Newton the justification for supposing that the world machine operated according to immutable natural law, and that any interference with its normal mode of operation would disturb its nicely balanced machinery and bring the world down in chaos.

The republican philosophers had built their theory of government on the same fundamental assumptions. They supposed that every man was free to order his person and property as he thought fit, and that any interference with this natural state of things was bound to be harmful to the progress of man. They therefore built their scheme of government somewhat after the image of the world machine which Newton had constructed, and sought to create a mechanism in which each species of property or sovereignty might be represented, while providing at the same time for a perpetually recurrent legislative machine in which no single part, by an omnivorous growth of its power, could throw the machinery of government out of gear. The machinery of government was thus a mechanism for preserving and harmonizing the various types of sovereignty and property which the republic was designed to represent, and it was so constructed that neither majorities nor minorities could tyrannize over one another. The resulting conception of government presupposed an immutable body of law, which, while capable of development and diversification, would not fundamentally alter the principles upon which government rested. The machinery of government was designed to attain through its progressive legislation a theoretical public good, which was the result of the compromise of the various types of sovereignty represented in government. The political science of the age of reason thus presupposed a stable and orderly representation of the various species of property and types of sovereignty without any fundamental change in their character. The conflict of factions, of species of property, and of types of representation was therefore taken as an essential factor in effecting an ultimate harmony of the antagonistic parts through scientific legislation.

The development of social Darwinism and the growth of the social sciences brought with them, however, an inquiry into the genesis and articulation of the metaphysical presuppositions of eighteenth-century political science. All of these inquiries, in so far as they regard the political state, had as their outcome speculation on the effects of the evolutionary rise of industrial capitalism and its attendant development of technology upon the mechanistic conception of government. The resulting critique of mechanism in political science showed the common fallacies of the age of reason, and also called into question the assumption that all factions and species of property could be equally represented. The fact was that the rise of industrial capitalism had brought to the fore a revolutionary rupture in the concepts of the eighteenth century. Political pressures were mounting whose effect was to transform the conception of the realm of government. These new conceptions of government were in turn a reflection of the fact, hardly foreseen by the republican theorists of the eighteenth century, that one species of property had come to dominate all others. First in the form of industrial capital and then eventually in the form of financial capital, one species of property had come to dominate agricultural and commercial forms. This was a result evidently not intended by the founders of the American constitutions; for they had presupposed an equal representation of the different species of property and of the antagonistic factions which were their virtual representatives. Thus, in a field of inquiry remote from Darwinian science, the evolution of new forms and the origin of new species out of the favorable variations of the old and dying species had proved to be a fundamental truth, and appeared to call for a corresponding advance in public administration.

2. *The Modern State*

Republican theory had presupposed that, because all men possess equally the inalienable rights of life, liberty, and property, these could be equally represented through the mechanism of government. The representative principle of government was supposed to apply equally, though diversely, to the different factions which were to be represented. But the political theorists, following out the evolutionary clue, soon discovered that financial and banking factions, which had become the heirs of industrial capital, were more fully represented by their weight in public councils than any other faction of the community. The community was thereupon divided up into spheres in order to display the prevalence of the contending factions, and theorists invented the term "business community" to cover the depredations of financial circles on the representative principle. They also imagined that the "agricultural community" and the "laboring community" were not equally represented, but were in fact under the common dominance of finance capital. Though these vague terms of evolutionary politics covered up a host of evils, and rather confused than clarified a more fundamental struggle between capital and labor, they had at least the advantage of bringing the eighteenth-century theory of factions up to date, and of reminding the "communities" suffering a disadvantage of the lapse from the older principle of equal representation. In the terms developed by the theorists of evolutionary politics, then, the modern state was seen to be dominated by one faction, not to the exclusion, but at least to the disadvantage of the others. This was itself a reflection of the fact, supported by Darwinian science, that the older forms of property—the agricultural, the petty producer, the small enterprise, and the waning commercial interest—were being driven to the wall and destroyed by the tremendous evolutionary expansion of the industrial capitalism.

"Representative government means, chiefly, representation of business interests," wrote Thorstein Veblen. "The government commonly
works in the interest of the businessmen with a fairly consistent single-
ness of purpose. And in its solicitude for the business man's interests it
is born out by current public sentiment, for there is a naïve, unques-
tioning persuasion abroad among the body of the people to the effect
that, in some occult way, the material interests of the populace coincide
with the pecuniary interests of those business men who live within the
scope of the same set of governmental contrivances. This persuasion is
particularly secure among the more conservative portion of the community, the business men, superior and subordinate, together with the
professional classes, as contrasted with those vulgar portions of the community who are tainted with socialistic or anarchistic notions. But since
the conservative element comprises the citizens of substance and weight,
and indeed the effective majority of law-abiding citizens, it follows
that, with the sanction of the great body of the people, even including
those who have no pecuniary interest to serve in the matter, constitutional government has, in the main, become a department of the business organization and is guided by the advice of business men." [98]

The evolutionary theorists thus reached the strange conclusion that
the boundaries of eighteenth-century republicanism were being tram-
pled on, not by the protesting classes who might have had some reason
for questioning its metaphysical assumptions, but by the financial faction itself. The expansion of the pecuniary interests of such a class,
extending beyond the limits of the state and the nation into the international sphere, required the intervention of government in economic affairs, not simply to regulate the antagonisms of the competing
factions, but principally to provide a common council for the guidance
of their national and international operations. The older principle of
laissez faire, designed to keep the government neutral as respects the
contending interests, was now seen to be destroyed by the revolutionary
ruptures of the social fabric attending the rise of industrial capitalism.
Here was a strange result for the evolutionary politics, because it assumed that the laissez-faire principle had been discarded, so that the
state might more effectively minister to the common needs of the financial faction; by a strange twist on modern language usage, the theorists
employed the expression "police state" to indicate, not a modern totali-
tarian state, but the abandoned laissez-faire state of the eighteenth century. Despite the vague language of evolutionary politics, however, the
result of their inquiries was a realization that the modern state was by
no means a replica of the neutral mechanism of the eighteenth century,

and that the principle of laissez-faire had fallen into decay coincidentally with the development of a complex technology and the rise of industrial capitalism.

3. *The Passing of Laissez Faire*

The dream of a laissez-faire government passed into oblivion as the causes mounted for the intervention of the state in economic affairs. The assumption of the eighteenth century that every man was the best manager of his own business, that the life, liberty, and estate of each man should be meddled with no further than to protect them, now came in for a critique at the hands of the disciples of evolutionary politics. The ideal of laissez faire was called into question not only by the popular protest of the majority who were suffering from the ravages of unregulated economic enterprise, but also from the minority whose uncoördinated activities had threatened to bring anarchy into the public market. The strange fact of the age was that all classes were calling for government intervention in economic affairs, though each possessed a different reason and intended to reap a different advantage. On the one hand, there were the disintegrating forms of enterprise suffering from the domination of their larger monopolistic competitors, and who therefore called for a return to the days of free and equal competition. The contradiction of their position was that they called for a return to the days of laissez faire by means of a violation of its fundamental principle. On the other hand, the larger monopolistic enterprises, while upholding the principle of laissez faire in name, called for government aid whenever their positions were threatened, and particularly in the sphere of international relations, increasingly became identified with state policy. On similar grounds, labor organizations called for government intervention for the sake of protecting their wage gains from the hazard of spiraling inflations. However much, then, this or that faction might cling to the ideal of laissez faire, all groups were more or less drawn by the vortex of economic development into a silent destruction of it.

In the form of popular mythology, however, as a fundamental assumption that the public good could be effected by a natural and unregulated economy, the principle of laissez faire came in for direct and open attack. The economic theorists attacked its metaphysical assumptions, and more or less proved that crises, depressions, and cycles in the business world were a normal rather than abnormal state of its existence. It was discovered that the depression and exaltation of the business cycle were more or less bound up together, so that the economy of nature, far from being a harmonious and balanced order, was proved to be hostile and threatening to the economic well-being of man. This lack of faith in the inherent, self-regulating powers of nature corresponded to the scientific discovery that a principle of uncertainty lurked in the atomic world, so that on both counts man's faith in the order of nature, in the self-governing and automatic character of the economic world, was shattered as inevitably as the advances of modern science had shattered the mechanistic categories of Newtonian science. Classical political economy had in fact assumed that the hand of providence would guide the order of nature, and thus produce through the mysterious workings of its economy, the well-being or public good that was its intended effect. Eighteenth-century theory, as we have seen, assumed that the world was a machine, and that any interference with its abstract economic machinery would produce only harmful effects. In this form, the principle of laissez faire meant that the state should not intervene in the private economic pursuits of individuals, except to encourage and protect them as fundamental rights of nature. The crises and depressions of the twentieth century soon produced a lack of faith in unregulated capitalism, and called into question the principle of laissez faire.

Though the remedy of this situation appeared to Thorstein Veblen to justify the encouragement of monopoly, it was in any case clear that the metaphysical assumptions of classical economic theory were no longer tenable—that the laissez-faire principle, which had played in economic theory the role played in religious theory by the principle of separation of church and state, now enjoined, not a separation of the state and economic enterprise, but indeed their close association. The outcome was that the state could not stay out of economic enterprise, nor could economic enterprise stay out of the state. With the state of the union now identified with the state of the economy, the political power of the state became increasingly the prize of the fierce struggle for political power. But the contest more and more isolated from the indistinguishable mass the two chief classes which were henceforth contenders for the state power. The aristocracy of wealth, with its monopoly of capital, and the aristocracy of labor, with its monopoly of labor power, were henceforth the chief contending classes in the struggle for political power; but the contest was so equally divided between them, that less distinct groups of public interest became the makeweight in public policies. In any case, the principle of laissez faire and the metaphysical assumptions upon which it had rested were shattered forever, and labor, capital, and agriculture, each in its own way, urged the intervention of the state for the sake of some particular advantage to itself.

4. *The Struggle for Power*

The inevitable result of the speculations of evolutionary politics was that the realm of government duplicates the struggle for existence in the biological world, in which new species, classes, and forms of life, aided by their favorable variations, contest with the old forms for dominance. Translated into political terms, this meant simply that the various classes and factions of society struggle with one another to possess the state and shape its policies. But the principle of natural selection, by which in Darwinism favorable variations are produced, seemed to imply that the contest was unequal, for some species and classes are more favored than others. This development of evolutionary political theory had the uncomfortable result of calling into question the traditional principle of equality, not to mention the liberty and fraternity, upon which the eighteenth-century state had been founded. Some of the political Darwinists saw nothing in society but the reflection of the natural struggle for dominance, and they traced the genesis of the various political structures to the dominance of this or that class in its historical struggle for existence. The state therefore appeared to be the prize of political warfare, and the means of reducing competing classes to a position of servility.

"At the end of the last century a great revolution took place in which the bourgeoisie wrested political power from the nobles," wrote William Graham Sumner. "The peasants and the town mob shared in the revolution and the latter finally got control of it. When the excesses had provoked reaction and order was restored, the bourgeoisie, as the most intelligent and capable section of the population, took control and secured, to some extent, their own ideal of civil liberty and economic prosperity. Their writers have generally agreed, therefore, in regarding the revolution as a great blessing, attended by some most lamentable, but perhaps inevitable excesses. It may yet be necessary to pay a heavy price for the revision of this opinion, for it is now claimed that the revolution is a proper and, in fact, the only true and possible mode of social reform; that the bourgeoisie have arrogated to themselves all the gains of the last great revolution, and that another is needed to wrest from them, in turn, what they wrested from the nobles. The proletariat is, in fact, the faction which is formed for this assault. It finds its recruits where it can get them—among the discontented, the hot-headed, the ill-balanced, the ambitious, those who have nothing to lose, the flatterers of rising power, and other such persons who naturally gravitate toward a revolutionary party. It is plain that the thing to be struggled for is political power, not reform; in all great political struggles this is the real object, to gain political power and control of the force of the state." [99]

In common with the other disciples of evolutionary politics, Sumner saw the struggle for political power in terms of majority and plutocracy, and the problem of the reconciliation of their interests as the most pressing of his epoch. But he traced the evils of the republican system to its broadening of the franchise, which produced by its appeal to numbers a war between the majority and the plutocracy. On the assumption of eighteenth-century principles that each of the numerical units was to be equally represented, the contest was an unequal one, and the democratic majority would in the end be able to seize the state. "The majority interest, by numbers, seizes the power of the state and proceeds to realize its own interest against all others in the most ruthless fashion," he wrote. "That capital has means of defense is unquestionable; that it will defend itself is certain; that it cannot defend itself without resorting to all the vices of plutocracy seems inevitable. Thus the issue of democracy and plutocracy, numbers against capital, is made up. It is the issue which menaces modern society, and which is destined to dispel the dreams which have been cherished, that we were on the eve of a millennium."

The means which lay open to oligarchy in securing its hold on the state in the face of the rising power of numerical majorities, Sumner discovered in the graft, corruption, and bribery attendant upon the control of elections by political machines. "The principle of plutocracy is that money buys whatever the owner of money wants, and the class just described are made to be its instruments," he wrote. "At the same time the entire industrial development of the modern world has been such as to connect industry with political power in the matter of joint stock companies, corporations, franchises, concessions, public contracts, and so on, in new ways and in great magnitude. It is also to be noted that the impersonal and automatic methods of modern industry, and the fact that the actual superintendent is often a representative and quasi-trustee for others, has created the corporate conscience. An ambitious Roman used to buy and bribe his way through all the inferior magistracies up to the consulship, counting upon getting a province at last out of which he could extort enough to recoup himself, pay all his debts, and have a fortune besides. Modern plutocrats buy their way through elections and legislatures, in the confidence of being able to get powers which will recoup them for all the outlay and yield an ample surplus besides." [100]

The outcome of the inquiries of evolutionary politics revealed that the dream of romantic democracy of the transcendental age was doomed by its utopian hopes to a vast disappointment. The rise of industrial capitalism had doomed, not only the hope for romantic democracy, but also the promise of a simple, self-regulating mechanism of government; so that both the eighteenth-century promise and the nineteenth-century hope were shattered on the theories of evolutionary politics. The metaphysical presuppositions of the age of reason had not reckoned with the development of a machine technology nor with the growth of one faction of the community above all others. Its slogan of liberty, equality, and fraternity, which presumed not only an equal but a harmonious interest in the operations of government, turned out to be a dissolving segment of the domain of ideology, no longer capable of reflecting the state of affairs in the twentieth century. The new age presumed, on the contrary, a fundamental cleavage of interests in society, a discontinuity in the social fabric, a principle of uncertainty in its social physics. When these uncertainties and discontinuities were reflected in the new physics of Einstein and Planck during the early decades of the twentieth century, the political theorists found a scientific warrant for their uncertainty in the face of an evolving society, and were brought, as the republican disciples of Newton had been, under a new set of metaphysical assumptions.

5. The Critique of Republicanism

The theorists of evolutionary politics undertook a critique of eighteenth-century republicanism as a result of their inquiries into the nature and constitution of the modern state. The romantic age had undertaken a similar critique, but its objections were directed more at the sensational philosophy upon which republicanism rested than upon the structure of its government. When the theorists began to think of government in terms of the evolution of its forms, therefore, they submitted their opinions to a candid world and announced that its metaphysical assumptions were baseless; and that in any case it did not effect the objects of legislation for which its founders had intended it. The philosophy of natural rights expressed in the Declaration of Independence was discovered to be a transfer of divine rights from the English king to the republican magistrates. "The notion that there are such things as 'natural' rights is due to the fact that rights originated in the mores, and may remain there long before they can be formulated (because it requires some mental development to be able to formulate them) in philosophical propositions, or in laws," wrote Sumner. "The notion of 'natural' rights is the notion that rights have independent authority in absolute right, so that they are not relative or contingent, but absolute."

The claim of natural right by which the republican citizen became the absolute lord of his life, liberty, and estate was now seen to be a metaphysical assumption engendered by a practical situation, but nevertheless necessary in the evolution of the republican form of government. Similarly, the idea of the fundamental equality of men with respect to these rights, the theory of rights inalienable from human nature because they were of the substance of human nature, was an observation calculated to reinforce republican government but hardly entitled to the status of a metaphysical reality. "Modern notions of equality are no doubt to be explained historically as revolts against medieval inequality and status," wrote Sumner. "Natural rights, human rights, equal rights, equality of all men, are phases of a notion which began far back in the Middle Ages, in obscure and neglected writings, or in the polemical utterances of sects and parties. They were counterassertions against the existing system which assumed that rights were obtained from sovereigns, from which it resulted that perhaps no two men had the same or equal rights. The case became different when, in the eighteenth century, the medieval system was gone, the fighting value of the doctrine of equality was exhausted, and it was turned into a dogma of absolute validity and universal application." [101]

Republicanism was thus stripped of all its spurious claims by the disciples of evolutionary politics; the doctrine of equality, the philosophy of natural rights, and the sovereignty of the proprietor of a personal estate, were all established to have been only the historical products of eighteenth-century society. This discovery conferred upon many sacred rights and immunities an air of historical relativity, and called into question the metaphysical assumptions of eighteenth-century republicanism. It thus appeared that the republic was supported by a number of legal fictions and metaphysical assumptions common to the eighteenth century but hardly in keeping with the twentieth. Nothing was too sacred for the disciples of evolutionary politics; for they had discovered as their fundamental principle that the rise of industrial capitalism and its attendant machine discipline had completely transformed the basis of the republican state. Those who attended the machine had no conception of natural rights, no fancy dreams of liberty, no idyllic notions of equality before the law; for the discipline of the machine process, together with the necessary discipline of trade-union organization, had given rise to conceptions fundamentally different from the eighteenth-century philosophy of natural rights. Hence the fundamental presupposition of republicanism, freedom of will, basic alike to property rights and natural rights, appeared to the worker in opposition to the basic determining relation he bore to the machine process. By a strange contradiction, therefore, the mechanistic presuppositions of the natural rights philosophy were called into question by assumptions which were themselves dictated by the mechanistic processes of machine production.

It happened, accordingly, that the discoveries of evolutionary politics, combined with the notions generated by the discipline of the machine process, served to call into question the fundamental assumptions upon which the theory of republicanism had rested. The philosophy of natural rights proved itself to have been relative to the historical struggle of the republicans in countering the dogma of divine rights. The doctrine of equality, with its assumed subsidiary notion of equality before the law, was said to have been undermined by the rise of industrial capitalism and its attendant technology. The idea of liberty seemed idyllic to those who were disciplined by the machine process, while the presupposition of freedom of the will proved to be no freedom at all when it was dictated by the requirements of production. The world view of the eighteenth century, the whole philosophy of republicanism, was called into question, while the theorists busied themselves with the problem of finding a new basis for the republican form of government. But the older categories descended from the eighteenth century were shattered beyond repair. All that remained was to insist upon the legal fictions and metaphysical assumptions of republicanism with a kind of dogmatic persistence. The superstructure of theory, upon which the republican ideas had rested, was destroyed by the disciples of evolutionary politics; and nothing remained by to search for a new basis for the republican way of life.

6. *The Theory of the Public*

Of those who wrestled with the problem of providing republicanism with a new theoretical basis, only John Dewey deserves to be taken seriously. The other theorists, after destroying the older mechanistic categories and calling the metaphysical assumptions of eighteenth-century government into doubt, found themselves without a suitable substitute. The fact is that a sociologist is not a philosopher, and the task of refurbishing republican theory called imperatively for a philosopher. For Dewey, the fundamental fact was not the historical relativity of the older concepts, but the problem of what meaning the concepts de-

scended from an earlier day might still retain in his. The term *republic,*
it will be remembered, meant *res publica,* the public good, or more
literally, the public thing. The eighteenth-century republicans, however,
took the private interest to be identical with the public good; the public
good was accordingly a mere quantitative summation of numerous private goods. The best course of republican government was summed up
in the slogan, that that government is best which governs least, an obvious political expression of the fundamental laissez-faire dogma of
eighteenth-century economics. For Dewey, however, a public is formed,
and hence a public concern is generated, whenever the indirect consequences of a private action or transaction are such as to affect those beyond the immediate circle of the transaction.

Now in psychological theory this conception is similar to the spread
of effects, and hence is identical with what Dewey means by intelligence.
To sum up effects and to govern a number of particular cases under one
general law is also a philosophic definition of the generalizing function
of intelligence. Dewey's theory of the formation of a public, of consequences which demand a public concern, is therefore the equivalent
of the embodiment of intelligence in social action. "Indirect, extensive,
enduring and serious consequences of conjoint and interacting behavior
call a public into existence having a common interest in controlling
these consequences," he wrote. "But the machine age has so enormously
expanded, multiplied, intensified and complicated the scope of the indirect consequences, has formed such immense and consolidated unions
in action, on an impersonal rather than a community basis, that the
resultant public cannot identify and distinguish itself. And this discovery is obviously an antecedent condition of any effective organization
on its part. Such is our thesis regarding the eclipse which the public idea
and interest have undergone. There are too many publics and too much
of public concern for our existing resources to cope with. The problem
of a democratically organized public is primarily and essentially an intellectual problem, in a degree to which the political affairs of prior
ages offer no parallel." [102]

Here then was a noble attempt to bolster up the theory of republicanism descended as a heritage from the eighteenth century. A public is
formed, and hence the need of public concern is indicated, whenever
actions transcend by their consequences the boundaries of an immediate transaction; in brief, whatever affects the public is a public concern, and accordingly a matter for a republic. But the public cannot be
thus formed while it is kept in ignorance of what affects it, so that the
theory of the public presupposes a widespread enlightenment on social
problems; it presupposes, in fact, the same kind of widespread enlight-

enment which the founding fathers originally proclaimed to be essential to the functioning of the republican system. This in its turn depended upon the establishment of a public system of schools, where the chief concern was public enlightenment, the dissemination of information vital to a solution of the problems that were forming publics. In the new theory of republicanism, therefore, the basic idea that the republic concerns itself with the public good as distinguished from the private good is retained; however, at the same time, the new definition of republicanism does not prescribe a realm of sacred private affairs which the republic may not violate. In brief, while the new theory of republicanism retains the fundamental idea of the public good, it disposes of the idea of laissez faire, which precluded government interference in economic affairs. For economic affairs, more vitally than many other concerns, were public in their character and growing more and more to be the concern of the community which was affected by them. The new theory of republicanism, then, does not preclude government interference in economic enterprise, but at the same time it does not require such intervention. Its standard remains the public good, the affair which has become public by virtue of the indirect consequences it has generated, and whose effects must be systematically cared for as a *res publica*, a public thing.

CHAPTER TWENTY-THREE

THE GREAT EXPERIMENT

1. *The New Education*

Now at long last the fatal cleavage between the school and society began to reveal itself. The traditional school, long slumbering beneath the weight of formal subject matter, showed no recognition of the impending crisis in education. It remained for a handful of pioneers, hidden away in their tiny experimental schools, to demonstrate that just because intelligence was a social product, individual appropriation of the dead capital of a formal subject matter only heightened and intensified the crisis. Recognition of this fact, and the birth of the "New Education," may be dated from the publication of John Dewey's *School and Society,* about the turn of the century. At that time, just as a sea of social problems threatened to inundate all past conceptions of education, the fatal cleavage between the school and society widened, threatening to leave the school a crippled and ineffective institution. At that moment the program of the New Education was proclaimed in meager outline, but the suggestions were enough to orient the development of American education during the remainder of the century. Slowly at first, but with increasing vigor and promise, the educators announced the growing program of reform. To the traditional education, upon which the blame for the fatal cleavage between school and society was placed, was opposed Progressive Education, or sometimes the New Education. The modification it effected in curriculum, teaching, and method seemed at first only the legitimate product of a changed social situation, from which, proclaimed the disciples of Progressive Education, a new society was at last emerging.

In all this, however, the proponents of the New Education were inclined to trace the genesis of the separation of the school and society to the rise of industrial capitalism. The great gains made in the scientific-technological revolution which accompanied the growth of capitalism they consciously honored; but the guiding ideal which they seemed to have placed before themselves was one appropriate to the age of Rousseau and, consciously or unconsciously, they enshrined in their hearts the picture of the tranquillity and virtue of family life in the age of domestic production. The disciples of the New Education noted that in the age of petty production educational purposes were achieved unconsciously, through intimate acquaintance with nature at a primary level of experience, in the manipulation of objects and the use of the faculties in primitive and undifferentiated processes of production. The answer to the educational problems of the age thus seemed to lie in a return to the ideal of a small community, such as the family, sustaining itself by its own private production and developing its abilities more or less unconsciously as a by-product of its functions. The school might then model itself on the idea of a close and intimate life in which occupations exacted personal responsibilities and welded the family into a single unit in the performance of its productive processes. While the school was now to be a model community, engaging in processes of production, carrying on its activities toward common goals, it was also, and above all else, to be a child-centered school. This characteristic, its child-centeredness, distinguished the school conducted according to the model of the New Education from the traditional school which it proposed to reform. Child-centeredness was to be focused upon the native activities of the child; the aim of the teacher was to employ the native liberty of the child as the motive power of some worth-while task, to use his natural interest in play activities as the motivation for more serious work.

From this premise followed another characteristic conception of the New Education. If the child is taken as the center of the school program, it is his experience that is uppermost in the minds of pedagogues. Henceforth, education was conceived as growth, so that the interest of the child was the center from which the radius of experience stretched out to its circumference. Such was the nature of that romantic protest against the separation of the school and society, which bewailed the plight of the school in the system of modern industrial capitalism and sought to return to the primitively idyllic conditions of domestic production, where the family was the unit of production, and where there was no fatal cleavage between the school and society because there was no school. The birth of the New Education meant that Jean Jacques had once again stirred in his corner, and that the laissez-faire education was once again upon the horizon. The reforms proposed by the New Education take us back to Rousseau's protest against eighteenth-century formalism. Progressive education sought to establish in the school the laissez-faire conditions which had already been banished from society. It happened, accordingly, that the New Education met with the strongest resistance; but here and there, now in an experimental school, then again in a public school, slowly insinuated itself into professional strongholds of the modern pedagogue, only to be taken up more or less unconsciously as an ingredient of his technical vocabulary.

2. *The New Psychology*

Just as the New Education was being conceived in distant experimental schools, a New Psychology was given birth; and its connection with the New Education was immediate and apparent. The New Psychology was soon proclaimed as the modern parent stem of educational psychology, so that a connection was made into an entity and the science of educational psychology announced its birth. The American phase of this development can be illustrated by the case of William James, whose *Talks to Teachers on Psychology* may be taken to mark the birth of a native educational psychology. It was a functional psychology differentiating itself, for example, from the genetic psychology of G. Stanley Hall and the vague eclecticism of Francis W. Parker. The New Psychology was above all a functional psychology, which attempted to embody the evolutionary and biological concepts of the nineteenth century in a functional theory of mind. The immediate and important fact for the New Psychology was the stream of consciousness, the flow of impressions, feelings, desires, knowledge, and ideas. Introspective interest in the content of consciousness produced the notion that the mind has currents of its own, in which successive mutations, the birth of one field of focus and the dissolution of another, is a process of growth, of synthesis, in which a conscious unity is sought. The various fields of consciousness flow into one another, gradually dissolving the old field or giving rise to a new field, through which the focus seems to be the sensations arising out of the activities in which the organism is engaged. An important shift had thus been introduced into psychology, from the mind's purely rational or theoretic function, as in classical psychology, to the pragmatic, instrumental, role of the mind forced upon psychology by the theory of evolution. Consciousness thus seemed not a mere reflection, a mechanical reproduction, of sense impressions flowing from the environment, as with Locke, but rather an active field, a stream of consciousness, in which the content is the result of the interaction between the organism and its environment, and is particularly focused in moments of organic activity.

There was, however, a contradiction which the New Education would derive from the New Psychology, though even now few pedagogues seem to be aware of it. The epoch-making work of James had really represented a wave theory of consciousness, which contradicted the determinism of Locke's association psychology almost as much as the theories of Einstein and Planck were contradicted by the older Newtonian physics. The field or functional psychology of James had introduced the principle of indeterminism into psychology, thus shattering the mechanism and determinism of Locke's association psychology. However, James himself, though dimly aware of the contradiction, was unwilling to give up altogether the mechanism of eighteenth-century theory; for the mechanical assumptions still remaining in James were revealed in his practical advice to teachers: "Your pupils, whatever else they are, are at any rate little pieces of associating machinery," he wrote. "Their education consists in the organizing within them of determinate tendencies to associate one thing with another—impressions with consequences, these with reactions, those with results, and so on indefinitely. The more copious the associative systems, the completer the individual's adaptations to the world." The deterministic and mechanical view of psychology, James seemed dimly aware, was contradicted by the flow of the stream of consciousness, by the indeterminism of its active and formative state. "Meanwhile," he wrote, "it is a matter of commonest experience that our minds may pass from one object to another by various intermediary fields of consciousness. The indeterminateness of our paths of association *in concreto* is thus almost as striking a feature of them as the uniformity of their abstract form." [103]

Here, then, was the contradiction which the New Psychology contributed to the New Education. Education considered as experience, as formation from without, gives rise to determinism; while education considered as growth, as development from within, gives rise to indeterminism. The program of the New Education was shattered on this contradiction, and only Dewey, in a later stage of his thought, attempted a solution of it. For James, however, at the moment of the birth of the New Psychology, there could be no question of a complete departure from eighteenth-century mechanism; but at the same time he was forced, as a result of his analysis of the fields of consciousness, to introduce a principle of indeterminism. The principle of determinism was a heritage of empirical psychology, and the principle of indeterminism was the novel contribution of functional psychology. But before an adequate solution of the problem had been achieved, the program of the New Education shattered itself on the rocks of this psychological contradiction and fell into such ridiculous fallacies as to become the laughing stock of more stable and learned generations.

3. *The Progressive Education*

When the psychological developments of the New Education coalesced with the passing of the genteel tradition and the revolt against formalism in social thought, Progressive Education took both tendencies under the wings of its widespread program of reform. On the psychological side, it was a continuation of the evolutionary education and a further development of functional psychology; but as a form of social revolt, it represented the same attack upon formalism which its predecessor Rousseau had represented to the eighteenth century. Almost from the beginning it declared war on absolutism, authoritarianism, and regimentation in education; and intellectually, it was a part of the nominalistic and empirical reaction against the absolute idealism descended from transcendental philosophy. It stressed the reality of the flux, the subjective flow of consciousness, and like the eighteenth century, considered the rights of individuals, whether as students, parents, or citizens, as inviolable. It was on the political side a resurrection of the republican doctrine of the sovereignty of man over himself, and stood with republicanism on the capacities of man for self-government. The political side of the progressive doctrine was expressed in the doctrine of interest, which presupposed an order of development or growth in the child which, like Adam Smith's invisible hand of providence, was inviolable. It followed, also, that in matters of discipline self-government was to be both means and ends, and that the teacher, in the performance of the normal routine of his work, ought not to interfere with either the developing interests of the child or with his inviolable right to govern himself. In brief, Progressive Education represented the economic doctrine of laissez faire in the realm of learning, and proposed a Whig program of encouragement to native industry, but refused to enforce any program to hamper or restrain the unregulated growth of its capital interests.

Despite the rather lax discipline of the progressive school, which was the legitimate product of its doctrine, this part of the progressive program might have gone unchallenged had it not been that progressive educators were progressively draining the intellectual content from the schools. This outcome was also a legitimate part of progressive doctrine; for, on the one hand, its functional psychology tended to reduce knowledge to behavior and learning to doing, while on the other hand, its attack against absolute idealism and its general revolt against the genteel tradition in learning predisposed it to regard with scepticism any broad concept which might smack of metaphysics. Progressive

Education, then, may be said to have represented the varying intellectual traditions of nominalism, empiricism, positivism, and pragmatism, but in any single phase of its diverse growth it was concerned to call into question the generous metaphysical entities which had summed up the loyalties and maintained the wisdom of older and more stable generations. The children who emerged from such schools were as restless as the flux in which they had been educated; they had a kind of neurotic insight into a great many things which children were formerly not a party to, but the traditional subject matter of the schools they had bypassed almost completely, and in extreme cases lacked even the simple abilities of reading, writing, and spelling. Though these fundamental skills were a matter merely of mechanical skill to be learned mechanically, the flux of experience had enjoined a revolt from mechanism which could not at the moment be questioned.

On yet another side, Progressive Education represented the tradition of individualism and conceived itself to be progressive, not only on the count that it aided the evolutionary process, but also on the claim that it was the friend of American democracy. The innocent observer soon discovered, however, that by democracy was meant radical individualism which, like James's doctrine of radical empiricism, seemed a symbol of a society in which nothing was real but individuals. One of the paradoxes of Progressive Education was that it was conceived as a movement of radical individualism in education, while yet it attacked the system of modern industrial capitalism as crowding in upon the absolute rights of individuals. In brief, it celebrated the individualism to which capitalism had given birth, while denouncing the restraints upon individuals in which it was supposed to have eventuated. The progressive educator apparently regretted the fact that capitalism had outgrown its eighteenth-century swaddling clothes, and secretly wished that it be returned to its state of infancy. In political form, then, the progressive movement in education was allied with the progressive movement in politics, and represented the protest of a segment of society which at that moment was being carried into a small corner by the growth of capitalism. Jean Jacques Rousseau was thus the true father of Progressive Education; for to him individualism was a new and refreshing form of absolutism, while he dreamed of an education according to nature, where the individual might grow freely, unhampered by the restraints of civilized society.

But the heritage of Rousseau also contained the paradox of Rousseau, which took the form, in the progressivist pedagogy, of parallel yet contradictory conceptions of education. Education was conceived both as growth, as development from within, and as experience, as formation from without. This basic contradiction in the program of the progressive school led it into a sea of troubles. One side of the contradiction required that the child should be thought of as a living, growing organism, who in the course of his growth developed different needs, interests, and abilities. But there was no standard for achievement beyond growth itself; needs, interests, and abilities were the normal manifestation of growth, yet growth itself could not be measured except in terms of further growth. The other side of the contradiction supposed that the materials of growth might be supplied by experience; that by passing along a line of continuity from experience to experience the child might engage himself as a result of this insight as an instrument of his own growth. The chief end of education, therefore, was to supply a living, growing, desire for more growth, while supplying through experience some of the means to make it possible. In the early development of this contradiction, experience was regarded as being an end rather than having an end. In its early days, Progressive Education overlooked the social content of experience; it forgot that the criteria of development were already contained in social experience, so that, otherwise, a child might perfect his skill in burglary, develop a real need for it, grow a genuine interest in it, and achieve a reputation for his nefarious activities. In brief, the program of Progressive Education contained a hidden premise, namely, that experience is social, so that instead of *being* an end it really *contained* an end. It remained for Dewey to clear up some of the paradoxes of progressive education, while at the same time absolving himself from responsibility for some of its more ludicrous performances.

4. *Education as Experience*

The publication of John Dewey's *Experience and Education* was a milestone in the development of modern pedagogical theory, although most of the progressives took it as a substantial defense of their own practice. While specifically absolving himself from many of the absurd practices of the progressives, Dewey entered into an examination of the conflict between the proponents of the traditional education and the disciples of Progressive Education. But in the course of his analysis he fell upon the need, long denied to Progressive Education, for a theory and for criteria of experience; and admitted, by indirection, that society supplies its own values, standards, and criteria of growth, noting also the very real need for searching for authority within experience. Though experience was conceived in terms of personal flux, the indeterminate flow of subjective consciousness, still this was a notable advance, because the invitation to seek for authority within experience was a more or less tacit reminder that this authority might turn out to be social in nature. Moreover, the admission that not all experiences are educative, that some are "miseducative," was a more or less unconscious admission that growth could not provide its own inherent standard without the presupposition of the hidden premise that the standard was ultimately social. What indeed had been lacking in Progressive Education was a framework of judgment and value; its radical individualism and subjective empiricism had denied authority beyond the flux, resting discipline on impulse and government on an interest in the self.

Education has been marked by the conflicting concepts that education is development from within and that it is formation from without, wrote Dewey; and the current conflict between the traditional and the progressive programs of education represents a recurrence of this eternal conflict. Traditional education may be defined, he wrote, in the following terms: "The subject matter of education consists of bodies of information and of skills that have been worked out in the past; therefore, the chief business of the school is to transmit them to new generations. In the past, there have also been developed standards and rules of conduct; moral training consists in forming habits of action in conformity with those rules and standards. Finally, the general pattern of school organization (by which I mean the relations of pupils to one another and to teachers) constitutes the school a kind of institution sharply marked off from other social institutions." Similarly, Progressive Education may be defined in the following terms: "To imposition from above is opposed expression and the civilization of individuality; to external discipline is opposed free activity; to learning from texts and teachers, learning through experience; to acquisition of isolated skills and techniques by drill, is opposed acquisition of them as means of attaining ends which make a direct vital appeal; to preparation for a more or less remote future is opposed making the most of the opportunities of present life; to static aims and materials is opposed acquaintance with a changing world." [104]

Now in the opposition between traditional and progressive education Dewey hoped to effect a compromise, to work out a mediating position, which would take into account the best contribution of each program of education. His development of the theme that there was a need for a theory and criteria of experience, which he happily supplied, was in fact the disguise through which the external discipline of traditional education entered the door of the school without any admitted departure from progressive principles of growth. In other words, experience is defined so as to include both sides of the former conflict, development from within and discipline from without. The principle of growth, of development from within, now becomes the principle of continuity; and the principle of experience, of formation from without, now introduces itself as the principle of interaction. The contradiction upon which the progressive program had shattered itself was thus given theoretical solution by broadening the simple proposition that there can be no genuine growth without experience and no genuine experience without growth. But in fact the hidden premise of progressive theory, that experience has its own standards, that it is social in content, and hence supplies the criteria of evaluating further experiences and measuring further growth, was somewhat disguised by the abstract proposition that group activities are valuable types of educative experience. Individual growth was furnished criteria by the fact that through social experience the individual comes to accept a coöperating or interacting role. In brief, the criteria of growth are already in experience when that is taken to be social, and hence it is not growth that is relative to more growth that is to be the criteria, but rather that the group supplies its own criteria of growth and orients the whole development of the individual in the light of its values. In fact, we are back to the paradox of Rousseau, which at the same time is the contradiction of all modern public education, namely, that you cannot make the man and make the citizen at the same time, unless you assume an identity of interests between the individual and society, which neither Rousseau nor the whole of the modern epoch has been willing to assume, because it would be the death of individualism, and the birth of socialism, while challenging man's capacity for self-government in the democratic state.

5. *Education in the Democratic State*

All conceptions of modern pedagogy come to a new synthesis and happy fruition in a single classic work. Dewey's *Democracy and Education* reflects all the multicolored themes with which the previous generation enlivened the tapestry of contemporary opinion. That single work contains the themes of evolutionism, the genetic and organic interest in education, the revolt from mechanism and formalism, the pragmatic way in education, and the traditional American interest in individualism, brought up to date and synthesized in a broad concept of democracy. The work is addressed to the biological conception in education, and reveals that the generation of the first decades of the twentieth century had not yet finished with Darwin. Education is seen as a necessity of life, as a tool of adaptation, an instrument of evolution; and it is conceived not alone as individual but as social, as the means by which social organisms transmit the body of their experience and the corpus of their values to the growing generation of the young. "Society exists through a process of transmission quite as much as biological life," wrote Dewey; and society educates not only in the direct modes of tuition through the agency of the church, the school, and the press, but also by virtue of its tangle of communication. "Men live in a community in virtue of the things which they have in common," wrote Dewey. But communication is hampered, and the all-around growth of each member of society is thwarted, because some relationships are neither shared nor communicated. "A large number of human relationships in any group are still upon the machine-like plane. Individuals use one another so as to get desired results, without reference to the emotional and intellectual disposition and consent of those used."

The environment, not only the social but the physical environment as well, is conceived to be educative; it produces in the individual a certain disposition of action, a certain system of behavior, which corresponds to the broad features of the environment, and also reflects the acquired dispositions and needs of the individual. Through language, however, sentience is taken up into a system of meanings, so that intelligence is primarily social; mind is the realm of funded and shared meanings. It follows, also, if mind is the realm of funded and shared meanings shaped primarily by the course of practical conduct, by the problems faced by the group in its struggle for survival, it must be the primary means of social control. The attempt of the mature to shape and guide the experiences of the young is thus a form of social continuity. Only where the activities engaged in involve a sharing of tools, materials, outcomes, and meanings, only where there is some common purpose in the work of production, does the educative significance of language make its presence felt. "Only by engaging in joint activity, where one person's use of material and tools is consciously referred to the use other persons are making of their capacities and appliances, is social direction of disposition attained."

Thus conceived in biological and social terms, education took on the drama of endless perspectives of growth; and it led Dewey to his most famous, and most controverted, theme: "Since in reality there is nothing to which growth is relative save more growth, there is nothing to which education is subordinate save more education." Education conceived as growth is then differentiated from the different meanings which have historically been attached to it, with the result that while education is to mean the continuous reconstruction of experience, it is recognized that some social environments lend themselves more readily to the growth of individuals than others. The problem of education thus becomes a part of the problem of politics, so that the structure of institutional life is a factor, as social environment and the source of meanings, in the eventual level of growth attained by the individual. Thus began the search for the meaning of democracy in terms of the meaning of education; for if it could once be decided what form of political organization was most conducive to the all-around growth of each member of society, such a society would fulfill an educational criterion. To decide this question, two criteria were proposed—on the one hand, how numerous and varied were the interests which could be consistently shared; and on the other, how full and free was the interplay of the primary form of association with other forms of association?

"The devotion of democracy to education is a familiar fact," wrote Dewey. "The superficial explanation is that a government resting upon popular suffrage cannot be successful unless those who elect and who obey their governors are educated. Since a democratic society repudiates the principle of external authority, it must find a substitute in voluntary disposition and interest; these can be created only by education. But there is a deeper explanation. A democracy is more than a form of government; it is primarily a mode of associated living, of conjoint communicated experience. The extension in space of the number of individuals who participate in an interest so that each has to refer his own action to that of others, and to consider the action of others to give point and direction to his own, is equivalent to the breaking down of those barriers of class, race, and national territory which kept men from perceiving the full import of their activity. These more numerous and more varied points of contact denote a greater diversity of stimuli to which an individual has to respond; they consequently put a premium on variation in his action." [105]

Here then was a new form of that spiritual socialism and spontaneity which the elder Henry James had proclaimed a generation before; but it was also a new synthesis of all the diverse trends that had entered into the building of the concept of democracy. It represented a renewal of the tradition of democratic diversity which the romantic age proclaimed, and at the same time it recalled Darwin's emphasis upon individual variations or differences as the steps by which new forms and species arose. Considered in yet another light, it counteracted the republican theory of private property in opinion by the fact that language was a social product, and meanings a part of the funded social capital. It recalled no existing form of society, and yet, like Plato's republic, was an ideal guide to some remote society of the future. On this ideal plane, it was hardly calculated, except by way of embarrassment, to reform society; yet by the strength of its appeal it lent criticism of the mechanical forms of social relationships that had grown up. The significance of the problem it considered lay in the fact that it was a revival of the republican doctrine of government by enlightenment. It was in fact the intellectual program of eighteenth-century republicanism brought up to date by the transcendental tradition of spiritual socialism and spontaneity, as these would seem to a generation just emerging from the first cosmic influences of evolutionary science, and not yet embarked upon a period of recurrent war and depression. Nevertheless, it was the happy symbol of the traditional interest of Americans in the role that education ought to play not only in increasing democratic diversity but also in building a democratic state.

CHAPTER TWENTY-FOUR

THE PRAGMATIC TEMPER

1. *The Revolt from Dualism*

The advancement of science precipitated a crisis among philosophers of nature. They were now to be driven by their speculations into a revolt from dualism, from the fatal antinomies of mind and matter, of spirit and substance, of man and nature, which had plagued philosophy from its birth, but which also had received a narrow justification through the categories of eighteenth-century mechanism. Behind the many dualisms with which philosophy had been encumbered, however, lay a fundamental cleavage of subject and object, a cleavage all the more pronounced by the metaphysical assumption of the mechanical world view. Darwinian biology and Einsteinian physics both called for a reconstruction of the older doctrines; for the monism of the world seemed established both by the organic unity of the universe and by its transcendental geometry, while the principle of uncertainty appeared to establish that the activity of knowing was a factor in what was eventually known. "Throughout the history of philosophy the subject and object have been treated as absolutely discontinuous entities," wrote James; "and thereupon the presence of the latter to the former, or the 'apprehension' by the former of the latter, has assumed a paradoxical character which all sorts of theories had to be invented to overcome. Representative theories put a mental 'representation,' 'image,' or 'content' into the gap, as a sort of intermediary. Commonsense theories left the gap untouched, declaring our mind able to clear it by a self-transcending leap. Transcendentalist theories left it impossible to traverse by finite powers, and brought an absolute in to perform the saltatory act. All the while, in the very bosom of finite experience, every conjunction required to make the relation intelligible is given in full." [106]

The effect of the disruption of the mechanical world view, descended from Newton, was to lead philosophy into the finite world of experience in search of the leading principle which would unite the subject and object in a common bond. But it was discovered that the common bond had all along existed in experience itself; that the fact of consciousness was itself the result of the conjunction and interaction of subject and object. With this discovery, the finite world of experience took on the immense importance it had once enjoyed in transcendentalism, but with the difference that the absolute is banished, and the relation of subject and object is alone taken as real. This discovery was a part of the quest for certainty, and it meant that the philosopher, having found the mechanistic categories shattered beyond repair, seeks the other side of the coin, the subject, and finding that to exist with the object only on the conjunction of the two, posits a third, a law or relation of the universe, which is then taken to be the only reality. In the course of this somewhat singular development of philosophy, then, not only has the object, as a thing-in-itself, become unknowable, but the subject likewise, as a thing-in-itself, has been banished. There was left to philosophy, accordingly, only the relation which unites subject and object in a new dimension, and gives birth to mind, law, or order in the universe. What then was left to philosophy was the relation of the subject and object existing apart from its terms, so that appearance, phenomena, the conscious field, could alone be taken as real. In Peirce, this discovery is expressed as law or mind, the absolute third; in Mead, it is the generalized other, without which neither subject nor object could exist; in Dewey, it is the active relation which unites the ideal and the real; and in James it is pure experience, the *materia prima,* which is the common ground of both subject and object.

Radical empiricism thus became a native form of positivism; the dualisms which accompanied all previous philosophy were reduced to a single relation, and the subject and object have been banished for the sake of their relation. But the outcome of this development was to place all phenomena upon an equal plane of validity, for in radical empiricism there is no real difference between thought-stuff and thing-stuff. Hallucinations, dreams, the fables of the subconscious mind, are all equivalent as phenomena, all have an equal claim upon consciousness. Hence, the pragmatist seeks to impose the empirical test upon these conflicting though equal claims to truth; but his test resolves itself into the simple fact that some phenomena or groupings of phenomena work better than others, have a superior functional validity, and hence are entitled to the name of truth. Truth becomes therefore not an absolute, but the meaning of an idea in human experience, and especially its functional validity in the struggle for existence. In radical empiricism, in pragma-

tism, some appearances are found to correspond better, or rather function better, in the intercourse of the mind with reality, but these appearances are still phenomena, still appearances. Thus the work theory of
truth and the cash-value of ideas with which pragmatism and radical
empiricism are associated represent a minimum theory possible; it is
really an American version of positivism, and when logically carried
out brings us back to the subjective idealism of Berkeley and the scepticism of Hume.

"*Material substance* was criticized by Berkeley with such telling effect
that his name has reverberated through all subsequent philosophy,"
wrote James. "Berkeley's treatment of the notion of matter is so well
known as to need hardly more than a mention. So far from denying the
external world which we know, Berkeley corroborated it. It was the
scholastic notion of material substance unapproachable by us, *behind*
the external world, deeper and more real than it, and needed to support
it, which Berkeley maintained to be the most effective of all reducers
of the external world to unreality. Abolish that substance, he said,
believe that God, whom you can understand and approach, sends you
the sensible world directly, and you confirm the latter and back it up
with divine authority. Berkeley's criticism of 'matter' was consequently
absolutely pragmatistic. Matter is known as our sensations of colour,
figure, hardness, and the like. They are the cash-value of the term. The
difference matter makes to us by truly being is that then we get such
sensations; by not being, is that we lack them. These sensations then are
its sole meaning. Berkeley doesn't deny matter, then; he simply tells
us what it consists of. It is a true name for just so much in the way
of sensations." [107]

2. *The Pragmatic Mind*

The theory of pragmatism was at one of its levels an empirical idealism,
a modern and sophisticated version of Berkeley's phenomenalism, and
coincident with the development of European positivism; but at another level it far transcended positivism in its appeal to practice, and
this was in fact its most original contribution. Though it inevitably fell
into a fallacy of reducing ideas to sensations, knowledge to practice,
and learning to doing, it also, in the midst of its most fatal assumptions,
gave birth to a new theory of meaning. Pragmatism arose originally, as
its advocates announced, as a method of settling metaphysical disputes,
and in that disguise represented the common attack of positivism upon
all forms of metaphysics; but its method had the healthy result of tying
theory to practice, and hence of healing a fatal breach between theory

and practice which had been inherent in immediately preceding philosophies. "The pragmatic method is primarily a method of settling metaphysical disputes that otherwise might be interminable," wrote James. "Is the world one or many?—fated or free?—material or spiritual?—here are notions either of which may or may not hold good of the world; and disputes over such notions are unending. The pragmatic method in such cases is to try to interpret each notion by tracing its respective practical consequences. What difference would it make to any one if this notion rather than that notion were true? If no practical difference whatever can be traced, then the alternatives mean practically the same thing, and all dispute is idle." [108]

While denouncing the metaphysical assumptions of all former philosophies, pragmatism employed its method to develop a new metaphysic, and thereby proved, not that metaphysical questions were idle, but that it preferred a different world view. Pragmatism had in fact a preference for certain metaphysical assumptions, which its method did not so much create as justify. Its preference was for the metaphysical assumptions of Darwin and Einstein rather than for those of Newton and Descartes, and this preference was ingrained with the history of the epoch; for pragmatism was a faith in the science of its epoch, a faith in practice and in the outcome of experimental intervention in nature. It rejected the deterministic universe of Newton and Jonathan Edwards, and differentiated between the meaning of causality and that of determinism. In the Newtonian universe, determinism is taken to be equivalent to causality; for every event is strictly predetermined, action and reaction are equal, and the ultimate causality of the universe is traced by an infinite regress back to the power of God. But in pragmatism the universe is not strictly predetermined; it is a world open to intervention, experiment, and practice, and these represent an evolutionary rupture in the normal course of its development. For pragmatism there is no immutable law of nature, as in eighteenth-century mechanism; in fact, natural law is constantly developing, and the activity of man, his experimental intervention in the order of nature, is a factor in the growth of the universe.

This element in pragmatism represents a dialectical view of the world rather than a mechanistic one, and means simply that the world is no longer to be conceived as a machine but as the scene of dialectic activity characterized by the endless perspectives of growth. It means that the world was neither wholly necessary nor wholly contingent, neither strictly determined nor absolutely free, neither a complete order nor a complete disorder, neither wholly rational nor wholly irrational, neither wholly material nor wholly spiritual. This side of pragmatism is represented by experimentalism, and is associated with Dewey rather than James. To Dewey the world is dialectical through and through; it is an experimental world, open to the active intervention of man in its processes, partly problematic and partly determinate in its character. "The conjunction of problematic and determinate characters in nature renders every existence, as well as every idea and human act, an experiment in fact, even though not in design," he wrote; and he proposed to heal the fatal breach between theory and practice by the creation of theory out of practice. The dialectical element in pragmatism was also its historical element, so that not only was eighteenth-century mechanism called into question but the unhistorical character of its thought stood condemned. In brief, the empirical content of science had burst through all former categories of thought, and called imperatively for a new metaphysics of science. But the resulting experimentalism had the uncomfortable result of destroying all the metaphysical assumptions upon which the age of reason had built not only its science but its politics, morals, and religion as well. The metaphysics of experimentalism had in fact called into question the metaphysical assumptions of the system of unregulated, laissez-faire capitalism and the theory of republicanism which had been erected upon it. All that remained of eighteenth-century thought was its faith in universal enlightenment, which at the same time was a faith that the chief freedom was intellectual, the freedom of inquiry, so that practice would not be blinded for lack of theory.

3. *The Theory of Technology*

There is an important difference between the pragmatism of James and the experimentalism of Dewey which was crucial to the development of a native expression-spirit in philosophy. James was not yet freed from mechanism; his psychology was an eclectic mixture of mechanism and evolutionism, though he was headed in the direction of functionalism, and was an early representative of the pragmatic temper of mind. With Dewey, however, consciousness is not merely phenomenal, and the cash-value of ideas is not the only test of their validity. This eventuated in an important metaphysical difference in the pragmatic camp, which marks Dewey out from the stream of contemporary positivism. The positivism of James made his pragmatism only a modern and sophisticated form of Berkeley's idealism, which still revealed the separation of the subject from the object and a detachment from the active causal relation of knowing. The pragmatic element in James's theory, it is true, brought his phenomenalism close to the test of practice, and caused him to reject one grouping of phenomena in favor of another grouping because of the cash-valued validity which one set of phenomena supported over another. But aside from the practical test, James had no way of distinguishing the flux of phenomena, no way of marking out the terms of the stream of consciousness, so that his world was still fashioned partly of the stuff of dreams; and even in practice some ideas, like God, freedom, and immortality, may be found to have a certain cash-valued validity. This fallacy in the early and undeveloped pragmatism of James was avoided by Dewey's technological theory of knowledge.

"From the standpoint of the operational definition and tests of ideas," he wrote, "ideas have an empirical origin and status. But it is of *acts* performed, acts in the literal and existential sense of the word, deeds done, not reception of sensations forced on us from without. Sensory qualities are important. But they are intellectually significant only as consequences of acts intentionally performed. A colour seen at a particular locus in a spectral band is, for example, of immense intellectual importance in chemistry and astro-physics. But *merely* as seen, as a bare sensory quality, it is the same for the clodhopper and the scientist; in either case, it is the product of a direct sensory excitation; it is just and only another colour the eye has happened upon. To suppose that its cognitive value can be eked out or supplied by associating it with other sensory qualities of the same nature as itself, is like supposing that by putting a pile of sand in the eye we can get rid of the irritation caused by a single grain. To suppose, on the other hand, that we must appeal to a synthetic activity of an independent thought to give the quality meaning in and for knowledge, is like supposing that by thinking in our heads we can convert a pile of bricks into a building. Thinking, carried on inside the head, can make some headway in forming the *plan* of the building. But it takes actual operations to which the plan, as the fruit of thought, gives instrumental guidance to make a building out of separate bricks, or to transform an isolated sensory quality into a significant clue to knowledge of nature." [109]

Ideas are definitions of operations, plans of action, not the mere flow of phenomena in the subjective consciousness; and this development, known as the instrumental theory of knowledge, is in fact a theory of technology as well. The quest for certainty with which the age began is thus brought to a new stage by the answer that secure values can only be realized by perfecting methods of inquiry and action. It is the answer of Bacon to the question of Spencer, what knowledge is of most worth? It is the answer of Bacon that knowledge is power, and the rejoinder of Dewey that power is know-how; and as the end of knowledge, security of values, depends upon the perfection of methods of action, it is the answer that the knowledge of most worth is the knowledge of technique by which values can be reached or restored. In this form, of course, the instrumental theory unites the traditional American interests in mechanism and idealism at a higher and more abstract level. At this level the subject and object are drawn together in the active, causal relation of knowing, and the activity of knowing is seen to be a participant in what is finally known. Ideas are embodied in matter by way of technique, and every advance in technology, in perfected methods of inquiry and production, brings the possibility of realizing secure values ever closer. Such is the philosophy in which the long history of American ideas culminates; for the instrumental theory is a technological theory both of knowledge and value.

In this form, accordingly, the instrumental theory was the final culminating triumph of mechanism; it meant that through mechanism ideas could be given a material embodiment and values a natural home. But the unity of experience and nature, and the interpenetration of the subject and object in the active causal relation of knowing, so far transcends eighteenth-century mechanism as to be its exact opposite. It runs beyond eighteenth-century mechanism because it reflects a developed technology, and passes beyond the simple handicraft stage in its conception of causation. Although the stamp of machine technology is clearly upon it, the instrumental theory is not concerned with the mechanical equivalence of cause and effect, but rather with the end or outcome which defines the purpose. The machine, then, has become a purpose in operation, a mechanism of purpose, whose complex processes represent the conditions under which values are to be realized. The interest centers almost exclusively on technique, because the conditions of full and equal competition are no longer in force, and the realization of value may depend entirely on the technological advantage of one industry over another. The instrumental theory is thus a reflection of a society with a highly developed technology, and the inherent mechanism of its conceptions reproduces at a higher and more abstract level the mechanism originally induced by the handicraft production of the eighteenth century.

If then you would understand the Americans, you must remember that the philosophy of technology is more than a mere static reflection of a technical civilization. It is a metaphysical doctrine and it means, not only with Bacon that knowledge is power, but also with Whitman that the democratic Me is united with the alien Not Me in the active causal relation of knowing. The philosophy of technology means that man enters through his knowledge into the making of his own destiny; that none of his values can be final because they are all transition points

in their own eventual outcome. The unity of theory and practice, of
ends and means, through machine production, is only revolutionized
by the introduction of more and more complex machines, and to this
succeeds a further revolutionizing of technology by means of technology.
Technology is thus both ends and means; it is both a value in itself and
a means to the realization of further values. The atomic age promises to
complicate an already complex technology by the introduction of a new
source of power, bringing to completion a philosophy of technology
which is indigenous to America. Thus arises a final contradiction in the
native expression-spirit of America, and gives birth through its travail
to the materials with which a new atomic age will refashion the assumptions of former epochs of thought. On the one hand, nuclear physics has
released a source of power so godlike in its proportions that only the
total mobilization of social capital through public agencies can exploit
this new divinity for man's benefit. What then becomes of the private
capitalist? On the other hand, the new science of cybernetics has introduced the concept of the fully automatic factory, which needs at most
the services of only a few technicians to keep it going. What then becomes of the laborer?

NOTES

[1] Jonathan Edwards, *Works,* ed. by Austin (Worcester, 1808), IV, 287.

[2] John Davenport, "A Sermon Preach'd at Election," *Publications of the Colonial Society of Massachussetts,* X, 6; quoted in Perry Miller and Thomas H. Johnson, *The Puritans* (New York: The American Book Co., 1938), p. 190. Quotations from this book are printed by permission of the publisher.

[3] Brooks Adams, *The Emancipation of Massachusetts* (Boston, 1887), p. 276.

[4] Thomas Hooker, *The Soules Preparation* (London, 1632), p. 66.

[5] Edward Johnson, *The Wonder-Working Providence,* ed. by Jamison (New York, 1910), p. 128.

[6] Oratio Comitalis (manuscript), Harvard University Archives. Cited in Samuel Eliot Morison, *The Founding of Harvard College* (Cambridge: Harvard University Press, 1935), p. 250. Quotations from this book are printed by permission of the publisher.

[7] *Ibid.,* p. 177.

[8] Edwards, *op. cit.* (New York, 1829), I, 706.

[9] Thomas Jefferson, *Writings,* ed. by Ford (New York, 1892-1899), V, 89-90.

[10] Thomas Cooper, *Elements of Political Economy* (Columbia, 1826), pp. 54-55.

[11] Jonathan Mayhew, *Discourse Concerning Unlimited Submission* (Boston, 1750), pp. 29, 52.

[12] Thomas Paine, *The Complete Writings of Thomas Paine,* ed. by Philip S. Foner (New York: The Citadel Press, 1945), I, 12-14. Quotations from this book are printed by permission of the publisher.

[13] *Ibid.,* I, 24-26.

[14] *Ibid.,* I, 489.

[15] Isaac Newton, *Mathematical Principles of Natural Philosophy* (London, 1803), preface.

[16] Isaac Newton, *Opticks* (London, 1721), p. 344.

[17] Paine, *op. cit.,* I, 464-466.

[18] *Ibid.,* I, 600.

[19] John Adams, *Works,* ed. by C. F. Adams (Boston, 1850-1856), II, 5.

[20] Thomas Jefferson, *Writings,* ed. by Bergh (Washington: Thomas Jefferson Memorial Association, 1903), XV, 266.

[21] Ethan Allen, *Reason the Only Oracle* (Bennington, 1784), pp. 26–33.

[22] Paine, *op. cit.,* I, 369–370.

[23] *The Federalist,* No. 10.

[24] *The Federalist,* No. 51.

[25] John Adams, *op. cit.,* VI, 68–69, 280, 65, 321.

[26] *Ibid.,* VI, 276.

[27] *Ibid.,* IV, 548.

[28] *Ibid.,* VI, 128.

[29] Benjamin Rush, *Thoughts on the Mode of Education Proper in a Republic* (Philadelphia, 1786), pp. 14, 20.

[30] *Ibid.* (1791 edition), p. 77.

[31] Benjamin Rush, *Essays* (Philadelphia, 1798), pp. 21, 25, 39, 43.

[32] *Ibid.,* 39.

[33] Samuel Knox, *Essay on Education* (Philadelphia, 1799), p. 74.

[34] Noah Webster, *On the Education of the Youth of America* (New York, 1788), p. 161.

[35] Rush, *Essays, op. cit.,* pp. 47–49.

[36] *Ibid.,* pp. 71–72, 136.

[37] Knox, *op. cit.,* p. 49.

[38] Samuel Smith, *Remarks on Education* (Philadelphia, 1798), pp. 15–16.

[39] Noah Webster, *Miscellaneous Papers* (New York, 1794), p. 21.

[40] Du Pont de Nemours, *National Education in the United States* (Philadelphia, 1800), p. 24.

[41] Knox, *op. cit.,* p. 20.

[42] Du Pont de Nemours, *op. cit.,* p. 46.

[43] Knox, *op. cit.,* pp. 70–71.

[44] Lafitte du Courteil, *National Plan of Education* (Philadelphia, 1797), pp. 24–25.

[45] Knox, *op. cit.,* pp. 12, 76.

[46] Benjamin Rush, *Selected Writings,* ed. by Runes (New York: The Philosophical Library, 1949), pp. 91–94. Quotations from this book are printed by permission of the publisher.

[47] Jefferson, *op. cit.* (Ford edition), IX, 425–428.

[48] Rush, *Selected Writings, op. cit.,* p. 181.

[49] Jefferson, *op. cit.* (Bergh edition), XIV, 143–144.

[50] Thomas Cooper, *Elements of Political Economy* (Columbia, 1826), pp. 188–190.

[51] Jefferson, *op. cit.* (Ford edition), VI, 480–483.

[52] *Ibid.,* II, 100–103.

[53] James Madison, *Writings,* ed. by Hunt (New York: G. P. Putnam's Sons, 1910), VI, 103. Quotations from this book are printed by permission of the publisher.

[54] Paine, *op. cit.,* I, 580, 367–368.

[55] Theodore Parker, *Works,* Centenary Edition (Boston: The Beacon Press, 1907–1913), VI, 37–38. Quotations from this book are printed by permission of the publisher.

[56] *Ibid.,* VI, 23.

[57] *Ibid.,* VI, 9–10.

[58] Ralph W. Emerson, *Works,* Centenary Edition (Boston: Houghton, Mifflin Co., 1903–1904), I, 4–5. Quotations from this book are printed by permission of the publisher.

[59] Walt Whitman, *Complete Writings* (New York: G. P. Putnam's Sons, 1902), V, 135. Quotations from this book are printed by permission of the publisher.

[60] Emerson, *op. cit.,* I, 95–96.

[61] Whitman, *op. cit.,* V, 98.

[62] Emerson, *op. cit.,* IV, 28.

[63] William E. Channing, *Works* (Boston, 1867), I, xii–xiii.

[64] Parker, *op. cit.,* I, 187.

[65] Channing, *op. cit.,* I, xiii.

[66] Parker, *op. cit.,* VI, 365–366.

[67] *Ibid.,* I, 153.

[68] Parker, *op. cit.,* VI, 11–14.

[69] Emerson, *op. cit.,* IV, 46–47.

[70] Walt Whitman, *Specimen Days in America* (New York: Oxford University Press, 1931), pp. 276–279.

[71] Emerson, *op. cit.,* II, 133.

[72] *Ibid.,* II, 152.

[73] Channing, *op. cit.,* I, 372.

[74] Emerson, *op. cit.,* X, 143.

[75] *Ibid.,* VI, 140–141.

[76] Channing, *op. cit.,* I, 243–244.

[77] Emerson, *op. cit.,* IV, 8.

[78] William T. Harris, *Psychological Foundations of Education* (New York, 1898), p. 22. Quotations from this book are printed by permission of Appleton-Century-Crofts, Inc.

[79] Whitman, *Writings, op. cit.,* pp. 181–182.

[80] *Ibid.,* IX, 175–177.

[81] *Ibid.,* IX, 179–181.

[82] *Ibid.,* IX, 169–173.

[83] Emerson, *op. cit.,* III, 76–77.

[84] Charles Darwin, *The Origin of the Species* (London, 1859), p. 50.

[85] Charles Darwin, *Variation of Animals and Plants under Domestication* (London, 1868), I, 6.

[86] Chauncey Wright, *Philosophical Discussions* (New York, 1877), p. 7.

[87] Darwin, *Descent of Man* (London, 1871), p. 48.

[88] John Fiske, *The Idea of God as Affected by Modern Knowledge* (Cambridge, 1887), p. 149.

[89] Edward D. Cope, *The Origin of the Fittest* (New York, 1887), p. 237.

[90] Darwin, *Descent of Man, op. cit.,* p. 612.

[91] John Fiske, *Outlines of Cosmic Philosophy* (New York: Houghton, Mifflin Co., 1903), IV, 237–238. Quotations from this book are printed by permission of the publisher.

[92] Charles S. Peirce, *Collected Papers of Charles Sanders Peirce,* ed. by Charles Hartshorne and Paul Weiss (Cambridge: Harvard University Press, 1931–1935), VI, 187.

[93] John Dewey, *A Common Faith* (New York: Yale University Press, 1934), pp. 18–19. Quotations from this book are printed by permission of the publisher.

[94] *Ibid.,* pp. 78–79.

[95] William James, *Pragmatism* (New York: Longmans, Green & Co., 1921), pp. 299–300. Quotations from this book are printed by permission of the publisher.

[96] Lester Ward, *Psychic Factors in Civilization* (New York: Ginn and Co., 1902), p. 239.

[97] Brooks Adams, *Theory of Social Revolution* (New York, 1914), pp. 203–204. Quotations from this book are printed by permission of the estate of Brooks Adams.

[98] Thorstein Veblen, *The Theory of Business Enterprise* (New York: Charles Scribner's Sons, 1904), pp. 286–287. Quotations from this book are printed by permission of the publisher.

[99] William G. Sumner, *Earth Hunger and other Essays* (New Haven: Yale University Press, 1913), pp. 163–174. Quotations from this book are printed by permission of the publisher.

[100] *Ibid.,* pp. 288–289, 294.

[101] *Ibid.,* pp. 79, 87–88.

[102] John Dewey, *The Public and Its Problems* (New York: Henry Holt and Co., 1946), p. 126. Quotations from this book are printed by permission of the publisher.

[103] William James, *Talks to Teachers on Psychology* (New York: Henry Holt and Co., 1901), pp. 82–84. Quotations from this book are printed by permission of the publisher.

[104] John Dewey, *Experience and Education* (New York: The Macmillan Co., 1938), pp. 2–3. Quotations from this book are printed by permission of the publisher.

[105] John Dewey, *Democracy and Education* (New York: The Macmillan Co., 1923), pp. 6, 47, 101. Quotations from this book are printed by permission of the publisher.

[106] William James, *The Meaning of Truth* (New York: Longmans, Green & Co., 1910), pp. 102–103. Quotations from this book are printed by permission of the publisher.

[107] William James, *Pragmatism* (New York: Longmans, Green & Co., 1921), pp. 89–90. Quotations from this book are printed by permission of the publisher.

[108] *Ibid.,* p. 45.

[109] John Dewey, *The Quest for Certainty* (New York: G. P. Putnam's Sons, copyright 1929 by John Dewey), pp. 109–110. Quotations from this book are printed by permission of the publisher.